RELIGIONSPHILOSOPHIE

PHILOSOPHY OF RELIGION

SCHRIFTENREIHE DER WITTGENSTEIN-GESELLSCHAFT

VOLUME 10/2

BAND 10/2

PHILOSOPHY OF RELIGION

PPROCEEDINGS OF
THE 8th INTERNATIONAL WITTGENSTEIN SYMPOSIUM
PART 2

15th TO 21st AUGUST 1983
KIRCHBERG AM WECHSEL (AUSTRIA)

EDITOR

Wolfgang L. Gombocz

VIENNA 1984
HÖLDER-PICHLER-TEMPSKY

RELIGIONSPHILOSOPHIE

AKTEN DES
8. INTERNATIONALEN WITTGENSTEIN SYMPOSIUMS
TEIL 2

15. BIS 21. AUGUST 1983
KIRCHBERG AM WECHSEL (ÖSTERREICH)

HERAUSGEBER

Wolfgang L. Gombocz

WIEN 1984
HÖLDER-PICHLER-TEMPSKY

Wir danken dem österreichischen Bundesministerium für Wissenschaft und Forschung und der Kulturabteilung des Amtes der Niederösterreichischen Landesregierung für die finanzielle Unterstützung bei der Drucklegung dieses Werkes.

Distributors for
Austria, Switzerland and the Federal Republic of Germany
VERLAG HÖLDER-PICHLER-TEMPSKY
A-1096 Wien, Postfach 127, Frankgasse 4

Distributors for the U.S.A., Canada and Mexico
D. REIDEL PUBLISHING COMPANY, INC.
Lincoln Building, 190 Old Derby Street, Hingham, Mass. 02043, U.S.A.

Distributors for all other countries
D. REIDEL PUBLISHING COMPANY
P.O.Box 17, Dordrecht, Holland

CIP-Kurztitelaufnahme der Deutschen Bibliothek

Relgionsphilosophie / Hrsg. Wolfgang L. Gombocz. − Wien: Hölder-Pichler-Tempsky, 1984.
(Akten des 8. Internationalen Wittgenstein-Symposiums; Teilbd. 2) (Schriftenreihe der Wittgenstein-Gesellschaft; Bd. 10)
ISBN 3-209-00548-6
NE: Gombocz, Wolfgang [Hrsg.]; Österreichische Ludwig-Wittgenstein-Gesellschaft: Schriftenreihe der Wittgenstein-Gesellschaft

CIP-Kurztitelaufnahme der Deutschen Bibliothek

Ästhetik, Religionsphilosophie: Akten d. 8. Internat. Wittgenstein-Symposiums / Hrsg. Rudolf Haller; Wolfgang Gombocz. − Gesamtausg. − Wien: Hölder-Pichler-Tempsky, 1984.
(Schriftenreihe der Wittgenstein-Gesellschaft; Bd. 10)
ISBN 3-209-00549-4
NE: Haller, Rudolf [Hrsg.]; Internationales Wittgenstein-Symposium <08, 1983, Kirchberg, Wechsel>;
Österreichische Ludwig-Wittgenstein-Gesellschaft: Schriftenreihe der Wittgenstein-Gesellschaft

ISBN 3-209-00548-6

Gestaltung und Mitarbeit: Erich Péhm
Satz: Baroschrift, 1100 Wien
Druck: Manz, Wien

INHALTSVERZEICHNIS
TABLE OF CONTENTS

PREFACE

The Wittgenstein Conferences at Kirchberg (in Austria) are coming of age. Having started in 1976 with so-called "Wittgenstein-Tage", the Austrian Ludwig Wittgenstein Society will be completing its first decade of Wittgenstein research and exchange[1] within a couple of years. In 1983 Kirchberg invited the international philosophic community to make contributions in the fields of *Aesthetics* and *Philosophy of Religion*. More than 90 of these are published in two separate volumes. This is the latter of these.

The *Opening Address* of the conference was given by Professor Joseph M. Bocheński of Fribourg, Switzerland. In what he called "an old man's proposal what philosophy of religion should (not) be" the *emeritus* from Fribourg University developed twelve postulates (P1–P12) concerning the nature, subject matter, and method of any philosophy of religion. For Bocheński, philosophy of religion essentially is (or should be) *logic of religion* (P3), i.e. reconstruction of religious systems by means of logic in general. And since it is *only* reconstruction, it can be neither a *substitute* nor a *support* of religion (P1). Therefore, philosophy of religion does not include theodicy (or, for that matter, anti-theodicy) as one of its branches (P2). Philosophy of religion is to be based on empirical grounds (P10), and Bocheński suggests that "we should stimulate" research in that direction. Thus, according to Bocheński, philosophy of religion has a dual basis, at once empirical and logical, and, therefore, universal. Nevertheless, one has to take into account the *uniqueness* of religion (P5), i.e. one should, in principle, expect *specific rules of meaning* and truth (P6). Faced with this *proprium* of religion (and of theology) Bocheński hopes to limit the possible pluralism of meaning and truth by recourse to the most general rules of deduction and semiotics (P7). Several postulates directly concern the subject matter. P8 opposes "parochialism" by postulating that philosophy of religion is to be based on the totality of religions and on their most general manifestations. Furthermore, philosophy of religion should take into consideration not only single aspects but the entire complexity of religious phenomena (P9). And since the findings "of the theologians' and buddhologists' thoughts . . . should be known before we start research in a certain area" (P11), philosophy of religion should also be a forerunner of the various sciences of religion and carry out with them partial syntheses (P4).

The main part of the *Opening Address* explains and discusses these postulates, which resemble a quite *ascetic* view of the discipline, a sort of descriptivism.[2] In obvious contrast to this ascetic character of philosophy of religion, and in significant contradistinction to postulates 1, 2, and 3, the catholic priest (of the religious order to which Albert the Great and Thomas Aquinas belonged) adds a twelfth postulate to the list, a postulate which does not as much address scholarship as *ethical conduct:* Philosophers of religion *must have a firm Weltanschauung;* i.e. agnostics, skeptics, seekers, and persons who practise philosophy of religion in order to find support for their personal belief or disbelief are to be eliminated (P12). And Bocheński adds: "This goes without saying."

Three plenary sessions of the 1983 Kirchberg meeting were dedicated to *Philosophy of Religion*. Terence Penelhum's talk on *Religious Belief and Life after Death* argued that belief in a life after death is a necessary component of religion, and should not be explained away in the manner of liberal (Protestant) theology as merely supernatural. Penelhum insists on the view that the transformation in human personality that religion requires is such that it does not make sense unless one keeps to (a literal understanding of) the idea of a future life, i.e. of an *existence post mortem*. John H. Hick adopted Wittgenstein's concept of "seeing-as" in order to analyse the epistemology of faith and religious experience. Whereas Wittgenstein introduced the concept of "seeing-as" for the analysis (and explanation) of exceptional cases of ambigious perception, Hick so generalised it that *all* situations of human experience are cases of "experiencing-as". Objects and situations of everyday life thus become seen-as (experienced-as), and so display religious significance and meaning. Alvin Plantinga[3] explained *Ockham's Way Out* of the dilemma between, on the one hand, divine precognition (and predestination) and, on the other, human free will. William of Ockham reconciles God's precognition with freedom of human will *in all cases,* according to Plantinga, in a consistent way; both philosophers re(de)fine God's predestination in terms of *necessitas per accidens.* In doing so, William and Alvin must presuppose that God acts in continouos time, thereby excluding (or, at least, ignoring) the famous Boethian way out of the dilemma.

When Bocheński concluded his talk with the "conviction that those who are true to the ideal of philosophy of religion described by *my postulates* are present in large numbers" [e.g. in Kirchberg 1983], he could not have been thinking of Hick, Penelhum, and Plantinga for the following resasons: Penelhum's (quasi-)theological axiom regarding *post mortem* existence is in conflict with Bocheński's extreme descriptivism and, in consequence, could at best be the object of a philosophy of religion in peace with P3 and P2. Plantinga's approach smacks too much of theodicy for the ones "present in large numbers", besides being in conflict with P1. Hick, experiencing our universe as a religious one, takes himself to be a philosopher of religion, whereas the brave postulates of the "large numbers" would render him the object of investigations according to P5 and P6. (They get considerably better marks, however, within a framework of somewhat different *definientia* of religion and, therefore, of philosophy of religion, which emerged from the discussions at Kirchberg, for instance *transcendence, immanence, immortality, cosmodicy, totalitarism, anti-idolism, theology, liturgy,* and others. These I take up in my German preface.[4])

Yet, very many contributions to this volume show how widely accepted Bocheński's postulates are. Whereas A. Kasher is even more radical than Bocheński, others approach him in analytic zeal. Such are M. Engel *et al.* (analysing and criticizing R. Taylor's "Kiefer-Argument"), J. Ross and J. Gellman (developing an epistemology of faith and belief), and W. Leinfellner and O. Muck, to give just a few examples.

The editor would be remiss if he did not express his gratitude to one of the editors of the *Schriftenreihe der Wittgenstein-Gesellschaft,* Dr. Elisabeth Leinfellner, who helped in the preparation of this volume and also translated J. M. Bocheński's *Opening Address* into English, and to Professors J. M. Bocheński and R. Haller for their help and support. Herr E. Péhm of the Hölder-Pichler-Tempsky publishing house worked with admirable efficiency on the whole project. The reader who wants to make best use of this book might begin by reading the *Opening Address.* Another good and very different way into the subject would be to start with Asa Kasher. For a fuller summary of the contents of this volume see also my German *VORWORT.*

ENDNOTES

[1] Cf. notes 1–4 of my German preface *Religionsphilosophie in Kirchberg* for a detailed bibliography.
[2] I give a more detailed outline of this ascetic descriptivism (with some ciritique) in my German preface.
[3] The editor very much wanted to include this piece. The author felt it needs further revision.
[4] For detailed analysis cf. the last pages and the list containing the *definientia* R1 to R12. Notes 7–10 give references.

* * *

RELIGIONSPHILOSOPHIE IN KIRCHBERG

Ein Vorwort von
Wolfgang L. Gombocz
Karl-Franzens-Universität, Graz

Es war zu erwarten, daß das Internationale *Wittgenstein-Symposium*, welches seit 1977 alljährlich im August in Kirchberg am Wechsel (in Österreich) stattfindet, einmal auch die *Religionsphilosophie* zum Thema wählen würde. Was zu Ostern 1976 als „Wittgenstein-Tage 1976" begann[1] (und retrospektive als *erstes* Symposium gezählt wird), dann in zwei weiteren Kongressen über die Themen „Wittgenstein und sein Einfluß auf die gegenwärtige Philosophie" (1977) und „Wittgenstein, der Wiener Kreis und der Kritische Rationalismus" (1978) sich internationale Anerkennung verschaffte,[2] führte in den weiteren Symposien von Wittgensteins Philosophie insofern weg, als Themen aus der systematischen Philosophie aufs Programm gesetzt wurden, ohne daß von den Vortragenden ein Bezug zu Wittgenstein gefordert wurde. Seit damals ist die Philosophie des zeitweiligen Volksschullehrers in den Kirchberg benachbarten Ortschaften Otterthal (1924−26) und Trattenbach (1920−22) nicht mehr *ausschließliches*, aber immer noch *eines* der Themen bei jedem Wittgenstein-Symposium. 1979 handelte man über „Sprache, Logik und Philosophie", 1980 wählte man „Ethik" zum Thema, um „Sprache und Ontologie" (1981) sowie „Erkenntnis- und Wissenschaftstheorie" (1982) folgen zu lassen, wobei ein Großteil der Beiträge zu diesen Symposien bereits von Wittgensteinscher Philosophie absieht.[3]

Für 1983 hatte die Österreichische Ludwig-Wittgenstein-Gesellschaft (ÖLWG)[4] erstmals *zwei* Themen auf das Programm gesetzt, *Ästhetik* und *Religionsphilosophie*; außerdem gelang es der ÖLWG, den Nestor der kontinentaleuropäischen Religionsphilosophie, Joseph M. Bocheński aus Freiburg in der Schweiz, für den Eröffnungsvortrag zu gewinnen. Die (übrigen) Plenarvorträge verteilten sich gleichmäßig auf beide Disziplinen. Der hier vorliegende Halbband vereinigt in sich Beiträge zur Religionsphilosophie (und ihren Randgebieten),[5] während ein anderer Halbband, besorgt von Rudolf Haller, die Akten zur Ästhetik enthält.

Joseph M. Bocheński (1.1; englische Übersetzung von E. Leinfellner 1.2) trug in seinem Referat „Zur Religionsphilosophie" (so der Titel laut Programmheft, S. 6) zwölf Postulate (P1−P12) über Wesen, Gegenstand und Methode der Religionsphilosophie vor; diese Postulatenliste nennt der Emeritus aus Freiburg sein *eigenes Testament*. Bocheński versteht Religionsphilosophie im wesentlichen als Logik der Religion (P3),[6] als eine Rekonstruktion religiöser Aussagenzusammenhänge unter Berücksichtigung einer allgemeinen Logik. Deshalb kann und darf Religionsphilosophie weder Stütze noch Ersatz (P1) für Religion sein, d.h. Theodizee (oder Anti-Theodizee) ist als eine Disziplin der Religionsphilosophie (P2) auszuschließen. Eine so als Logik der Religion gefaßte Spezialwissenschaft mit der Möglichkeit, Teilsynthesen (P4) vorzulegen, hat ein *Proprium* von Religion (und auch von Theologie) zu akzeptieren (P5), d.h. Religionsphilosophie muß mit der Möglichkeit besonderer Wahrheits- und Sinnregeln innerhalb ihres Forschungsbereichs (P6) rechnen. Bocheński legt aber großen Wert darauf, solche in einen (möglicherweise unerwünschten) religionsphilosophischen Pluralismus führende Eigenartigkeit der Religion zu begrenzen (P7); dies geschieht am zielführendsten durch die allgemeinen Regeln des Schließens und der Semiotik. Postulat 8 wendet sich gegen den „Parochialismus" in der Religionsphilosophie, indem es die Einengung auf die abendländische Tradition ablehnt. Die Gesamtheit der Religionen (P8) und das Allgemein-(st)e in ihnen ist der gesuchte Gegenstand (P9); nicht bloß Aspekten, sondern der gesamten Komplexität religiöser Phänomene ist nachzuspüren, wobei von empirischen Grundlagen (P10) auszugehen ist. Während Postulat 11 forschungsökonomisch mahnt, die „Ergebnisse" von Theologen, Buddhologen und anderen Einzelwissenschaftlern zur Kenntnis zu nehmen, *bevor* man mit eigener Forschung beginnt, ist im abschließenden, letzten Postulat Bocheńskis radikalste Forderung ausgesprochen: In auffälligem Kontrast zu den Postulaten 1–3 über den Charakter der Religionsphilosophie als Logik der Religion stellt der katholische Priester aus dem Dominikanerorden in Postulat 12 ein – wie er es nennt – „moralisches" Gebot auf, welches er den elf „wissenschaftlichen" hinzufügt: Ein Religionsphilosoph darf kein Sucher oder Agnostiker oder Skeptiker sein, er muß eine feste Weltanschauung haben, sei es eine Religion, sei es eine Anti-Religion. Denn Bocheński hält einen Menschen *ohne* Weltanschauung, wie er betont, für einen Mythus; jeder hat eine Weltanschauung, und genau diese nicht zu bestreitende Einsicht sei der Hauptgrund für das Postulat: Diejenigen, die sich der Religionsphilosophie zuwenden, können ihre Weltanschauung nicht loswerden. Ja, sie sollen eine *feste* Weltanschauung haben, d.h. einen Glauben, der so unerschütterlich ist, daß er keine Forschung fürchtet. Nur mit solchen Menschen kann man nach Bocheński echte, wissenschaftliche Religionsphilosophie treiben. Diejenigen aber, die in oder mittels der Religionsphilosophie eine Stütze für den eigenen Glauben, oder die Widerlegung einer spezifischen Religion, oder einen Ersatz für Religion, oder gar Beweise für die Existenz (oder auch Nicht-Existenz) Gottes finden wollen, sollen aus dem Betrieb der Religionsphilosophie *ausgeschlossen bleiben* (P12).

Prima facie scheint P12 einer extrem asketischen Auffassung von Religionsphilosophie zu huldigen, indem eine so verstandene Religionsphilosophie *alles läßt wie es ist*. Doch zeigt ein weiterer Blick, daß Bocheńskis abschließendes Postulat *mehr* ist. Einerseits ist es verschieden von Norwood R. Hansons Attacke[7] gegen den Agnostizismus (bzw. Skeptizismus) in der Religionsphilosophie; Hanson will ja den Agnostizismus als eine unmögliche, d.h. unvernünftige Antwort auf die Frage nach der Existenz einer Gottheit herausstellen. Andererseits geht es Bocheński nicht darum, den Agnostizismus als „Kapitulation des Geistes und des Innenlebens vor dem momentan Gegebenen" abzuqualifizieren. Schließlich ist er weit davon entfernt, eine neuthomistische Auffassung von Religionsphilosophie zu vertreten. Was er vor Augen zu haben scheint, ist vielmehr die Forderung nach einer *klaren Trennung* von religionsphilosophischer Tätigkeit als einer wissenschaftlichen Erörterung und Durchdringung ihres Gegenstandsbereichs, d.i. *aller* religiöser Phänomene, und den Wissensansprüchen gewisser derartiger religiöser Systeme, welche in apologetischer Absicht sich religionsphilosophischer Methoden zu bedienen bemühen. Die Frage lautet: Kann bzw. soll ein religiöses bzw. theologisches Axiom in den Aussagenzusammenhang der Religions*philosophie* eingehen? Bocheńskis Antwort ist negativ; wenn aber Religion und Unreligion nicht dürfen, wo diese doch jeweils ein klares System von Ansprüchen vortragen, dann dürfen *a fortiori* Zweifler, Sucher, Skeptiker, kurz die „Lauen" *nicht*, weil sie eben einen systematischen Forderungskatalog (für Bocheński) nicht vorlegen können. Vielmehr scheinen die Ausführungen zu P12 zu untermauern, daß bei Nichtvorliegen einer solchen klaren „weltanschaulichen Position" (Bocheński nennt sie auch einen „unerschütterlichen Glauben") religionsphilosophische Tätigkeit (notwendigerweise?) sich auf die Suche nach einem *Ersatz* begibt, was ja bereits durch P1 (und P2) ausgeschlossen wurde.

Drei der insgesamt sieben Kirchberger Plenarvorträge waren religionsphilosophischen Themen gewidmet. Terence Penelhum (2.1) war mit Engagement dafür eingetreten, daß der Glaube an ein Weiterleben nach dem Tode wesentlicher und unaufgebbarer Bestandteil religiösen Glaubens, d.h. jeder Religion sei. Beide Glauben können für Penelhum nicht getrennt werden; die (in Mode gekommene) Ausscheidung des Glaubens an ein Weiterleben als unnötige übernatürliche Zugabe wird als Irrtum in wenigstens zweifacher Hinsicht abgelehnt: Einmal irren sich diejenigen, die die Aussagen über eine Existenz *post mortem* als Erklärung über die persönlichen Engagements des in Frage stehenden Gläubigen *reduzierend* (um-)deuten, weil sie die Folgen des religiösen Engagements mit dem Wesen von Religion verwechseln, da nur bei wörtlichem Verstehen der Erwartungen eines Weiterlebens dies eine ausreichende Garantie für das religiöse Engagement sei. Zum anderen übersehen solche Umdeuter das Erfordernis von religiösen Idealen, wie z.B. Wiedergeburt aus dem Geist oder Abtötung des (irdischen) Selbst, sobald Religion der real-irdischen Wirklichkeit der religiösen Person eine phänomenale (z.B. eschatologische) gegenüberstellt. Ohne ein wörtliches Verständnis ist (eschatologische) Religion schal.

Inwieweit Penelhums *religionsphilosophischer* Anspruch Bocheńskis Postulaten genügen kann, bleibt nur insofern unklar, als er P12 (in der hier vorgelegten Rekonstruktion bezüglich einer Trennung der Ebenen und eines asketischen Deskriptivismus) schwerlich wird Rechnung tragen können. *Ein* theologisches (religiöses) Axiom gelangt in den religionsphilosophischen Aussagenzusammenhang von Penelhum. Bocheński stellte sich mit P12, P1 und P2 zumindest außerhalb der kontinentaleuropäischen Auffassung von Religionsphilosphie. Als eine eigene philosophische Disziplin wurde die Religionsphilosophie (sieht man einmal von Bernard Bolzano ab) vom Neukantianismus begründet. Die Neukantianer führten Religion auf ein besonderes religiöses Apriori (im Menschen) zurück. Der (Neu-)Thomismus konnte dem zustimmen, mußte allerdings dem Neukantianismus insofern widersprechen, als dieser dem Gegenstand der Religion das Sein absprach. Für Bocheński sind derartige Fragestellungen aus der Religions*philosophie* auszuschließen; traditionell wurden (und werden) sie im Rahmen einer natürlichen Gotteslehre (*theologia naturalis*) abgehandelt. Penelhum, sicherlich kein Neukantianer oder Neuthomist, steht einer solchen Auffassung von Religionsphilosophie allerdings aufgeschlossen gegenüber.[8]

John H. Hick (2.2) hatte am gleichen Tage wie Penelhum seine Ausführungen über den „religiösen Blick" auf die uns umgebende Welt vorgetragen. Dabei legte er Wittgensteins Begriff des „Sehens-als" einer epistemologischen Analyse von Glauben und religiöser Erfahrung zugrunde. Während Wittgenstein den Begriff des Sehens-als nur in Ausnahmesituationen zur Anwendung brachte, verallgemeinert Hick ihn auf *alle* Situationen menschlicher Erfahrung. Dabei werden Gegenstände, aber auch Situationen, welche *per se* objektiv mehrdeutig, d.h. der Deutung zwar bedürftig, aber oft unzugänglich sind, „erfahren-als" mit einer religiösen Bedeutung behaftet. Waren Penelhum und Kasher (siehe dazu unten) mit Bocheńskis Postulaten in Konflikt geraten, so ist Hicks Vortrag, verstanden als ein Beitrag zur Religionsphilosophie, bestenfalls Untersuchungsgegenstand einer Religionsphilosophie im Sinne Bocheńskis.

Alvin Plantinga hatte den dritten Plenarvortrag beigesteuert, der leider nicht in die Akten aufgenommen werden konnte;[9] ausgehend von einem Zitat Augustins (*De libero arbitrio*), in welchem der Kirchenvater sich mit Evodius auseinandersetzt, hatte Plantinga dem Problem göttlichen Vorherwissens als Vorherbestimmung nachgespürt. Dabei scheint die menschliche Willensfreiheit unter die Räder zu kommen, eine Problematik, die sich im besonderen auch für die reformatorischen Theologien in der augustinischen Tradition stellt. Nach kurzen Erörterungen der Positionen von Augustinus, Thomas von Aquin, Petrus Damianus und Jonathan Edwards, wandte sich Plantinga Wilhelm von Ockham zu, mit dessen Hilfe er Gottes Vorherwissen mit der Freiheit des menschlichen Willens *in allen* Fällen und konsistent zusammenbringen will. Dabei wird im besonderen der Begriff des Vorherwissens durch Aufteilung in mehrere Spezies erweitert, wobei gleichzeitig die Beziehungen zwischen Vorherwissen und Vorherbestimmen stark reduziert werden, sowie der Begriff der Vorherbestimmung mittels der *necessitas per accidens* eingegrenzt wird. Die Voraussetzung eines Zeitkontinuums ist dabei für Ockham (und Plantinga) unerläßlich, eine Lösungsmöglichkeit im Sinne z.B. des Boethius damit aber ausgeschlossen.

Durch den Ausfall dieses Beitrages ist die philosophische Gotteslehre (4.) in diesem Halbband noch weniger vertreten; schon beim Kongreß selbst fiel die geringe Anzahl von Beiträgen dazu auf. Dies mag als ein Indikator dafür gelten, daß Kashers Programm (2.4) eines religionsphilosophischen Minimalismus (unter Ausschluß (quasi-)theologischer Fragestellungen soweit wie möglich) in Kreisen der (analytischen) Religionsphilosophie Einzug gehalten hat. Trotzdem sind bemerkenswerte Einzeluntersuchungen vorgelegt worden, wie z.B. E. R. Kraemers (4.1) Ausführungen über göttliche Intentionalität, A. Z. Bar-Ons (4.2) Analyse des ontologischen Gottesbeweises im Anschluß an Anselm von Canterbury, und M. R. Engels *et al.* (4.3) Widerlegungsversuch einer erst jüngst vorgetragenen Variante eines teleologischen

Gottesbeweises, die durch Richard Taylor populär wurde. Weiters sind W. Leinfellners (4.4) und F. M. Wuketits' (4.5) Beiträge zum Thema „Evolution und Schöpfung" hier angefügt worden, da sie einzelwissenschaftliches Material im Zusammenhang des kosmologischen Gottesbeweises vorlegen. Ob Biologie tatsächlich den Schöpfungsgedanken ablehnen *muß*, wie Wuketits (4.5) ausführt, mag kontrovers bleiben, durchaus wertvoll aber sind die Materialsammlungen und Hinweise beider Autoren zugunsten einer skeptisch-agnostischen Ausrichtung bezüglich der „Beweisfrage". Nobelpreisträger und andere angesehene Wissenschaftler haben seit längerem die Hypothese vorgetragen, daß Leben *nicht* auf der Erde *entstand*, sondern daß Leben (über die Vermittlung von Kometen z.B.) aus dem Kosmos auf diesen Planeten gebracht wurde. Falls diese Hypothese etwas für sich hätte, fiele der Druck der „magischen" vier Milliarden Jahre für die „Kosmogonie" weg: Es ist ein weiter Weg — der Weg zurück zum ersten Beweger.

Von den offensichtlich religionsphilosophisch relevanten Beiträgen in Gruppe 3 verdienen besonders die J. J. Ross' (3.1) und J. I. Gellmans (3.2) Erwähnung. In „Crediting, Taking for Granted, and Quasi-Belief" argumentiert Ross für eine feinere Unterscheidung (als sie weithin üblich ist) mehrerer Glaubensbegriffe. Dabei wird klar, daß das propositionale Element von Glauben in der Mehrheit von Analysen bisher überbewertet worden ist. Gellman (3.2) legt eine Studie institutionellen Glaubens (im religiösen Kontext) vor, wobei gezeigt wird, daß weder institutioneller Glaube noch Glaube *simpliciter* propositional zu sein brauchen. Gruppe 5 vereinigt die Beiträge über Wittgensteins Auffassung von Religion und Religionsphilosophie, wobei T. J. McKnight (5.3) den Wunderbegriff bei Thomas von Aquin und Wittgenstein vergleicht, H. Hellerer (5.4) den Nachweis versucht, daß Wittgensteins persönliche „Religion" tolstoisch ist, während Hubík (5.7) Wittgenstein und Karl Marx zusammenbringt. „Religion und Praxis" ist der Titel für die in Gruppe 6 vereinigten Beiträge, während neun Aufsätze zum Verhältnis von Religion und Wissenschaft den Band beschließen (7.). Hier sind sowohl Studien über das Verhältnis von Religion (bzw. Theologie) zu Einzelwissenschaften anzutreffen (z.B. 7.3 und 7.4), wie auch Beiträge zum Begriff des religiösen versus wissenschaftlichen Weltbildes, wobei auch Wittgensteins Auffassung (7.6) zur Sprache kommt.

Den Begriff einer (analytischen) Religionsphilosophie hatte Bocheński durch Postulate zu ihrem Wesen einzugrenzen versucht; andere Beiträge setzten allerdings einen stärker normativen (wie z.B. Kasher), bzw. einen stärker theologischen (wie z.B. Penelhum), oder apologetischen Begriff (wie z.B. Hick) voraus. Der Begriff der Religion selbst blieb dabei aber (wie *de facto* überhaupt auf diesem Symposium) unterbestimmt. Nach verbreiteter Auffassung gibt es weder eine Liste notwendiger noch eine akzeptierter hinreichender Bedingungen für Religion; es liegt aber nahe, jedes Element (R1 bis R12) der nun folgenden Aufstellung (des Herausgebers) als solches einzuschätzen, daß es als Eigenschaft von X hilft, dieses X zunächst und prüfend für einen Kandidaten von Religion zu halten, sowie günstigenfalls bei Vorliegen von Eigenschaftsbündeln (im bes. aus R1 bis R7) dieses X *als eine Religion zu identifizieren*:

(R1)
(Transzendenz)

Der Glaube an (ein) übernatürliche(s) Wesen.

(R2)
(Anti-Idolismus)

Die Unterscheidung von Heiligem und Profanem (Säkularem); von wahrer Gottesverehrung und Idolatrie.

(R3)
(Schriftautorität)

Die Hinordnung des einzelnen Gläubigen (wie der Gemeinschaft, s. R4) auf einen heiligen Text, welcher verehrt wird, und im bes. als autoritativ akzeptiert ist (bei sog. Buchreligionen).

(R4)
(Bundesidee)

Das Bilden einer Gemeinschaft aufgrund von R1–R3; ein solcher „Bund" erlaubt Grade der Zusammengehörigkeit von quasi-freiwilligem Anschluß bis zu total(itär)em Zwang (innerhalb eines „Gottesstaates").

(R5) (Kosmodizee)	Eine Gesamtdeutung des (sichtbaren) Kosmos, seines Ursprungs und der Stellung des (in einer Gemeinschaft lebenden) Menschen in ihm aufgrund von R1−R3, wobei R4 begründet, zumindest aber miteinbezogen wird.
(R6) (Moralkodex)	Eine (gewöhnlicherweise weitreichende und) durch Sanktionen seitens der Gemeinschaft der Gläubigen (bzw. ihrer internen Autoritäten) gestützte Morallehre unter Bezugnahme auf R3−R5.
(R7) (Totalitarismus)	Die Disposition in den gläubigen Individuen, ein (mehr oder weniger, *idealiter* aber vollständig) geordnetes Leben aufgrund von R6 zu führen.
(R8) (Esoterik)	(Typische, d.h. als artbildend anzusehende) Gefühle, wie Schuld, Reue, Vergebung, Teilhabe am Geheimnis, Auserwählung u.a.
(R9) (Immanenz)	Gebete sowie andere Formen der „Kommunikation" mit dem Transzendenten.
(R10) (Liturgie)	(Ritual-)Handlungen bezogen z.B. auf heilige Gegenstände, auf heilige Tage, oder auch auf Heiliges (in einem nichtgegenständlichen Sinn).
(R11) (Immortalität)	Der Glaube an ein Weiterleben nach dem Tode.
(R12) (Theologie)	Die rationale Durchdringung des Glaubenssystems, bzw. ein Postulat der Verträglichkeit (Über- bzw. Unterordnung) von Glaube und Vernunft.

Bocheńskis dominant *deskriptive* Deutung einer wissenschaftlichen Religionsphilosophie konzentriert sich auf Rekonstruktion und immanente Evaluation von Aussagenzusammenhängen der Art R1, R4, R5 und R6, erklärt die Tätigkeiten bzw. „Fakten" von R8, R9 und R10 zum Untersuchungsgegenstand selbständiger Teildisziplinen, die auch unter den Namen *Religionspsychologie*, *Religionssoziologie* oder (allgemein) *Religionswissenschaft* bekannt sind. *Postulatorisch* bleibt aber eine klare Trennung zwischen der Religion als Objekt und der Religionsphilosophie als „Meta-Theorie" bestehen, wobei allerdings die Abgrenzung gegenüber der *Theologie* (vgl. R12) unterbestimmt bleibt. Penelhums (2.1) Erweiterung bzw. Abweichung (im Vergleich mit Bocheński) besteht nun darin, daß er immanente Postulate z.B. für R5 diskutiert, um eine bestimmte Religion überhaupt als *Religion* auszuweisen, wenn er als *Religionsphilosoph* verlangt, daß der Glaube an ein Weiterleben nach dem Tode (wie in R11) *conditio sine qua non* für eine religiöse Weltdeutung bzw. Deutung des Individuums und seiner Erwartungen (im Sinne von R5) ist. Und auch Hick (2.2) versteht sich als Religionsphilosophen und nicht etwa als Theologen (Abgrenzung von R12 gegenüber P10), wenn er eine Begründung für eine „spezifische" Plausibilität von R5 (auf empirischer Basis?) gibt.

Kasher nun (2.4) propagiert ein Reduktionsprogramm für Religionsphilosophie: Verlagerung der Forschungstätigkeit weg von den traditionellen Problemen der natürlichen Theologie und hin zu „conceptual studies of religious forms of life". Zum Gegenstand einer wissenschaftlichen Erörterung wird Religion dann in ihren Aspekten als „irdische" Verhaltensform oder Begründung von Handlungen, nicht aber „als Schatztruhe derartiger Paradoxa" wie Allwissenheit und Allmacht des transzendenten Gegenüber. Auszuschließen aus dem religionsphilosophischen Forschungsprogramm sind nach Kasher jene *theologischen* Teile der Religion (R12), die sich nicht in der religiösen Praxis wiederfinden, im bes. der Begriff „Gott". Was bleibt, läßt sich in drei Gruppen beschreiben:

(a) *Nichts* ist Gegenstand der Religionsphilosophie, wenn es nicht in der religiösen Praxis aus-gedrückt wird. D.h. der Inhalt der Religion tritt zu Tage durch Ausübung, nicht durch Defini-tion oder (akademische) Theologie (*Primat der Praxis*).

(b) Besondere Beachtung verdienen jene Religionen, welche bezüglich R6 (und R7) dem *Ideal der Totalität* nahekommen, d.h. Religionen, in welchen die „Ideologie" (der Code) reli-giöser Lebensführung im Prinzip komplett ist, indem er (sie) Regeln für *jeden* Bereich menschlicher Tätigkeit enthält.

(c) Minimalistische Religionsphilosophie studiert Religionen hinsichtlich ihrer Opposition zu Formen der *Idolatrie* (vgl. R2) als einer Form religiöser Praxis, welche nicht bloß die Vereh-rung Baals (im auserwählten Volk des Alten Testamentes) oder des Zeus ausschließt, sondern die Bekämpfung jeder Art von Lastern und „Süchtigkeit" — Egoismus und Nationalismus, Reichtum und Macht, „love and lust" — einschließt.

Kasher nennt diese „essentiellen Ingredientien" jeder Religion Konstitutivität (a), idealen Totalitarismus (b) und Anti-Idolismus (c). Diese wohl als hinreichende Bedingungen zu deu-tenden Ingredientien reduzieren obige Liste auf R2, R7 und vielleicht R9/R10. Religionsphi-losophie ist damit zur Religionssoziologie geworden. Sie läßt *nicht nur alles wie es ist, sie küm-mert sich um Vieles*, vielleicht um das Meiste, *gar nicht* mehr. R1 degeneriert zu R9/R10 (oder weniger), R5 wird — wegen des Postulates nach Ausdruck in der religiösen Praxis — vermut-lich irrelevant, wenn nicht inexistent. (Da aber R7 unmittelbar R6 und mittelbar R5 voraus-setzt, darf man Kashers Reduktionismus als — teilweise — inadäquat und verbesserungsbe-dürftig ansehen.) Alvin Plantingas meisterliche Analyse der Kompatibilität von Gottes Vor-herwissen (und Vorherbestimmen) mit der Freiheit des menschlichen Willens (s. oben) fällt aus dem Rahmen einer so verstandenen Religionsphilosophie hinaus, nachdem sie bereits Gefahr gelaufen war, durch Bocheńskis Postulate in den Objektbereich gedrängt zu werden.[10] Argumente, wie das des Hl. Anselm (analysiert von Bar-On in 4.2) oder von James Kiefer (vgl. Engels Kritik in 4.3), ja überhaupt *philosophische* Anstrengungen um eine Gotteslehre zerrinnen zu nichts, da es für Kasher beispielsweise „no practical indication of genuine reli-gious interest in problems of divine immutability, of divine lack of responsibility for human sins . . ., and even of the existence of God" gibt.

* * *

Eine Sammlung religionsphilosophischer Abhandlungen — mit in der Tat bemerkenswerter Abbildung der Postulate Bocheńskis einerseits und des Programms Kashers andererseits — wird somit der Öffentlichkeit vorgelegt. Der Herausgeber dankt der ÖLWG und vor allem Frau Elisabeth Leinfellner, die u.a. auch Professor Bocheńskis Ansprache ins Englische über-trug, für die Unterstützung bei der Vorbereitung des Bandes, sowie den Herren Joseph M. Bocheński, Rudolf Haller und Erich Péhm für die entgegenkommende Zusammenarbeit. Herausgeber und Verlag sind allen Autoren und Mitarbeitern für ihre konstruktive Koopera-tion zu Dank verpflichtet.

ANMERKUNGEN

[1] Vgl. Adolf Hübner (Hrsg.): *Ludwig Wittgenstein. Ein österreichischer Philosoph*, 1889—1951. Schrift zur 25. Wiederkehr seines Todestages, Kirchberg 1976, 40 S. (Mit einem Beitrag von Werner Lein-fellner: Wittgensteins Philosophie, S. 11—21).

[2] So mußte wegen der großen Nachfrage z.B. der Kongreßband des 2. Symposiums in zweiter Auflage herausgebracht werden: E. u. W. Leinfellner *et alii* (Hrsg.): Wittgenstein und sein Einfluß auf die

gegenwärtige Philosophie. Akten des 2. Internationalen Wittgenstein-Symposiums . . . 1977, Wien
²1980 (¹1978). − Weiters: H. Berghel *et alii* (Hrsg.): *Wittgenstein, der Wiener Kreis und der Kritische Rationalismus. Akten des 3. Internationalen Wittgenstein-Symposiums* . . . 1978, Wien 1979.

[3] Vgl. P. Weingartner u. H. Czermak (Hrsg.): *Erkenntnis- und Wissenschaftstheorie. Akten des 7. Internationalen Wittgenstein-Symposiums* . . .1982, Wien 1983. − W. Leinfellner *et alii* (Hrsg.): *Sprache und Ontologie. Akten des 6. Internationalen Wittgenstein-Symposiums* . . .1981, Wien 1982. − E. Morscher u. R. Stranzinger (Hrsg.): *Ethik − Grundlagen, Probleme und Anwendungen. Akten des 5. Internationalen Wittgenstein-Symposiums* . . . 1980, Wien 1981. − R. Haller u. W. Graßl (Hrsg.): *Sprache, Logik und Philosophie. Akten des 4. Internationalen Wittgenstein-Symposiums* . . . 1979, Wien 1980.

[4] Sie ist die eigentliche Veranstalterin dieser Symposien, wobei ihr Präsident, Dr. Adolf Hübner, die Hauptlast der Organisation trägt.

[5] Die mehr als 40 Beiträge sind in *sieben* thematischen Gruppen gesammelt; für mein Vorwort lege ich den Zitaten diese Ordnung zugrunde, wobei „1.1" bedeutet „erste Gruppe, erster Beitrag" etc. − Einige der Beiträge haben keinen erkennbaren, direkten Bezug zur Religionsphilosophie, wie z.B. 3.5 bis 3.9 oder 7.8. Die in Gruppe 3 zusammengefaßten Arbeiten betreffen jedoch den Zusammenhang von Wissen und Glauben im (streng) erkenntnistheoretischen Sinn, wenn einmal der religionsphilosophische Aspekt ausfällt.

[6] Vgl. auch sein Buch: *Logik der Religion* (Köln 1968).

[7] Hanson, Norwood R., *What I Do Not Believe and Other Essays* (Dordrecht 1971), S. 303−8: The Agnostic's Dilemma; S. 309−31: What I Don't Believe.

[8] Vgl. auch sein Buch: *God and Skepticism* (Dordrecht 1983).

[9] A. Plantinga (briefliche Mitteilung) findet, daß „Ockham's Way Out" weiterer Bearbeitung bedarf, für welche er derzeit nicht genug Zeit hat. − Der zunächst von Plantinga in Aussicht genommene Vortrag „On Taking God as Hypothesis", welcher sich mit J. L. Mackie auseinandersetzen wollte, ist ein weiterer religionsphilosophischer Titel, auf welchen der Hrsg. die Aufmerksamkeit lenken möchte. Man muß wünschen, daß beide Beiträge bald der Fachwelt zugänglich gemacht werden.

[10] Mackie, J. L., *The Miracle of Theism* (Oxford 1982), würde z.B. nach Kashers „Minimalprogramm" überhaupt nichts Religionsphilosophisches enthalten.

* * *

ABKÜRZUNGEN DER TITEL VON WITTGENSTEINS SCHRIFTEN
ABBREVIATIONS OF THE TITLES OF WITTGENSTEIN'S WRITINGS

BBB	=	*Blue and Brown Books*
BF	=	*Bemerkungen über Farben*
BLB	=	*Blue Book*
BRB	=	*Brown Book*
BFGB	=	*Bemerkungen über Frazers „The Golden Bough"*
BGM	=	*Bemerkungen über die Grundlagen der Mathematik*
LCA	=	*Lectures and Conversations on Aesthetics, Psychology and Religious Belief*
LE	=	*Lecture on Ethics*
LFM	=	*Lectures on the Foundations of Mathematics*
LO	=	*Letters to Ogden*
LRKM	=	*Letters to Russell, Keynes and Moore*
NB	=	*Notebooks 1914–1916*
NL	=	*Notes for Lectures on Private Experience and Sensedata*
OC	=	*On Certainty*
PB	=	*Philosophische Bemerkungen*
PG	=	*Philosophische Grammatik / Philosophical Grammar*
PI	=	*Philosophical Investigations*
PR	=	*Philosophical Remarks*
PT	=	*Prototractatus*
PU	=	*Philosophische Untersuchungen*
RC	=	*Remarks on Color*
RFM	=	*Remarks on the Foundations of Mathematics*
RLF	=	*Some Remarks on Logical Form*
RPP	=	*Remarks on the Philosophy of Psychology*
TLP	=	*Tractatus Logico-Philosophicus*
TB	=	*Tagebücher 1914–1916*
ÜG	=	*Über Gewißheit*
VB	=	*Vermischte Bemerkungen*
WV	=	*Wörterbuch für Volksschulen*
WWK	=	*Wittgenstein und der Wiener Kreis*
Z	=	*Zettel*

1. Eröffnungsansprache

1. Opening Address

ERÖFFNUNGSREDE ZUM ACHTEN INTERNATIONALEN WITTGENSTEIN-SYMPOSIUM 1983*

Joseph M. Bocheński
Freiburg, Schweiz

Meine sehr verehrten Damen und Herren, und Sie, hochverehrte Vertreter der Behörden!

Erlauben Sie mir zwei rein persönliche Bemerkungen: Wir sprechen von Sprachphilosophie und Sprachkritik, und wir müssen ein bißchen Kritik auch an meiner Sprache üben. Ich spreche nämlich einen Dialekt, der in irgendeiner Weise Ihrer schönen deutschen Sprache ähnlich ist. Aber das sagen die Freunde . . . Wollen Sie mir, bitte, verzeihen! Ich hoffe, daß Sie mich wenigstens teilweise verstehen werden! Das ist die erste Bemerkung.

Die zweite ist aber, daß ich in Schwierigkeiten bin. Von meinen Vorrednern hat Herr Hübner sehr tief und nicht ohne Witz gesprochen, und Herr Wallner mit wunderbarem Witz und nicht ohne Tiefe. Nun, was bleibt mir? Ich werde das folgende sagen: Ich bin sehr alt; der bekannte große österreichische Philosoph, der jetzt seine 80 Jahre gefeiert hat, Sir Karl Popper, ist jünger als ich. Ich bin ein Großvater. Ich gebe einige Ratschläge, bäuerliche Ratschläge ohne Tiefe, ohne Witz, Ratschläge eines alten Bauern, der sein Feld bebaut hat und jetzt weggehen muß, und der den Jüngeren diese paar Ratschläge geben möchte. Das sind so rhapsodisch – wie Kant sagte – zusammengesetzte Wünsche des Opas, des alten Vaters, aber ohne jede Tiefe, ohne Witz. Das waren die persönlichen Bemerkungen.

Ich komme jetzt zur Sache selbst. Vor genau 200 Jahren (1783) ist in Riga ein Werk mit dem merkwürdigen Titel *Prolegomena zu einer jeden künftigen Metaphysik, die als Wissenschaft wird auftreten können* erschienen. Kant glaubte damals, daß die Metaphysik an einer Wende ist. Man müsse eine ganz neue Metaphysik machen. Es ist meine Überzeugung, daß wir in Hinblick auf die Religionsphilosophie in einer ähnlichen Lage sind. Wir sind an einer Wende, am Anfang einer neuen Periode. Und es wäre – hätten wir so einen Geist wie Kant – gut, wenn jemand Prolegomena dazu schreiben könnte. Ich kann es leider nicht. Ich kann nur einige rhapsodische Wünsche oder (wissenschaftlich gesagt) Postulate formulieren. Meine Absicht ist also diese: Einige Postulate für jede künftige Religionsphilosophie zu formulieren, die als Wissenschaft wird auftreten können. Mein Vortrag wird aus drei Stücken bestehen: (1) Über die Natur der Religionsphilosophie, (2) über ihren Gegenstand, nämlich die Religion, (3) über die zu gebrauchende Methode. Die Einteilung ist ein bißchen schief, denn es handelt eigentlich nur von der Methode. Es ist aber immer schön und gut, wenn man drei Teile haben kann. Also: Natur, Gegenstand und Methode; am Ende noch eine Zusammenfassung mit Schlußwort.

1. Meine verehrten Damen und Herren, wir kommen jetzt zu unserem ersten Punkt, nämlich zur *Natur*. Und hier muß ich einige Bemerkungen über die Beziehungen zwischen der Philosophie und der Religion machen. Denn hier gerade ist der Wendepunkt: Wie waren diese Beziehungen bis jetzt, bis zum Aufkommen der Analytischen Philosophie? Die Antwort lautet: Sie waren nicht koscher. Sie waren trübe. Hier war es ganz anders als, sagen wir, bei der Philosophie der Kunst. Die Philosophie der Kunst hat sich ruhig entwickelt, die Philosophie der Religion nicht. Warum? Weil die Philosophie ständig als eines von zwei Dingen erschien: entweder als ein Ersatz für die Religion, oder als eine Stütze für die Religion. Und deshalb waren diese Beziehungen nicht koscher. Warum war es so? Die Antwort ist sehr einfach: Erstens gerade deshalb, weil die voranalytische Philosophie nicht analytisch, sondern synthetisch war. Sie versuchte, eine Synthese der gesamten menschlichen Erfahrung aufzubauen, und damit wurde sie zur Trägerin einer Weltanschauung. Schon gar nicht spreche ich

davon, daß gewisse Philosophen, wie z.B. Comte, sich bewußt als Träger einer Weltanschauung verstanden haben. Aber auch wenn sie das nicht getan haben, wie z.B. Spinoza, so waren sie doch im Begriff, einen Ersatz für die Religion zu fabrizieren. Das ist der eine Grund.

Der zweite Grund ist, daß diese Philosophien im großen und ganzen objektsprachlich ausgerichtet waren. Sie sprachen von denselben Dingen wie die Religion selbst, z.B. von Gott, der Weltseele usw. Das war der Grund, warum die meisten Philosophen entweder einen Ersatz für die Religion oder aber eine Stütze für dieselbe fabrizieren wollten. Es gibt natürlich Ausnahmen. Eine große Ausnahme ist Aristoteles in seinem vollständigen Ignorieren der Religion — sie existiert für ihn nicht. Es ist daher ein historisches Wunder, daß gerade Aristoteles auf drei Religionen einen so großen Einfluß gehabt hat: die jüdische, die christliche und den Islam. Für ihn existieren die Religionen einfach nicht; sie interessieren ihn nicht. Dies ist die eine Haltung. Eine andere mögliche Haltung ist die von Thomas von Aquin. Für ihn ist die Philosophie weder Ersatz, noch Stütze der Religion, sie macht vielmehr eine Teilsynthese, welche in die allgemeinste Synthese der Theologie eingebaut wird.

Nun, meine Damen und Herren, der erste Gedanke des alten Bauern auf diesem Feld ist, daß dies alles vorbei ist. Wir leben im „age of analysis". *Die* Philosophie ist heute die Analytische Philosophie — alles andere gehört zur Geschichte. Und das darf hier am Orte, wo Wittgenstein gelebt und gewirkt hat, ganz klar gesagt werden: Die alte Philosophie ist vorbei. Wir leben im Zeitalter der Analytischen Philosophie, und diese Philosophie kann weder ein Ersatz, noch eine Stütze für die Religion sein. Warum? Die Antwort ist wieder ganz einfach: denn, erstens, ist sie *Analytische* Philosophie auch in dem Sinne, daß sie an keine allgemeine Synthese glaubt. Wir bauen Teilsynthesen auf, wir treiben vor allem Analysen, aber ein Gesamtbild der Welt wird kein Analytischer Philosoph bieten. Und zweitens ist die Analytische Philosophie im großen und ganzen — sagen wir: im wesentlichen — metasprachlich. Sie spricht nicht von der Welt, sie spricht von der Sprache. Ich will nicht übertreiben: Ich bin nicht der Meinung jener Kollegen, die glauben, daß die Philosophie nur Beiträge zum *Oxford Dictionary* liefern sollte; ich glaube, daß hie und da auch etwas Objektsprachliches gesagt werden kann. Aber im wesentlichen sind wir metasprachlich und deshalb ist keine Rede von einem Ersatz oder einer Stütze der Religion.

Folgerung, also Postulat: Die Theodizee, die Verteidigung Gottes — oder die Anti-Theodizee — ist kein Teil der Religionsphilosophie; sie sollte aus dieser Philosophie ausgemerzt werden; sie hat damit nichts zu tun. Damit ist nicht gesagt, daß die Theodizee, die natürliche Theologie, nicht möglich wäre. Ich glaube persönlich, daß sie möglich ist. Aber im Lichte unserer Logik ist sie erstens sehr schwierig, zweitens ohne große Plausibilität, und drittens ist, wie Whitehead einmal schön sagte, was sie hervorbringt, nicht „very useful for religious uses", nicht sehr nützlich für den religiösen Gebrauch, wie z.B. die Götter Aristoteles' oder wie der Gott von Whitehead selbst. Deshalb sage ich, daß eine Theodizee zwar gut ist, aber mit Religionsphilosophie hat sie nichts zu tun. Ein Gläubiger glaubt an Gott und braucht keine philosophische Stütze. Das wäre also das erste Postulat.

Es ist aber ganz negativ; es besagt, was die Religionsphilosophie *nicht* sein sollte: keine Stütze, kein Ersatz für die Religion. Man darf aber fragen, was soll die Religionsphilosophie denn positiv sein? Mein Vorschlag wäre: Religionsphilosophie soll im wesentlichen die Logik der Religion, wenn wir die Logik der Religion weit fassen und nicht eng, wie z.B. die formale Logik. Wir verstehen die Logik der Religion dann im Sinne der *allgemeinen* Logik, die, wie Sie wissen, aus drei Stücken besteht: 1. reine oder formale Logik, dann angewandte Logiken, d.h. 2. Logik der Sprache, Semiotik, und 3. Logik des Denkens, allgemeine Methodologie. Der Vorschlag lautet: Religionsphilosophie sollte im wesentlichen die Logik der Religion sein. Ich sage, „im wesentlichen", weil es nicht ausgeschlossen ist, daß sie jene beiden Funktionen ausüben könnte, welche die Philosophie (auch unsere moderne Philosophie) traditionellerweise immer ausgeübt hat:

Erstens die Funktion der Voläuferin; die Philosophie hat immer als Vorläuferin der Wissenschaft gewirkt. Es ist nicht unmöglich, daß z.B. die zahlreichen Arbeiten zur religiösen Sprache, die jetzt entstanden sind, Vorläufer sind für eine Linguistik der Religion. Zweitens aber hat die Philosophie immer die Funktion des Interdisziplinären gehabt, nämlich der Teilsynthese. Es gibt viele Religionswissenschaften: die Religionssoziologie, die Religionsgeographie, die Religionspsychologie, die religiöse Linguistik usw. usw. Wir empfinden das Bedürfnis nach einer Synthese dieser, und in dieser Hinsicht könnte die Religionsphilosophie etwas leisten. Das wären also, meine Damen und Herren, Vorschläge über die Natur, der Religionsphilosophie: Nicht Ersatz, nicht Stütze für die Religion, dagegen Logik der Religion.

2. Damit komme ich zum zweiten Stück, zum Gegenstand: dieser ist die Religion selbst, ein sehr großes und erhabenes Thema. Es wird daher hier und heute viel Zeit in Anspruch nehmen.

Meine verehrten Damen und Herren, über die Religion kann Verschiedenes gesagt werden, ich würde aber glauben, daß für unsere Zwecke, für die Zwecke der Religionsphilosophie, drei Kennzeichen der Religion besonders betont werden sollten: die Eigenartigkeit, die Allgemeinheit und die Komplexität. Ich werde klarmachen, was ich damit meine. (Ein Freund von mir sagte, wenn wir in *klaren* Worten sprechen, wie ist da ein Dialog möglich? Aber bei den Philosophen − wenigstens bei jenen, die sich zu Wittgenstein bekennen − herrscht die Unsitte vor, wenigstens klar sprechen zu versuchen. Und dann sagen die anderen: Oberflächlich, oberflächlich, da ist keine Tiefe. Meine verehrten Damen und Herren, das tiefste aller Dinge ist das Leere.) Versuchen wir also, klar zu sein!

Als erstes erörtern wir das Postulat der Anerkennung der Eigenartigkeit. Die Religion soll als ein Komplex von eigenartigen Phänomenen angesehen werden, als etwas besonderes. Vielleicht zeigt dann später die Analyse, daß man sie doch auf etwas anderes reduzieren kann, daß sie z.B. Ethik ist wie bei Kant, oder etwas anderes; aber man soll das nicht a priori voraussetzen − im Gegenteil: Der Vorschlag ist, man soll an das Gebiet mit der Voraussetzung gehen, daß − wenn sich das Gegenteil nicht zeigen läßt − die Religion so etwas Eigenartiges ist. Dieses Postulat ist ein Apriori; vielleicht können wir später etwas anderes sagen, aber zunächst sollte der Zugang vom Gesichtspunkt der Eigenartigkeit gemacht werden.

Was bedeutet das? Das bedeutet, daß wir a priori die Möglichkeit von ganz besonderen Sinn- und Wahrheitsregeln zulassen sollten. Dies ist wiederum ein ganz konkretes Postulat. Vielleicht zeigt sich später, daß es anders ist; aber a priori haben wir keinen Grund, anders vorzugehen. Die Religion scheint etwas Einzigartiges zu sein, die religiöse Rede ist etwas Einzigartiges, und wir sollten die Möglichkeit ganz besonderer Sinnregeln und ganz besonderer Wahrheitsregeln zulassen. Das wird leider öfters nicht getan und man hat verschiedene Formen des Reduktionismus in die Welt gesetzt. Dagegen ist der Vorschlag hier im Sinne des methodologischen Pluralismus formuliert. Das setzt voraus, daß wir einen allgemeinen philosophischen Pluralismus annehmen und die Möglichkeit von verschiedenen Sinnregeln, von verschiedenen Wahrheitsregeln zulassen.

Vielleicht erlauben Sie mir ein paar Randbemerkungen über diesen Pluralismus. Obwohl die Philosophie der Gegenwart Analytische Philosophie ist, so muß man doch an dieser Stätte, wo einer ihrer bedeutendsten Vertreter gewirkt hat, sagen, daß sie nicht mit dem Pluralismus angefangen hat. Was nun Moore auch immer gedacht haben mag, Russell war jedenfalls ein extremer Monist. Und der W. I, der Tractatus-Wittgenstein, ist so ein extremer − ich würde sagen: absurder − Monist. Sein Einfluß auf den Wiener Kreis führt zu dem extremen Monismus dieser Philosophie: nur *ein* Begriff von Satz, nur *ein* Begriff von Sinn, nur *ein* Begriff von Wahrheit usw.; die einzige Sprache, die zulässig ist, ist die Sprache der Wissenschaft. Das hat sich aber geändert. Und zwar ist hier natürlich der Einfluß der Sprachspiele von Wittgenstein, von W. II, sehr bedeutend, aber nicht allein. Es konvergieren in dieser Haltung des modernen Philosophen eine ganze Reihe von Faktoren. Da ist zuerst die formale Logik − oder, wenn Sie wollen, genauer: die Methodologie der Deduktion − die uns ad oculos gezeigt hat, wie wir verschiedene Axiomatisierungen machen können. Das vor allem ist das Ergebnis der gesamten Kritik der Wissenschaften, und zwar nicht gerade so wie bei den Paradigmen von Kuhn, sondern der ganzen kritischen Entwicklung von Boutroux an bis auf ihn. Es ist das Verdienst der Sprachphilosophie und, last but not least, dieses Gedankens von Wittgenstein über die Sprachspiele, da wir heute durchgehend Pluralisten im methodologischen Sinne sind, und zwar so sehr, daß wir, meine verehrten Damen und Herren, Gefahr laufen zu übertreiben. Man ist so pluralistisch, daß jeder auf seiner eigenen Trompete spielt, seine eigene Logik hat, seine eigene Sprachlehre usw., und man fällt in eine vollständige Skepsis. Was den Philosophen dann bleibt, wäre zu beschreiben, wie die religiösen Menschen sprechen; dann müßte man annehmen, daß jede Art von Aberglauben ebenso wichtig sei wie die Wissenschaft und die Religion.

Nach der Formulierung des Postulats vom Pluralismus möchte ich diesen Pluralismus nun begrenzen und als zusätzliches Postulat das der Begrenzung nennen. Nach ihm hat die Eigenartigkeit der Religion ihre Grenzen. Wo liegen diese Grenzen? Dies ist ein schwieriges philosophisches Problem. Aber ich würde im Augenblick soviel sagen: Sie liegen sicher in den allgemeinsten Schlußregeln und allgemeinsten Prinzipien der Semiotik, allgemeinsten Schlußregeln im Sinne der *Philosophy of Logic* von Quine. Ich zitiere mit Absicht den Namen des Meisters, damit klar werde, daß nicht alle Analytiker im Sinne der extremen Skepsis sind. Ich glaube, es wäre der Ruin, das Ende der Religionsphilosophie, wenn wir *alles* Mögliche annehmen würden. Grenzen muß es geben; aber innerhalb dieser Grenzen scheint das Postulat des Pluralismus angemessen zu sein. Das wäre *ein* Kennzeichen, nämlich die Eigenartigkeit.

Was das andere Kennzeichen, das ich etwas ungeschickt „Allgemeinheit" genannt habe, betrifft (hier werde ich schimpfen; ein Philosoph muß von Zeit zu Zeit schimpfen, das macht sich gut), so glaube ich, daß hier eine Unsitte getrieben wird mit dem, was die Engländer „parochialism" nennen: Man sieht nur *unsere* Religion und macht sich z.B. vor, der Gegensatz zur Religion wäre der Atheismus, obwohl es atheistische Religionen gibt, so den Hinayāna-Buddhismus. Das Postulat der Allgemeinheit wäre, daß der Gegenstand der Religionsphilosophie nicht eine bestimmte Religion, sondern das Allgemeinste in den Religionen sein sollte. Was dieses Allgemeinste ist, worin es besteht, wenn Sie, z.B. das Christentum und den Hinayāna-Buddhismus unter einen Hut legen sollen, und finden sollen, was ihnen gemeinsam sein soll, das ist ein großes Problem. Sie wissen, daß dieser Buddhismus keinen Begriff der Gnade, keinen Begriff des Gebetes kennt, keinen Gott hat – eines der Grunddogmen ist: es gibt keinen Gott, es gibt keine Seele –, und doch kann man nicht leugnen, daß er eine Religion ist. Das Postulat des alten Bauern lautet: Meine Damen und Herren, bitte, keinen *parochialism*! Keine Beschränkung auf die christliche Religion! Die Philosophie geht immer auf das Allgemeinste, und wir wollten das Allgemeinste in der Religion untersuchen, das allen großen Religionen gemeinsam ist. Das wäre also das Postulat der Allgemeinheit.

Endlich ein Wort über das dritte Kennzeichen, die Komplexität. Die Religion ist etwas ungeheuerlich Komplexes, etwas unglaublich Komplexes. Wahrscheinlich überschauen wir bis jetzt nicht alle diese Verhaltensweisen und Formen des Denkens, Sprechens usw., die dem religiösen Menschen eigen sind. Nun, hier hat auch der Reduktionismus Unheil gestiftet. Ein bestimmter Typ des Reduktionismus ist z.B. sehr klar durch den Marxismus-Leninismus vertreten: Die Religion sei ein Inbegriff von phantastischen Vorstellungen über die Natur; dies ist die Reduktion der Religion auf etwas rein Kognitives. Evidenterweise falsch, wie so viele andere Dinge im Marxismus-Leninismus. Dieser Haltung ist eine andere entgegengesetzt, die bei uns verbreitet ist, nämlich der Emotivismus, die Reduktion der Religion auf rein Emotives. Ich habe einmal versucht, zu zeigen, daß das den Tatsachen widerspricht. Erlauben Sie, daß ich wiederhole, was ich da geschrieben habe, über mein Experiment mit dem Araber – die Kollegen aus Israel sollen mir verzeihen. Es ist ein armer Mann, dem ich in der Wüste begegne, und ich fasse ihn am Bart und frage ihn, ob Allah existiert. „Ja", sagt der Araber, „ja selbstverständlich". Dann drehe ich das Ganze um und frage, ist es wahr, daß Allah existiert? „Ja", sagt der Beduine, und er fährt fort, „selbstverständlich, er muß da sein". Und das kann nur eine Aussage sein, etwas Kognitives – daraus folgt, daß die Gläubigen glauben, in ihrer Sprache kognitive Ausdrücke zu haben. Es ist falsch, dies auf das Emotive zurückzuführen. Vielleicht kann man zeigen, daß der Gläubige sich geirrt hat, usw., aber das Postulat lautet: Keine Reduktion a priori durchzuführen, sondern versuchen, die Religion in ihrer gesamten Komplexität zu erforschen, sich nicht nur auf einen Aspekt festlegen.

3. Das war das zweite Stück. Ich erinnere: das erste war die Natur, das zweite der Gegen-

stand und jetzt kommt – ich bin bald am Ende – das dritte Stück: die Methode. Tatsächlich habe ich die ganze Zeit hindurch von der Methode gesprochen, und die Einteilung ist natürlich mehr oder minder willkürlich. Daher habe ich nur zwei eher nebensächliche Bemerkungen über die Methode und über gewisse Unsitten, die von unseren Religionsphilosophen mit der Methode getrieben werden, zu machen. Die zwei Postulate, die ich hier gegen diese Unsitten formulieren möchte, sind die folgenden:

Erstens: Ich möchte vorschlagen, daß die Religionsphilosophie eine empirische Grundlage haben sollte. Wie wird's gemacht? Sehr oft, bei verschiedenen hochverehrten Theologen usw., so: Es wird ein Begriff der Religion konstruiert, im Arbeitszimmer des Herrn Religionsphilosophen oder Theologen, und wenn dieser Begriff so schön konstruiert ist, dann treibt man eine Analyse dieses Begriffes. Das ist selbstverständlich eine sehr angenehme Beschäftigung, aber mit Wissenschaft hat es überhaupt nichts zu tun. Die Religion ist ein reales Phänomen; man kann sie liebhaben oder nicht liebhaben, aber eines kann man nicht leugnen, daß es so etwas wie Religion, oder, genauer gesagt, religiöses Verhalten, religiöses Sprechen von Menschen gibt, und es ist – verzeihen Sie das Wort – ein Unfug, unseren eigenen, herausspekulierten Begriff der Religion anstelle dieser Realität zu analysieren. Das Postulat wäre, die Religion als etwas Reales anzusehen; man soll also nicht über unsere Begriffe sprechen, sondern über die Realität. Das aber bedeutet, daß wir eine Kenntnis der religiösen Verhältnisse haben, eine empirische Kenntnis haben. Schauen Sie, werden Sie mir sagen, eine kolossale Bücherei ist über das religiöse Verhalten der Menschen geschrieben worden. Das ist schon wahr, aber gerade nicht über die Dinge, die uns als Philosophen interessieren. Es gibt ein paar gute Werke empirischer Art über die religiöse Sprache, aber viel weniger als man gerne haben möchte. Eine Anregung des abtretenden alten Mannes für die jüngere Generation lautet daher: Wollen Sie, bitte, die empirische Forschung in diesem Gebiet fördern und gebrauchen, weil das eine notwendige Grundlage für die Religionsphilosophie ist. Das wäre das eine, denn ich glaube, diese empirische Grundlage ist nicht nur nützlich, sie ist notwendig: damit wir eine Wissenschaft haben, brauchen wir eine empirische Grundlage.

Der andere Vorschlag, das andere Postulat ist nicht so kategorisch. Ich sage, daß eine historische Grundlage nützlich sein würde, und diese fehlt kolossalerweise. Schauen Sie, meine verehrten Damen und Herren, über die Religion haben sehr zahlreiche, oft geniale Denker in unseren und in anderen Kulturkreisen gedacht; ein ungeheures Quantum an Scharfsinn, Erudition usw. wurde gebraucht, um zu verstehen, was z.B. der Glaube ist, und zwar sowohl in der katholischen Theologie wie auch z.B. bei den Brahmanen. Man denke nur an die Werke eines Uddyotakara oder eines Shankara, um nur zwei zu nennen.

Nun, das Postulat ist das folgende: Es wäre nützlich, wenn die Religionsphilosophen nicht versuchen würden, offene Türen einzurennen und dort Forschungen zu betreiben, wo es sich um Probleme handelt, die seit Jahrhunderten gelöst sind. Und leider wird dieser Unfug immer wieder getrieben. Ein paar Beispiele, denn ich will nicht Behauptungen ohne Grundlagen aufstellen: Herr High hat eine Entdeckung gemacht, daß Glaube-an und Glaube-daß nicht dasselbe sind. Sehr schön. Nun, dies findet sich bei Augustinus und ist bei Anselm ausgearbeitet, und bei Thomas von Aquin steht dieselbe Sache, über die damals ein Student im Ersten-Semester-Examen gefragt wurde, und zwar viel scharfsinniger und eingehender als bei Herrn High. Was er darüber sagt ist freilich richtig; aber er rennt offene Türen ein: man soll nicht das zu lösen versuchen, was andere gelöst haben. Das ist nur ein Beispiel.

Ich werde hier noch zwei Männer nennen, die ich sehr schätze; Herrn Tillich und Herrn Ricoeur. Diese sprechen von Symbolen in allen Abwandlungen. Die religiöse Sprache soll symbolisch sein; Tillich und Ricoeur haben tiefe, sehr tiefe Betrachtungen darüber gemacht. Ich habe mich bemüht zu verstehen, was sie eigentlich damit sagen wollen, weil es bei diesen nicht-analytischen Denkern die Sitte ist, nicht klar zu sagen, was sie meinen. Man muß sich anstrengen, sie zu verstehen. Nun glaube ich, sie verstanden zu haben. Sie meinen genau dasselbe, was die Scholastiker unter dem Namen „Analogie" vortrugen. Nur machen sie es schlecht; ich sage Ihnen, sie würden im 13. oder sogar im 16. Jahrhundert im Ersten-Semester-Examen der Theologie durchfallen. Wenn Sie so ein kleines Werkchen von Cajetan nehmen, *De nominum analogia*, da ist hier unvergleichbar mehr drinnen als im ganzen Tillich und Ricoeur zusammen. Ich sage das trotz aller Reverenz für diese eminenten Denker. Was ich also anregen möchte – und das nicht nur im Hinblick auf unsere scholastische Tradition; wir haben ungeheure Massen von solchen Betrachtungen z.B. auch bei den Indern – ist folgendes: Es ist notwendig, eine empirische Grundlage zu haben, und es wäre sehr nützlich, wenn wir auch die historische Grundlage nicht vernachlässigen würden.

Das ist alles.

Ich habe nur ein paar Ratschläge formuliert, und, wenn Sie es mir erlauben, werde ich wiederholen, was ich gesagt habe. Ich habe nämlich aus meiner kleinen didaktischen Erfahrung gelernt, daß es manchmal gut ist zu wiederholen.

Wir haben elf Postulate genannt. Da aber 11 eine unschöne Zahl ist, soll am Ende noch ein 12. angefügt werden. Zunächst aber die schon genannten elf:

1. Die Religionsphilosophie soll weder ein Ersatz, noch eine Stütze für die Religion sein.

2. Sie soll keine Theodizee und keine Anti-Theodizee enthalten.

3. Sie sollte im wesentlichen eine Logik der Religion sein.

4. Vielleicht dürfte sie auch zwei andere Funktionen ausüben, nämlich jene der Vorläuferin für Spezialwissenschaften und jene der Teilsynthese.

5. Die Religionsphilosophie sollte die Eigenartigkeit der Religion berücksichtigen, und zwar wenigstens als Ausgangspunkt. Das bedeutet,

6. daß sie die Möglichkeit besonderer Sinn- und Wahrheitsregeln anerkennen sollte.

7. Dieser Pluralismus der möglichen Sinn- und Wahrheitsregeln sollte jedoch Grenzen haben, und diese Grenzen sehe ich persönlich in den allgemeinsten Regeln des Schließens und in der allgemeinen Semiotik.

8. Die Religionsphilosophie sollte sich auf die Gesamtheit der Religionen, auf das Allgemeinste in der Religion, und nicht nur auf unsere lokale Religion beziehen.

9. Sie sollte die gesamte Komplexität der religiösen Phänomene berücksichtigen und sich nicht auf einen einzigen Aspekt festlegen.

10. Sie sollte eine empirische Grundlage haben, und die Forschungen in diesem Gebiet sollten angeregt werden.

11. und letztens: Die Ergebnisse des Nachdenkens der Theologen und Buddhologen der Vergangenheit sollten bekannt sein, bevor wir an die Forschung in einem Gebiet gehen.

Das sind, meine verehrten Damen und Herren, einige rhapsodische – wie Kant sagte – Gedanken, die ich mir in einem Feld gemacht habe, das ich so nebenbei auch bebaute, und die ich aussprechen möchte bevor ich sterbe. Ich hoffe, daß die jüngere Generation die Forschung in diesem Sinn übernimmt. Und ich bin den Organisatoren sehr dankbar, daß sie mir die Gelegenheit gegeben haben, Ihnen so eine Art Testament vorzutragen.

Damit wir aber 12 haben – komme ich noch zu einem letzten Postulat; es soll das Schlußwort sein. Dieses letzte Postulat ist von einer anderen Art; es ist nämlich ein Postulat, das sich nicht so sehr auf das Wissenschaftliche, sondern auf das Moralische richtet, das Moralische des Forschers im Gebiet der Religionsphilosophie. Die Religionsphilosphie gehört, meine verehrten Zuhörer, zu jenen Disziplinen, die durch eine Art von Menschen infiziert ist, die nicht hierher gehören. Es gibt mehrere solche Disziplinen, z.B. die Indologie. Wenn Sie versuchen, etwas über das indische Denken zu erfahren, dann werden Sie sehen, was für Ungeheuerlichkeiten da vorkommen. In unserem Gebiet haben wir es immer mit einem Typus von Mensch zu tun, der eine Weltanschauung hat − sei es eine Religion, sei es eine Anti-Religion; oft ist er sich aber dieser Weltanschauung nicht sicher; er hat keinen festen Glauben. Er treibt Religionsphilosophie, um eine Stütze für seinen Glauben zu finden. Er glaubt an Gott; und möchte in der Religionsphilosophie einen Beweis für die Existenz Gottes finden, oder so etwas, weil sein Glaube schwach ist. Oder jemand ist ein Anti-Religiöser und möchte von der Religionsphilosophie einen Beweis haben, daß die Religion falsch ist. Ich bin der Meinung, daß diese Art von Menschen aus der Religionsphilosphie ausgemerzt werden sollen. Sie sind keine echten Wissenschaftler. Sie schaffen nur Unruhe und Verwirrung. Sie werden mir entgegenhalten, daß eine neutrale Haltung ja nicht möglich ist. Das ist selbstverständlich. Ein Mensch, der keine Weltanschauung hat, ist ein Mythos. Jeder von uns hat eine Weltanschauung, das soll nicht bestritten werden. Das wird hier gerade postuliert; es ist mein zwölftes Postulat: Diejenigen, die an die Religionsphilosophie gehen, können freilich ihre Weltanschauung nicht loswerden. Aber sie sollen eine *feste* Weltanschauung haben, einen Glauben, der so fest ist, daß er keine Forschung fürchtet. Nur mit solchen Männern kann man eine echte wissenschaftliche Religionsphilosophie treiben.

Leider ist die Lage bei weitem nicht so schön, und viele Menschen, die Religionsphilosophie treiben, treiben sie aus unreinen Motiven. Meine Damen und Herren, ich bin einer von jenen, der Schriften von Verschiedenen unter Ihnen gelesen hat, und ich darf der Überzeugung Ausdruck geben, daß hier jene Leute, die dem Ideal der hier umschriebenen Religionsphilosophie treu bleiben, zahlreich vertreten sind; deshalb darf ich auch der Hoffnung Ausdruck geben, daß in diesem Symposium echte und nützliche Arbeit über Religionsphilosophie geleistet werden wird.

ANMERKUNG

* Vom Tonband transkribiert und leicht bearbeitet von Elisabeth Leinfellner. − Vom Verfasser durchgesehen und unter Mitwirkung des Herausgebers für den Druck eingerichtet.

* * *

OPENING ADDRESS OF THE EIGHTH INTERNATIONAL WITTGENSTEIN SYMPOSIUM 1983*

Joseph M. Bocheński
Fribourg, Switzerland

Ladies and Gentlemen, Representatives of the Government!

Permit me two personal remarks. We speak of philosophy of language and critique of language, and we have to apply some criticism also to my language. Namely, I speak a dialect which, in some way, resembles your beautyful German language. But that's what my friends say ... Please, forgive me. I hope that you will at least partially understand me. This is the first remark.

But the second remark is that I am in trouble. Of the two speakers before me Mr. Hübner has spoken with great profundity and not without wit, and Mr. Wallner with wonderful wit and not without profundity. Now, what's left for me? I will say the following: I am very old. The famous, great Austrian philosopher who has just celebrated his 80th birthday, Sir Karl Popper, is younger than I am. I am a grandfather. Thus, what I am going to do is to give advice, rustic advice, without profundity, without wit, rustic advice from an old peasant who has tilled his field and who now has to go away and wants to give some advice to the younger generation. They are wishes of the old gramps, of the old father, but without any profundity, without wit; they are rhapsodically – as Kant has said – pieced together. Please forgive me. These were the personal remarks.

Now I come to the subject matter itself. Exactly 200 years ago (1783) a book appeared in Riga, with the strange title *Prolegomena zu einer jeden künftigen Metaphysik, die als Wissenschaft wird auftreten können (Prolegomena to Any Future Metaphysics Which Will Have the Character of a Science[1])*. At this time, Kant believed that metaphysics was at a turning point. A completely new metaphysics should be established. As regards philosophy of religion, it is my conviction that we are in a similar situation. We have reached a turning point, the beginning of a new period. And–if there existed such a mind as Kant–it would be good if he would write prolegomena to this new philosophy of religion. Unfortunately, I am unable to do this. I can formulate only a few rhapsodic whishes, or, expressed in a scholarly way: postulates. My subject matter is the following: I want to formulate a few postulates for any future philosophy of religion which will have the character of a science. If you permit me, I will proceed as follows: in three parts. Firstly, on nature, that is, postulates on the nature of philosophy of religion, secondly: on the subject matter of philosophy of religion, namely, religion; and thirdly: on method. This division is somewhat lopsided, since everything is on method. But that's the way it is: it is always good and fine if we can have three parts. Thus we have: nature, subject matter, and method, and at the end a summary with an afterword. To summarize is a custom with philosophers.

Ladies and gentlemen, now we come to our first point, namely, *nature*. If you permit me, I have to make here a few remarks on the relationship between philosophy and religion. Exactly here is the turning point, and the first point is: How were these relations until now, until the rise of Analytic Philosophy? The answer is: They were not kosher. They were tarnished. The situation was completely different compared to, let's say, the situation in philosophy of art. Philosophy of art developed quietly, philosophy of religion didn't. Why? Because philosophy constantly appeared as either one of two things: either as a substitute for religion, or as a support of religion. Therefore, these relations were not kosher. Why was that so? The answer is very simple: firstly, exactly for the reason that pre-Analytic philosophy was not analytic but synthetic. This philosophy attempted to build up a synthesis of all human experience; thus it became the vehicle of a *Weltanschauung*. I do not even talk about the fact that certain philosophers, let's say, Comte etc. consciously understood themselves to be representatives of a *Weltanschauung*. But even if they did not do that—men, for instance, like Spinoza—they were nevertheless about to fabricate a substitute for religion, this synthesis which any religion brings along in some way. This is the first reason.

The socond reason is that, by and large, these philosophies were expressed in object language. Thus they spoke of the same things as religion itself, for instance, of God, the world soul, etc. This was the reason why most philosophers wanted to fabricate either a substitute for religion, or a support of it. Of course, there are exceptions. One great exception is Aristotle: he completely ignores religion—religion does not exist for him. It is a sort of historical miracle that it is Aristotle who had such great influence upon three religions: Judaism, Christianity, and Islam. But for him, religions simply do not exist; they do not interest him. This is one attitude. Another possible attitude is the one of Thomas Aquinas. For him, philosophy is neither a substitute, nor a support, but philosophy produces a partial synthesis which is built into the most general synthesis of theology.

Now, ladies and gentlemen, the first thought of this old man in this field is that this is all over. We live in the age of analysis. Today's philosophy *is* Analytic Philosophy—everything else belongs to history. And here, in this place where Wittgenstein has lived and worked, we may express this with all clarity: The old philosophy is a thing of the past! We live in the age Analytic Philosophy, and this philosophy can be neither a substitute for, nor a support of, religion. Why? Again the answer is very simple, since, firstly, this form of philosophy is *analytic* also in the sense that it does not believe in a general synthesis. We produce partial syntheses, above all we analyze, but no Analytic philosopher will offer an all-inclusive picture of the world. Secondly, by and large,—let's say, essentially—Analytic Philosophy is in metalanguage. Analytic Philosophy does not speak of the world; it speaks of language. I do not want to exaggerate: I am not of the opinion of those of my colleagues who believe that philosophy should only contribute to the *Oxford Dictionary*; I believe, now and then we are in a position to say something in object language, too. But essentially we are oriented towards metalanguage and there is, therefore, no talk of a substitute or support.

Conclusion, that is, postulate: Theodicy, the vindication of God,—or anti-Theodicy—is not a part of philosophy of relgion; Theodicy should be eradicated from philosophy of religion; it has nothing to do with it. By this I do not mean to say that Theodicy, the natural theology, is not possible. I personally believe that it is possible. But in the light of our logic theodicy appears, firstly, as being very difficult; secondly, without great plausibility; and thirdly, as Whitehead once said so beautifully: What theodicy produces is "not very useful for religious uses", examples being the gods of Aristotle or even Whitehead's God. Therefore I say, theodicy is good, but in any case it has nothing to do with philosophy of religion. A believer believes in God and in theodicy and does not need a philosophical support of this belief. This is my postulate as regards theodicy.

Now, this is negative, the old man's proposal what philosophy of religion should not be: no support, no substitute. But positively: What is philosophy of religion? Another proposal would be the following: Essentially, philosophy of religion is logic of religion, if we understand by logic of religion something more comprehensive and not as narrow as, for instance, formal logic alone. We then understand logic of religion in the sense of general logic which, as you know, consists of three parts, namely: (1) pure or formal logic; then, applied logic, namely (2) logic of language or semiotics; and, (3), logic of thinking, that is, general methodology. The proposal would be: Essentially, philosophy of religion should be logic of religion. I say, essentially, since we cannot exclude that philosophy of religion should carry out the two functions which philosophy traditionally has always carried out: One of these functions is the forerunner function; philosophy has always served as a forerunner of the sciences. It is not impossible that, for instance, the many works of religious language which recently have originated are simply forerunners of a linguistics of religion. Therefore, philosophy of religion could carry out the function of being a forerunner of other, specialized sciences. Secondly, philosophy has always had an interdisciplinary function, namely the function of partial synthesis. There are so many religious sciences: there is sociology of religion, geography of religion, psychology of religion, linguistics of religion, etc., etc. We feel the need to somehow synthesize these sciences; it is possible that philosophy of religion could accomplish something in this respect. These, ladies and gentlemen, have been my proposals of an old man as regards the nature of philosophy, of philosophy of religion. Therefore, please: no substitute for, no support of, religion! To this we compare philosophy of religion as logic of religion.

With this I come to the second part. Perhaps you remember: the second part was to be the subject matter, namely, religion, a vast and sublime topic. It will need a lot of time here.

Ladies and gentlemen, here is the long part: the subject matter. Various things can be said about religion, but I am inclined to believe that for our purposes, for the purposes of philosophy of religion, we should especially stress three characteristics of religion. By this I mean uniqueness, generality, and complexity. I will make clear what I mean by that. (A friend of mine said, if we speak in clear words, how is a dialogue possible? But among philosophers—at least among those who are followers of Wittgenstein—the bad habit prevails to attempt to at least speak clearly. And then the others say: Superficial, superficial, there is no profundity. Ladies and gentlemen, the most profound thing of all is the void!) Now, let's attempt to be clear about it. At first, we have here the postulate of acknowledging religion's uniqueness. Religion should be seen as a complex of unique phenomena, as something special. Perhaps analysis will show later on that religion can, nevertheless, be reduced to something else, that it is, for instance, ethics (as in Kant) or something else; but one should not presuppose this a priori—on the contrary: The proposal—again this old man's—is: In case we cannot demonstrate the opposite, we should approach the field with the presupposition that religion is something unique. This postulate is an a priori; of course, later on you may perhaps change the postulate. But in the beginning the approach should be made from the standpoint of uniqueness.

What does this imply? This implies that we have to admit a priori the possibility of many different specific rules of meaning and of truth. This is again an entirely concrete postulate. Perhaps later on it will appear that it is otherwise; but a priori we have no reason for proceeding in another manner. Religion seems to be something unique, and we should admit the possibility of very specific rules of meaning and very specific rules of truth. Often this is not done and various kinds of reductionism have come into existence. Compared to this, this thesis, this proposal, this wish of the old peasant has been formulated in the sense of a methodological pluralism; this presupposes that we postulate a general philosophical pluralism and admit the possibility of different rules of meaning and of different rules of truth.

Perhaps you permit me a few comments on this pluralism. Although today's philosophy is Analytic Philosophy one has, nevertheless, to express—in this place where one of its most prominent representatives has worked—that Analytic Philosophy did not initiate this pluralism. Whatever Moore might have thought, Russell was, in any case, an extreme monist. And W. I, the Wittgenstein of *Tractatus*, is such an extreme—I should like to say: absurd—monist. His influence upon the Vienna Circle leads to the latter's extreme monism: There is only one concept of sentence, only one concept of meaning, only one concept of truth, etc.; the only admissible language is the language of science. But here a change has ocurred. Of course, the influence of Wittgenstein's, W. II's, language games is here very important, but not exclusively. An entire series of factors converges in this attitude of the modern philosopher. There is, firstly, formal logic—or, if you prefer, more exactly: the methodology of deduction—which has clearly demonstrated how we can make different axiomatizations. This is, above all, the result of the comprehensive criticism of the sciences, not only as found in connection with Kuhn's paradigms, but as found in the entire development of criticism from Boutroux to Kuhn. It is the merit of philosophy of language and, last but not least, of Wittgenstein's idea of language games that today we are pluralists throughout, in the methodological sense of the word; we are pluralists to such a degree that we, ladies and gentlemen, run some risk to exaggerate. We are so pluralistic that everyone plays his own trumpet, has his own logic, his own theory of language, etc., and then we fall into a complete skepsis. What would be left for the philosopher is to describe how religious people speak. As a result we would have to assume that every kind of superstition is just as important as science and as religion.

After I have formulated the postulate of pluralism, I would like to restrict pluralism; as an additional postulate I adduce the postulate of restriction. According to this postulate, the uniqueness of religion has limits. Where are these limits? This is a difficult philosophical problem. But at the moment I would say as much: They certainly lie in the most general rules of deduction and the most general principles of semiotics, "most general rules" understood, for instance, in the sense of Quine's philosophy of logic. I quote the great master's name so that it be clear that not everybody is such a pluralist in the sense of extreme skepsis. I believe it would be the ruin, the end of philosophy of religion, if we could postulate everything imaginable. There must be limits; but within these limits the postulate of pluralism seems to be appropriate. This was *one* characteristic, namely, uniqueness.

As regards the other characteristic, which I have called, somewhat clumsily, "generality" I happen to believe that we do assume here often an attitude which the English call "parochialism": We see only *our* religion and pretend to ourselves, for instance, that the opposite of religion is atheism, even though there are atheistic religions, for instance, Hinayānā Buddhism. The postulate of generality is, then, that philosophy of religion's subject matter is not one specific religion but the most general phenomena common to all religions. What these most general phenomena are, what they consist in, if you should bring under one heading, for instance, Christianity and Hinayānā Buddhism and should find out what is common to both of them, this is a great problem. You know that Hinayānā Buddhism has no concept of grace, no concept of prayer, no God—one of the basic dogmas is: there is no God, there is no soul—and we nevertheless cannot deny that it is a religion. Thus, the postulate, again of the old peasant, is: Ladies and gentlemen, please: No parochialism! Do not restrict yourselves to the Christian religion. Philosophy always aims at the most general phenomena, and we want to examine the most general phenomena of religion which are, if I may say so, common to the great relgions. This has been the postulate of generality; let's call it the second characteristic. It is, accordingly, a postulate for the future philosophy of religion.

Finally a word about the third characteristic, complexity. Religion is enormously complex, incredibly complex. It is likely that we are still not able to grasp all the attitudes and forms of thinking, speaking, etc. which are a characteristic of a religious person. Here, too, reductionism has caused mischief. A certain type of reductionism is very clearly represented by Marxism-Leninism: Religion is a kind of embodiment of fantastic ideas about nature; thereby religion is reduced to something purely cognitive. This is obviously false, like so many other things, not only religion's reduction to the cognitive: To this attitude is opposed another one which is widespread in our countries, namely, emotivism, the reduction of religion to purely emotive expressions. Some time ago I have attempted to show that this contradicts the facts. Permit me to repeat what I have written on my experiment with the Arab—I ask my colleagues from Israel to forgive me. It is a poor man whom I meet in the desert and I grasp his beard and ask him whether Allah exists. "Yes", says the Arab, "Yes, of course". Then I turn the whole matter around and ask, "Is it true that Allah exists?" "Yes", says the Beduin, and he says, "Of course, he must exist". This can only be a statement, something cognitive—the believers, therefore, believe that in their language they have something cognitive. It is absurd to reduce this obviously cognitive utterance to something purely emotive: We can perhaps show that we have made an error, etc., but the starting point is here, and the postulate says that we should not a priori carry out a reduction, but should attempt to have religion researched in all its complexity, not commit ourselves to only one aspect.

This was the second part. I remind you: the first part was nature, the second, subject matter, and now comes—I'll come to an end shortly—the third part, that is, method. In reality, I have talked the whole time of method, and the division is, of course, more or less arbitrary.

Therefore, I have to make only two, rather incidental, remarks on method and on certain forms of how our philosophers of religion abuse method. The two postulates which I here want to formulate against these forms of abuse are the following:

Firstly: I would like to propose that philosophy of religion should have an empirical basis. How is this brought about? Very often, by various venerable theologians, like this: A concept of religion is constructed, in the study of Mr. Philosopher of Religion or Mr. Theologian, and when this concept has been so nicely constructed, then an analysis of this concept is carried out. Now, it goes without saying that this is a very pleasant occupation, but it has nothing at all to do with science. Religion is an empirical phenomenon; we can like it or dislike it, but one thing we cannot deny: that there exists something like religion or, expressed more accurately: religious behaviour, religious speech of human beings. It is—pardon the expression—a nonsense to analyze, instead of this reality, a concept of religion which we, ourselves, have found by speculation. The postulate would be to look at religion as something real; we should not speak philosophically about the concept but about reality. But this supposes that we possess a knowledge of religious phenomena, that is, an empirical knowledge. You will tell me, "A colossal library has been written about humankind's religious behaviour"—this is true, but exactly not about those matters which are interesting for us as philosophers. There exist very few empirical works on religious language, such as one would like to have. Thus, the abdicating old man's suggestion for the younger generation: Please further and use empirical research in this field, since it is a necessary basis for philosophy of religion. This is one of the two proposals, since I believe that this empirical basis is not only useful but also necessary: In order to have a science, was need an empirical basis.

The other proposal, the other postulate is not as categorical. I say that a historical basis would be useful, and this basis is lacking in a colossal way. Ladies and gentlemen, many, and often genial, thinkers in our and in other cultures have thought about religion. An enormous amount of acumen, erudition, etc. was needed in order to understand what, for instance, faith is. This concerns Catholic theology as well as, for instance, Brahamanism, if you consider, e.g., the works of Uddyotakara or Shankara, to name only these two.

Now, the postulate would be as follws: It would be very useful if the philosophers of religion would not attempt to carry coals to Newcastle and to do research in areas whose problems have been solved centuries ago. Unfortunately, this abuse is practiced again and again. A few examples, since I do not want to make assertions without foundations: Mr. High has made a discovery, that belief-in and belief-that are not the same. Very good. Now, the whole thing is to be found in Augustine and has been elaborated in Anselm, and in Thomas Aquinas the same problem is to be found. Students were asked about it in a first-semester exam, and, to be sure, much more acutely and thoroughly than in Mr. High's writings. Now, Mr. High's attempt is on the right track, it is correct, but he is, of course, carrying coals to Newcastle: We should not solve what others have solved already. This is only one example.

I will now mention two men which I highly esteem, namely, Mr. Tillich and Mr. Ricoeur. Now, they speak of symbols in all shadings. Religious language is said to be symbolic; Tillich and Ricoeur have deeply, very deeply reflected upon this. I have tried to understand what they really want to say, since it is the custom with non-Analytic thinkers to not clearly say what they mean. We have to make an effort to understand them and I believe that I have understood them. They believe the very same thing which in the scholastic philosophers goes by the name of "analogy". Only, they do it badly; I tell you, in the 13th or even in the 16th century they would flunk the first-semester exam in theology. If you look at Cajetan's little book, De nominum analogia, there is incomparably more in it than in all of Tillich and Ricoeur taken together. I say this despite all my respect for these eminent thinkers.

What I want to suggest here—and this not only with our scholastic tradition in view; we have an enormous amount of such reflections for instance in India—is the following: It is necessary to have an empirical basis, and it would be very useful if we would not neglect the historical basis, too.

That's all.

I have formulated only a few recommendations and, if you permit me—this is from my narrow didactic experience: it is good to summarize—I want to summarize what I have said here.

We have noted down 11 postulates. It is not good to have 11—therefore a 12th one will be added at the end—but we have had 11, and they go like this:

1. Philosophy of religion should neither be a substitute for, nor a support of, religion.

2. Philosophy of religion should contain no theodicy and no anti-theodicy.

3. Essentially, philosophy of religion should be logic of religion.

4. Perhaps philosophy of relgion should be permitted to carry out also two other functions, namely, the function of being a forerunner of the special sciences, and the function of partial synthesis.

5. Philosophy of religion should take into consideration religion's uniqueness, at least as a starting point. This means

6. that it should acknowledge specific rules of meaning and of truth, at least the possibility thereof.

7. This pluralism of possible rules of meaning and rules of truth should, however, have limits. I personally see these limits in the most general rules of deduction and in general semiotics.

8. Philosophy of religion should be based on the totality of all religions, on the most general phenomena of religion, and not only on our local religion.

9. Philosophy of religion should take the entire complexity of religious phenomena into account and should not be tied down to a single aspect.

10. Philosophy of religion should have an empirical basis and we should stimulate research in this area.

11. and last: The results of the Theologians' and Buddhologists' thoughts of the past should be known before we start research in a certain area.

Ladies and gentlemen, these are some rhapsodic—as Kant put it—thoughts which I have entertained in a field which I have also tilled, besides other fields, and which I would like to express before I die; I hope the younger generation will take over. And I am very grateful to the organizing committee that they have given me the opportunity to present to you a kind of testament.

But—in order to have 12—I will mention a last postulate; it shall function as an afterword. This last postulate is of a different character, namely, it is a postulate which does not as much address scholarship but ethical conduct, the ethical conduct of the researcher in philosophy of religion. Ladies and gentlemen, philosophy of religion belongs to those disciplines which are infected with a kind of person who does not belong here. There are several of such disciplines; one of them is, e.g., the study of India's culture. If you attempt to learn something about Indian thought then you'll see what monstrosities will turn up. In our area I am referring to a type of person who has a *Weltanschauung*—be it this religion or anti-religion etc., anyway a *Weltanschauung*. This person is, however, unsure of his *Weltanschauung*; he has no firm belief and practices philosophy of religion in order to find support for his belief. Let's say, there is someone who believes in God; now he wants to find in philosophy of religion a proof for

God's existence or something like that, since his belief is weak. Or someone is against religion and wants a proof that religion is false. I tell you, this kind of person should be eliminated from philosophy of religion; they only cause unrest and confusion, they are not true scientists. You'll tell me, "Yes, indeed, but a neutral attitude is not possible". This goes without saying. A human being who has no *Weltanschauung*, that is a myth. Each of us has *Weltanschauung*, I do not want to deny this. But that's exactly what will be postulated here, and it is my last postulate: Those who approach philosophy of religion, can and should not get rid of their *Weltanschauung*. But they should have a *firm Weltanschauung*, a belief which is so firm that it is not afraid of any research. Only with such men one can carry on a genuine scientific philosophy of religion. Unfortunately, the situation is by far not so good, and many persons who practice philosophy of religion do so from impure motives.

Now, ladies and gentlemen, I am one of those who has read works written by various authors from among you and I may express the conviction that those who are true to the ideal of philosophy of religion described by my postulates are present in large numbers. Therefore, I also may express the hope that at this symposium genuine and useful work in philosophy of religion will be carried out.

Translated by Elisabeth Leinfellner.

ENDNOTES

* Translated from a tape transcript; slightly edited (E. L.).
1 The term 'science' is used as a translation for 'Wissenschaft'; 'Wissenschaft' means both the sciences and the humanities (E. L.).

* * *

2. Grundlagen und Methoden der Religionsphilosophie

2. Foundations and Methods of Philosophy of Religion

RELIGIOUS BELIEF AND LIFE AFTER DEATH

Terence Penelhum
University of Calgary, Alberta

I wish to argue that belief in a life after death is a necessary component of religious commitment, and is not a superfluous, supernatural addition to it. I shall take Christianity as my main example, but I think that what I say will fit several other major religious traditions as well, with adjustments.

The position I shall take is opposed to a quite common kind of argument in Twentieth-Century theology and philosophy of religion. I shall first indicate the defects in that form of argument, and then present a positive case for my own view.

I

It is possible for someone to believe in an afterlife for reasons that are not religious. Some people think there is life after death because they have been impressed by the record of Psychical Research (or Parapsychology). Others may think there is life after death for philosophical reasons, such as those given by Plato or McTaggart. It is possible to think that an afterlife is just another pleasant (or unpleasant) natural fact, without religious significance. Such opinions are uncommon, but they exist; and they show that belief in an afterlife is not a sufficient condition of religiousness. I wish to argue that it is, however, a necessary condition of it, or at least of a very pervasive form of it.

Some apologists for religion have argued that it is not necessary to believe in life after death. Why would religious apologists think this? Whatever their individual differences, they share a conviction with which it is easy to sympathise, and with which I do myself, have quite strong sympathy. They are convinced that many of the obstacles that prevent reflective and educated people from embracing religion in our day are the result of their misunderstanding what the claims of religion really are. These claims are still presented in forms which combine them with outmoded cosmologies, or Greek metaphysics, or culture-bound sexual chauvinism—details which were not a problem, perhaps, in the First Century, but which prevent hearers in the Twentieth Century from recognising the real intent of the religious message.

If religious apologists feel this, they will try to re-interpret the religious tradition they represent, in order to eliminate those aspects of it which they judge to be outmoded. There are many such aspects which do not concern me here. But sometimes the attempt to remove antiquated hindrances from religion takes the from of attempting to expunge from it all obvious references to the supernatural, and when this happens one supernatural element which is marked for elimination is the belief in a life after death. Roughly, those who wish to eliminate it tell us that it is really no more than a form of symbolism representing certain transformations in human personality that are the central concern of religious faith here and now.

I shall take a theological version of this position, and then proceed to look at a more recent philosophical version of it. After presenting some general philosophical arguments against them, I shall proceed to my positive argument. The positive argument will be that the transformation in human personality that religion requires is one which does not make clear sense unless we reintroduce the idea of a future life when we explain it.

II

My first example is the famous theological debate that centred round Rudolf Bultmann's proposal to *demythologise* the Christian proclamation.[1] Bultmann pointed out that the reader of the Gospels finds in them a world-view which fills our environment with evil spirits, and assumes we live in an three-storey universe, with heaven above, hell beneath, and the world of man in between. Salvation is understood as the rescue of mankind from the dominion of the evil spirits, who owe allegiance to the devil who lives below in hell; this rescue is accomplished by the son of God, who comes down from heaven above, dies, is resurrected, and then ascends once more to the top storey. We cannot believe this world-view; so the whole message of salvation has to be recast in a form that does not assume it, and is free of the myths that encumber it.

To recast it, one has to express it in new terms. As is well-known, Bultmann's attempt to do this uses the language of the philosophical tradition most readily available to him: that of existentialist philosophy. The gospel message then becomes an expression of mankind's urgent need to change from a self-centred, protective, anxiety-ridden form of life, to one that is free, authentic, and open to love and sacrifice.

The problem with this translation is that the original documents say a great deal more than this. They tell their readers that the change in themselves that is so urgent is *possible*. It is possible for a specific reason: that the work of the god-man continues among us after his death, because of his resurrection. Can *this* claim be reinterpreted, or does it have to be abandoned? If it is to be retained, it will have to be reinterpreted in a way that leaves out the raising of the god-man from death. So we are told that the events associated with the stories of Easter in the Gospels are mythological presentations of the fact that the life and death of Jesus inaugurated a new human community, the church, whose life and preaching can transform those who turn to it into free and authentic personalities. These transformations are not due to supernatural events and realities; the language of these events and realities are traditional expressions of the power of the preaching which leads to these changes in its hearers. In Bultmann's own words: "The faith of Easter is just this—faith in the word of preaching".[2]

What has taken place here is that the transforming effects of religious faith are taken to be the content of the message to which faith is the response. Bultmann sees that in the early days the response came about because those who heard the message were reassured by the stories that God had come to rescue them, and that his son had risen from the dead and would sustain them. So he looks for a desupernaturalised version of this reassurance. It turns out to be the power of the church and its preaching. But the church is the community of those who have responded and have undergone the personal change demanded. Without the cosmic grounds for reassurance, the content of the church's preaching is just the demand for change, minus the grounds that make it possible. To repeat, the personal consequences of accepting the claim that the world has been saved by God are now presented as the whole content of that claim. Paul van Buren is clearer than Bultmann himself about this, when he says in his book *The Secular Meaning of Gospel*, which follows Bultmann in many respects, that "Freedom . . . is not the consequence of faith. It is its logical meaning".[3]

At the risk of labouring the obvious, let me make this point in another way. In the Gospels, Jesus is often portrayed as telling his hearers that they do not have enough faith, and that if they did, all things would be possible for them. The sign that they do not have enough faith is that they are beset by anxieties—about their safety, or their possessions, or their family obligations. If they had enough faith, they would be able to *take no thought* for these things. Now, however one responds to this, it is clear that someone who was able to take no thought for these things would be free to give himself in other ways, free to sacrifice and to love. It is easy to read these sayings as commands to be like this. But they are not presented simply as commands. Two other things are said. One is that one should be sacrificial and loving because that is how God behaves to us. The natural response to this, of course, is to say that this is all very well for God, but is too hard for me. So something else is added: since God does act this way towards us, we can be assured that if we do take no thought for what worries us now, and live more openly and sacrificially, no real harm will come to us—even though we may be cheated, or persecuted, or even killed. So if Jesus' hearers really believed God cared for them (as they said they did), they would be reassured enough to be free to live in the way God wants them to. This reassurance is as critical a part of the transformation of the person as the self-negating behaviour it makes possible. Without it Jesus would be making demands that are utopian in the worst sense: he would be telling them to act in ways which would be wonderful if everyone else acted in those ways too, but merely foolhardy in a world where they do not. This is what is commonly said about Jesus' ethics, of course; and if the part about God's reassuring concern is false, the criticism is quite correct. How we are to know that what Jesus says about God's behaviour is true is another matter, and it is not dealt with in the Gospels, where he assumes it to be a consequence of the Judaic tradition which he shares with his hearers and reinterprets to them. But if we, now, reinterpret his preaching as a mere demand for personal transformation, with no cosmic grounds for its viability, we take away what enables anyone to do what it asks.

In a sentence, the demythologising programme, as I read it, seeks to translate the content of religious proclamations into a language made up solely of terms referring to the supposed consequence of accepting them. To use Austin's language, I think it involves a confusion between the perlocutionary force of religious utterances and their illucutionary force: between what the hearing of religious utterances is intended to do to people, or is intended to get them to do, and what is said to them in order to get them to do it.[4] With regard to those religious utterances that are about the resurrection, Bultmann's programme seems to me to treat the claim that it has happened, and may happen also for us, as a mere mythological restatement of the demand that we change ourselves in a way that we could only achieve if we were reassured that it *had* happened. To recognise this is not to say that we have to return to the world-views of the First Century in order to take religious claims seriously. But it is to admit that there are limits to what we can jettison from those views if we wish to continue using the symbols of the tradition without self-deception.

III

I want now to turn to a similar form of argument, centred more directly on the belief in life after death, and couched in the idiom of analytical philosophy. I refer to the proposed reinterpretation of the belief in an afterlife that we find in the work of D. Z. Phillips. He is probably the best-known practitioner of a mode of interpretation of religious discourse that claims descent from Wittgenstein. In spite of the obvious differences, I interpret him, and others who argue similarly, as having an underlying motive like that of Bultmann: that of trying to put aside unreal obstacles to the religious life that are the result of misunderstandigs of its nature and demands.

The obstacles which Phillips seeks to put aside are not mythological fantasies from a bygone age. They are thought, instead, to come from the corrupting influences of philosophical theory. This inclines us to interpret the language of immortality and eternal life in terms of continued personal existence after death. Since such a theory has so many scientific and philosophical difficulties in its way, it is a clear service to religion to show that the elements of religious discourse that have been thought to express it, have quite a different role from this in the form of life of the believer.

A brief comment on the Wittgensteinian ancestry of this position. It is clear that Wittgenstein himself, who respected simple and sincere religious persons, was emphatic that the way they held their faith was not at all like the way in which others hold scientific hypotheses or metaphysical theories. This has naturally led some of his followers to favour understandings of religion which minimise its doctrinal aspects and emphasise the ways in which its commitments issue in distinctive forms of life. Those who have tried to use some of Wittgenstein's insights to attack religion have tended, on the whole, to treat it in the way in which he himself treated philosophical constructions: as requiring us to dislodge our language from the normal settings which give it sense, and resulting in the appearance, not the reality, of coherent communication. Among those who see Wittgenstein's thought as a source of sympathetic interpretation of religion, the common factor seems to be the application to religion of the insistence that it is a deep error to demand philosophical foundations for our beliefs and commitments. If this is applied to religion, it leads to the stance that there is no ground for reproach in the fact that independent grounds for the religious life (such as proofs of the existence of God) cannot be found. This stance does not, by itself, entail rejection of the supernatural content of religious utterances; only of the expectation that they can be established philosophically. But although some Wittgensteinian philosophers of religion, such as Malcolm, do not attempt to desupernaturalise faith, Phillips does do so. I incline to think that in doing so he is closer to the way Wittgenstein himself speaks when talking of religion, as distinct from philosophy, though it is important to bear in mind that this is not the only possible way of developing what he says.

Phillips, then, maintains that the language of immortality and eternal life has a role in religious practice quite different from the one it would have if it told us of a life to follow our physical death. He is not suggesting that such language cease to be part of the religious form of life; he is leaving religion "as it is". He is maintaining that, as it is, religion does not embody this supernatural belief. How can he maintain this?

His argument is partly negative: that if religious commitment did involve supernatural beliefs, these would corrupt what we can see to be its true character. He argues this in two books, *The Concept of Prayer*, and *Death and Immortality*.[5] In each one he maintains that the religious feature he examines is one that could not have the point it does have, if the supernatural understanding of it were true. If we think that prayer is a matter of addressing requests to a supernatural being, we miss its point. Its point is *internal to its practice*. If the person praying were petitioning a supernatural being, then he would only achieve the purpose of what he does if God interrupted the normal processes of nature to give him what he wants. But the point of prayer is realised when the believer sees that the world has no obligation to him, that nothing is his due: when he radically accepts what happens to him. So a supernaturalist understanding of prayer would hinder its *proper practice*, not merely misinterpret what that practice is. He says similar things about the belief in immortality. If this is understood as continuance of life after death, we shall interpret what the believer says and does as an attempt to order his life now so that he can enjoy rewards hereafter, and this will submit his religious practice to the demands of his ego. But the proper understanding of religious practice, and therefore of the language of eternal life, is in therms of the *destruction* of the ego: "The immortality of the soul by contrast refers to a person's relation to the self-effacement and love of others involved in dying to the self. Death is overcome in that dying to the self is the meaning of the believer's life".[6] The point is extended in the following passage from the same work:

> I am suggesting, then that eternal life for the believer is participation in the life of God, and that this life has to do with dying to the self, seeing that all things are a gift from God, that nothing is ours by right or necessity. At this point, however, many philosophers will say that I have yet to prove the existence of God . . . To speak of the love of God is not to prove the existence of a God of love. To say that everything is a gift from God is not to prove the existence of the Giver. I believe these popular philosophical objections to be radically misconstrued. In learning by contemplation, attention, renunciation, what forgiving, thanking, loving, etc. mean in these contexts, the believer is participating in the reality of God; *this is what we mean by God's reality.*[7]

This last sentence makes it clear that the secularising thrust of this interpretation of religious discourse extends far beyond the elimination of the belief in a hereafter. But I will confine myself to that.

I have three philosophical criticisms of this position. (1) First, we find here, as in the case of Bultmann, an unargued assumption that one can understand *what is said* in a particular set of utterances by discovered *what saying it does* to its speakers or its hearers. So the content of talk about eternal life is to be construed entirely in terms of the personality-changes that it induces in those who use it. (2) Second, when Phillips tells us that a supernaturalist understanding of prayer, or of talk of immortality, hinders their proper practice, he is telling us that only those who do not interpret it this way are praying as they should, or approaching death as they should. This is not to leave religion as it is, but to select some preferred religious phenomena and attitudes as normative for religion as a whole. (3) My third criticism is that those religious attitudes that Phillips, and I think Bultmann, take as normative in this way imply an expectation of an afterlife in the very form they tell us to reject. The rest of the paper will present my positive case for this thesis.

IV

I take as my starting point Phillips' statement that eternal life is dying to the self; and his opinion that believing in the perpetuation of life beyond the grave only feeds the demands of the ego, instead of releasing us from them. I do not doubt that the belief in an afterlife can serve such a purpose, and often does—for example, in the hands of the more crass sort of evangelist. What I shall try to maintain is that, in spite of this danger, such a belief is an inescapable component of the conviction that eternal life, and dying to the self, are real human possibilities.

Construing talk of eternal life without including life after death within it requires us to think of eternal life as a transformed state of a human personality here and now. Such a transformed state will either be one in which the person's attitudes and responses and wants are altered (becoming unanxious and outgoing, instead of egocentric, for example), or one in which the person adopts radical moral resolutions and pursues radical moral ideals in a determined way. These two possibilities are clearly not exclusive of one another. But it is characteristic of states like these that they admit of degrees and fluctuations: one person's wants and attitudes can show a greater degree of emancipation from anxiety and egocentricity than another's do, and each of them may have their spiritual ups and downs as life goes on; similarly one person's resolution to follow a less self-absorbed mode of life and conduct will be more successful on some days than others. But there is an absolute quality about the language of eternal life, and, I think, that of dying to the self, which is not matched in the descriptions of those states to which one might be tempted to reduce them. I find it odd to talk as though one person might have more eternal life than another person, or that somebody might have a little less of it today than he did yesterday. Either one has attained it or one has not. Similarly, "dying to the self" is a success-term of a special kind. My attitudes can be egocentric one day and selfless another day, and I can match my resolutions better in one year than in another. But either a person has died to the self or that person has not. It does not seem possible to reverse such an act, or repeat it. I do not wish to place too much weight upon idiomatic differences, but it helps a philosophical theory to be able to account for them. What I would hope to account for, in part, then, is the fact that while those who ascribe the attainment of eternal life to themselves, or to others, do indeed discern its attainment in certain transformations of the personalities of those to whom they ascribe it, there is a difference between identifying these psychological transformations on the one hand and describing them in these particular religious terms on the other. Thus far I have only said that the difference consists in the religious ascriptions not admitting qualifications of degree. I shall now try to explore this further.

While I am following Phillips in talking primarily of the Christian religion, it is commonplace that salvation, or liberation, is conceived in several of the major religious traditions of the world as consisting in emancipation from egocentricity. On the surface, talk of conquering egocentricity seems to be wholly psychological: to be about a morally lofty form of mental health. This is why it is so tempting, when expounding the teachings of the major faiths, to use medical analogies—for example, to say that the first three of the Four Noble Truths of

Buddhism express the Buddhist diagnosis of the human predicament, and the Fourth, together with the Noble Eightfold Path, embody its prescriptions for dealing with it. It is characteristic of the religions that in their diagnostic phase they offer a radically gloomy account of the state of unregenerate human beings; an account that seems pathologically pessimistic, and even misanthropic and life-denying, to secular common sense. A famous western example is St. Augustine's description of the sinful state of his soul at the time in his boyhood when he stole the fruit from the pear tree. Many people feel, reading such accounts, that too much fuss is being made altogether; that although we do have the faults that are identified, they are not as *important* as this. My concern now, however, is with the other side of the religious story of human nature: the description of what happens to someone who has accepted the diagnosis and followed the prescription. For it is to this phase of the story that the language of eternal life, and associated expressions, belong. I think it is fair to say that the common-sense response to these religious estimates, both of the saints and of other regenerate believers, is that not only were they not so bad as their tradition claims them to have been before their conversion, but they are not so mightily improved as it says they are afterwards. Someone who is not determined to overlook such things can still find signs of self-regard, insensitivity, manipulation, lust and self-deceit, even though these factors are now muted and rearranged. Yet the religious language used to talk of the new personality is one that seems to imply a thoroughgoing and decisive transformation. In a way that reminds one of so many discussions of religious interpretations of life, it seems as though the negative facts are not allowed to count, just as the signs of goodness were not allowed to count before.

This appearance is correct, and its causes show that it is not a merely psychological change that the language of eternal life is intended to describe.

But let us begin with the surface psychology of this change. I think this can be captured by saying that the subject sees him- or herself as having been, hitherto, a chronic servant of a tendency he now wishes to reject. Perhaps this is identified as pride, or self-absorption, or compulsive craving. He sees it as having infected all his detailed wants, aversions, and choices, although he will probably say that he has not fully realised its pervasiveness until now. Now that he does admit it, he feels towards it roughly the way an addict feels towards the habit that controls him: he still wants what it tells him to want, but he also, even more, now wants not to have it, and to be freed from the desires it generates. But this is only part of the story; we have included the self-knowledge that is a part of his condition, but if that is all there is the most we will find will be moral conflict. In addition to this we must recognise a second element: somehow he thinks he has decisively begun to free himself from the old compulsions, not merely fight them.

The idioms we use to talk about such moral development are idioms in which we speak of the subject himself and the desires and compulsions he has as though they are distinct entities: so that formerly he was controlled by them, whereas now he is not. He has, we might say, externalised them.[8] This does not entail that he no longer has them, or that he no longer yields to them. Though it cannot be taken seriously if he has them, and yields to them, as much as he ever did, it is consistent with their still winning over him on occasions. But these occasions are now *lapses*, and do not, if he contends with them, show that he is not emancipated from the inner forces he rejects.

So far, there is nothing intrinsically religious about this story. At least, a story like it could be told about anyone who reforms in a radical way, or resolves internal conflict of a deep sort, at the wholly secular level. Conversion to a secular system of political or psychological thought can frequently involve one in a vision of understanding one's inner compulsions for the first time, and turning one's back on them. Sometimes such convulsions are dubbed "religious" on this ground alone, but that is tendentious and question-begging. Even if we were to adopt this nomenclature, there is still a key feature of the language of eternal life, and of death to the self, that is not present in these other cases. I shall call this its *utopian* aspect.

The claim that one has freed oneself from an alien internal force is highly vulnerable. Somebody who talks of some desire within him, or some aversion within him, as though it is an external force is doing this in the face of the obvious fact that it is a desire, or aversion, that he, and no one else, has; so he is open to the charge that his idiom is designed for blatant self-deception. To refute this charge, there has to be some way of cashing his claim that he is in some manner dissociated from that desire or aversion, ever though the evidence shows that he gives way to it from time to time. This has to be provided by showing that the ideal towards which he now directs himself is one towards which substantial progress can be made; and that even though he may end his life without being greatly different, to the outward eye, from what he was before, it is possible for him, given moderately favourable circumstances, to move markedly towards achieving it. In other words, his vision of himself as potentially free of the tendencies he rejects is not absurd, even if he may not match it in practice.

This is a test which many of us fail. It is quite common for us to say of someone that he has devoted his life to objectives whose pursuit is alien to him, and that he does not have the "inner resources" to sustain a life dedicated to them, even though in choosing them he has resolved inner conflicts and uncertainties within him, and may have released spiritual energies that were dormant before, and appear happy in expending them. We may say of him that he is just mistaken to suppose that he can dissociate himself from those factors in his nature that he now claims to reject. To take an obvious case, someone who embraces the rigours of an ascetic way of life is often judged to be rejecting what cannot be rejected and embracing what cannot be embraced, to be denying his own spiritual composition or to be rejecting his own humanity. This sort of criticism can either take the form of claiming that his choice is one that is at odds with his particular nature, even though it might be consistent with some other persons', or it can take the form of claiming that no human being at all can sustain the way of life he claims to follow. When we make criticisms of this kind, I suggest we commit ourselves to a distinction between the real and the phenomenal personality. This need not be a highly metaphysical distinction. It is between the personality that each of us develops for himself and is known to fellows and intimates, and a deeper personal structure that the critic claims to lie beneath it; and this latter may as well be defined through psychology or genetics as through theology. There is no shortage of disciplines that tell us what we are really like, and enable us to make judgments about how far our fellows have come to terms with these alleged realities.

Suppose I am judged by some such scheme, and fail the test. This failure will entail that, in the critic's eyes, those lapses in my acts and feelings which I think I am entitled to discount actually reveal that I am not emancipated from the inner powers I claim to have rejected, and never will be. Nothing will happen to justify my present tendency to write them off. I have misjudged my real nature in sopposing that the compulsions I try to say "no" to are alien to it.

It is in this context that we have to understand what I have called the utopian aspect of the language of eternal life. The sort of criticism we have just considered has the effect of limiting human aspirations, of reminding us that there are inner limits to idealism. But this seems exactly opposite to the way in which the language of eternal life works. For it is used to tell us that someone can, and has, been emancipated from tendencies and compulsions which the very same tradition insists are more deeply ingrained within us than we recognise. It is these ingrained tendencies, not the more readily dislodgeable ones, that it says that person is now freed from, and recognises as alien. Their very depth and persistence generates a bountiful sequence of lapses, in which that person loses to them still. But in spite of this, these lapses are not judged to be indicators of how the person really stands spiritually. They are residual manifestations of the alien power from which that person is now free. The real nature of that person is not to be defined to include them, even though all the empirical evidence indicates that it does.

So to have attained, or to have been granted, eternal life is to have broken away in principle from powers and tendencies within you that have infected your real nature, and are now exposed as alien. These very powers are ones which seem to most realistic observers to define the limits of what human nature is. Egocentricity can at most be reduced, surely, not eliminated? Yet it is this elimination that the language of eternal life claims to have happened, and somehow to have happened already.

I suggest that if this claim were true, it could only be because the utopian vision of human nature totally uncontaminated by those allegedly alien powers was, after all, realistic—that the doctrine that our real nature is devoid of them was correct. Now one traditional way of trying to show this is through myths of primal innocence. The golden or paradisical period in the past was thought to display the original, or essential, nature of man prior to the corrupt infections of pride. But such stories are false, and even if they were not, they would not show what the language of eternal life claims, that the corruption is something from which we can escape. But if we look in the opposite temporal direction, to the future, we can suppose that allegedly real nature of human beings is a future possibility, of which the person said to have gained eternal life now shows manifest signs. But this cannot be a general future paradise in which human nature in general will be transformed; for what we want to provide truth-conditions for is the claim that *this individual* has attained eternal life. For that to be true *this individual* must manifest signs of participation in the future transformation. Since the transformation is, thus far, incomplete, and he lapses so often, only a future individual existence can provide the conditions of that participation. The concept of eternal life is what it has always been taken to be: an eschatological concept that links a changed quality of life now with *an expectation* for the future.

V

I conclude with two comments—the first about the scope of the argument I have offered, and the second about its application to non-Christian religious traditions.

I have tried to show that the language of eternal life, and that of dying to the self, cannot be used of someone without the traditional implication that that person has a future in which the transformation begun here and now will be completed, and the gap which still exists between the ideal he espouses and his present spiritul condition, can be finally closed. Without this implication, the person is only reformed, not saved, and to ascribe eternal life to anyone under such conditions would be to state something false.

Perhaps ascriptions of eternal life *are* always false. I have not tried to show them to be true, only to say something about the conditions of their truth. In many realms of discourse it may be possible to discern the truth of statements one makes without any idea of their truth-conditions. I can be in a position to state truly that my television set is in working order, without having any understanding of what makes it go. In religious discourse there are the strongest reasons for denying that even the devout fully understand the truth-conditions of the claims they make, since they are claims about the transcendent or supernatural. But this does not show that the claims believers make about their spiritual state can be made with no cognisance of their truth-conditions at all. I have been arguing that the special way in which those who participate in the discourse that includes the ascription of eternal life, discount the continuing spiritual defects of those to whom they ascribe it, requires them to assert continued personal existence after death, as traditionally they always have done. An external critic can say that there are insuperable difficulties in the way of asserting that anyone survives death. If he can show this to be true, then he has refuted the belief in the possibility of eternal life, because he will have demonstrated that the truth-conditions of ascribing it correctly to anybody cannot ever obtain. He might believe, still, that those who believe in it are morally better for doing so, even that they could never improve as much if they did not do so; but he would nevertheless have demonstrated that their own way of describing their improved spiritual condition is erroneous.

I have kept to Christian concepts, but have alluded to the fact that egocentricity is the fundamental human ill that is identified in several of the greatest traditions, and liberation is understood as the conquest of it. The pattern of analysis I have suggested for some key Christian concepts can clearly not stand unamended when the nature of liberation in these traditions is examined. But it is easy to show that the concept cannot be reduced to psychological and moral terms either. In the Hindu tradition of Advaita Vedanta, and in most Buddhist traditions with which I am acquainted, the persisting individual self is, roughly speaking, viewed as itself a product of egocentric drives, not merely as a reality that such drives can corrupt. This obviously precludes defining liberation in terms of the continuance of the individual self. But a parallel pattern to the Christian one can still be discerned. In Advaita, the phenomenal, egocentric personality is seen as a misleading manifestation of a real self which is not a human individual, and enlightenment is seen as the experience and realisation of that deeper reality, which is present here and now, yet still, in individual terms, in the future. In Buddhism, the traditional rejection of speculation makes it improper even to use the distinction between the phenomenal and the real, but it is still safe to say the *anatta* doctrine tells us that egocentric experience and thought is shot through with error and falsehood, and that in enlightenment one transcends these, and thus transcends the temporal barriers that the egocentric personality refuses to accept. In both cases the participant's understanding of the partial transformation of the disciple is one that cannot be articulated without transcending psychological and moral descriptions of it. Here too I would argue, therefore, that the religious understanding of the spiritual state of the participant is an irreducibly eschatological understanding.

ENDNOTES

[1] Bultmann, Rudolf, "New Testament and Theology", in: H. W. Bartsch (ed.), *Kerygma and Myth*, trans. R. H. Fuller (London 1972), p. 1ff.
[2] Bultmann (1972), p. 41.
[3] Buren, Paul van, *The Secular Meaning of the Gospel* (London 1966), p. 124.
[4] Austin, J. L., *How to Do Things With Words* (Oxford 1962), esp. Chapter VIII.
[5] Phillips, D. Z., *The Concept of Prayer* (London 1965), and *Death and Immortality* (London 1970).
[6] Phillips (1970), p. 54.
[7] Phillips (1970), p. 54f.
[8] Some of the arguments I use here are developed more fully in Terence Penelhum, "Human Nature and External Desires", *The Monist*, Vol. 62 (1979), p. 304ff. These in turn were responses to two important essays by Harry Frankfurt. See Harry Frankfurt, "Freedom of the Will and the Concept of a Person", *Journal of Philosophy*, Vol. 68 (1971), p. 5ff., and "Identification and Externality", in: A. Rorty (ed.), *The Identities of Persons* (Berkeley and Los Angeles 1976), p. 239ff.

* * *

SEEING-AS AND RELIGIOUS EXPERIENCE

John Hick
Claremont Graduate School, Claremont, California

Much has been written during the last twenty years or so under the stimulus of Wittgenstein's remarks on religion. Indeed we have in the writings of D. Z. Phillips and others what is often referred to as the neo-Wittgensteinian philosophy of religion, according to which religious language constitutes an essentially autonomous 'language game' with its own internal ceiteria of truth, immune to challenge or criticism from those who do not participate in that language game. From a religious point of view it is an attractive feature of this position that it acknowledges the right of the believer to his/her beliefs and practices. On the other hand, however, in doing this it (in my view) cuts the heart out of religious belief and practice. For the importance of religious beliefs to the believer lies ultimately in the assumption that they are substantially true references to the nature of reality; and the importance of religious practices to the practitioner lies in the assumption that through them one is renewing or deepening one's relationship to the transcendent divine being. The cost, of course, of making such metaphysical claims in the secular world of today is that they inevitably provoke controversy; and a corresponding benefit of the contrary view is that such controversy is avoided. Thus when a Humanist or a Marxist tells a believer that it is foolish to pray to God, because there is no God to pray to, the neo-Wittgensteinian philosopher of religion will tell both atheist and believer that they are playing different language games and that there can therefore be no controversy between them. The believer is thus left secure in his belief, protected from outside attack, but only on the understanding that his beliefs do not depend for their validity upon the universe being structured in one way (a theistic way) rather than another (an atheistic way).

I am personally not convinced that Wittgenstein, were he alive today, would have endorsed this neo-Wittgensteinian development. I have the impression that he respected ordinary life and speech too much to accept a theory which so blatantly contradicts the normal intentions of most religious language users. To deny, for example, that the language of petitionary prayer is normally meant to presuppose the reality of a divine being who exists in addition to all the human beings who exist, is (in my view) to contradict the natural meaning of such language. Convictions about the character of the universe, and hence about the most appropriate way to live in it, are turned by this neo-Wittgensteinian analysis into expressions of emotion and attitude whose appropriateness depends upon their expressing the feelings and attitudes of the religious person rather than upon their being appropriate to the nature and structure of reality independently of human feelings and attitudes. It is true that religious people commonly use language in metaphorical ways, and indeed that religious pictures of the universe are typically mythological in character, so that their affirmations concerning God, creation, judgment, heaven and hell, and so on are generally to be construed as pointers rather than as literal descriptions. But the pointers are undoubtedly intended to point to realities transcending the metaphors and myths; and to suppress this intention is to do violence to religious speech and to empty the religious 'form of life' of its central and motivating conviction. This does not seem to me to be in the spirit of Wittgenstein. However I am not an expert on his writtings and am conscious that I may be mistaken at this point. I would accordingly only say that, in my view, the neo-Wittgensteinian philosophy of religion embodies a misinterpretation of religion, and possibly also a misinterpretation of Wittgenstein's utterances on religion.

There is however another aspect of Wittgenstein's work that has, I believe, constructive implications for the philosophy of religion. This is his discussion of 'seeing as' and related topics in the second Part of the *Philosophical Investigations*. I want to suggest that this helps us to place the distinctively religious way of experiencing life on the epistemological map, as a form of what I shall call 'experiencing-as'; and helps us to understand religious faith, in its most basic sense, as the interpretative element within this distinctively religious way of experiencing life. I shall not attempt to extract a doctrine from Wittgenstein's pages, but only to show how his thought can be fruitful in ways which he himself may or may not have had in mind. I leave the question of the extent to which Wittgenstein would have approved or disapproved this suggestion to others who are more fully conversant with the Wittgenstein corpus. Such a procedure is perhaps in line with his own words in the Foreward to the *Investigations*: 'I should not like my writting to spare other people the trouble of thinking. But, if possible, to stimulate someone to thoughts of his own'.

First, then, I suggest that Wittgenstein was right in the implicit judgment, which pervades his references to religion, that what is important and to be respected here is not the conventional religious organizations and their official formulations but the religious way of experiencing and participating in human existence, and the forms of life in which this is expressed. It is in relation to this 'religious way of experiencing life and of participating in human existence' that the concept of seeing-as is relevant. Wittgenstein's Cambridge disciple John Wisdom opened a window in this direction in some informal remarks which I heard him address to the Socratic Society in Oxford around 1949. This was before the publication of the *Investigations*, although there had been a reference to the idea of seeing-as in the *Brown Book*; but in any case I presume that Wisdom's wider use of the concept had been stimulated by discussions with Wittgenstein himself.

Wittgenstein points to two senses of the word 'see'. If I am looking at a picture, say the picture of a face, in sense number one I see what is physically present on the paper—mounds of ink, we might say, of a certain shape, size, thickness and position. But in sense number two I see the picture of a face. We could say that in this second sense to see is to interpret or to find meaning or significance in what is before us—we interpret and perceive the mounds of ink as having the particular kind of meaning that we describe as the picture of a face, a meaning that mounds of ink, simply as such, do not have. The interpretative activity which is integral to seeing in this second sense, but which is absent from seeing in the first sense, is particularly evident when we are looking at a puzzle picture. As Wittgenstein says, 'we *see* it as we interpret it' (*Philosophical Investigations*, trans. G. E. M. Anscombe, Oxford 1953, p. 193). As he also puts it, in seeing-as an element of thinking is mixed with pure seeing in sense number one. When we see the duck-rabbit as a duck and then as a rabbit Wittgenstein speaks of these as aspects, and he says that 'the flashing of an aspect on us seems half visual experience, half thought' (*Ibid.*, p. 197).

We can, I suggest, immediately expand the concept of seeing-as, which is purely visual, into the comprehensive notion of experiencing-as. For the finding of meaning does not occur only through sight. We can hear a sound as that of a passing train; feel the wood as bamboo; smell the cloud as smoke; taste what is in our mouth as peppermint. In our everyday perception of our environment we use several sense organs at once; and I suggest that we adopt the term 'experiencing-as' to refer to our ordinary multi-dimensional awareness of the world. Like seeing-as (or seeing in sense number two), experiencing-as involves thought in the form of interpretation, i.e. becoming aware of our environment in terms of the systems of concepts embodied in what Wittgenstein sometimes called language games. He points out the important fact that the capacity to apply concepts to percepts is a necessary condition for having certain kinds of experience (such as seeing a particular triangle on paper as suspended from its apex) but not for having certain other kinds, such as feeling a toothache (*Ibid.*, p. 208).

The distinction between experiencing and experiencing-as, like that between seeing and seeing-as, or 'seeing' in sense number one and in sense number two, is however seldom actually exemplified. For we hardly ever experience, as distinguished from experiencing-as. Even so stark an experience as feeling pain is often linked by conceptual filiaments with the sytems of meaning that structure our lives. Pains can be experienced as threats to our holiday plans, or to our career, or our financial security, and so on. Perhaps, in very early infancy there is entirely unconceptualized experience. And perhaps there are kinds of aesthetic experience which are not forms of experiencing-as. But I think it is safe to say that ordinary human experiencing is always experiencing-as, always a perceiving of that which is present to us as having a certain recognizable character, which I am calling its meaning or significance. I take it that one of Wittgenstein's basic insights was that the system, or perhaps better the living organism, of meanings in terms of which we live is carried in the language of a certain linguistic community.

Wittgenstein himself seems to have been inclined to restrict the notion of seeing-as to manifestly ambiguous cases, such as puzzle pictures. It would not, he says, make sense for me 'to say at the sight of a knife and fork "Now I am seeing this as a knife and fork"' . . . One doesn't 'take' what one knows as the cutlery at a meal for cutlery' (*Ibid.*, p. 185). On the other hand he recognises that there are occasions when I would not say '*I* am seeing this as an *x*' but when nevertheless someone else might properly say of me, '*He* is seeing that as an *x*'. And this is true, I would suggest, of the ordinary everyday seeings-as, or experiencings-as, in which we recognize familiar objects such as knives and forks. If a stone age savage is shown the cutlery he will not see it as cutlery, because he lacks the concepts, which are part of our culture but not of his, of cutlery, knife, fork, etc., together with such other surrounding concepts as eating at table with manufactured implements, and so on. We could therefore say of him 'He is not experiencing it as cutlery'—but, perhaps, as something utterly puzzling or maybe as a set of magic objects. And in contrast we could say of a member of our own culture, 'He/she *is* seeing it as cutlery'.

I therefore hold that, apart perhaps from certain marginal cases, all human experiencing is experiencing-as. And I would further suggest—in general conformity, I think, with Wittgenstein's insights—that the awareness of entities as having this or that kind of significance always has a practical dispositional aspect. To experience the thing on the table as a fork is to be in a dispositional state to behave in relation to it in a certain range of ways, namely those that consist in using it as a fork. And, in general, to perceive what is before us as an *x* is to be in a state to treat it as an *x*, rather than as a *y* or a *z*.

We next have to notice that in addition to the kind of meaning exhibited by individual physical objects, such as knives and forks, ducks and rabbits, people and books, there are the more complex kinds of meaning exhibited by situations. 'Situation' is a relational notion. A situation, for X, consists of a set of objects which are unified in X's attention and which have as a whole a practical dispositional meaning for X which is more than the sum of the meanings of its constituent objects. Thus our present situation in this session this morning can be described in purely physical terms, corresponding to reports of what is seen in Wittgenstein's sense number one. Here we would describe each physical object in the room, including both human bodies and inanimate furniture, and their several shapes, sizes, positions and movements. But another kind of report is also possible, using such higher level concepts as *Gesellschaft*, philosophy, discussion, academic paper, criticism, etc. Human consciousness normally functions at this situational level, and it is here that we find the distinctively human dimensions of meaning over and above those that we share with the other animals

These distinctively human dimensions of meaning or significance, transcending the purely physical meaning of our environment, appear to be of three kinds—ethical, aesthetic and religious. I shall say a little about ethical meaning, very little about aesthetic meaning, and then rather more about religious meaning.

The ethical or moral meaning that we may experience a situation as having could also be called its social or its personal significance. For morality has to do with the interactions and relationships between persons. A purely physical account of a situation involving people would include a number of mobile organisms; but at the personal or ethical level we interact with these organisms as persons—as centres of consciousness, feeling, will, beings whose very existence imposes a potential moral claim upon us. For example, suppose I am present at a street accident, when someone is struck by a car and is lying in the road bleeding and in pain.

If we can imagine someone experiencing this situation purely at the physical level of meaning they would observe the body and the flowing blood and hear the cries and moans; and that would be all. But as ethical beings we are also conscious in all this of a fellow human being in pain and danger, urgently needing first aid. We are perceiving the ethical meaning of the situation. We are experiencing not only in natural but also in moral terms. And the practical-dispositional aspect of this form of experiencing-as is expressed in the action which our distinctively moral awareness renders appropriate—in this case to do whatever we can to help the injured person.

Clearly, ethical presupposes natural meaning and can in this precise sense be described as a higher order of meaning. For ethical meaning is always the further meaning of a physical situation. And to experience a situation as having this or that kind of moral significance is to be in a dispositional state to behave within it in a way or ways appropriate to its having that significance. These dispositional responses may of course be weakened or cancelled out by some contrary self-regarding concern. But to be a moral, as distinguished from an amoral, being is to be conscious of moral obligations, whether or not or to whatever extent one's actions are guided by them. And to say that we are moral creatures is to say that we are liable to experience human situations as having this kind of significance.

Aesthetic meaning sometimes presupposes physical meaning (as in paintings of natural scenes and of people), but sometimes seems not to (as in much music and in abstract art). And to experience something as having aesthetic significance sometimes has a practical-dispositional aspect, affecting our attitudes, and sometimes seems not to but to be purely contemplative. The varieties and complexities here are daunting, and I do not propose to enter upon them. But to say that human beings are aesthetic as well as ethical creatures is to say that they are liable to experience aspects of their environment as having aesthetic significance.

Moving now to religious meaning, to describe man (as has often been done) as the religious animal is to say that human beings have apparently always displayed a tendency to experience individuals, places and situations as having religious meaning. Throughout a good deal of religious life individuals have been experienced as divine—usually kings, as in many primitive societies and in ancient Egypt (where the Pharaoh was divine), ancient Babylon (where the king embodied divine power), and ancient Israel (where the king was adopted at his enthronement as 'son of God'); and in Christianity Jesus of Nazareth is seen and devotionally experienced as divine. Many places have likewise been experienced as numinous and holy—hills, mountains, trees and rocks among many primitive societies, and within the great world religions such places as Benares, Bodh-Gaya, Jerusalem, Bethlehem, Mecca, Lourdes, and other places of pilgrimage. But the kind of experiencing-as that I should like more particularly to consider is situational. It is a feature of monotheistic religion that any human situation may, in principle, be experienced as one in which one is living in the unseen presence of God. For God is omnipresent, and in all that one does and undergoes one is having to do with God and God with oneself. In the case of saints this consciousness of existing in God's presence has been relatively continuous and pervasive; in the case of more ordinary believers it is occasional and fleeting. In the Hebrew scriptures a particular thread of history is described throughout in religious terms. The escape of a band of alien slaves from Egypt and their wanderings in the Sinai desert and eventual settlement in Canaan, their national consolidation and subsequent conquest and dispersion, are all presented as God's dealings with his chosen people. Their political ups and downs are seen as his encouragement of them when they were faithful and disciplining of them when unfaithful. This is often referred to as the prophetic interpretation of Hebrew history. But this interpretation is not, or not basically, a theoretical interpretation, historical schema imposed retrospectively upon the events of the past. It has its origin in the experience and then the preaching of the prophets concerning the meaning of events that were currently taking place around them. To give just one example, when in the time of Jeremiah a hostile Chaldean army was investing Jerusalem, to the prophet this was God wielding a foreign power to punish his erring people. As one well-known commentary says, 'Behind the serried ranks of the Chaldean army [Jeremiah] beheld the form of Jahweh fighting for them and through them against His own people'. Jeremiah did not, I take it, literally see the visible form of Jahweh; but he did experience what was taking place as having the religious meaning of divine punishment. And it is this kind of experience reported by the prophets that, in Jewish understanding, provides the clue to the meaning of all history.

Again, the New Testament centers upon the disciples' experience of Jesus as the Christ— which originally meant the messiah (God's anointed agent to bring in the Kingdom) but which in later Christian thought was elevated to mean the Second Person of a divine Trinity. In experiencing Jesus as the messiah the disciples were experiencing him in a way that was significantly different from that of those who perceived him, for example, as a heretical rabbi or a political agitator; and the New Testament documents reflect this apostolic interpretation of Jesus as the Christ.

This word 'interpret' can function in two senses or on two levels; and we should now distinguish these. There is the second-order sense in which an historian interprets the data, or a detective the clues, or a lawyer the evidence, or indeed in which a metaphysician may interpret the universe. This is a matter of conscious theory-construction. At this second-order level there are religious interpretations or, as we call them, theologies and religious philosophies, consisting in metaphysical theories which offer interpretations of the universe in which the data of religious experience are given a central and controlling place. Wittgenstein seems to have regarded these—rightly, in my view—as religiously much less important than the religious experiencing of life, and above all the dispositional aspect of this in attitudes of trust and acceptance and in acts of worship and service. For this second-order kind of interpretation presupposes the more basic, or first-order, interpretative activity which enters into virtually all conscious experience of our environment. In this first-order sense we are interpreting what is before us when we experience this as a fork, that as a house, and the other as a cow, or again when we experience our present situation as one of participating in a session of philosophical discussion; or yet again, when some of us might, in a moment of reflection, be conscious in and through this same situation of being at the same time in the presence of God. Interpreting in this sense is normally an unconscious and habitual process resulting from negotiations with our environment in terms of the set of concepts constituting our operative world of meaning. To interpret in this primary sense involves, as a I suggested earlier, being in a dispositional state to behave in ways appropriate to the perceived meaning of our situation. Thus, in the case of the Chaldean threat to Jerusalem, the appropriate response was one of national repentance; and it was to this that Jeremiah called his fellow citizens. In the case of the disciples' experience of Jesus as the Christ, their dispositional response was one of reverence and obedience, of openness to his teachings and of radical readiness to change their lives in following him.

We observe in these examples that that which is religiously interpreted and experienced is in itself ambiguous—in this respect like a puzzle picture,—in that it is also capable of being perceived non-religiously. A secular historian, describing the events recorded in the Hebrew scriptures, would speak of the rise and fall of empires, and of economic, political and cultural pressures, but would not speak of God as an agent in ancient Near Eastern history. Likewise, in addition to those who experienced Jesus as the Christ there were others who perceived him under quite other categories; so that the Jesus phenomenon was capable of being perceived in these contrary ways. One can see very clearly in such a case the hierarchy of interpretations that can occur. At the most basic level there was awareness of the physical existence of Jesus as a living organism. Superimposed upon this there was, at the human and social level of awareness, Jesus' life as a human being interacting with others in the Palestinian society of his day. And superimposed upon this there was, for the specifically Christian mode of experiencing-as, Jesus as the Christ. At this third level the Jesus phenomenon was importantly ambiguous, capable of being experienced in a number of different ways. This ambiguity is characteristic of religious meaning. On a larger scale we can say that the world, or indeed the universe, is religiously ambiguous—able to be experienced by different people, or indeed by the same person at different times, in both religious and naturalistic ways. This is not of course to say that one way of experiencing it may not be correct, in the—perhaps un-Wittgensteinian—sense of being appropriate to its actual character, and the other incorrect. But if so, the true character of the universe does not force itself upon us, and we are left with an important element of freedom and responsibility in our response to it. From a religious point of view this connects with the thought that God leaves us free to respond or fail to respond to him. I would suggest that this element of uncompelled interpretation in our experience of life is to be identified with faith in the most fundamental sense of that word. All forms of experiencing-as embody cognitive choices and are thus acts of faith; and religious faith is that cognitive choice which distinguishes the religious from the secular way of experiencing our human situation. This element of cognitive freedom in relation to God has been stressed by many religious thinkers. For example, Pascal, speaking of the incarnation, says, 'It was not right that he should in a manner manifestly divine, and completely capable of convincing all men; but it was also not right that he should come in a manner so hidden that he could not be recognized by those who sincerely seek him. He has willed to make himself perfectly recognizable by those; and thus, willing to appear openly to those who seek him with all their heart, and hidden from those who flee from him with all their heart, he so arranges the knowledge of himself that he has given signs of himself, visible to those who seek him, and not to those who do not seek him. There is enough light for those who only desire to see, and enough obscurity for those who have a contrary disposition.' (Pensées, No. 430).

It should be noted that this account of faith as an uncompelled interpretation or mode of experiencing-as is neutral as betwen religious and secular understandings. The theist and the atheist might agree to this epistemological analysis of faith whilst making their own different cognitive choices, the believer trusting that the religious way of experiencing-as into which he or she has entered will ultimately be vindicated by the future unfolding of the character of the universe.

A point which Wittgenstein would, I imagine, want to stress is that the way in which we experience our environment depends upon the system of concepts that we use, and that this is carried from generation to generation in the language in terms of which we think and behave. There is thus a relativity of forms of experience to what Wittgenstein sometimes called language-games or, as I should prefer to say, cultures. This helps to explain how it is that there is not just one form of religious experiencing-as, with its own superstructure of theological theories, but a plurality, which we call the different religions. Given the concept of God—that is, the concept of the ultimate reality and mystery as personal,—and given a spiritual formation within a theistic tradition, the religious person is likely to experience life as being lived in the unseen presence of God, the world around him as God's creation, and moral claims as divine commands. Such a person may be, for example, a Jew or a Christian or a Muslim or a Sikh or a theistic Hindu. But given the very different concept of Brahman, or of the Dharma, or Sunyata, or the Tao—that is, a concept of the ultimate reality and mystery as the non-personal depth or ground or process of existence,—and given a spiritual formation within a non-theistic tradition, the religious person is likely to experience life as the karmic process leading eventually to enlightenment and the realization of reality. Such a person may be, for example, an advaitic Hindu or a Theravada or Mahayana Buddhist. Thus if we ask why it is that Christians, Buddhists, Jews, Muslims, Hindus report such different perceptions of the divine, the answer that suggests itself is that they are operating with different sets of religious concepts in terms of which they experience in characteristically different ways. This is of course a neutral account of the situation. It could be that the religions are all experiencing erroneously, projecting different illusions upon the universe. And it could on the other hand be that they are each responding to an infinite divine reality which exceeds our human conceptualities and which is capable of being humanly thought and experienced in these fascinatingly divergent ways.

My suggestion, then, is that Wittgenstein's concept of seeing-as, enlarged into the concept of experiencing-as, applies to all our conscious experience of our environment, including the religious ways of experiencing it. Such a view does justice to the systematically ambiguous character of the world, capable as it is of being experienced both religiously and naturalistically. These are radically different forms of experiencing-as. Such a view also does justice to the fact that the religious experiencing of life can itself take different forms. The world may be experienced as God's handiwork, or as the battlefield of good and evil, or as the cosmic dance of Shiva, or as the beginningless and endless interdependent process of *pratitya samut-pada* within which we may experience nirvana; and so on. These are different forms of religious experiencing-as. Thus Wittgenstein's original concept can be fruitful in perhaps unexpected ways when it is brought into connection with the concrete religious forms of life.

* * *

DER BEITRAG DER WISSENSCHAFTSTHEORIE ZUR KLÄRUNG DER RATIONALITÄT VON GLAUBE ALS LEBENSTRAGENDER ÜBERZEUGUNG

Otto Muck
Universität Innsbruck

Die folgenden Überlegungen beziehen sich auf lebenstragende Überzeugungen oder, synonym damit verstanden, auf *Weltanschauung* (WA). Wenn auch meist religiöse Rede und metaphysische Formulierungen Gegenstand der Analyse und Kritik waren, so soll durch Berücksichtigung von WA die Frage allgemeiner und grundsätzlicher gestellt werden. Denn religiöse Rede wird als besondere Weise des Ausdrucks von WA verstanden und Metaphysik als Versuch einer philosophischen Entfaltung von Strukturen von WA.

Als Beispiel für Forderungen der *Rationalität* werden die syntaktischen und semantischen Ansprüche gesehen, nach denen der Logische Empirismus religiöse Rede und metaphysische Formulierungen gemessen und kritisiert hat: Unter logisch-syntaktischer Hinsicht die Forderung nach Explizierbarkeit der Sätze gemäß einer Logik im Sinne der *Principia Mathematica*, bezüglich der Sinnhaftigkeit und des kognitiven Gehalts das empiristische Verifikationsprinzip.

Daß diese Forderungen als Rationalitätskriterium verwendet wurden, ergibt sich aus den Folgerungen: Äußerungen lebenstragender Überzeugungen kommt danach kein kognitiver Sinn zu, nur emotiver. Das hat weiters zur Folge, daß derartige Äußerungen nicht begründbar oder kritisch diskutierbar sind, weil der Folgerungsbegriff Aussagen voraussetzt. Deutlich wurde auch das Fehlen von kognitivem Gehalt dadurch, daß diese Äußerungen Wertaussagen oder Normen formulieren oder gar begründen wollen.

Eine Folge dessen, daß Formulierungen von WA kognitiver Gehalt abzusprechen sei, ist, daß sich eine wissenschaftliche Beschäftigung mit WA nicht auf den Inhalt beziehen könne, man müsse WA vielmehr als Ausdruck einer früheren, überholten, jetzt nicht mehr akzeptierbaren Weltsicht auffassen. Wenn derartige Äußerungen heute dennoch auftreten, dann sei dieses Auftreten mit genetisch-erklärenden Methoden zu untersuchen, etwa psychologisch, wissenssoziologisch bzw. ideologie-kritisch.

Für das Verständnis der Struktur von WA ist es interessant, an solchen kritischen Positionen folgendes festzustellen:

1. Der zu Beginn des Logischen Empirismus erhobene *Ausschließlichkeitsanspruch* bezüglich der genannten Forderungen der Rationalität hat durch diesen Anspruch selbst den Charakter einer WA. Dieser Anspruch wird jedoch nicht mit der Methode, die für Rationalität gefordert wird, gerechtfertigt. Diese Inkonsistenz hat dazu geführt, jene Forderungen eher methodisch zu verstehen und als „Abgrenzungskriterien" für Sätze eines bestimmten Bereichs, z.B. für empirisch gehaltvolle Sätze in Erfahrungswissenschaften. Damit eröffnet sich aber die Frage, ob andere Kriterien der Rationalität formuliert werden können, die nicht nur für einen besonderen Bereich gelten.

2. Auffallend ist, daß manche dieser wissenschaftstheoretischen und bezüglich WA ablehnenden Positionen selbst mit einer bestimmten *deutenden Theorie* verbunden sind: sei es ein geschichtsphilosophisches Konzept im Sinne des Dreistadiengesetzes von A. Comte, sei es eine Deutung menschlichen Erkennens im Sinne des empiristischen Erkenntnismodells oder einer evolutiven Erkenntnisauffassung. Auch diese Theorien sind nicht durch die in Anspruch genommene Methode begründet. Es fehlt eine entsprechende kritische Diskussion und Entfaltung solcher Auffassungen wie auch die Klärung ihrer Voraussetzungen. Dazu gehörte auch die Frage nach der eigentümlichen Rationalität und Struktur von WA. Deshalb einige kurze Hinweise zur Struktur solcher Theorien:

Eine vorsichtige pragmatische Rechtfertigung von Forderungen A der Rationalität für einen Bereich a – z.B. für die Erfahrungswissenschaften – zeigt, daß diese Forderungen sich als nötig erwiesen haben, um bestimmte Probleme oder Antinomien in a zu bewältigen. Solche Forderungen finden in einer deutenden Theorie eine Art von teleologischer Erklärung: diese enthält eine Deutung der Elemente von a, z.B. der Erfahrungssätze als Information über die Wirklichkeit; weiters ein Ziel, z.B. die Verläßlichkeit und Optimierung der Information. Mittels der Zusammenhänge eines vorausgesetzen begrifflichen Rahmens (z.B. daß Informationsgewinn nur über die Sinne möglich, aber durch andere Beobachter prüfbar sei) wird daraus abgeleitet, was Inhalt der methodischen Forderung ist, z.B. intersubjektive empirische Prüfbarkeit.

Solche Theorien können *bloß deutend* sein, indem sie die methodisch pragmatisch gerechtfertigte Forderung nachträglich im vorausgesetzten Begriffssystem deuten. Interesse besteht dafür, weil dadurch die Plausibilität vergrößert wird, indem die methodischen Forderungen in den vorausgesetzten begrifflichen Rahmen eingeordnet, integriert werden. Eine solche Erklärung hat daher *integrierende Funktion*. Zugleich besteht jedoch die Gefahr, daß Plausibilität mit Berechtigung verwechselt wird und weitere methodische Differenzierungen und Korrekturen durch eine solche Theorie erschwert werden.

Solche Theorien können aber auch dazu verwendet werden, Forderungen *neu abzuleiten* – mit heuristischem Zweck oder mit dem Ziel der Begründung solcher Normen. Besonders im zweiten Fall zeigt sich die Problematik einer mangelnden Klärung der Stuktur solcher Theorien und des ungeklärt vorausgesetzen begrifflichen Rahmens.

Nach anfänglicher Verabsolutierung der Forderungen A, denen die Sätze von WA (Bereich b) nicht entsprechen, wurde besonders in der Analytischen Philosophie im einzelnen die Eigenart religiöser Rede und damit von WA herausgearbeitet, also von eigenen Forderungen B, die von A wenigstens teilweise verschieden sind. Ein *Reduktionismus* sieht die Forderungen B der Rationalität von b als bloße Anwendung von A auf b und spricht daher in den Fällen, in denen B von A verschieden ist, b Rationalität ab. Wird dem Reduktionismus gegenüber die Verschiedenheit der Forderung A und B wegen der Verschiedenheit der Bereiche a und b herausgestellt, kommt es leicht zu einer unbefriedigenden Trennung der Bereiche. Deshalb wird vorgeschlagen, die Forderungen A als *Anwendung allgemeiner Forderungen* der Rationalität C auf a zu verstehen und die Forderungen B als Anwendungen von C auf b. Selbst wenn die Formulierung von C auf Schwierigkeiten stoßen sollte, kann diese Auffassung wenigstens als heuristisches Ideal dienen. Beispiele für Versuche einer Formulierung von C finden sich im Kritischen Rationalismus und im Konstruktivismus, unter ausdrücklicher Berücksichtigung von WA z.B. bei I. M. Bochenski[1] und F. Ferré[2].

Deutende Theorien für A sind ein Hindernis für eine solche Öffnung von A hinsichtlich C und damit B, besonders wenn der vorausgesetzte begriffliche Rahmen ungeklärt ist. Hier könnte eine deutende Theorie für C helfen, die aber wohl noch schwerer zu formulieren ist als C. Wo jedoch eine solche Theorie fehlt, sollte man Theorien für A gegenüber vorsichtig sein. Übrigens scheint mir die Formulierung einer solchen Theorie für C sowohl das Anliegen einer Metaphysik zu sein als auch deren Schwierigkeit verständlich zu machen.

Welche *Eigentümlichkeiten von WA*[3], also von b, bedingen nun eine Modifikation der in einer Wissenschaft, also in a, gängigen Rationalitätsforderung A? In der Diskussion der Analytischen Philosophie in Anschluß an die *New Essays in Philosophical Theology* wurden u.a. der wesentlich *persönliche* und *praktische* Charakter einer WA herausgestellt. WA ist dabei durch die Funktion charakterisiert, nicht nur eine theoretisch, oft bildhafte symbolisch ausgedrückte, sondern vor allem auch das Entscheiden und Handeln orientierende praktische Deutung alles dessen zu geben, womit sich ein Mensch auseinanderzusetzen hat (Strukturierung und Bewertung der Lebenserfahrung).

Der persönliche Charakter hat zur Folge, daß man gewöhnlich nicht bezüglich einer WA als ganzer – wenn auch bezüglich mancher aus ihr herausgelöster Zusammenhänge – eine Argumentation mit dem Ziel interpersonaler Übereinstimmung anstreben kann. Gehen wir nämlich davon aus, daß in einer Argumentation die Geltung eines Satzes gemäß Argumentationsregeln auf Argumentationsgrundlagen zurückgeführt wird, dann setzt ein interpersonales Argumentieren gemeinsames Akzeptieren der Argumentationsregeln und -grundlagen voraus. Wir sehen von dem philosophischen Problem ab, das sich aus der Frage ergibt, ob die Übereinstimmung nur faktisch ist.

Persönlich soll dann eine Begründung heißen, in der die Beweisgrundlagen wenigstens zum Teil nicht gemeinsam akzeptiert sind. Argumentationsziel eines Dialogs, in dem ein Partner seine persönliche Begründung zu entfalten sucht, wird zunächst eine Verbesserung des Verständnisses der betreffenden persönlichen Überzeugung sein. Zugleich treten hier interpersonal diskutierbare Zusammenhänge auf, z.B. Fragen nach Schlüssigkeit, Widerspruchsfreiheit, Bezug zu gemeinsamer persönlicher Erfahrung und deren Strukturierung. So ist sowohl der Aufweis der allgemeinen Strukturen von WA, die sich aus ihrer Funktion ergeben, wie auch eine Anzahl von Zusammenhängen, die aus konkreter WA herausabstrahiert sind, durchaus interpersonaler Argumentation zugänglich. Aus der allgemeinen Struktur von WA ergeben sich Folgerungen für die Eigenart von Begründungen. Genannt seien hier die Erfahrung als „Lebenserfahrung" und der Bezug zur Erfahrung durch die eigentümliche Art von „Erklärung":

Damit eine WA ihre Funktion erfüllt, muß ihre Erfahrungsbasis nicht nur die von den Erfahrungswissenschaften berücksichtigte umfassen, sondern auch alltägliche Erfahrung der verschiedensten Lebenssituationen und auch spontane Werterfahrung. Diese „Lebenserfahrung" ist in dem Sinn umfassend, als sie nicht von vornherein bestimmte Bereiche dessen, womit Menschen sich in ihrem Leben auseinanderzusetzen haben, ausschließen soll. Der persönliche Charakter der konkreten Lebenserfahrung eines Menschen schließt nicht aus, daß aus dieser Lebenserfahrung vielfach gemeinsame Züge herausgearbeitet werden können, besonders was die soziale und kulturelle gemeinsame Lebenswelt betrifft wie auch typische Grenzsituationen menschlichen Lebens. Die Offenheit, Unabgeschlossenheit der Lebenserfahrung ermöglicht grundsätzlich, daß weitere Erfahrungen rationale Grundlage für eine Modifikation einer WA sind.

Für die Eigenart von Argumentation in WA ist auch zu beachten, daß der Bezug zur Erfahrung nicht den Charakter einer an Prognosen prüfbaren Erklärung hat, sondern eher den Charakter einer auf Angemessenheit zu prüfenden Systematisierung und einer integrativen Erklärung, wie sie auch in deutenden Theorien auftritt. Bezüglich einer in einer WA auftretenden deutenden Theorie, die von den indikativen Sätzen einer WA vorausgesetzt wird, ist zu beachten, ob sie nachträglich deutend oder eigenständig normenbegründend ist. Besonders im zweiten Fall ist für eine kritische Diskussion eine entsprechende Prüfung des begrifflichen Rahmens nötig. Jedenfalls aber sind die Formulierungen in ihrem Bezug zu der durch eine WA getragenen Lebenspraxis bzw. Lebensform zu verstehen. Es wäre aber auch verfehlt, die Aussagen und referierenden Ausdrücke einer WA rekonstruieren zu wollen, ohne dabei die Eigenart der in der WA verwendeten deutenden Theorien zu berücksichtigen[4].

Die vorgelegten Überlegungen sollten aufzeigen, daß die Rationalität von WA nicht durch Reduktion auf die Methodologie einzelner Wissenschaften geklärt werden kann. Zugleich sollte aber auch einer zu starken Trennung von der Wissenschaftstheorie vorgebaut werden: durch das von der Wissenschaftstheorie Herausgearbeitete und durch ein begründetes Abheben von bereichsspezifischen Forderungen können die allgemeineren Forderungen der Rationalität wie auch die der WA eigenen deutlicher formuliert und verständlich gemacht werden. Das Herausarbeiten von Besonderheiten von WA zeigt, daß dabei nicht ein allgemeiner Rahmen der Rationalität verlassen werden muß, daß aber anderseits konkret gezeigt werden kann, warum manche in einzelnen Wissenschaften bewährte Forderungen einer speziellen Methodologie angehören und nicht unbesehen auf WA übertragen werden dürfen.

ANMERKUNGEN

[1] Bochenski, I. M., *The Logic of Religion* (New York [1]1965) und P. Weingartner, *Wissenschaftstheorie I: Einführung in die Hauptprobleme* (Stuttgart—Bad Cannstatt [1]1971).
[2] Ferré, F., *Language, Logic and God* (New York [1]1961).
[3] Muck, O., *Philosophische Gotteslehre* (Düsseldorf 1983), S. 78—102.
[4] Vgl. z.B. M. Gatzemeier, *Theologie als Wissenschaft I: Die Sache der Theologie* (Stuttgart—Bad Cannstatt 1974).

* * *

MINIMALISM:
PHILOSOPHY OF RELIGION WITH MININAL THEOLOGY

Asa Kasher
Tel-Aviv-University, Tel-Aviv

Minimalism is a philosophical research programme we would like to propose, outline and defend, within philosophy of religion. Usually, newly suggested research programmes rest on a combination of discontent or disenchantment with inspired hope, and Minimalism is no exception. Thus, at the roots of Minimalism are a dissatisfaction with prevalent research programmes in philosophy of religion, mostly centred upon theological concerns, and an educated suggestion that attention should be shifted, within philosophy of religion, at least in part, from the traditional problems of Natural Theology to internal, conceptual studies of religious forms of life.

To form an impression of the philosophical discontent from which Minimalism stems, recall one of Karl Popper's insights into history of philosophy in general: Every philosophical school, tradition or branch is liable to degenerate as a consequence of inbreeding, "the consequences of the mistaken belief that one can philosophize without having been compelled to philosophize by problems which arise outside philosophy—in mathematics, for example, or in cosmology, or in politics, or in religion, or in social life . . . Genuine philosophical problems are always rooted in urgent problems outside philosophy, and they die if these roots decay."[1]

As a matter of fact, there is no practical indication of genuine religious interest in problems of divine immutability, of divine lack of responsibility for human sins being compatible, or incompatible, with our freedom of the will, and even of the existence of God.

In one of his letters to Norman Malcolm, Wittgenstein asked "what is the use of studying philosophy if all that it does for you is to enable you to talk with some plausibility about some abstruse questions of logic, etc. and if it does not improve your thinking about the important questions of everyday life . . ."[2]. Clearly, the important questions of common religious life are related, first and foremost, to earthly forms of behaviour or reasons for action, rather than to paradoxes of omnipotence and omniscience.

Within different religions one encounters fairly recent norms, validly enacted by a person or a council, without any recourse to revelation, prophecy or any other mystery. For a practicing member of such a religion, it might be an important question of everyday life whether such a norm is binding upon him or her. A philsosphical study of religious language-games can improve one's thinking on such a question, if it contributes to better understanding of the nature of systems of religious norms, of normative development, of institutional authority, infallibility and revision, of spurious decrees, and the like. Sometimes, a newly introduced norm marks the attitude of a religious tradition towards unprecedented situations. A genuine attitude is grounded on a deep value judgement which, in turn, is implicitly expressed in a variety of traditional norms. Again, philosophy of religion can improve one's thinking on such judgements, if it elucidates conceptual relationships between values and norms which are meant to embody them, and the like.

Several concepts, such as prayer, scriptures, punishment or worship, are amenable to theological analysis: Prayer is an address to God, etc. The methodological point of Minimalism is that philosophical analysis of such concepts should avoid, as much as possible, resort to purely theological concepts, in particular to the most difficult and problematic of all, i.e. the concept of God.

We turn now to a sketch of a minimalistic analysis of a family of religious concepts. The 'hard core' of the minimalistic research programme[3] consists of several assumptions about religion and about religious practices. We briefly sketch three of them, which are going to serve in the sequel as background for the ensuing minimalistic analysis.

First, there is nothing in the religions under consideration that is not expressed in their respective practices. The latter are governed by constitutive norms. Whatever is part and parcel of such a religion is shown in one way or another in the overt conduct of not only the pious but also in that of an observant follower of the religion.

Notice that that principle of Minimalism is not of an operationalistic character, because we require that the content of a religion be expressed in rather than defined by the religious practices.

Secondly, attention is presently drawn to religions which are, in a sense, ideally total; that is to say, where the ideal code of religious conduct is on principle complete, including regulations, whether general or particular, with respect to each and every sphere of given human activity. Religions are never practically total, but where they are interested in rendering human life fully meaning-laden, they are ideally total.

Thirdly, and from a minimalistic point of view perhaps most importantly, it is assumed that the point to be ascribed to religious practices is their being embodiments of extreme opposition to any kind and form of idolatry, in the broadest sense of the term: Since excessive devotion to anything in the world may render it being worshipped, such religious antagonism with idolatry is not confined to classical idols, such as Baal, Zephyros or Luna, but is meant to apply also to any form of addiction, be it to wealth or strength, love or lust, self and nation, or what have you. Roughly speaking, the code of practice of such a religion consists of a variety of institutions of self-restraint, each directed against certain forms or dangers of idol worshipping or absolute devotion to something worldly.

The three essential ingredients of the religions here under consideration are, thus, constitutivity, ideal totalism and anti-idolism. We believe that various religions contain at least a core of such a minimalistic nature. This is the case for certain denominations in Islam and Judaism, to mention just two examples.

To show that Minimalism is viable, as applied to some actual religions, one should clarify how Minimalism copes with a prevalent feature of major historical religions, namely talk of God. Indeed, Minimalism does not rule out any talk of God, because a philosophical research programme does not rule out any phenomenon from its own natural field. To use Wittgenstein's famous expression, "Philosophy . . . leaves everything as it is." (PI, 124.)

Talk of God, during the history of any religion, is often conspicuously diverse. Could such a common diversity of expression be distilled and made into a distinct, minimalistic way of talk of God? The name of the key to our affirmative answer is indeed constitutivity. Not every phrase used by members of a religion with relation to their religion strictly belongs to that religion, committing everyone who is attempting to draw an accurate picture of the religion to include in it an explanatory logic or history of that phrase. According to the minimalistic point of view, the content of a religion is expressed in its code of practice. Hence, just those expressions should be considered, when the religion itself is depicted, that play a constitutive role in the code of practice, i.e., in one of the institutions of the religion.

Now, in many cases there are two major texts which include ample talk of God and which have been granted a formal religious function, namely Holy Scriptures and prayer books. We should, then, consider the nature of talk of God in such books, in order to get an impression and then form a view of talk of God in Minimalism.[4]

Consider talk of God in the Bible, for example. From a minimalistic point of view, differences between, say, talk of God in *Genesis* and talk of God in *Job* or the *Song of Solomon* might turn out to be of no particular significance. From that point of view, no reading of a verse, interpretation of a chapter or analysis of a book may be ascribed to the religion itself, rather than to certain persons who observe it, unless reflected in the religious code of practice. Thus, whatever reasons one might adduce for uses of talk of God in Holy Scriptures, the religious significance of these uses of talk of God has to be couched in terms of the religious functions of the Holy Scriptures taken as a whole.

To find the functions of the holy writ, consider the way in which a traditional code of practice can develop. When a new problem is encountered as to whether a certain action should be regarded as legitimate under some circumstances, a natural route is usually followed towards an appropriate solution of the given problem: very simple problems are decided by one's normative intuition; problems of higher complexity are litigated and then decided on the grounds of some explicit norms and implicit principles; but every once in a while a brand-new problem appears, solution of which requires new legislation rather than litigation or intuitive judgement. Legislation, in turn, may take the form of applying rather deep-seated, basic norms, but sometimes it requires recourse to the very foundations of the whole code of practice, in the last resort. This happens when the problem posed bears no significant similarity to any of the previously solved religious problems. The scarcity of such occasions does not preclude them from contributing in an important way to the development of the related code of practice, much beyond what meets the eye. Notice, that such a need to reach the very normative roots of a code of practice is none too natural when the code of practice is ideally total.

Thus, sacred writings serve as normative roots of practice-oriented, ideally total religions, according to the present analysis. However, since scriptures are usually amenable to different interpretations, holy scriptures provide their religion with an outline of its limits: Whatever belongs to the religion has to be either compatible with these scriptures, under an appropriate interpretation, or else be incompatible with them in an internally justified way.

It is our view that the Old Testament can be taken as expressing, first and foremost, strong anti-idolism. Under such an interpretation of it, many religious practices which stem from a tradition which is related to those Holy Scriptures are rendered meaningful.[5]

Thus, talk of God in the Holy Scriptures serves no assertoric purpose, be it theological, historical, scientific or what have you, as long as it serves a normative purpose, directing the follower to observe an anti-idolist code of practice.[6]

In a nutshell, the logic of talk of God in such Holy Scriptures thus interpreted, is normative and exclusionary. It is normative in the sense that every significant case of talk of God in the Holy Writ has normative consequences, and thus, as we all have learned from Hume, it has also some normative ingredient. The normative grain of talk of God may be expressed by taking phrases of the form 'this-and-that is not God' to stand for 'this-and-that ought not to be worshipped'. Distinctly, an idol is not a God, *ergo* no idol may be worshipped.

Talk of God, according to the present point of view, is exclusionary, in the sense that the Holy Scriptures, by using talk of God, should be taken to discredit the ascription of some property to anything in our world, rather than crediting with the same property some being elsewhere, whatever that means.

ENDNOTES

[1] Popper, Karl R., *Conjectures and Refutations* (London 1963), pp. 71–2.
[2] Malcolm, Norman, *Ludwig Wittgenstein, A Memoir* (London 1958), p. 39
[3] Lakatos, Imre, "Falsification and the Methodology of Scientific Research Programmes", *Criticism and the Growth of Knowledge*, I. Lakatos and A. Musgrave (eds.) (Cambridge 1970), pp. 132–4
[4] In a longer version of the present paper, as delivered in the conference, the case of talk of God in Liturgy was also considered. It will be presented in detail in our forthcoming "Talk of God and Liturgy: A Minimalistic Approach".
[5] In the longer version of the present paper we discussed the examples of the story of creation, as presented in the book of *Genesis*, the verse "Let my people go" in its biblical context, and the seemingly paradoxical end verses of *Ecclesiastes*.
[6] The present view is *not* a positivistic one, because of differences in the roles played by values according to positivistic views and according to the one presented in this paper.

* * *

RELIGIONSPHILOSOPHIE NACH WITTGENSTEIN

Kurt Wuchterl
Universität Stuttgart

1. Wittgenstein hat keine explizite Religionsphilosophie (RP) entwickelt. Dennoch kann selbst seine Frühphilosophie als eine Antwort auf die Frage nach der Möglichkeit einer RP angesehen werden. Der „Traktat" enthält alle Konsequenzen, die eine autonome logische und naturwissenschaftliche Denkmethode nach sich zieht. Er stellt eine Theorie strenger Analytizität des Denkens dar und erhält seine religionsphilosophische Bedeutung dadurch, daß er sich selbst aufhebt. Wer Kontingenzerfahrung (v.a. das Staunen über die Existenz der Welt, das Gefühl der absoluten Geborgenheit, die Erfahrung des persönlichen Schuldgefühls) als wirklich akzeptiert, widerspricht sich selbst, sofern er die Wirklichkeit im Sinne des „Traktats" als wertfreies Ensemble von Tatsachen und Sachverhalten samt deren logischen Relationen interpretiert. Was bleiben kann, ist eine *stumme* Religiosität.

Die Denkfigur Wittgensteins beweist die Inkonsistenz eines Denkens, das religiöse Phänomene mit den strengen Methoden der modernen Wissenschaften allein sprachlich korrekt angehen und diese zugleich bis ins Letzte verstehen will.

2. Das Thema kann auch so interpretiert werden, daß Gedanken und Methoden Wittgensteins von dessen Nachfolgern verwendet werden, um eine explizite RP zu entwickeln. Dieser Versuch betrifft nur die Spätphilosophie. Es lassen sich Grundformen religionsphilosophischer Entwürfe unterscheiden: Reduktive Formen − Sprachspielkonzeptionen − Entwürfe mit Religiosität als integratives Element einer Lebensform. Diese drei Grundformen widersprechen sich zwar wechselseitig, können sich aber in jedem Falle auf Aussagen Wittgensteins berufen. Sie orientieren sich zugleich an Wittgensteins These von der Unhintergehbarkeit der Sprache. Der Sprachgebrauch ist zugleich einzige Rechtfertigungsinstanz.

3. Die dritte Interpretation des Themas bezieht sich auf eine zwar an Wittgenstein anknüpfende, diese aber zugleich transzendierende RP. Diese soll hier entwickelt werden.

Zunächst einiges zum Grundproblem der RP. Diese fällt aus dem Disziplinenkanon insofern heraus, als sie als einzige einen geradezu paradoxen Anspruch erhebt: Sie will etwas verstehen und in ein vernünftiges Grundkonzept einordnen, das von seinem Wesen her, eben weil es sich auf Religiöses bezieht, gerade nicht voll begreifbar gemacht werden kann. Dieses Dilemma hat verschiedene Konsequenzen. Häufig geht man ausschließlich kritisch vor und interpretiert die religiösen Phänomene so, daß sie ihren spezifischen Charakter des Transzendenzbezugs verlieren (vgl. Feuerbach, Marx; Albert, Bartley; Braithwaite). Bei anderen bezieht sich die Uminterpretation nicht auf die Phänomene, sondern auf die Philosophie selbst. Sie wird so umgedeutet, daß sie die Paradoxie aufzunehmen vermag (vgl. die mystische Seinsprophetie Heideggers). Eine dritte Möglichkeit läßt einerseits die religiösen Phänomene in ihrer Eigenständigkeit stehen und versucht andererseits, diese in ihren Wechselwirkungen mit der allgemeinen philosophischen Vernunft zu beschreiben. Man setzt also einen konsistenten methodischen Kontext (Logik, Sprachanalyse, intersubjektive Verständlichkeit) voraus, der als notwendige Bedingung für Philosophie fungiert.

4. *Entwicklung der Aufgabe einer RP unter diesen Voraussetzungen und mit Rückgriff auf einige Gedanken Wittgensteins*: Von Wichtigkeit ist dessen Gedanke, daß es zahlreiche funktionierende Kommunikationseinheiten oder „Sprachspiele" gibt, in denen religiöse Phänomene in ein allgemeines Sinngefüge eingeordnet sind. Im Gegensatz zu PU § 23 handelt es sich in religiösen Kontexten nicht um zeitlich begrenzte, sprachlich vermittelte Verhaltensweisen, sondern um eine Lebensform im Ganzen. Wir nennen sie deshalb im Anschluß an T. S. Kuhn Paradigmen.

Es gibt sehr verschiedenartige Sprachspiele oder Paradigmen dieser Art: Mythologien, Offenbarungsreligionen, aber auch säkularisierte Weltanschauungen und sich auf Wissenschaft berufende Gesamtdeutungen. Sie alle verstehen die religiösen Phänomene je verschieden. Die genannten Deutungen vollziehen faktisch eine Kontingenzbewältigung, d.h. die zunächst allen menschlichen Sinn transzendierenden Phänomene werden durch die in Lebensformen eingeordneten Sprachspiele mit Sinn und Bedeutung versehen. Diese Sinngebungen betreffen nicht nur am Rande liegende Spekulationen und nebensächliche Beliebigkeiten, sondern sie durchdringen alle existenziell relevanten Bereiche dieses Kommunikationszusammenhangs. So wirkt sich beispielsweise der Glaube an das Jüngste Gericht auf das Gesamt*verhalten* des Christen aus. Die genannten Kontingenzbewältigungen sind demnach zugleich Kontingenznormierungen für das Gesamtverhalten. Sie sind handlungsleitend und konativ im Sinne Hares.

Kontingenz heißt eigentlich Zufälligkeit. Sie enthält für uns ein Moment des Unvermeidbaren und ein Moment des über unsere Verfügungsgewalt Hinausgehenden. Kontingente Ereignisse können wir durch unsere Handlungen nicht abwenden; deshalb brauchen wir symbolische Konstruktionen, um sie in den Griff zu bekommen und sie sinnvoll erscheinen zu lassen.

RP hat nun die Aufgabe, die verschiedenen Kontingenzbewältigungen und Kontingenznormierungen zu analysieren. Sie zeigt, welche Leitbegriffe diesen Deutungen zugrundeliegen, wie diese ihre begründende Funktion ausüben und sich gegenseitig ergänzen; ob die Zusammenhänge methodisch korrekt nachvollzogen werden können, usw. (Vgl. die organisierenden Bilder von Ferré). Dem gehen die elementaren Betrachtungen der Sprachanalyse voraus. Sie fragt: Wie funktioniert religiöse Sprache? Welches sind ihre spezifischen Sprachregeln? Sind diese Qualifikationen intersubjektiv verständlich?

Diese Analyse des religiösen Sprachgebrauchs ist eine *Vorstufe* und kein Selbstzweck. Die Hauptaufgabe der RP bezieht sich auf die Darstellung der Struktur des Sinngefüges religiöser Aussagensysteme[1] und auf die Darlegung der normativen Kraft jener Leitbegriffe.

Ein Beispiel: Eine RP, die sich auf die Analyse *christlicher* Kontingenz-Bewältigungen bezieht, wird vor allem auf die beiden Leitbegriffe der Liebe und Gerechtigkeit stoßen. Denn jede nicht-reduktive, Transzendenz berücksichtigende RP geht formal von den Prämissen der Existenz und der Bestimmtheit Gottes aus. Diese Bestimmtheit wird in der christlichen RP mit Christus in Zusammenhang gebracht. Die nähere Charakterisierung dieser Bestimmung läuft dann meistens auf die genannten Leitbegriffe hinaus. Aus ersterem lassen sich alle Konsequenzen einer altruistischen Lebenspraxis verstehen; zugleich enthält der Gedanke der Liebe Gottes auch die Vorstellung der Geborgenheit des Einzelnen in der Gesamtheit des Natur- und Geschichtsablaufs. Daneben normiert aber auch der Leitbegriff „Gerechtigkeit Gottes" das Leben, z.B. in der Form einer praktischen Vernunft im Sinne Kants. Das Theodizeeproblem zeigt, daß die Leitbegriffe in einem gewissen Spannungsverhältnis zueinander stehen und gleichursprünglich sind. Denn wie kann ein *liebender* Gott das Leid Unschuldiger zulassen? Und wie kann andererseits ein *gerechter* Gott die Brutalitäten von Massenmördern ihrer Eigengesetzlichkeit überlassen, und dann noch von Gnade gesprochen werden?

5. Durch die Analyse verschiedener solcher Kontingenz-Bewältigungen wird den Religionsphilosophen bewußt, daß *erstens* die Prämissen solcher Bewältigungen nicht in unserer Disposition stehen, also selbst kontingent sind; daß aber *zweitens eine* solche Realisierung — und sei sie noch so skeptisch (wie bei Schlette[2]) oder zurückhaltend (wie bei Camus[3]) — die unverzichtbare Bedingung für *jede* Lebensform bedeutet. Somit ist RP selbst keine Kontingenz-*Bewältigung*, sondern nur Kontingenz-*Identifikation*. Ein Religionsphilosoph muß nicht selbst die einzelnen Glaubenssätze glauben, sondern geht davon aus, daß überhaupt Glaubenssätze geglaubt werden. RP hat mithin die Aufgabe, die Leitbegriffe als kontingente Setzungen zu erkennen und ihre Rolle als notwendige Regulative für methodisches Denken und praktisches Handeln darzulegen. Sie läßt alles, wie es ist.

Wenn jemand religiöse, also *objektsprachliche* Begründungen für existenziell relevante Phänomene sucht, so wird er sich dabei stets an dem durch die Leitbegriffe gegebenen Rahmen orientieren. Letztere fungieren gleichsam als Axiome, allerdings nicht im streng deduktivven Sinne. Denn die Begründung wird meist nur angedeutet und als *möglich* vorausgesetzt. Man ist überzeugt, daß es einen Bezug zu den Leitbegriffen gibt, ohne diesen in jedem Fall darstellen zu müssen.

6. Die hier angedeutete RP läßt sich vorteilhaft mit Hilfe des Paradigmenbegriffs präzisieren[4]. Deshalb gibt es keine *metasprachliche* Begründung für die Wahl der Leitbegriffe. Vernünftigkeit erscheint als Möglichkeit der Einordnung in einen durch ein Paradigma gegebenen Rahmen. Kontingenz-Normierung ist in diesem Sinne „übervernünftig".

Die RP hat ihre Aufgabe dann erfüllt, wenn sie zu zeigen vermag, daß ihre Aussagen wirklich die konkreten religiösen Intentionen betreffen und daß sie in ihren Beispielen die verschiedenen Möglichkeiten sinnvoller reflexiver Existenz in einer historisch gewachsenen Gemeinschaft beschreiben kann.

Argumentationen, die sich auf den naheliegenden Leitbegriff des Humanum berufen und so in der Gegenwart von größter Überzeugungskraft sind, stehen auf dem Boden eines speziellen Paradigmas und sind daher nicht mehr religionsphilosophisch, sondern objektsprachlich zu interpretieren. Die religionsphilosophische Aufgabe der Analyse der vorgegebenen Glaubenssysteme wird dann ergänzt durch eine bestimmte, aus der heutigen Situation und der eigenen Lebenserfahrung erwachsene Bewertung. Dieses heute weit verbreitete Paradigma eines kritischen Humanismus muß aber selbst wieder der Analyse standhalten, das heißt, Gegenstand der allgemeinen Religionsphilosphie werden. Während gewisse *notwendige* Bedingungen das Verwerfen oder Akzeptieren von vorgegebenen Lebensformen im Sinne eines Bewährungskriteriums ermöglichen, ist es vergeblich, *hinreichende* Bedingungen zu finden.

ANMERKUNGEN

[1] Vgl. dazu z.B. J. M. Bocheński, *Logik der Religion* (Köln 1968).
[2] Schlette, H. R., *Skeptische Religionsphilosophie* (Freiburg 1972).
[3] Camus, A., *Der Mythos von Sisyphos* (Hamburg 1959).
[4] Vgl. dazu K. Wuchterl, *Philosophie und Religion* (Bern–Stuttgart 1982), S. 81ff. Im 3. Teil wird eine paradigmenbezogene RP entwickelt. Einen Überblick über die gesamte analytische RP findet man bei H. Schrödter, *Analytische RP* (Freiburg–München 1979).

* * *

THEOLOGIE UND KRITISCHE RATIONALITÄT

Kurt Weinke
Universität Graz

Im Rahmen einer „kritsch-rationalen" Betrachtung theologischer Fragen sind zeitgenössische Versuche bemerkenswert, (sprachphilosophisch gesehen) das Unsagbare in sprachliche Kategorien zu gießen, (metaphysik-kritisch betrachtet) Fragen die Transzendenz betreffend wissenschaftlich abhandeln zu wollen; dies sind Versuche, das Wittgensteinsche Diktum: „Worüber man nicht sprechen kann, davon muß man schweigen" zu umgehen. Als „pars pro toto" derartiger Bestrebungen darf das umfängliche Werk von Hans Küng „Existiert Gott?" gelten, das eine Fülle an Problemen aufwirft, die Antwort auf seine eigene, zentrale Frage aber, ob Gott tatsächlich existiert oder nicht, schuldig bleibt, obwohl Küng in einem Kapitel den Titel „Gott existiert" vorsah, und im Unterkapitel („Gott als Wirklichkeit") von bloßen Hypothesen (offensichtlich von allem bisher Gesagten) zur Wirklichkeit (der Gottes eben) kommen möchte. Sonderbar mutet − in zwei Punkten zusammengefaßt − seine grundsätzliche Überlegung an, die jederzeit von Neopositivisten, Marxisten, Feuerbachianern, kritischen Rationalisten und Agnostikern auch in gleicher Form behauptet werden könnte, nämlich erstens: „Ein Nein zu Gott ist möglich. Der Atheismus läßt sich nicht rational eliminieren: Er ist unwiderlegbar!" Zweitens: „Auch ein Ja zu Gott ist möglich. Der Atheismus läßt sich nicht rational etablieren: Er ist unbeweisbar!"[1] Interessanter ist der Begleittext dazu, der zwischen diesen beiden Punkten steht und eigentlich in kurzer Form eine Antwort auf die Frage des gesamten Werkes gibt: Es soll nicht zynisch gemeint sein, wenn ich feststelle, daß diese Küngschen Ergebnisse äußerst mager sind und eigentlich nicht mehr ausdrücken, als daß es eine zutiefst eigene, persönliche Entscheidung ist, die wohl auch das berühmte „credo, quia absurdum" einschließt, wenn man an Gott glaubt und vice versa. Es sei nochmals betont, daß gegen eine solche Ansicht auch traditionell metaphysik-freie (oder metaphysik-feindliche) Strömungen nichts einzuwenden haben. Von einem kritisch-rationalen Gesichtspunkt aus gesehen müßte ein derartiger Standpunkt bloß mit der richtigen Bezeichnung, nämlich „Dezisionismus", versehen werden − doch gerade darum geht es Küng nicht. Im Verhältnis zu diesen Ausführungen Küngs, in denen fast in penetranter Weise Urvertrauen, Hingabebereitschaft, existentielle Öffnung zur Transzendenz in wissenschaftlichem Kontext zur Rede stehen und sich dort eigenartig ausnehmen, sind Versuche, sprachphilosophische Überlegungen in die Problematik der Quasi-Gottesbeweise einzubeziehen, erfolgsversprechender, wenn auch letztlich nicht überzeugend. Vor allem haben es der Wittgensteinsche Begriff des „Sprachspiels" und die „Philosophie der gewöhnlichen Sprache" allgemein dazu gebracht, von Theologen aufgegriffen und wohl auch für arteigene, theologische Zwecke adaptiert zu werden. Wim de Pater hat im Anschluß an Ian Ramsey und dessen Zentralbegriff der „disclosure" in seinem Werk „Theologische Sprachlogik" versucht, das Sprechen über Gott als ein Sprachmodell „sui generis" darzustellen; er schreibt: „Offensichtlich reden wir über Gott in einem bestimmten Zusammenhang, in einer Sprache, die sich von derjenigen unterscheidet, mit der wir Tische und Stühle beschreiben oder das Wetter voraussagen."[2] Das mag durchaus stimmen, doch ist dieser Standpunkt von einem kritisch-rationalen Gesichtspunkt aus nicht haltbar, da nicht angegeben wird, worin die methodische „differentia specifica" besteht. Die inhaltliche Verschiedenheit ist damit sicherlich nicht konstituiert (wie auch in anderen Bereichen nicht), womit es sich um eine willkürliche, nicht akzeptable Aufspaltung in zwei Gebiete, analog der Trennung von Geistes- und Naturwissenschaften handelt. Somit dürfte die Dichotomisierung, die de Pater vorschlägt, vom immanent-kritischen, also letztlich religiösen Standpunkt aus gesehen, berechtigt sein, um das Arteigene der religiösen Aussage erhalten zu wollen, von einem transeunt-kritischen Standpunkt aus gesehen, etwa jenem des Kritischen Rationalismus, ist diese Trennung nicht akzeptabel. Dies mußte vorausgeschickt werden, um die folgende Stelle in ihrer gewollten Ambivalenz einzusehen: „Die große Gefahr bei der religiösen Sprache besteht darin, daß man die ihr eigene Logik vergißt, indem man nur auf ihre verbale Übereinstimmung mit anderen Sprechweisen achtet. Dem Wortlaut nach ist die Aussage ‚Christus sitzt zur Rechten des Vaters' der anderen ähnlich: ‚Peter sitzt rechts vom Vater' . . . Theistische Sprache ist eine eigene Art des Sprechens, hat also ihre eigene (nichtformale) Logik, was z.B. einschließt, daß der Aufweis oder die Widerlegung solcher Aussagen auf andere Weise geschieht als bei ihren verbalen Parallelen.“[3] Das allerdings ist, und zwar nicht nur vom Standpunkt eines Kritischen Rationalismus aus, vor allem deswegen abzulehnen, da man nicht in der Lage ist, diese „eigene Art des Sprechens“ mit der „eigenen (nichtformalen) Logik“ intersubjektiv einsichtig zu begründen. Es besteht somit der dringende Verdacht, daß es sich hier um einen Rückzug in eine Privatsprache mit eigener Methodik handelt, die sich von der üblichen Sprache und Logik abkapselt, oder, besser gesagt, immunisiert, um einer möglicherweise vernichtenden Kritik zu entgehen: Daher wohl findet sich stets der Hinweis auf den nicht-deskriptiven, dafür aber *evokativen* Gebrauch der religiösen Sprache, womit allerdings die reine Subjektivität impliziert ist – ein Ergebnis, das der Hauptforderung der Theologie, allgemein verbindliche Aussagen tätigen zu können, kraß widerspricht. Dies wird allerdings nicht zugegeben, da es jede theologische Sprache auf eine des Glaubens (im Extremfall auf jene der Mystik) reduzierte, womit zum Modell zweier Sprachwelten geschritten und zwei differente Logiken konstruiert würden, die auch für den metaphysischen Bereich der Wunder gelten sollten.

Doch auch bei jeder noch so distanzierten Einstellung zu positivistischen Überlegungen (die von Metaphysikern gern als „platt“ und „oberflächlich“ apostrophiert werden), muß doch derartigen Versuchen, die letztlich auf einen privilegierten Zugang zu den tiefen, metaphysischen Erkenntnissen hinauslaufen, engegengehalten werden, daß die anvisierte methodische Alternative nirgendwo explizit gemacht wird; jeder Rekurs auf einen „performativen Gebrauch“ der Sprache oder die terminologische Einkleidung „Evokation“ sind mißglückte Hereinnahmen von Gebrauchsweisen und Begriffen spezieller Bedeutung in die theologische Sprache.

Es kann sicherlich als allgemein akzeptiertes, wissenschaftliches Verhalten angesehen werden, wenn es auch vom Kritischen Rationalismus mit besonderem Nachdruck ausgesprochen wird, gerade jene Ansichten, die zum Kern des liebgewonnenen Systems gehören, einer besonders harten, permanenten Prüfung zu unterziehen – auch wenn dabei Revisionen großen Stils notwendig werden sollten. Gerade diese intellektuelle Redlichkeit ist es, die den Ausführungen Küngs und de Paters fehlen, wie aus folgendem Zitat ersichtlich ist: „Der Glaube enthält sicher Objektivität, aber nur für den, der ‚sieht': eine Erschließungsobjektivität. In einer Erschließung gibt es nämlich etwas, das uns trifft, uns auffällt, uns anzieht. Wir selbst sind dabei verhältnismäßig passiv, es kommt auf uns zu, es wird uns gegeben.“[4] Wenn in diesem und in ähnlichen Kontexten *bloß* von der „Gnade des Glaubens“, von der „Glaubenserleuchtung“ gesprochen würde, gäbe es keinen Punkt der Kritik; es handelte sich ja um den Versuch, subjektive Glaubenserlebnisse verbal einzukleiden, das dabei Sagbare einem Kreis von anderen Gläubigen kundzutun. Den Autoren geht es aber um eine „theologische Sprachlogik“, um den Versuch, mit Hilfe der wissenschaftlich anerkannten Methoden gültige Aussagen über das „Unsagbare“ zu tätigen. In diesem Zusammenhang ist der Vorgang Ian Ramseys zu loben, der klarstellt, daß metaphysische Kategorien nur bis zu einem bestimmten (nicht genauer fixierbaren) Punkt mit Hilfe der Umgangssprache beschrieben werden können, daß aber stets dahinter (darüber hinaus) ein X bleibt, das sich unseren verbalen Repräsentationsweisen prinzipiell entzieht.

In welcher Form auch immer neuzeitliche theologische Versuche angestellt werden, das hochmittelalterlich-scholastische Problem des Erweises der Existenz Gottes einer Lösung zuzuführen, muß eingestanden werden, daß im wesentlichen die Methode, ja sogar viele Argumente in unveränderter Form übernommen wurden. Somit ist es nicht verwunderlich, daß auch die erzielten Ergebnisse gleichermaßen unbefriedigend geblieben sind.

Darüber kann auch die moderne „Aufmachung" der Beispiele und die Hereinnahme wissenschaftlicher Methoden, die meist bloß ancillarische Bedeutung erlangen, nicht hinwegtäuschen. Das gibt de Pater auch einschränkend zu: „Daraus folgt nicht nur, daß Theologie ein äußerst riskantes Unternehmen ist, sondern auch, daß sie (mit den nötigen Einschränkungen) in andere Spachspiele eindringen kann, ohne sich mit einem davon zu identifizieren".[5] Diese hier als Stärke der theologischen Position ausgegebene Ansicht erweist sich gleichermaßen als Schwäche, da sie dokumentiert, daß eine Theologie stets mehr erklären und beweisen will, als es irgendein Sprachspiel-Modell kann. Diesem Verdikt sind wohl alle letztlich unbefriedigend gebliebenen Entmythologisierungsversuche primär protestantischer Provenienz zum Opfer gefallen. Es war das verständliche Bemühen, mittels sprachlichen Transfers in moderne Kontexte und neuer Erklärungsweisen das Mythische vom Rationalen zu trennen, um mit Hilfe einer Ausdifferenzierung in primär (unverzichtbar) Gültiges und sekundär Wichtiges das jeder Kritik zu Entziehende vom Kritisierbaren abzuheben. Zu Recht wendet sich der Kritische Rationalismus gegen ein derartiges Halbieren der Kritik, die letztlich dazu angetan ist, bestimmte Bereiche gegen eine zerstörende Kritik abzuschirmen.

Die Theorie von Sprachspielen, Entwürfe alternativer Logiken, sowie dem klassisch rationalistischen oder empiristischen Einheitsmodell der wissenschaftlichen Methodik gleichrangige Methoden (in Medizin, Psychologie usw.) legen es anscheinend nahe, eine arteigene theologische Methode (siehe Bochenski) zu postulieren; dies werde (im vorliegenden Fall) vom Gegenstand selbst, von der Eigenart des Religiösen, das besondere Wahrheitsregeln erfordere, verlangt. Doch ist hier wohl zweierlei zu unterscheiden: Niemand wird die Behauptung in Frage stellen, daß verschiedene Gegenstände (Mathematik, Naturwissenschaft, interpretierende Geisteswissenschaft) im Sinne Bochenskis auch methodische Differenzen aufweisen; doch hat die negativ zu bewertende Dichotomisierung zwischen Geistes- und Naturwissenschaften (die auch vom Gegenstand selbst her zu rechtfertigen sei) gezeigt, daß ein methodologischer Monismus keine simple Reduktion im Gefolge hat, sondern Phänomene besser erklären kann, somit unbedingt anzustreben ist. Dies schließt durchaus die Notwendigkeit einer differenzierten Behandlung der sehr komplexen Religionsproblematik ein, entbindet jedoch die Theologie nicht, sofern sie mehr sein will als ein Glaube, entweder die Regeln der Wissenschaft auf sich anzuwenden (Prinzipien der Logik, Semantik usw.), ohne die ein rationaler Diskurs nicht möglich erscheint, oder alternative Methoden zu entwerfen, die ihrerseits Anspruch auf Generalisierung über Religionen hinaus zeitigen müßten . . . und diese Leistung muß von der Theologie erst erbracht werden.

ANMERKUNGEN

[1] Küng, Hans, „Existiert Gott?" (Piper, München 1978), S. 625.
[2] De Pater, Wim A., „Theologische Sprachlogik" (Kösel, München 1971).
[3] Ebd., S. 19.
[4] Ebd., S.106.
[5] Ebd., S. 88.

* * *

ZUR AKTUALITÄT DER RELIGIONSKRITIK SCHOPENHAUERS

Reinhard Margreiter
Imst, Österreich

Obwohl rezeptionsgeschichtlich von weit geringerer Bedeutung als die einschlägigen Äußerungen von Feuerbach, Marx, Nietzsche und Freud, gehören Schopenhauers über sein Gesamtwerk verstreute, an zwei Stellen gleichwohl konzentrierte[1] Überlegungen zum Phänomen Religion ebenfalls in den Rahmen der klassischen deutschen Religionskritik und stellen zu dieser – die trotz all ihrer Mängel nach wie vor für die materiale Diskussion des Gegenstands als bestimmend angesehen werden kann – ein wichtiges Korrektiv dar durch die Abkehr von kämpferischem Atheismus, hegelianischer Geschichtsauffassung und anthropozentrischer Spekulation. Darüberhinaus erinnern sie sachliche Aspekte, die in der heutigen Diskussion in Gefahr geraten, vergessen zu werden: so die Frage nach dem Ursprung der Religion, nach der Wahrheit religiöser Vorstellungen und Normen und nach der Notwendigkeit religiöser Institutionen bzw. nach dem Konstitutionsverhältnis von subjektiver Religiosität und sozialer Organisationsform des Glaubens. Die folgende, in vier Themenkreise zusammengefaßte Kurzdarstellung der Schopenhauerschen Religionskritik will daher im Interesse einer kritischen Religionsphänomenologie zum Versuch einer geläuterten, sachgerechten Reformulierung der klassischen Religionskritik beitragen. Dabei wird ‚Phänomenologie‘ keineswegs im Sinn R. Ottos verstanden, sondern als regulativer Anspruch, Phänomene möglichst sachnah und ohne überflüssige Theoriekorsette zu beschreiben, und demgemäß sollen auch die systematischen Zusammenhänge mit der spekulativen Willensmetaphysik nach Möglichkeit ausgeklammert werden. Die vier Themenkreise befassen sich mit dem anthropologischen Motiv, der Wahrheitsfrage, der praktischen Funktion und der geschichtlichen Zukunft von Religion.

1. Das anthropologische Motiv. Anlaß zur Erfindung von und zum Festhalten an Religion ist nach Schopenhauer eine dreifache menschliche Disposition: seine ‚metaphysische Anlage‘, die Grundgefühle ‚Furcht und Hoffnung‘ und das ‚moralische Bewußtsein‘ (P II 396). Das ‚metaphysische Bedürfnis‘ zeige sich in der Verwunderung über die gewöhnlichen Dinge, über das eigene Dasein, im Bedenken von Leiden und Tod und im Interesse an Glück und Unsterblichkeit. Im Sinne Kants wird Metaphysik bestimmt als „jede angebliche Erkenntnis, welche über die Möglichkeit der Erfahrung, also über die Natur, oder die gegebene Erscheinung der Dinge, hinausgeht, um Aufschluß zu erteilen über das, wodurch jene . . . bedingt wäre" (W II 212), somit als Anspruch, zumindest die Grundlinien jener lebensweltlichen Ganzheit zu erkennen, die unser Dasein bestimmt und zwangsläufig mehr umfaßt als das unmittelbar Gewisse. Nicht eine eigene ‚religiöse Natur‘, aber eben dieses ‚metaphysische Bedürfnis‘, das schlechthin Befriedigung verlange, sei für den Menschen konstitutiv, „weil der Horizont seiner Gedanken abgeschlossen werden muß, nicht unbegrenzt bleiben darf (P II 395). Ein solcher Abschluß bzw. die Reflexion des Abschlußproblems werde aber nun von zwei konkurrierenden Instanzen angeboten: von Philosophie und Religion. Letztere, mit Platon als ‚Volksmetaphysik‘ bezeichnet, sei maßgeblich für das Gros der Menschheit, da Philosophie „Nachdenken, Bildung, Muße und Urteil" verlange und allein schon aus Gründen der sozialen Realität „nur einer äußerst geringen Anzahl von Menschen zugänglich" (W II 212) sei. Stütze sich Philosophie auf die Urteilskraft menschlicher Vernunft und auf moralische Selbstverantwortlichkeit des einzelnen, so Religion auf Autorität und Offenbarung, verlange also, wenn nötig unter Restriktion der Vernunft, blinde Übernahme. Daher seien so viele ihrer Argumente Drohungen und Wunschversprechen.

Das metaphysische Bedürfnis der Menschen erkannt und sich das Monopol der weichenstellenden frühkindlichen Erziehung gesichert zu haben, sei die ‚Urlist' der Priester, die ihren Lebensunterhalt und auch ihre gesellschaftliche Macht dem metaphysischen Bedürfnis verdanken: als „Monopolisten und Generalpächter desselben" (W II 209), als „sonderbares Mittelding zwischen Betrügern und Sittenlehrern" (P II 428). Die menschlichen Grundgefühle Furcht und Hoffnung seien für die Entstehung von Götter- und Dämonenvorstellungen entscheidend gewesen, da diese Orientierungsgestalten für das drohend Unbekannte aus Natur und Gesellschaft darstellen würden, zu dem so der Mensch ein zumindest teilweise Sicherheit versprechendes Regelverhalten aufbauen konnte durch Pflichten, Gebote, Beschwörung, Gebet und Ritus. Als drittes Motiv der Religion nennt Schopenhauer schließlich noch eine eigene – aus der (unbewußten) Überzeugung von der Einheit alles Lebendigen abzuleitende – ‚moralische Anlage' des Menschen, die zwar im Prinzip unabhängig sei von Religion, historisch aber und unter den Bedingungen der Reflexionslosigkeit der meisten Menschen an ihr Halt und Bestätigung gefunden habe und im falschen Bewußtsein des religiösen Menschen sogar mit ‚dem Religiösen' identifiziert werde.

2. Die Wahrheitsfrage. Während Nietzsche und Freud in der Religion eine Anhäufung von Irrtümern und allenfalls die verzerrte Widerspiegelung menschlicher Grunderfahrungen sehen, liegt für Feuerbach und Marx in ihrem Projektionscharakter – der Projektion von Glück, Vollkommenheit, Weisheit, Güte, Harmonie – antizipatorische Wahrheit, weil sie als Möglichkeit menschlicher Selbstverwirklichung zu begreifen sei. Weitab von solch anthropozentrischem Geschichtsoptimismus stellt sich Schopenhauer in die Tradition der seit der Antike geläufigen allegorischen Mythendeutung und konzediert den religiösen Votstellungen sogenannte ‚allegorische Wahrheit'. Wahrheiten können demnach entweder sensu stricto/proprio oder sensu allegorico, direkt oder indirekt formuliert werden. Das eine tue Philosophie, das andere Religion, die somit neben gemeinsamem lebensweltlichem Ursprung und gemeinsamen Fragestellungen auch gemeinsame Antwortmöglichkeiten aufweisen. Drei Beispiele: Das Dogma der Erbsünde drücke die konstitutive Schuldhaftigkeit und Erlösungsbedürftigkeit alles Lebendigen aus. Daß die gesamte Menschheit in Adam gesündigt habe und in Christus erlöst werde, beinhalte, daß das eigentliche Wesen des Menschen nicht seine Individuation sei, sondern die Gattung bzw. platonische Idee derselben. In den beiden Civitates des Augustinus finde sich die über Kant bis zu Platon und den Indern zurückgehende philosophische Wahrheit der zwei Welten, deren Bürger der Mensch gleichzeitig sei.

Zwei Einwände sind hier nicht zu unterdrücken. Zum einen scheint es für eine Decodierung von Allegorien keine strengen und verbindlichen Regeln zu geben. Zum anderen kann Schopenhauers dogmatischer Philosophie- und Wahrheitsbegriff, demgemäß auf Anschauung gegründete Metaphysik mit unumstößlichem Wahrheitsanspruch möglich und in seiner, Schopenhauers, Philosophie auch verwirklicht sein soll, kaum akzeptiert werden. Was aber im phänomenologischen Interesse festzuhalten bleibt, ist der Grundgedanke der symbolischen Wahrheit und der metaphysischen (und dann auch ethischen) Parallelaussagen von Philosophie und Religion.

Das Verhältnis beider zueinander sei freilich problematisch, denn „Glauben und Wissen vertragen sich nicht wohl im selben Kopfe: sie sind darin wie Wolf und Schaf in *einem* Käfig" (P II 464). Zwar könne Philosophie die allegorisch verpackten Wahrheiten der Religion freundlich würdigen, nie aber deren bedingungslosen Glaubens- und Autoritätsanspruch anerkennen. Sie kann selbst dem Widersprüchlichen und Skurrilen im mythischen Denken eine sinnvolle Funktion zuweisen – als „Andeutung ihrer allegorischen Natur" sei in der Religion „eine kleine Beimischung von Absurdität ein notwendiges Ingredienz" (P II 429) –, den Widerspruch aber nicht im eigenen begrifflichen Denken akzeptieren. Sie muß das Geheimnis der letzten, dem menschlichen Denken strukturell verschlossenen Wirklichkeit – auf Schopenhauers Mittelposition zwischen Kantischer Grenzziehung der Erfahrung und Hegelscher Spekulation kann hier nicht eingegangen werden – strenger und sachgemäßer hüten als die im Element von Mythos und Allegorie verbleibende Religion. Der „schlimme Punkt für alle Religionen" sei, „daß sie nicht eingeständlich, sondern nur versteckterweise allegorisch sein dürfen", was „einen fortgesetzten Trug herbeiführt und ein großer Übelstand" (P II 430) sei.

Um ihre Autorität unter den Gläubigen zu erhalten, müsse die Religion die Wahrheit ihrer Mythen und Dogmen als direkt und unmittelbar behaupten und gerate damit in Konflikt mit der säkularen Vernunft. Im Leugnen der Allegorizität trete dann Wahrheit im Gewand der Lüge auf, als pia fraus, und der Priester sei notwendig auch Betrüger. In den Verdacht unredlicher Absicht gerate dann auch jede Religionsphilosophie, die den Glauben vorschnell mit Vernunft und Erfahrung versöhnen will. Die Wahrheitsfrage in der Religion wird von Schopenhauer also nicht nur als theoretisches, sondern auch vor allem praktisches, das soziale Funktionieren religiöser Institutionen betreffendes Problem gesehen. Sie redlich stellen und beantworten heißt aber nichts anderes, als Religion als Dogma, Ritus und Institution abzulehnen. Diese sind nicht bloße Äußerlichkeiten, sondern ihr wesentlich, da der innerliche, gefühlsmäßige, existentielle ‚Kern‘ des Religiösen nichts genuin Eigenes darstellt, sondern das dem metaphysischen Bedürfnis entspringende Streben sei und von der Philosophie weit sachgerechter behandelt werden könne. Obwohl von namhaften Schopenhauer-Interpreten bestritten[2], scheint mir dieses Insistieren auf dem für die Religion konstitutiven Zugleich von subjektivem Erleben und objektiven Formen nicht bloß ein aufklärerischer Traditionsrest zu sein, sondern eine wesentliche phänomenologische Einsicht, die die Religion, wie sie lebensweltlich ist, nicht zugunsten einer Wunschvorstellung, wie Religion sein sollte, aus dem Blick verliert.

3. Die praktische Funktion. Die Bedeutung der Religion liege aber nicht in ihrer intellektuellen, sondern ihrer praktisch-moralischen Funktion. Erst als handlungsleitende, Ethik implizierende sind die metaphysischen Aussagen über die Struktur der Wirklichkeit an sich relevant. Als „Richtschnur für das Handeln" und als „Beruhigung und Trost im Leiden und im Tode" (P II 383) entspreche Religion den Bedürfnissen und der Fassungskraft der großen Menge.Sie sei „das alleinige Lenkungs-, Bändigungs- und Besänftigungsmittel dieser Rasse vernunftbegabter Tiere, deren Verwandtschaft mit dem Affen die mit dem Tiger nicht ausschließt" (P II 402), ihre Aussagen Regulative oder Hypothesen zu praktischem Zweck, und eben nur als funktionierende soziale Institution sei sie fähig, das ansonsten recht schwache moralische Bewußtsein der Menschen zu stützen. Daß sie in der Regel revolutionäre Potentiale entschärft und schon von Macchiavelli als „Stützen der Throne" (P II 424) empfohlen wird, registriert Schopenhauer, ohne es, als politisch Konservativer, abzulehnen. Eher stört ihn, daß sie den Fortschritt der Wissenschaften hemmt und letztlich keine freie, einzig der Vernunft verpflichtete Philosophie neben sich dulden kann. Doch liegt sein Hauptinteresse darin, in welchem Ausmaß und in welcher Weise sie Moral transportiert.

Trotz vieler rühmender Stellen bescheinigt er ihr hierin keine durchgängig positive und verläßliche Rolle. Ihrer intellektuellen Ambivalenz, der Vermengung von Wahrheit und Aberglauben, entspricht eine praktische, die Vermengung von wahrhafter Moral und größter Unmoral, die erst vom Philosophen klar erkannt und geschieden werden könne. Ein Beispiel: Durch Erfahrung und Begriff gelangt der Philosophierende nach Schopenhauer zur metaphysischen These der Alleinheit des Lebendigen und damit zum Mitleid als ethischer Forderung, Solidarität mit jedem lebenden Wesen zu üben. Für den Gläubigen wird aber Ethik gewöhnlich über religiöse Vorstellungen und Gebote vermittelt. Der Christ liebt seinen Nächsten — wobei er überdies das Tier ausklammert — auf Gottes Geheiß. Befiehlt aber derselbe Gott Kreuzzug, Ketzerverfolgung und Inquisition, predigt er Fanatismus und Rache, so beruft sich der Gläubige in methodisch gleicher Weise auf seine Gehorsamspflicht und fühlt sich in seiner allfälligen Gemeinheit und Grausamkei auch noch gut und gerecht. So gibt es neben dem unbestritten moralischen auch einen demoralisierenden Einfluß der Religion aufs menschliche Handeln und neben unbestrittener Befriedigung des metaphysischen Bedürfnisses auch dessen Mißbrauch, neben der Förderung auch ein Verschütten der moralischen Anlage. Ob im ganzen gesehen das eine oder andere überwiegt, bleibt im berühmten Dialog zwischen Philalethes und Demophiles, der das Religionskapitel in den *Parerga* einleitet, offen, da sich Schopenhauer hier offensichtlich des Urteils nicht sicher ist. Er trifft allerdings eine Rangordnung der verschiedenen Religionen nach dem Kriterium ihrer ethischen Grundsätze. Seine eigene Ethik, die den schonenden Umgang mit allem Lebendigen und eine Humanität jenseits anthropozentrischer Anmaßung fordert, scheint mir angesichts der ökologischen Krise und der mörderischen Auswirkungen der derzeitigen Weltwirschaftsordnung durchaus aktuell zu sein.

4. Die Zukunft. Auch Schopenhauer teilt, aufs erste gesehen, die unrichtige Einschätzung der klassischen Religionskritik vom Ende der Religion. Das Christentum – es wird allerdings nur von Europa gesprochen und nicht von anderen Weltteilen – gehe allmählich seinem Ende entgegen, da es „unmöglich bestehen kann, sobald einiges Nachdenken unter die Leute gekommen" (P II 465) und bloße, auf Auktorität, Wunder und Offenbarung gestützte Glaubenslehren eine nur dem Kindesalter der Menschheit angemessene Aushülfe" (P II 409) darstellten. Als „Kinder der Unwissenheit, die ihre Mutter nicht lange überleben" (P II 463), müßten die Religionen dem Fortschritt der Wissenschaften und der Aufklärung Platz machen, sie seien mit Schonung beiseitezuschieben. Schopenhauer verkennt hier zweifellos die zumindest pragmatische Vereinbarkeit von Wissenschaft und Religion, und die bis heute gemachte und in absehbare Zukunft vorblickende geschichtliche Erfahrung der Zählebigkeit, ja teilweisen Regenerationsfähigkeit der Religion läßt vermuten, daß sie sich die ganze weitere Menschheitsgeschichte hindurch zumindest in Residuen wird erhalten können. Zuzugestehen aber ist, daß der Trend der Rückläufigkeit der Kulturbedeutung von Religion anhält und daß – nach allen Erfahrungen mit den Versuchen, den Menschen Atheismus zwangszuverordnen – der *schonende* Umgang mit ihr, die vielleicht nicht stirbt, aber gleichwohl schrumpft, der angemessenste ist.

Was dennoch Schopenhauers These vom Ende der Religion bedeutsam macht, ist der antihegelianische Kontext, in dem sie steht, ist seine pessimistische Anthroplogie. Denn er verbindet mit dem Ende der Religion ausdrücklich keine geschichtsphilosophische Heilserwartung, kein eschatologisches Reich der Freiheit, keine Selbstverwirklichung des Menschen. Auch die Herrschaft der Vernunft werde nur die Hölle auf Erden bedeuten. Der anthropozentrische Mythos sei lächerlich, der Mensch dem Leiden unentrinnbar und nicht Herrscher, sondern integrativer Teil der Gesamtwirklichkeit. Indem Schopenhauer der Menschheit im großen jene – von der Aufklärung bis zu Feuerbach, Marx und Freud unterstellte – Entwicklung hin zu immer größerer Intellektualität, Moralität und Eudämonie abspricht, sie als vom blinden, unbewußten Willen beherrscht und den Intellekt ausdrücklich nicht als autonome Instanz betrachtet, liefert er einen korrigierenden Beitrag zum Verständnis des anthropologischen Fundaments, auf das sich die klassische Religionskritik – im Prinzip zu Recht – bezieht. Feuerbachs radikale Reduktion des Religiösen auf das Menschliche, sein Aufbrechen jenes alten Zirkels der Argumentation, die immer den religiösen Menschen von Gott her und Gott vom religiösen Menschen her erklären und rechtfertigen wollte, wird erst dann zur sachgerechten phänomenologischen Einsicht, wenn besser und unverzerrter begriffen wird, *was der Mensch ist.* Ein solches Bgreifen, das zureichend wäre, steht nach wie vor aus. Ein Rückgriff auf Schopenhauer kann aber – das ist meine These – dazu Hinweise geben, da er sowohl konservative wie aufklärerische Illusionen des Menschen über sich selbst, die gleichermaßen den Blick aufs Phänomen verstellen, in ihre Schranken weist.

ANMERKUNGEN

[1] Es handelt sich um das 17. Kapitel („Über das metaphysische Bedürfnis des Menschen") im Zweiten Band von *Die Welt als Wille und Vorstellung* und um das 15. Kapitel („Über Religion") des Zweiten Bandes der *Parerga und Paralipomena.* Zur Zitation werden die in der Schopenhauer-Literatur üblichen Abkürzungen verwendet (W II; P II); die nachstehende Zahl bezieht sich auf die Seitenangabe, hier nach der Edition der Werke Schopenhauers von W. Löhneysen (Stuttgart-Wiesbaden 1965).

[2] Der Bogen reicht von P. Deussen, „Schopenhauer und die Religion", *Schopenhauer-Jahrbuch* Bd. 4 (1915), S. 8ff., bis A. Hübscher, *Denker gegen den Strom. Schopenhauer gestern-heute-morgen* (Bonn ²1982), S. 23f. Über weitere Literatur zum Thema vgl. das *Schopenhauer-Jahrbuch* Bd. 17 (1930) und A. Hübscher, *Schopenhauer-Bibliographie* (Stuttgart–Bad Cannstatt 1981).

* * *

3. Erkenntnistheoretisches zu Glaube(n) und Religion

3. Epistemology of Belief, Faith, and Religion

CREDITING, TAKING FOR GRANTED, AND QUASI-BELIEF

Jacob J. Ross
Tel-Aviv University, Ramat-Aviv

It is now generally conceded that the expressions "belief" and "knowledge" are fraught with ambiguity. But no agreed technical terminology has yet emerged which will unravel the ambiguities while yet being true to all the many distinctions embodied in ordinary language usages of these terms.

I want here to introduce a new term, "crediting", which lays no claim to being anything more than a name for something with which we are all perfectly familiar but have not, for the most part, taken the trouble to single out for attention. Partly because of its unpretentious nature, this term can, I hope, be accepted by most (or at least many) of the contending parties. And if so there might lie herein a modest contribution to the emergence of a greater measure of agreement regarding the proper mapping of this very familiar but still very treacherous area of discourse.

1. We are all, I think, familiar with the experience of coming to the conclusion, or deciding, sometimes on the basis of good evidence, and sometimes on the basis of mere guesswork, that something is the case (we shall call this "p"). In common parlance we are then said to believe that p, as may be evidenced by our readiness to declare that p is true, and to act accordingly. Unfortunately, ordinary usage does not make it clear whether the believing consists in the very coming to the conclusion that p (an occurrence); or in the readiness hereafter to declare that p, and to act accordingly (a disposition); or in the retained memory that p which we hereafter possess. This retained memory is sometimes thought to be spoken of in the expression "having a belief", and can be conceived, as by D. M. Armstrong, as traces "inscribed" in our brain. In this last sense believing is taken to be a state, rather than a disposition or an occurrence. This lack of clarity ordinarily disturbs no one, for our language, for everyday purposes, serves perfectly efficiently, without taking up any position regarding this question. But philosophers have tended to fix upon one or other of these designations as the primary meaning of "believing". Thus the whole of the Cook-Wilsonian tradition in British philosophy, down to and including H. H. Price[1], has regarded believing as primarily a mental occurrence and discussed, in detail, its relationship to other occurrences, such as entertaining, taking for granted, etc. I believe there is still much to be learned from these discussions, in spite of the widespread current rejection of the occurrent analysis of belief (which Price rightly called "the traditional view"[2]—at any rate insofar as British empiricism is concerned) and its displacement by the disposition theory, which was championed by C. S. Peirce[3]. F. P. Ramsey[4], R. B. Braithwaite[5] and others. The disposition theory owes much of its present popularity to the influence of G. Ryle[6]. The state theory of believing has recently been strongly supported by D. M. Armstrong[7], and has many adherents.

2. An irenic terminological reconciliation between the occurrent and the dispositional views may be achieved by distinguishing between "crediting", "believing proper", and "quasi-believing". The first of these terms will refer to an occurrence, while the second and third refer to dispositions, one when preceded by the said occurrence, and the other when not preceded by this occurrence, respectively. The most unfamiliar of these terms is "crediting" and it is with this that I shall be particularly concerned in this paper[8].

"Crediting", I offer, then, as a new technical term, in this context, and I stipulate that the expression "crediting p" be used to refer to the familiar experience of setting oneself to act as if p. Crediting is, thus, an occurrence, paradigmatically conscious and deliberate. But, we shall suppose, it may be the case that often one credits p unconsciously and without proper deliberation. This sort of thing may happen, for example, when p forms the background to, or is presupposed by, or is associated with, some other truth, or group of truths, which we consciously credit without singling out p for attention. Crediting, at all events, is something that we do—an act. And this I take to be the truth foreshadowed in the Cook-Wilsonian preoccupation with "believing" as a cognitive act.

3. When we try to identify crediting p in the well-known terminology which H. H. Price suggested[9], we find that it corresponds most closely to what Price called "assent" or "adoption", particularly to that factor of assent that Price calls "preferring p to q or r". However, Price himself dissociates assent from any necessary connection with setting oneself to act as if p. He denies that setting oneself to act as if p could be identified with "believing p" since one can decide to act as if p even though one does not believe p at all. The case he mentions is when we come to a fork in a road, and have no evidence as to which of the two branch-roads is the right one. He says: "We can only here decide to act as if road A was the right one. But we do not on that account believe it. For we feel no confidence about its being the right one"[10]. He goes on to say that we can even sometimes decide to act as if p were true when we disbelieve it or even because we disbelieve it—as when we act as if a particular scientific or archaeological theory were true in order to convince someone else that it is false.

These examples do indeed show that setting oneself to act as if p cannot be identified unambiguously wiht the ordinary language expression "believing p". But they have no bearing upon the legitimacy of my new term "crediting p". I should say that both in the case of the person who hesitantly opts for path A, as well as in the case of the person who acts as if a particular scientific theory were true in order to convince us of the opposite, it would be perfectly legitimate to say that we had here cases of "crediting p". What is at stake is simply the question how serious and unhesitant the deciding to act as if p must be in order to count as "crediting p". And I see no reason why we should not adopt a minimalist demand which allows these cases to count as "crediting" even though we might indeed hesitate ordinarily whether to count them as "believing", which in some usages, at any rate, seems to entail a fairly high degree of conviction and a sincere commitment to stick by p.

4. But it would be wrong to conclude from Price's cases that there is no necessary connection between the readiness to act as if p and what is ordinarily called believing p. For there are other uses which make the connection between these two absolutely plain. We should certainly not credit that A believed p if all his actions belied p. (This might be explained by insincerity or unconscious motives, etc.). Indeed it is cases like these which lend considerable support to R. B. Braithwaite's thesis[11] that a tendency to action is not merely a criterion but "part of the actual meaning" of believing. This thesis which Braithwaite found also in Alexander Bain[12], surely captures an important part of our ordinary usages. But it does not square with some of the others—as we can see from Price's cases. Since Braithwaite makes it plain that he is not speaking of a disposition to believe but to what he calls "actual belief", i.e. an occurrent belief, which, he thinks, consists of two parts: (i) entertaining p, and (ii) the disposition to act as if p were true, it seems to me that what Braithwaite had in mind is what I have called "crediting p", i.e. setting oneself to act as if p. From some of the things said by William James in his celebrated essay "The Will to Believe"[13]. I gather that James too, in speaking vaguely of "believing p", had in mind what I have called "crediting p".

There is, then, an occurrent act, something which people do, which is vaguely referred to in some of our ordinary uses of the expression "believing", and it is this act that, I suggest, we should refer to hereafter as "crediting p".

5. I want to argue, now, in opposition to H. H. Price, that "crediting p" should not be contrasted with what Price (following Cardinal Newman[14]), called "assenting to p" in a way which I regard as irrelevant. According to Price "assenting" is the primary component of belief in addition to what both he and Braithwaite call "entertaining p", i.e. simply thinking of p without either believing or disbelieving. When "entertaining p" is followed up by a process of deliberation in which we move, by weighing the evidence, with more or less confidence, to the acceptance that p, we then have "assenting to p". So believing proper, for Price, is some-

thing deliberate, reasoned and based on evidence. It is not, then, dependent on the will, and can arise only when we have rationally concluded that p. It is this view that, I suppose, leads Price to refer to what I call "crediting p" by the more pejorative term "preferring p to q and r", i.e. as part of the deliberative process.

But this is unwarranted. There is no reason to confuse what one is doing (i.e. "crediting") with the grounds (or the basis or the justification) for what one is doing. Such grounds may vary from the mere will to believe that p (i.e. laying stakes on p with little or no evidence at all) through thinking it more or less likely that p, to thinking, correctly, that one can prove that p. So in my view "crediting" takes the place of "assent", leaving the grounds (or even causes) for what we do to be discussed separately.

6. But Price's distinction between the reasons and the causes for adopting p nonetheless has some force, and we may still accept, with slight modification, his category of "taking for granted that p". This, for him, is the unthinking jumping to a conclusion, without any weighing of evidence or any consideration of alternatives, on the basis of some hint. Price's example[15] is that of seeing a man walking in front of us in the street, having red hair and a dark blue overcoat, and wrongly (and embarassingly) jumping to the conclusion that it is our old friend Smith, whom we proceed to slap on the back. It is the causal process of "association" that led to our conclusion, rather than the reasoned deliberation which, for Price, is a necessary part of the assent involved in believing. As Price correctly points out, there was, in this case, some evidence for the conclusion (i.e. the red hair, the blue coat, etc.); but it did not figure in our thinking as evidence but rather as a causal stimulus which set off the association. What is clear from this example, although Price does not point this out, is that the "jumping to the conclusion" involved in "taking for granted" showed itself in subsequent action-slapping the man on the back. So that we have here a case of what I call "crediting"—and this, and not simply the fact that there was some evidence in the background, is what makes the example similar to what we ordinarily call "believing p". If we did nothing about it—no overt action, no exclamation such as "That's Smith!"—and even failed to acknowledge to ourselves in any way that we took the man to be Smith, would this still count as "taking for granted"? It is not clear what Price would say about this. I want to suggest that we should speak of "taking for granted that p" whether we are ready to act upon it or not. In the former case, "taking for granted" would serve as a ground for "crediting p", in the latter as something less than crediting. In either event, I should prefer to regard "taking for granted", considered simply as a distinct occurrence, as a sort of half-way house lying between "crediting p" and the "quasi-belief that p". I think we shall understand "taking for granted that p" better, then, it we first understand what I call "quasi-belief"

7. I borrow the expression "quasi-belief" from some of the writings of C. D. Broad[16], and wish to designate thereby any case of acting as if p where it would be inappropriate, for one reason or another, to speak of "crediting p" (or, a fortiori, of "believing that p"). Extreme examples of quasi-belief are to be found in cases of the instinctive or natural readiness of any organism, including human beings, to act in a certain manner ("as if one believed that p"). Dogs behave as if they believed bones were tasty; babies act as if they believed that mothers' milk were necessary for their sustenance. Male dogs behave as if they believed that a certain scent indicated the proximity of a female dog in heat. From an early age I, like most other human beings, acted as if I believed I could lift my hands at will. In each of the above cases the phrase "as if" indicates a reservation about the appropriateness of regarding what is concerned as "belief". In the case of the dog this is because of a general reluctance to attribute beliefs to animals. In the case of the baby the reservation may stem from the assumption that a belief has to be something which a person could formulate to himself, even if in fact he did not do so. And babies, we assume, could not, at such an early stage creditably be regarded as formulating such thoughts to themselves. There has to be the possibility of conscious human thinking at work before we are ready to speak freely of "believing"[17]. But what about my "belief" that I can lift my hands at will? The reservation here seems to stem from the fact that this is not the sort of thing I would ever think about. It is, as it were, inscribed as a basic skill

in my genetic program; and, given the right stimuli, I naturally lift my hand. A quasi-belief, in short, may arise whenever by birth or by some other means (e.g. a brain operation, hypnosis, or drugs) I act as if p, without it being proper to ascribe to me any cognitive endeavour to credit p i.e. to set myself to act as if p.

What I here loosely call "cognitive endeavour" is the key to understanding the difference between crediting p and the quasi-belief that p. Cognitive endeavours may well be regarded as a continuum of possible acts, with crediting p as the upper limit, shading off below into pure quasi-belief, where no such effort (act or endeavour) exists. And if so, what I call "taking for granted that p" could be regarded as lying somewhere in the middle of this continuum. The cognitive endeavour here is less than crediting p; but we at least have some cognitive process—something the person has done. And so we have much more than mere quasi-belief. Whenever taking for granted leads to action, it will be regarded as a ground for the crediting of p which must have supervened. In such an instance, it might even be regarded as a sort of cause. In many cases the occurrence of the crediting might merely be a subsequent inference from the fact that I find myself acting as if p. Thus, in Price's example, the taking for granted that it is my friend Smith, based on a hurried glimpse of the red hair and the coat, might translate itself so rapidly into the action of slapping him on the back, that I only afterwards realize (too late!) that I had wrongly credited (i.e. set myself to act as if) p.

8. We may ask, finally, what might be gained from distinguishing, as I have here suggested, between "crediting p", "taking for granted that p", and the "quasi-belief that p"? Of the many possible benefits I believe to exist, I single out just one—and, in my opinion, not the most important one—for particular mention here.

In the contemporary controversy whether or not knowledge is equivalent to justified true belief, one of the arguments put forward by some of the deniers of this purported equivalence consists of pointing out that in ordinary language, the use of the term "belief" has an illocutionary force such that the statement "He does not believe it; he knows it" makes perfect sense. A person who knows p, then, cannot also be said to believe p. Many replies have been addressed to this argument (by Keith Lehrer[18] and D. Armstrong[19], for example) and it is, rightly, not regarded as particularly convincing. Its weakness can be clearly exposed by the use uf the terminology I have here suggested. For even if it were true (which seems most unlikely) that there were no ordinary usage of the term "believing" which did not have the illocutionary force of refusing to commit oneself as to whether one knew, the alleged difficulty disappears entirely if we substitute the term "crediting" in place of "believing" and propose that knowledge is equivalent to justifiably crediting something that is true. There is no usual illocutionary force to the term "crediting" as I have introduced it, especially if, as I have stipulated, it be used to designate an occurrent cognitive act (setting oneself to act as if). I should like to confess that I am also of the opinion (as hinted above) that the best way of sharpening and continuing to use the ordinary language locution "believing p" is to restrict it to its dispositional use, in which it refers to the readiness to declare and to act as if p. I should contend, however, that this be restricted to the case where the said disposition is consequent to consciously or unconsciously crediting p. If this terminology be adopted and we wish to speak of knowledge in its dispositional sense—which I think is its more usual sense in ordinary language—then we may revert to the more usual formula and say that knowledge is equivalent to justified true belief. This, indeed, is an equivalence which seems to me to hold true, of cognitive attributions, at any rate, though not necessarily of cognitive claims[20]. But that is another story.

What is clear, then, is that the adoption of a more precise terminology, such as I have suggested in the above paper, shows that there is no reason whatsoever to derive from one particular ordinary usage of "believing" (its performative use in very specific situations) the conclusion that if one knows p one cannot be said to believe p. One can credit p and come to believe it; one can then also sometimes be said to know p, at least in the sense that one's belief is recognized by all concerned to be justified and true. All these locutions now have precise meanings—and this is the advantage of an improved terminology, in which the term "crediting" occupies a central role.

ENDNOTES

[1] See particularly H. H. Price, *Belief* (London 1969), and his "Some Considerations About Belief", *Proceedings of the Aristotelian Society*, 35 (1934—5), reprinted in *Knowledge and Belief*, edited A. Phillips Griffiths (Oxford 1967), p. 41—59.

[2] Price (1969), p. 20.

[3] Peirce, C. S., "The Fixation of Belief", reprinted in *The Philosophy of Peirce*, edited J. Buchler (London 1940).

[4] Ramsey, F. P., *The Foundations of Mathematics* (London 1931).

[5] Braithwaite, R. B., "The Nature of Believing", *Proceedings of the Aristotelian Society*, 33 (1932—3), reprinted in Griffiths (1967), p. 28—40.

[6] Ryle, Gilbert, *The Concept of Mind* (London 1949), especially Chapter V.

[7] Armstrong, D. M., *Belief, Truth and Knowledge* (Cambridge 1973).

[8] May I say, paranthetically, that there is not much use that I can find in my terminology for the usual expression "concluding" or "coming to the conclusion that p". If these refer to the relationship between p and its logical premises, then we are not merely designating a mental occurrence but also pointing to its logical underpinnings; and if we are merely saying that we have accepted p in the sense of setting ourselves to treat p as true, then this is equivalent to what I call "crediting" or setting oneself to act as if p.

[9] See specially his "Some Considerations About Belief", loc. cit.

[10] Griffiths (1967), p. 47.

[11] In "The Nature Of Believing", loc. cit.

[12] *The Emotions and the Will* (London 1859).

[13] *In the Will to Believe and other Essays* (New York 1895).

[14] *The Grammar of Assent* (London 1870).

[15] Griffiths (1967), p. 48.

[16] See for example C. D. Broad, *The Mind and its Place in Nature* (London 1923), p. 215.

[17] This fits very well with Braithwaite's account, even though he was talking of the occurrent uses of "belief", whereas these examples are more readily applicable to the dispositional use. In each case the individual (dog or baby) acted as if p, but he could not properly be described as "entertaining p".

[18] Lehrer, Keith, *Knowledge* (Oxford 1974), Chapter 3.

[19] Armstrong, D. M., *Belief, Truth and Knowledge*, p. 140.

[20] For the importance of the distinction between knowledge attributions and knowledge claims see Alan R. White's paper "On Claiming To Know", included in Griffiths (1967), p 100—111.

* * *

INSTITUTIONAL BELIEF

Jerome Gellman
Ben Gurion University of the Negev, Beer-Sheva, Israel

A major task for philosophers of religion is to elucidate the meaning of "belief" in religion. I hope to make a modest contribution to this endeavor by discussing a sometimes neglected distinction between two kinds of belief-attributing sentences. The first you are likely to meet in a work on religion and may be illustrated by:

(1) "Buddhists believe that Gautama had a great awakening."

The second kind is illustrated by:

(2) "Buddhist believe they have arms and legs."

(1) ascribes to Buddhists a belief held *qua* Buddhists, within an institutional religion, (2) is not an institutional belief, and is not believed *qua* anything, except *qua* normal human being.

In what follows, I characterize the distinction between institutional and non-institutional belief, and argue that the type of proposition believed in the two cases is importantly different. Then I show how an awareness of the distinction undermines a major motivation for a view of religious language found in the Neo-Wittgensteinian tradition.

The distinction between institutional and non-institutional belief is suggested by Edmund Leach's discussion of the Tully River controversy in anthropology. W. E. Roth had reported that the Tully River Blacks of Australia were ignorant of the connection between copulation and pregnancy, because they attributed pregnancy to a woman's dreaming of having a child, and other such irrelevancies, as we believe. Leach protests that we cannot infer that the natives were really ignorant of the true cause of pregnancy . After all, Roth himself reports that they knew the cause of pregnancy in animals, and in societies well aware of the truth in man, there abound magical tales of conception. Instead, Leach argues that, "When an ethnographer reports that 'members of the X tribe believe that . . .' he is giving a description of an orthodoxy, a dogma, something which is true of the culture as a whole."[1]

Leach's view is that the Tully River Blacks very likely knew the true cause of pregnancy. Their statements to the contrary were in the realm of ritual. (Among the Walbiri tribe, in ritual contexts spirits are spoken of as causing conception, whereas in other contexts copulation is spoken of.) What a person says as a member of an institutional structure may differ from what he otherwise believes. This need not be because he is insincere about his institutional beliefs, and neither need there be a contradiction between the latter and his other beliefs. We must elucidate what it *means* to have an institutional belief and how the latter relate to non-institutional beliefs.

A promising direction comes from a study of the Ethyopian Dorze by Dan Sperber.[2] The Dorze, Sperber reports, believe the leopard is a Christian who observes the fasts of the Ethyopian Orthodox Church, including Wednesdays and Fridays. Yet, the Dorze is no less careful to guard his animals on those days than on other days of the week. He believes *both* that Leopards observe the fast days and also that they are always dangerous. How does the Dorze believe a contradiction? Sperber suggests that in their tradition there is no one definite proposition believed about the leopard. Rather the Dorze believes concerning the sentence:

(3) "The leopard is a Christian who observes Orthodox Ethyopian fast days"

that *for some interpretation or other* it is true, where typically the believer has no particular interpretation in mind. Let us call this a belief in the *affirmability* of (3), and say that the believer *affirms* the sentence (3). Belief in affirmability relates a person to a sentence in quotes, as it were, with an indefinite meaning. So what the Dorze really believes is:

> (4) "The leopard is a Christian who observes Orthodox Ethyopian fast days" is affirmable.

But (4) is so indefinite it cannot be inconsistent with the belief that the leopard is always dangerous. So the Dorze can guard his flocks and remain true to tradition.

I want to adapt Sperber's proposal to the distinction between institutional and non- institutional belief, with two modifications. First, in institutional belief not single sentences but networks of sentences are affirmed. To learn an institutional language is to learn a set of instructions on how to talk, where networks of sentences give semantic constraints on possible interpretations of individual sentences. Secondly, Sperber believes that "non-symbolic statements" are fully analyzed propositions, but the difference between institutional beliefs and others lies elsewhere. The central difference is that non-institutional belief generally includes a more or less agreed method of resolution of indefiniteness. If two believers affirmed the same non-institutional sentence but gave idiosyncratic interpretations, respectively, they would not have the *same* belief. But in institutional belief the sameness of belief is constituted by agreement over the affirmability of the institutional language, in disregard of individual disambiguations. The Dorze, for example, all have the same traditional belief as long as they believe (4), regardless of how or whether they disambiguate (3).

To summarize, institutional belief involves the belief in the affirmability of sentence-networks, with relative freedom on how to disambiguate affirmed sentences.

Religious belief is typically institutional. Often, to have the same religious belief just is to share a network of language, to follow the same instructions. What is believed is the affirmability of certain sentences in semantic relation to each other. Neither the interpretations nor an agreed method of resolution of the indefinite meanings is institutionally prescribed. Thus, religious language is open-ended by its very nature from the start. To suppose that it is progressively emptied of empirical content by qualifications is to fail to appreciate its institutional nature. Also, its indefiniteness precludes religion from being an hypothesis or theory, since it cannot face the test of confirmation or refutation. This feature also gives religious language the power to express such different attitudes and intentions.

Belief in God is typically institutional. What counts as the *same* belief in God is the common belief in the affirmability of "God exists" within a commonly affirmed language network. This makes possible different metaphysical views of God amongst co-religionists, where the metaphysics is not institutionally prescribed. On the institutional level, "God" functions as a referring term, since it plays the semantic role of a referring term in the language. In institutional terms, this *constitutes* being a referring term.

Dogmas, scriptual language, and ordinary religious talk all have an institutional character, making possible shared belief, individual interpretations of same, and a rich multiplicity of inner attitudes.

A recognition of the institutional nature of religion, undermines a view of religious language found in the Neo-Wittgensteinian tradition, which I shall call the "expressive view". It is represented by Peter Winch when he compares God-talk to pain-talk.[3] Just as pain-talk allegedly replaces and extends pain behavior, so God-talk, says Winch, replaces and extends ritual behavior. For Winch, ritual expresses peculiarly relgious feelings of "awe", "reverence", and "wonder", and God-talk follows the contours of ritual, expressing the same distinctive religious feelings and attitudes. D. Z. Phillips also has written of peculiarly religious inner attitudes, expressed in ritual and language, and his view will be discussed below. The expressive view, then, says that religious language expresses recognizable attitudes and feelings which are distinctively religious. A corrolary of this view is that "God" is not a typical referring term. With a typical referring term, substitutivity of co-referential terms is generally valid, but in expressive language the whole weight may be in using just these words and no others. No other terms may do the expressive job as well. Hence a term like "God" may not be substitutable for, and hence not be a typical referring term.

Now it seems to me that a major motivation for the expressive view is to avoid thinking of religion as an hypothesis or theory. In his well-known paper, "Religious Belief and Language Games", D. Z. Phillips, for instance, often contrasts religion with hypotheses and theories.[4] He asks us to consider a mother who places a garland on a statue of the Virgin Mary. Phillips thinks that if she considered the act prudential, then it would be superstitious. Why? Because, "All one needs is a comparison of the material fortunes of babies for whom the blessing of the Virgin has been sought, and the material fortunes of those who have received no such blessing. The results will be statistically random."[5] The act is superstitious for Phillips because it issues from a belief in causal connections easily confirmed not to exist.

Phillips suggests that the homage to the Virgin Mary can be *religious* rather than superstitious. This would be when "The mother seeks the protection of Mary's holiness; she wants the child's life to be oriented in [Mary's] virtues . . . This orientation is what the believer would call the blessing of the Virgin Mary."[6] Phillips is contending that there is an especially religious way to place a garland, in virtue of its expressing especially relgious attitudes. He seems to recognize a superstitious way of performing the ritual as the sole alternative to his "religious" interpretation of it. The implication seems to be that religion is saved from the charge of superstition only by embracing the expressive view.

If the thesis of this paper is correct, Phillips is mistaken. First, that the placing of garlands is neither superstitious nor expressive, but institutional, seems more plausible. As such, the ritual represents an institutional belief to the effect that:

(5) "Placing a garland is prudential," is affirmable.

Three people who place garlands, the first believing the benefit is somehow spiritual, the second believing it somehow physical, and the third having no thought beyond the indefinite belief in "some benefit or other", are all of them performing the *same* ritual, institutionally considered. Their participation in the ritual *pictures*, as it were, their agreement over (5). Institutionally speaking, they have the same belief. Not the expressive nature of the ritual but the indefiniteness of what is believed affirmable in (5) is what accounts for its not being a superstition: it cannot face the tribunal of empirical testing.

Moreover, even if the expectation of some benefit were as vividly definite as you like, this still need not be a superstition, since this expectation typically would not confront reality in isolation, but as part of a whole way of thinking. Placing a garland might be benefit-enhancing, but other actions benefit-inhibiting. Whether the expected benefit actually comes about will depend on a whole complex of actions any of which together or separately might inhibit the benefit accruing to the performance of one particular act. Typically religions work out the whole view rather incompletely—things are left on a level of great indefiniteness. So, belief in a definite benefit is consistent with indefiniteness over all, and again superstition is precluded.

Thus, a recognition of religious belief as institutional removes a major motivation for the expressive view, viz., the desire to distance religion from superstition. Institutional belief *cannot* be superstitious.

Finally, it is a mistake to suppose that what co-religionists *must* have in common is one recognizable inner attitude expressed in ritual and language. Rather, what their share is a belief- —in the *affirmability* of their institutional language.

Is institutional religion, then, a mere game, in which one just follows instructions? Is this not a sham rather than genuine religion? The answer lies in grasping the ritual nature of the human species. We are ritual animals, which is to say not only that we find rituals apt for expressing inner attitudes, nor only that we value the socially conforming power of ritual, but that it is our nature to engage in rituals as a form of seeking for a "point" in things. We ritualize our search, hoping or expecting that ritual will enhance our success and expression of the "point" once we find it. Ritual can precede any "point" we see in it, except for being the framework in which meaning is discovered and articulated. Neo-Wittgensteinian philosopers seem to insist that there must first be a "point" there to be expressed, which the ritual then articulates. This seems to be false to the institutional nature of religion, and denied by what I mean by calling humans ritual in nature.

Belief in affirmability shares the above character of ritual. It is a ritualized use of language, forming a common framework for mutual "point" seekers. But the meaning that each one discovers may be his own, and independent of the institutionally prescribed language.

Hence, institutional belief is no mere game, in the sense in which it can be dropped at whim. It is as serious as life, and utterly genuine, if we gauge genuineness by a true grasp of humanity. But at the same time, we are not *only* ritual animals, and religion is not restricted to the institutional level. The indefinitenes of religious belief is the occasion for human expression as well, ranging from the most gross superstition to sublime spirituality[7].

ENDNOTES

[1] Leach, Edmund, "Virgin Birth", in Leach, *Genesis as Myth* (London 1971), p. 88.
[2] Sperber, Dan, *Rethinking Symbolism* (Cambridge 1979).
[3] Winch, Peter, "Meaning and Religious Language", in: S. Brown, *Reason and Religion* (Ithaca 1979).
[4] Phillips, D. Z., "Religious Belief and Language Games", *Ratio*, 12 (1970), p. 26−46.
[5] Phillips (1970), p. 40.
[6] Phillips (1970), p. 42.
[7] I thank J. J. Ross for helpful comments, and W. L. Gombocz for a question that forced me to clarify an earlier version of this paper.

* * *

SOME PHILOSOPHICAL REMARKS ON THE RELATION BETWEEN KNOWING AND BELIEVING

Dennis M. Senchuk
Indiana University, Bloomington

Philosophical discussants of the relation between 'knowing' and 'believing' have sometimes gone to extremes. While some philosophers, in keeping with the standard analysis of knowledge as justified true belief, have held that 'knowing that p' entails 'believing that p'; others, some of whom also contend that 'knowing' is unanalysable, have held "that it is impossible to know and to believe the same thing at the same time". (H. H. Price, 1934, p. 230.) This range of opinion leaves plenty of room for debate.

But will such diametrically opposed colloquists inevitably talk past each other? A hopeful sign of common ground on which to join the issues might be found among some plausible motives for holding the conflicting extremes: the standard analysis of knowing may well need (something like) the belief condition, according to which 'believing that p' is a necessary condition for 'knowing that p', in order to secure proper *ownership* of the knowledge (for even if I have the right to be sure that p, *and* p is true; I might not be aware of my right or of p itself and, so, not really *know* that p—e.g., know that the square formed of sides equal to the diagonal of a given square has twice the area of the given square); while the view that knowing is an unanalysable, direct relation between knower and known, needs (or is thought to need) to rule out believing as a part of knowing, because believing seems an unsuitably *indirect* relation to what one knows (so, for example, Price concludes from the observation that others can at best truly *believe* him to be puzzled and, hence, cannot *know* him to be so, that simultaneously believing and knowing that p is impossible). Both sides, despite their great differences, can be viewed as appealing to (the presence or absence of) belief as a way of ensuring the right personal relationship to one's knowledge.

Assuming such a common motive, barely implicit in the one position and virtually explicit in the other position, it is evident that these contrary appeals to belief cannot both be sustained. Indeed, there is some reason to question the need for each appeal: the standard analysis could just as well secure proper ownership by suggesting that the knower, without actually believing that p, must nonetheless have some sort of cognizance, grasp, or (arguably only latent) mastery of the p which is known. The unanalysability position, on the other hand, is probably wrong to contend that a direct relation between knower and known precludes believing what one knows; for even if seeing isn't believing, seeing would not seem to be *incompatible* with believing, either. (Here it is not necessary to prove the point so much as to shift the burden of proof: what reason is there to contend that if John *knows*, having seen it happen, that the butler did it, then John cannot *believe* that the butler did it?)

What reason, indeed!? Does it follow from the fact of one's being directly related to something that one cannot also be indirectly related to it? If not, Price's argument requires further support.

Suppose one were to suggest, in possible furtherance of Price's position, that knowledge is the result of eliminating any need to believe? (This suggestion is in keeping with the sense, if not the intent, of Chisholm's remark (1957): "The relation of knowing to believing . . . is not that of falcon to bird or of airedale to dog; it is more like that of arriving to travelling." (p. 18)) Believing might be said to be something one has to do in lieu of knowing, to be a poor substitute for the genuine article. If so, then why would one insist upon retaining the undesired substitute after attaining the desired thing itself? That would be like wanting to retain possession of a voided I O U after it has already been redeemed for cash.

Reflecting upon Chisholm's above-mentioned comparison, Merrill Ring (1977) suggests: "When one has arrived, one is no longer traveling. Similarly when one does come to know what was previously believed, the believing, like the traveling, is over." (p. 59.) But although we might well agree with Ring that further believing, after one has reached one's final destination of knowing, is *unnecessary*, it does not follow from such a concession that continuing to believe what one already knows is *impossible*.

Is there any feature of knowing which precludes further believing? Ring suggests that a person "who knows cannot do what someone who believes can do." (Ibid.) Namely, the knower cannot try to find out what's already known; but "if someone believes something, . . . further inquiry bearing on what is believed is possible." (Ibid.) These suggestions are at least debatable: for one thing, belief has sometimes been viewed (by C. S. Pierce, for example) as a terminus of inquiry, as something that quiets the irritation of doubt; for another, a proponent of the standard analysis of knowing might regard Ring's suggestions as question-begging, might urge that even if most beliefs *do* allow for no possibility of further inquiry, perhaps those involved in instances of knowing, i.e., those beliefs which are both justified and true, *do not*. Ring could respond to the Piercean point by suggesting that belief is at best a psychological rather than logical barrier to further inquiry; but the charge of question-begging could not be dealt with so easily: for unless the *absence* of belief from cases of knowing can be shown to be the reason why knowing that p precludes trying to find out that p, the bare fact, if it is a fact, that knowledge precludes further inquiry will not establish Ring's (or Price's) conclusion "that knowing is necessarily not believing." (p. 56)

Still, some of Ring's observations may be relevant to a less extreme but more tenable account of the relation between knowing and believing. For although believing may not be *incompatible* with knowing, knowing may still qualify as a favorable *alternative* to believing.

In support of this account, one might appeal to certain locutions which seem to imply its truth−e.g. "I don't believe that 2+2 = 4; I know it." But it seems rather difficult to get contemporary philosophers to take such linguistic evidence seriously. Thus, Anthony Quinton (1967) admits that "If, knowing p, I am asked 'Do you believe that p?', I should reply "No, I know it.'" But if this is taken to show that knowledge isn't or can't be a kind of belief, Quinton insists it "is hardly a serious argument." He says ". . . If I know that p, I do not merely believe it, but I do believe it all the same. It is often wrong or misleading in certain circumstances to say something that is inquestionably true." (p. 346) The legacy of H. P. Grice (1961 and many other times since) is apparent: what's right or wrong to say in "certain circumstances", is alleged to be a purely pragmatic concern irrelevant to the literal truth of philosophically significant propositions−e.g., to the compound proposition "I know that p, *and* I believe that p."

A. R. White (1982) argues in much the same vein when he dismisses such remarks as "I don't believe it, I know it" and "It's not a question of believing, I actually know it." According to White, "what the remarks contrast is not belief and knowledge but 'mere' belief and knowledge, just as 'It's not big, it's huge' or 'It's not difficult it's impossible' mean that the first description is an understatement, only a part of what the second description mentions more fully or more accurately." (p. 92)

The following example, credited by Ring to J. K. Stephens, would seem to provide a handy rejoinder to White: "Hitler was not a very, very naughty man . . . Between being naughty and being evil there is a *categorical* shift . . . So too knowing is not a true belief which is very, very well supported." (p. 58) White himself, though, is ready with the reply that this doesn't show that knowing and believing mutually exclude one another. But be that as it may, just as being evil does not entail being naughty, so too perhaps knowing does not entail believing.

White's own examples range between corrections of what might be called undertstatements of *degree* ("It's not big, it's huge") and understatements of *kind* ("It's not difficult, it's impossible.") In the former cases, we might be willing to concede that the understatement does follow from the more appropriate locution; in the latter cases we would not concede such a thing. Now of course interpreting the claim "I don't believe, I know" as an attempt to correct an understatement of kind rather than degree can hardly be said to prove 'knowing' does not entail 'believing'; but that interpretation is at least plausible and does argumentatively parry the thrust of White's remarks.

Perhaps more telling is the locution, "I don't *have* to believe it, I *know* it." This locution is aggressively tendentious, insisting as it were that knowing does not necessitate believing, that knowing is a favorable alternative to believing. But rather than press the point so directly, only perhaps to be told of other philosophers' divergent linguistic intuitions, or to be chided instead for introducing irrelevant "pragmatic" considerations, let's make a modest detour over territory less well trod by analytic philosophers.

J.-P. Sartre once observed that belief carries with it the basis for its own destruction. The figure he used was, as I recall, that of a self-poisoning well. No matter how strongly one believes something, the suggestion goes, one has to admit that it's still a matter of belief: it's something one is forced to *believe* because one doesn't really *know*. And once one acknowledges that one doesn't really know, doubt seeps in, poisoning the well of belief. One moral of all this might be that if you're happy with your beliefs, perhaps you shouldn't think about them too much. But another way around the problem, a way that may be more psychologically than logically compelling is to insist, e.g., "I don't *believe* that God exists; I *know* it!"

Not everyone, of course, would accept these Sartrean remarks about believing. Wittgenstein for example, held a seemingly contrary view, insisting that one can't mistrust one's beliefs. But Wittgenstein uses this observation to disabuse us of the idea that beliefs, like sense impressions, might serve as evidence for our claims, as when we say: "I believe it's raining and my belief is reliable, so I have confidence in it." Wittgenstein's rejoinder to this idea is: "One can mistrust one's own senses but not one's own belief." (*P.I*, II, x) Without spelling out the logic of this rejoinder, suffice it to say that the sort of mistrust being denied by Wittgenstein is that which would be expressed by saying, if it made *sense* to say such a thing, that I believe it's raining, but I mistrust my belief. And Sartre's view does not specifically seem to license saying this, either; so the incompatibility of their views may be more apparent than real.

Knowledge, unlike belief, is surely not potentially self-destructive: the skeptic may supply us with reasons to call into question our knowledge; but its being knowledge could not be among those reasons for doubt. Belief and knowledge might peacefully coexist, even if the latter does not presuppose the former; but if both were in evidence, the acknowledgment that we also believe what we know would not lead us to doubt our knowledge. If belief is its own poison, moreover, then knowledge is the antidote: our knowledge can serve to prevent the cessation of our collateral belief.

Knowledge, then, might be said to provide a hospitable environment for belief—perhaps that is one reason why it sometimes seems that the one implies the other. But belief may be more affective than . . . well, cognitive; and that may be why it can be said, for example, that although she knows her son is a murderer, she just can't believe it. Must we believe what we know? Reasoned reflection may demand that we do so; but relatively unreasoned thoughts and feelings may lead us to ignore that demand. It is idle to suggest that, at some level, the woman of the example must believe what she knows; for, as suggested earlier, the knower can simply have some cognizance, grasp, or mastery of the known—the knower need not even *accept* (an arguably even more affective term than "believe") the known.

Can Sartre's view, if correct, actually serve to *prove* any of these contentions? Perhaps not; but his view is quite congenial to my major contention, that knowing is best viewed as an occasionally available, more favorable (assuming a desire for truth), non-exclusive alternative to believing. A proponent of the standard analysis of knowing may counter any claim to a proof, based on Sartre's view, of this contention; for were one to presuppose that knowledge is justified true belief, then one might suggest that those beliefs which are constituents of knowledge are attended by an antidote to their otherwise self-poisoning properties, an antidote supplied by their justified claim to truth. Still, Sartre's view does accord well with the sentiment expressed in the claim "I don't have to believe, I know!"; and although this doesn't really prove my claims about the relation between knowing and believing, I haven't yet discovered any reason to retreat from those claims, either. Defenders of the other, to my mind more extreme, alternative conceptions of that relationship might well say the same about their own views; but in a philosphical climate where too often the denial of proof for each position has been taken as direct support for the other extreme, perhaps yet a third way of viewing the matter will have its own philosophically bracing effect on the controversy.

REFERENCES

Chisholm, Roderick, *Perceiving: A Philosophical Study* (Ithaca, N.Y. 1957).
Grice, H. P., "The Causal Theory of Perception" *Proceedings of the Aristotelean Society*, Suppl. Vol. 35 (1961), 121–152.
Price, H. H., "Some Considerations about Belief" *Proceedings of the Aristotelean Society*, Vol. 35 (1934–5).
Quinton, Anthony , "Knowledge and Belief", in: P. Edwards (ed.), *The Encyclopedia of Philosophy* (New York 1967).
Ring, Merrill, "Knowledge: The Cessation of Belief" *American Philosophical Quarterly*, Vol. 14, No. 1 (1977).
White, Alan R., *The Nature of Knowledge* (Totowa, N.J. 1982).
Wittgenstein, Ludwig, *Philosophical Investigations* (Oxford 1953).

* * *

BELIEF, KNOWLEDGE, AND INFERENCE

Nigel G. E. Harris
University of Dundee, Scotland

To what extent should a person be said to believe or to know what can be deduced from propositions that he can, rightly, be said to believe or to know?

Because there can be cases in which someone believes a proposition p and yet is quite unaware of many of the propositions which can be validly inferred from p, it is generally accepted that a person should not be said to believe all the propositions that could be deduced from the propositions he can, rightly, be said to believe. And for a similar reason it is generally accepted that a person should not be said to know all the propositions that could be deduced from the propositions he can, rightly, be said to know. But it also seems to be a universally held view amongst modern epistemologists that if someone believes a proposition p, and if, also, he *validly infers* a proposition q from p, then he *should* be said to believe q; and that if someone knows p, and if, also, he *validly infers* q from p, then he *should* be said to know q. Indeed, this latter view is commonly treated as though it were so obvious that it needs no justification.

Far from being obvious, I think this view conflicts with some of our intuitions. I want to argue that there *are* cases in which someone who believes a proposition p and who validly infers another proposition q from p should not be said to believe q. Such cases arise when q is obtained directly from p by some weakening rule of inference such as Addition [inferring $p \lor q$ from p] or Existential Generalization [inferring $(\exists x)Fx$ from Fa]. (Cases of rules which would require p to be a conjunction of two or more propositions are not included—see below.) In these cases it is intuitively more plausible to say that someone's believing q is ruled out by his believing the stronger proposition p, rather than to say that it is possible to believe p and q simultaneously. One cannot, I think, come to have a belief which merely lacks the specificity possessed by a belief about the very same matter which one continues to hold.

Suppose you believe that I have a total of 9 children. From what you believe it follows that I have about 10 children, and this is something which you may infer from your belief and, perhaps, go on to assert. But it would seem very odd to say that as a result of making the inference you now believe not only that I have 9 children, but *also* that I have about 10 children. If you have a belief about the exact number of my children then this belief precludes you from having (at least whilst you have that exact belief in mind) a belief about the approximate number of my children. It is, of course, perfectly acceptable to describe a belief in approximate terms and to say, in this example for instance, that the number of children you believe me to have is about 10. But this is a rough description of a belief, not a description of a rough belief.

Rather than accepting my view it might seem tempting to say that if one believes p then one already as *part* of that belief believes any weaker proposition that is an immediate consequence of p, and which p might thus in some sense be said to contain. Thus in the example just discussed one would say that in believing I have 9 children you would *ipso facto* believe that I have about 10 children. But this will not do. Someone (such as a small child) with a limited repertoire of concepts might believe I have a total of 9 children, yet not be capable of believing that I have about 10 because he lacks any concepts to do with approximation.

The view I am advocating allows one to say that what have come to be known as Gettier examples[1] do not provide counter-instances to the traditional identification of knowledge with justified true belief.

Suppose a teacher, Smith, has as good reasons as anyone could normally be expected to have to back up his belief that one of his students, Jones, owns a Ford (Jones consistently claims it is his, he shows the registration book in his name, he and nobody else drives it, etc.). Yet, despite all the evidence, Jones does not own the Ford. However, quite unknown to Smith, another student of his called Brown *does* own a Ford. Gettier and many others have argued that if Smith were to infer that one of his students owns a Ford, then that is something that is both true and that he could be said to be justified in believing (since it follows, and he believes and is justified in believing that it follows, from his justified belief that *Jones* owns a Ford). Yet it seems that we should not say that Smith *knows* that one of his students owns a Ford, since the circumstances that make Smith's conclusion true have nothing to do with his grounds for drawing that conclusion.

Most commentators in the 20 years since Gettier's article first appeared have taken examples like this to show that knowledge cannot be defined as justified true belief. Only two ways of avoiding this conclusion have hitherto been suggested. One involves denying the validity of the inference from "Jones owns a Ford" to "Someone owns a Ford"[2]; the other involves denying that a belief inferred from a false proposition can be justified.[3] The first leads to an implausibly restricted logic.[4] The second is also too sweeping, for suppose on ample evidence from newspapers, etc., Smith comes to believe that all Ford cars have some fault, then if he is justified in believing that Jones owns a Ford he will surely be justified in believing that Jones has a car with that fault in it. My view, however, provides a third and better way out.

What seems wrong with the Gettier example above is the assumption that Smith must be taken to hold the belief that someone owns a Ford (in the sense of being taken to believe the proposition "Someone owns a Ford"). What Smith believes about the ownership of a Ford is that Jones owns a Ford, and that he has in mind this belief in respect of a specific person prevents him from additionally having the weaker belief that someone owns a Ford. We can, of course, say of Smith that he believes that someone owns a Ford *if* by this we are referring (somewhat vaguely) to Smith's belief that Jones owns a Ford and are *not* taking ourselves to be describing any of his beliefs *fully*.

A similar line can be taken about any other Gettier examples, since all involve attributing to someone simultaneous beliefs in a proposition and in some weak direct consequence of it. This is true even in the following case due to R. M. Chisholm[5]: a myopic man mistakenly thinks that a dog in a field is a sheep and concludes that there are sheep in the field, but this conclusion happens to be correct since there are sheep in part of the field out of the man's sight. In this case what the man believes is not the weak proposition that there are sheep in the field, but the stronger proposition that the object that he has observed in the field is a sheep.

I mentioned earlier that the cases in which someone who believes p and infers q from p should not be said to believe q do not include cases in which the rule of inference *requires* p to be a conjunction (cases, say, of applying Addition to a conjunction *are* to be included). I now want to discuss such cases.

Often when someone is said to believe p and q what is being claimed is that that person both believes p and believes q, without it being implied that he believes the conjunction p & q, for he may never have brought p and q simultaneously to mind. But it is obviously possible for someone to believe a conjunction of the form p & q. When someone has a belief that p & q he must *ipso facto* believe p and believe q. This is because someone who believes a conjunction must, if his belief *is* a belief in a conjunction, understand what a conjunction is, namely that it is merely a way of simultaneously presenting two propositions. It is thus appropriate to talk of the belief that p and the belief that q as constituents of the belief that p & q, whereas it would be quite inappropriate to say that the belief that I have about 10 children is a constituent of the belief that I have 9 children. So when someone believes that p & q and applies the rule of inference known as Simplification to obtain p, doing this will not give him a new belief that p, for p will be something which he can already be credited with believing.

When someone applies a 2-premiss rule of inference such as Modus Ponens to infer a proposition from two beliefs he holds, then this will produce a new belief. Thus, if you believe that if the train is more than an hour late you will miss your connection, and you then come to believe that the train is more than an hour late and infer that you will miss your connection, then you can be taken to believe that you will miss your connection. Here the proposition that you come to believe says something categorical about the missing of the connection which is not only not said by either of the propositions from which it is inferred when considered separately, but is not said (except through the inference) by the conjunction of those propositions. Thus there is a sense in which an inference from $p \mathbin{\&} (p \supset q)$ to q will produce a conclusion that is more forceful than its premiss, unlike inferences by Addition or Existential Generalization.

Finally, I want to mention the case of making inferences from beliefs by the rule known as Disjunctive Syllogism. This might seem to provide an example of believing both p and $p \lor q$ together. Suppose you believe that either Smith or Jones is dead, and you then come to believe that Smith is not dead. If you infer that it must be Jones who is dead and come to believe that proposition, then will you not now believe both that Jones is dead *and* that either Smith or Jones is dead?

I think it is most implausible to say in this case that you will still believe that either Smith or Jones is dead (in the sense of believing that disjunction) once you have come to believe that Smith is not dead. The coming to believe a stronger, more specific, proposition about who is dead will mean giving up the weaker proposition as something you believe; the stronger proposition will *replace* the weaker one.

ENDNOTES

1 Gettier, Edmund L., "Is Justified True Belief Knowledge?", *Analysis*, Vol. 23 (1963), pp. 121–3.
2 New, C. G., "Some Implications of 'Someone'", *Analysis*, Vol, 26 (1965), pp. 62–4.
3 Pailthorp, Charles, "Knowledge as Justified True Belief", *The Review of Metaphysics*, Vol. 23 (1969), pp. 25–47, and I. Thalberg, "In Defense of Justified True Belief", *The Journal of Philosophy*, Vol. 66 (1969), pp. 794–803.
4 Harman, Gilbert, "New Implications of 'Someone'", *Analysis*, Vol. 26 (1966), p. 206.
5 Chisholm, Roderick M., *Theory of Knowledge* (Englewood Cliffs, N. J. 1966), p. 23.

* * *

SOME LOGICAL INCONGRUITIES BETWEEN THE CONCEPT OF KNOWLEDGE AND THE CONCEPT OF BELIEF

Justus Hartnack
Helsingør, Denmark

If I state I know that p and it turns out that p is false then it is also false that I knew that p. I shall have to say that I thought I knew but apparently I did not. But if I say that I believe that p and it turns out that p is false it does not entail that it is false that I believed it. It is perfectly correct to say that I now realize that p is false but that nevertheless I did believe it. In other words, it would be a conceptual misunderstanding to speak of false knowledge and redundant to speak of true knowledge, but it would be neither a misunderstanding nor a redundancy to speak of true or false beliefs.

Both knowledge and beliefs are related to evidence. But they are so in different ways. The evidence available for a belief is evidence for the possible truth of the object of my belief; but it is not evidence for the existence of the belief. I may be a very irrational person who, accordingly, have all sorts of beliefs for which there is no evidence whatever. A psychoanalyst may be able to discover the psychological causes of my irrational beliefs. A psychological cause of a belief, however, belongs to another category than does evidence. Evidence is a non-psychological concept related to the concept of truth, which of course *par excellence* is a non-psychological concept. The evidence for knowledge, however, is evidence not only evidence for the truth of the object of knowledge; it is also evidence for the existence of knowledge. If the evidence for the truth of that which I claim that I know is not strong enough to entail the truth of the object of the alleged knowledge then there was no knowledge of it. To have the right to make a knowledge claim is conditioned by being able to answer the question how I know. I must reveal my evidence.

But here we are confronted with one of the problems connected with the use of the concept of knowledge. If I have a headache it seems preposterous to ask the question how I know that I have a headache—a question I only could answer by saying that I know it simply because I do in fact have a headache. And if I cannot answer the question adequately it means that I cannot say that I know that I have a headache. Which seems equally preposterous because I do not believe it, am certain, or am convinced that I have it. To say that I *know* seems to be the natural thing to say. Apparently we have a situation in which there is a discrepancy between what I cannot say and what in fact is the case. There is, however, no such discrepancy.

I order to see that there is no such discrepancy, it is important to notice that the concept of knowledge is not a psychological concept. To say that one knows something is not to report or describe a state of mind. In fact, the verb 'to know' or the expression "to have knowledge', behaves in important respects as a trouser-word. That is, it derives its meaning and its legitimacy from being a negation of a particular case of not-knowledge. If there are such particular cases I have the right to use the concept of knowledge. To the question "How do you know?" my answer will be to mention the things that gave me the right, i.e. the relevant instances of not-knowing. If there are no possible ways whatever to conceive of cases of non-knowing, the concept of knowledge can find no application at all. It would be, to use a by now classical expression, a violation of the logical syntax governing the concept in question. There is consequently no discrepancy. The reason it is preposterous to say that if I have a headache I do, or do not, know it, is not because I in fact know it or do not know it but because the concept of knowledge cannot meaningfully be applied in such cases. Wittgenstein's thought-experiment where, through some kind of nerve-connections, I can feel another person's pain does not entitle me to say that it is not my pain. Of course it is my pain. The cause of the pain is another person's body; but the cause of a pain is not the same as the pain. It does not, therefore, constitute an instance of not knowing, as it would do if my pain would not be mine if the cause is outside my body.

In his "A Defence of Common Sense" the first proposition which G. E. Moore says he *knows* with certainty to be true is that there exists at present a living human body which, as he says, is *my* body. Does Moore really Know it? Do I know that there is a body which is my body? And do you know that there is a body which is your body? Or to put it differently. Could Moore (or you or I myself) conceive of a situation of not-knowing? In the situation which Moore were describing it would be impossible to describe a particular situation which would constitute an instance of not-knowing. This does not mean that it would be inconceivable to describe situations which would be cases of not-knowing. Suppose that there were cases of out-of-body experiences and suppose that I and some others have such experiences and we see our bodies lying on the surface of the earth. I can then point to a certain body and say that I know that this body is my body. I can say that if one of the other persons disputes it, he may, falsely believe that it is his body.

When Wittgenstein first sentence in *On Certainty* is "If you do know that *here is one hand*, we'll grant you all the rest", he is of course referring to Moore's lecture: "Proof of an external world". Moore claims to be able to prove the existence of external objects by, as he says, "holding up my two hands, and saying, as I make a certain gesture with the right hand, 'Here is one hand', and adding, as I make a certain gesture with the left, 'and here is another'". And a few paragraphs later: 'I certainly did at that moment *know* that which I expressed by the combination of certain gestures while saying the words 'There is one hand and here is another' . . . How absurd it would be to suggest that I did not know it, but only believed it". Obviously, it would be absurd, as he says, if in this particular situation he had said that he believed that here is a hand. It would be absurd in the sense that he in fact did not believe it. To believe something implies that I have some evidence to assert that which in fact I do assert but that the evidence is not strong enough to guarantee its truth. Both does he *know* it? Could it, in the present case, be conceivable, that there could be an instance of not knowing? In unusual cases, yes. But in the particular circumstances under which Moore was holding up his hands, no. In very unusual or special cases one might imagine that a person has received one artificial hand, but that at this very moment he has forgotten which one it is. Then he makes sure and can then rightly exclaim "Now I know". But, as I said, this is an extremely unusual case. And under normal circumstances, certainly under the circumstances under which Moore was uttering the words, no instance of not-knowing case can be conceived. So we may conclude that Moore did not *know* the proposition that here is a hand. This does not imply that some other of the epistemological moderators, such as, 'I believe', 'I guess', 'I assume' will be appropriate. All that is left is the bare assertion. I neither believe, guess, or assume, as little as I know, that I have a headache. I simply have it, which I can report or be silent about.

Connected with the fact that knowledge in many respects behaves like a trouser-word is another fact: I use expressions such as 'I know' only if I am challenged—or could be challenged—which I am or can be only if an instance of not-knowing (i.e. of doubting, assuming, or believing) is conceivable. I do not prefix assertions or statements with an 'I know' phrase, as I may prefix them with 'I believe', 'I assume', etc. Compare the following statements: (1) "I believe it is a bank holiday tomorrow; (2) "It is a bank holiday tomorrow"; (3) "I know that it is a bank holiday tomorrow". One difference between (1) and (2) on the one hand and (3) on the other hand is this: Both (1) and (2) can be uttered without any special occasion for doing so. They can both be my first remark. I can enter a room and start my conversation by asserting either (1) or (2). But it would be an oddity if my first remark were (3). If it was, I would invite questions like: "Who says that there isn't?" In other words, we only use the expression: 'I know that p' if we have been challenged. If we have not been challenged we express that which we believe we know by asserting (2). If I say: "It is a bank holiday tomorrow" I can be challenged; and if I cannot show sufficient evidence to justify a knowledge-claim, I have said something more than I should have. I shall have to admit that I really should have said that I only believed or assumed it.

The fact that it is only when we are challenged that we use the expression 'I know that p', somehow also explains and gives plausibility to the Austinian claim that there is a performative force in the use of that expression. It is when we are challenged and want to emphasize that we do have sufficient evidence and want to emphasize that what we assert cannot be wrong that we us e the verb 'to know'. By using the expression 'I know that p', we, so to speak, guarantee that we have sufficient evidence to assert that we cannot be wrong. If, however, we are unchallenged, or do not expect to be challenged, we state that which we know without the use of the verb 'to know'. The fact that we possess knowledge does not call for the use of the expressions 'I know that p' but only of 'p'—that is, Knowledge is, at least ordinarily, stated without the use of the concept of knowledge. If I know that the cat is on the mat and consequently assert "The cat is on the mat", I use the concept 'cat' and the concept 'mat' but not the concept 'knowledge'—and this, incidentally, is parallel to the use of the concept of truth. We state that which is true without the use of that concept, and it is only if, in one way or another, we are challenged, provoked, or interrogated, that we use the concept.

It is often assumed that knowledge can be defined in terms of a completely justified belief. In his *Encyclopedia of Philosophy* article, Vol. 4 p. 346, Anthony Quinton asserts that "if I know that p, I do not merely believe it, but I do believe it all the same" and compares the difference between the concept of knowledge and belief to the difference between the concepts of "being married to" and "living with". As he says: "I should mislead people if I described my wife as "the woman I live with", and I might say, "No she is my wife", if I were asked whether she is the woman I live with. Nevertheless, my wife is the woman I live with. What is true is that I do not *merely* live with her. Likewise, if I know that p, I do not merely believe it, but I do believe it all the same". However, the person who objects to the description of his wife as 'the woman I live with' does so because, in this context, the expression 'the woman I live with' means precisely that I am not married to her. But if the use of knowledge and belief are differently related to evidence and therefore perform different jobs, it follows that a completely justified belief either is not belief or it is not knowledge.

It is against the logic of the concept of belief to use the expression I believe that p if the truth of p is in fact known. To say that I believe that p means that I could be wrong—however unlikely it might be. If it is not only unlikely but impossible that I should be wrong it is not just an expression of epistemological modesty if I say I believe instead of saying that I know. An apparent paradox arieses if I say that if I am entitled to say that I know that p then I am not entitled to say that I believe that p. In other words, I do not believe that which I know. The paradox, however, is only apparent. It is apparent because the expression 'I do not believe that p' may, in some contexts, mean that I disbelieve that p. Interpreted this way it would of course be a paradox. It is a paradox that I disbelieve that which I know to be the case. But the expression may also be interpreted differently. It may also mean that the force of the evidence transcends the limits of legitimate use of the verb 'to believe' and consequently requires the use of the verb 'to know'. And if I transcend the limits of the legitimate use of the verb 'to believe' it follows that I cannot say that I believe that which I know. In other words, all according to context, we have these two interpretations:

(1) I know that p and therefore I do not disbelieve it.
(2) I know that p and therefore I do not believe it.

This shows that a denial of the right to use the verb 'to believe' does not entail a disbelief. Or in other words, a denial of a belief does not entail a disbelief.

Nevertheless, it is, of course, the case that if I know that p I am in a psychological state of mind. This state of mind has been described differently, varying from 'believing that p', over 'accepting that p', 'to be sure that p' (cf. "Is justified true belief Knowledge?" by Edmund L. Gettier, *Analysis* Vol. 23). All of these concepts share the weakness that p may be false without falsifying the state of mind (i.e. I can say that despite the fact that p is false I did believe, I did accept, and I was in fact sure—whereas I cannot say that did know). Instead I propose to use the concept of disbelief. If I have evidence which is strong enough to a knowledge claim, it is, partly, a conceptual error to use the concept of belief, and it is a conceptual error and a conceptual impossibility to disbelieve. Whereas the concepts of knowledge and belief are incompatible, the concepts of knowledge and disbelief are not.

It may be maintained that both knowledge and belief are states of mind. This is not correct, however. None of them are states of mind, but both of them *imply* states of mind. There is, however, this difference. If I know something, it would be both a conceptual error and a psychological impossibility to disbelieve, whereas with respect to belief it is neither nor. There is an important simularity, however, between knowledge and belief. In both cases the right to make a knowledge statement and a belief statement is based on available evidence. It is the evidence which gives me the right to either. And it is the evidence that makes it either a conceptual error and an impossibility to disbelieve the truth of that which I claim to know or gives me the difficulties—small or great—to doubt its truth.

Despite often stated assertions it is not correct that a belief can be defined as a disposition. It is of course correct that to believe something implies tendencies to behave in relevant ways. If I believe that it is about to rain I may put on my raincoat, take in my laundry, issue proper warnings, etc. Nevertheless I shall argue that it is a mistake to take this as an analysis of what a belief is. There certainly is a difference between the assertion that if I have a certain belief I have a tendency to say and do an indefinite number of things, and the assertion that if I have a certain belief all that this means is that I have a tendency to say and do an indefinite number of things. According to the first view, the relation between my belief and my tendency to say and do the relevant things is one of implication; but according to the second view, the relation is one of identity. While the former is correct, the latter is mistaken. It may even be the case that the relation is one not only of implication but of equivalence. That is, if I believe that it is going to rain it may be inferred that I have a tendency to say and do certain things; and, furthermore, if I do have such a tendency it may be inferred that I have the corresponding belief. But because two statements are equivalent it does not follow that they have the same meaning.

The things I do out of a tendency or a disposition I may know that I am doing by *discovering* it. It is something which is classified as an act or as behavior. It therefore has no sense to ask for evidence or for truth-value. Beliefs, assumptions, and propositions have evidence and truth-value; behavior and acts have neither. There is a radical difference between the two concepts "to be disposed to assert" and "to have evidence for asserting". The concept of disposition belongs to the same family of concepts as "cause" and "law of nature". A disposition or a tendency can be expressed as a law-like statement. An occurrence, which is a manifestation of a disposition or a tendency, presupposes an event functioning as a cause.

The fact that I have a disposition to do certain things is known from my doing these things. The fact that I am vain is something I have discovered from my behavior. My behavior is the clue for knowing what dispositions (needs, interests, motives, etc.) I have. If I say I do as I do because I am vain I do so because I have discovered that the law-like statement expressing vanity applies to me.

If I assert that p I must either believe or know that p. And there is a radical difference between explaining a statement which expresses a belief and explaining behavior expressing a disposition. While I discover my dispositions from the acts I perform, the statements implied by my belief presuppose that my beliefs are known already. I do not discover that I believe it is going to rain from the fact that I say that it is going to rain.

This difference is connected with the previous mentioned fact that whereas I define my dispositions by my behavior, I do not define my beliefs this way. By a disposition I *mean* the different things I tend to do; by a belief I do not *mean* this, but imply it.

Some may object to my proposition that I do not discover my beliefs from the statements I make or from my acts but that my acts presuppose I already know my beliefs. It may be maintained that the true way to discover one's beliefs is to observe one's acts. I may believe that I love my brother, but my acts, my dreams, my slips, and the like may reveal that my belief is false; I do not love him; really, I hate him.

It is important, however, to notice the following difference. My belief that I love my brother is the belief that I have certain tendencies to act in certain ways. My belief that it is going to rain is a belief, not in certain tendencies to act in certain ways, but in the occurrence of a certain state of affaire, an occurrence which, obviously enough, is independent of my statements of acts. My statements and my acts can neither verify nor falsity my belief that it is going to rain. To say that I believe that I love my brother is the same as to say that there is evidence for the existence of a tendency to act in certain ways. Quite obviously, I cannot meaningfully say that the evidence I have for the existence of a tendency to act in a certain way is my reason for acting in this particular way. Yet it is different with belief that it is going to rain. To say that I believe it is going to rain is the same as to say that there is evidence that it is going to rain. The evidence is evidence, not for any tendency or disposition to act in certain ways, but for the occurrence of certain facts. It is meaningful to say that my reason for acting in a certain way is the evidence for the rainy weather, but it would be meaningless to say that the evidence for the rain should be my acts.

To be disposed to assert, therefore, is to discover the disposition by discovering that one makes certain statements. But this is impossible. It is impossible because to discover that one is making a statement is not to make a statement at all. I cannot *discover* that I assert that p. I can discover, more or less parrotlike, more or less mechanically, or more or less unknowingly, that I utter some sentences; but this is not to make an assertion. A parrot which utters that p is not asserting that p because it is not *using* language, The teacher who uses p as an example of a sentence with certain grammatical properties is not using p to assert that p. In order to assert that p it is not enough that the sentence 'p' is uttered. The sentence must be used with the intention to assert that p. And a necessary condition of doing something with intention is precisely that one does not *discover* that one is doing the intended thing. To say that one is discovering what one is doing is the same as to say that one is not doing it by intention.

If I discover that I am using a sentence 'p' it then follows that I cannot be asserting p. And if I do a thing from being disposed to do it it implies that I know that I am doing it from discovering it. Consequently, I cannot make assertions from being disposed to make them. The concepts of "*doing something from disposition*" and "*doing something by intention*" are incompatible concepts. The concepts of asserting is consequently incompatible with the concept of disposition.

Knowledge entails truth. We cannot say that p is an object of knowledge but that nevertheless p may not be true. This fact has created familiar puzzles such as that of the logical positivists who have been eager to emphasize that no empirical proposition can be an object of knowledge. An empirical proposition implies an infinite number of propositions, and as it is logically impossible to verify an infinite number of propositions we can never know whether there might not be a false proposition—and if just one is false the implicans is false. This is unacceptable. It surely is unacceptable that we never have the right to say that we know that p if p is an empirical proposition. So we feel we have to say with Austin: "surely . . . we are often right to say we know even in cases where we turn out subsequently to have been mistaken—and indeed we seem always, or practically always, liable, to be mistaken . . . It is naturally always possible ('humanly' possible) that I may be mistaken—but that by itself is no bar against using the expression 'I know'". To accept this Austinian line, however, also creates puzzles. To say that one has the right to claim that this book is my book must mean that the book is in fact my book. To have the right to say that I have passed the examination must mean that I have in fact passed it. To say that I have a right to assert that the proposition p is true must mean that the proposition is in fact true: so to say that I have the right to claim that I know that p must mean that I do in fact know p. Now suppose that I have the right to say that I know that p; suppose furthermore that p turns out to be false. If we grant Austin his point I shall be permitted to say that although p is false I nevertheless had the ritht to say that I knew that p. But surely I cannot say that I did know that p; because I cannot say that when I asserted that I knew p I did know it although my knowledge proved to be false. If Austin is right, therefore, there are situations in which I can say that I know that p despite the fact that I do not know that p. I cannot know that p if p is false. If p is false it is correct to say that I do not know that p. To say that I have the right to say that there are cases when I know that p even if p is false is to say therefore, that there are cases where I have the right to say that I know that p despite the fact that it is incorrect to say that I know that p.

This is, of course, unsatisfactory, to say the least. It is unsatisfactory that we can also have the right to say that we know in cases in which it is incorrect to say that we know—that is, in cases where in fact we do not know.

Of course, there are situations in which we have all the available evidence for a proposition, and therefore it is justifiable, at least so we think, to claim the truth of it. Nevertheless, later on, new evidence is discovered which definitely falsifies the proposition. It is evidence which it was impossible for us even to think of when we proclaimed that we knew the proposition. Could we say that we had the right so to proclaim? According to what I have argued, we could not. What we may say, or, rather, will have to say, is that in this particular situation it was *excusable* to claim that we knew. But a presupposition of using the word 'excuse' is precisely that something wrong has been done, or that an error or a mistake has been made. We cannot talk about excusing acts which were right. That is, Austin's statement that "we are often right to say we know even in cases where we turn out subsequently to have been mistaken" is correct if by the word "right" we mean the same as 'excusable'—but this is an interpretation which hardly is the one Austin had in mind.

Let me finish the paper with a few words about my alleged knowledge of my own existence. It is important, however, to distinguish between the sentence: "It is a fact that I exist", and the sentence: "I exist". The former sentence is a contingent sentence. It is contingent, among other things, on the fact that my parents met. The latter sentence, however, is not a sentence which can be used to make a genuine assertion. A presupposition of making any assertion or utterance is that I exist. I cannot, therefore utter the sentence "I exist" unless I exist. The sentence "I exist" has its own truth as a presupposition. The sentence, therefore, only states the presupposition for that it can be uttered at all. It is, obviously, a logical untenable situation. It consequently does not make sense to assert that I know that the sentence: "I exist" is a true sentence. Does it make sense to say that I know that it is a fact that I exist? I can say that I know that as a matter of fact I was my parents second child. I may also be able to prove to the satisfaction of any court that I know that I am in fact that person. But what this amounts to is the sentence: "I know that I am in fact identical with the person born at this particular time and place as a son of these particular parents." This is the kind of answer an Anastasia would give as her alleged proof that she was in fact the person she claimed to be. And this is of course something different from the sentence: "I know that it is a fact that I do exist"—provided that the existence talked about is not in terms of 'exist as so and so'. But if it is about my existence as such I cannot answer questions of how I know. We are back to the former sentence: "I exist" which, as we saw, presupposes its own truth in order to be uttered or even thought.

There is thus a logical difference between first-person pain-statements and first-person existent-statements. Pain-statements are informative but they cannot be prefixed with any of what I have called the epistemological moderators such as 'I know', 'I believe', or 'I am convinced'. First-person existence-statements are not only uninformative but they are expressions of a language which has gone off-track. And epistemological moderators are not used in front of sentences which are off-track.

* * *

CAVELL, WITTGENSTEIN, AND HUMAN FINITUDE

Gordon C. F. Bearn
Yale University, New Haven, Connecticut

According to Cavell the skeptic is correct: we do not know the existence of the world with certainty. Yet Cavell draws the moral of this truth in two incompatible moods. (a) In a *romantic* mood, he suggests that our primary relation to the world is deeper than knowledge; it is one in which the existence of the world is to be ". . . accepted, that is to say, received."[1] (b) In a *deflationary* mood, he rejects entirely the traditional problem of knowledge and hence both its traditional and its romantic solutions. This is the mood in which philosophy is given peace. (*PI* § 133)

I shall raise the threat of skepticism in terms of what Cavell calls the disappointment of criteria and then offer a deflationary treatment of Cavell's romanticism.

Far from providing an answer to the skeptic, Cavell argues that ". . . the fate of criteria, or their limitation, reveals . . . the truth of skepticism . . ." (*CR* 7)[2] Suppose we tried to answer skeptical doubts about our claim to know that a woman is in pain by citing criteria for being in pain, perhaps we point out that she is favoring her leg. The skeptic is not likely to be satisfied by this answer, for surely he knows the criteria, the grammar of the word 'pain.' What he demands is our reason for claiming that *this* is an instance of favoring. In *The Blue Book* at such a point, Wittgenstein said, "You will be at a loss to answer this question, and find that here we strike rock bottom, that is we have come down to conventions." (*BB* p. 24) In the *Investigations* at a similar stage of argument, he speaks not of conventions but of our agreement (Übereinstimmung) in judgments, which he says is not an agreement in opinions, but in form of life. (*PI* §§ 242, 241) Cavell refers to this agreement as ". . . our mutual attunement in judgments." (*CR* 31–2, 115)

Criteria had been expected to guarantee our claim to know that she is in pain. Now it appears that criteria can only guarantee such judgments if we already agree in the *further* judgment that the criteria are manifest in the present case. (*CR* 32) Although as a matter of fact we agree in our use of criteria—our judgments are attuned—our attunement is without foundation. Cavell:

> What is disappointing about criteria?
> There is something they do not do; it can seem the essential. I have to know what they are for; I have to accept them, use them. This makes my use of them seem arbitrary, or private—as though they were never shared, or as if our sharing them is either a fantastic accident or a kind of mass folly. (*CR* 83)

The disappointment of criteria comes to this: can our agreement in the application of criteria to the world be given a justification or is our agreement merely arbitrary? This problem suggests a path to its resolution. As the author of *Being and Time* might have put it, our attunement should be worked out in terms of the things themselves.[3] This is the path of romanticism.

(a) Cavell's *romantic* answer to the charge that our mutual attunement is arbitrary cannot be understood apart from a particular picture of that problem which motivates his writing. The picture is one of ". . . 'seeing ourselves as outside the world as a whole', looking in at it . . . as though it were another *object* . . ." (*CR* 236) Cavell says of this picture, as he might have of the problem of arbitrariness itself, that it is an expression of our wanting ". . . to know the world as we imagine God knows it." (*CR* 236)

In this mood, Cavell replaces the traditional quest to know the world as a God might, with a more accurate representation of our finite, human relation to the world. This is the truth of skepticism:

> . . . we think skepticism must mean that we cannot know the world exists, and hence that perhaps there isn't one . . . Whereas what skepticism suggests is that since we cannot know the world exists, its presentness to us cannot be a function of *knowing*. The world is to be accepted . . .[4]

'Acceptance' names a dimension of our human relation to the world-as-a-whole. A provocative footnote in Cavell's *The Senses of Walden* makes this dimension or category a little more clear: ". . . Kant . . . left unarticulated an essential feature (category) of objectivity itself, viz., that of a *world apart from me in which* objects are met. [This] . . . externality of the world is articulated by Thoreau as its nextness to me."[5] In company with the romantic poets, Cavell describes the ideal acceptance of the external world in terms derived from the ideal acknowledgment of others:

> What is next to us is what we neighbor. [Thoreau] . . . has spoken of finding himself suddenly neighbor to the birds; and he speaks of the pond in neighborly terms: "Of all the characters I have known, perhaps Walden wears best, and best preserves its purity" (IX, 25). Our relation to nature, at its best, would be that of neighboring it . . .[6]

By neighboring nature we are to overcome the charge that our attunements are arbitrary; this is Cavell's romantic resolution of the disappointment of criteria. My skepticism about Cavell's romanticism concerns the nature of the world we neighbor. *Either* our neighbors are within our natural habitat and neighboring them does not re-establish contact with a world beyond our attunement, *or* neighboring does establish contact with such a world but at the price of our no longer being able to give any account of *what* we are neighboring. If we wish to remain within the bounds of the utterable, we must count this romantic resolution of the problem of arbitrariness a failure.

(b) Resolving the problem of arbitrariness seems to require that our attunements be worked out in terms of a world underlying these attunements, yet in a *deflationary* mood Cavell suggests that ". . . nothing is deeper than the fact, or extent, of agreement itself." (*CR* 32) In this mood the problem of arbitrariness seems to evaporate.

To aid my discussion of the disappearance of this problem, I distinguish two ways in which our judgments may be attuned. (i) *Secure* attunements concern subjects, such as Moore's hands or elementary arithmetic, on which our attunement in judgment is non-diverging. (ii) *Insecure* attunements concern subjects, such as the moral status of abortion or the genuineness of a work of art, where there have been through history or across cultures diverging attunements.

(i) Cavell suggests that far from being arbitrary, our secure attunements are only natural. (*CR* 122–3) This is what gives criteria their "strength" and their "force". (*CR* 122, 207) It is natural, in the presence of suffering, to comfort. Not to do so would be, as we say, *inhuman*. Our secure attunements are not arbitrary; they are an expression of our humanity. We can do no other.

Concerning our arithmetical attunements Wittgenstein wrote: "The danger, I believe, is one of giving a justification of our procedure where there is no such thing as a justification and we ought simply to have said: *that's how we do it.*" (*RFM* III § 74) This does *not* make our secure attunements arbitrary. If there were an alternative to our secure attunements, then they might be arbitrary, but there is not; so they are not arbitrary. "Compare a concept with a style of painting. For is even our style of painting arbitrary? Can we choose one at pleasure?" (*PI* p. 230e) To fear that our secure attunements might be arbitrary is already to deny our human finitude. It is to imagine possibilities which are not human possibilities. (*PI* § 497) Cavell:

> The skeptic insinuates that there are possibilities to which the claim of certainty shuts its eyes . . . It is the voice, or the imitation of the voice, of intellectual conscience. Wittgenstein replies: "they are shut." (*PI* p. 224e) It is the voice of human conscience. It is not generally conclusive, but it is more of an answer than it may appear to be. In the face of the skeptic's picture of intellectual limitedness, Wittgenstein proposes a picture of human finitude. (*CR* 431)

96

(ii) What are we to make of Cavell's claim that this deflationary approach to our attune-ments is not generally conclusive? On my reading, this shows that although Cavell endorses a deflationary approach to our secure attunements, he does not endorse this approach to those of our attunements which are insecure.

> If the topic is that of continuing a series, it may be . . . enough to find that I *just do*; to rest upon myself as my foundation. [But where the question is] . . . Why are some people poor and others rich? . . . or Do you love black people as much as white people? . . . I may find my answers thin, I may feel run out of reasons without being able to say "This is what I do" . . . and honor that. (*CR* 125)

These insecurities recover the truth of skepticism but without the "theatricality" of imagi-ning ourselves outside the world-as-a-whole. (*CR* 236) The question they raise is simply: what *are* my attunements? Our insecurity is an expression of the fact that before certain questions we are unsure of what we want to say, of what we want to do; Cavell would say: of who we are. If these insecurities are the truth in skepticism then skepticism is not to be refuted but to be domesticated. The insecurities are not to be made secure, but to be made familiar. Philoso-phical peace will come when we are at home with our secure and insecure attunements, when we know our way about. (*PI* § 123)

Altough I have criticized Cavell's romanticism, his deflationary writings may still be charac-terized as a *purified romanticism*, that is, as an attempt to show that human and philosophical peace need not presuppose the paradoxical immanence of what is transcendent. The human alone may suffice.[7]

ENDNOTES

[1] Cavell, S., *The Senses of Walden* (San Francisco 1981), p. 133.
[2] 'CR 7' stands for: S. Cavell *The Claim of Reason* (New York 1979), p. 7.
[3] Heidegger, M., *Being and Time* (New York 1962), p. 195.
[4] Cavell, S., *Must We Mean What We Say?* (Cambridge 1969), p. 324.
[5] Cavell, S., (1981), p. 107n.
[6] Cavell, S., (1981), p. 105.
[7] This paper was much improved by the criticisms of Louis Goldring.

* * *

REDUCTIONISM – WHAT IT IS AND WHAT IT IS NOT

Sara Yaretzky-Kahansky
Tel-Aviv University, Tel-Aviv

The term 'reductionism' and its cognates are used to refer to different types of philosophical ploys and arguments. This unfortunately generates more heat than light in the discussions for and against reductionism. In this essay I shall try to shed some light on the nature of reductionism. I shall do this by distinguishing reduction from a number of other philosophical ploys and forms of argument with which it is often confused, such as deduction, explication, definition, and showing things, somehow thought of as non-identicals, to be identical. The type of exercise I shall be engaged in could be discribed using Gilbert Ryle's phrase as beginning to chart a map of "the logical geography"[1] of the concept of reductionism.

What is common to all arguments labelled reductionist is that an attempt is made to eliminate one type of entity or statement and replace it by another type of entity or statement. Any attempt to make a reductionist move, I shall call a reductionist theory. That is to say, I understand by 'reductionist theory' any attempt to reduce one type of entity or statement to another type of entity or statement. On this view many ordinary theories are obviously reductionist theories because those who formulate them see them as attempts to eliminate one concept from an area of discourse and replace it by another. The question as to whether it is possible to replace a concept in an area of discourse by another such that the replaced concept will have the same meaning as the concept which replaces it, is a question over which there is much dispute. However, and this is a principal point, unless this can be accomplished the reduction cannot be regarded as being successful. If one takes seriously the syntax which is used in reductionist moves, it is obvious that this is the intention of the people attempting reduction. They claim such things as X (the entity or statement they wish to eliminate or replace) is *nothing but, merely, nothing other than,* or simply *is* Y (the entity or statement by which they wish to replace X).

The notion of reduction is often run together with that of deduction. Nagel[2], Quine[3] and Woodger,[4] for example, claim that a successful reduction occurs when the concepts, or entities, or statements of one area of discourse (or theory or model) are replaced by concepts, or entities, or statements of another area of discourse, such that the prime concepts, suppositions and conclusions of the one can be deduced from the latter. Feyerabend[5], Kuhn[6] and Popper,[7] on the other hand, distinguish between reduction and deduction. They claim that a successful reduction entails only that the concepts, entities, statements, and conclusions of the reduced theory are explicated in terms of the reducing theory, and not that they are deduced from it. A successful reduction, on this view, occurs if the reducing theory explains what the reduced theory did in a lucid and comprehensive manner.

The first concept of reduction mentioned above implies that the reductionist move entails a deductive relationship between the concepts, or entities, or statements that are replaced and those which replace them. This has led some who adhere to this view to assert that reduction is a species of deduction. That is, they deduce from the premise that reductionist moves entail deductive moves the conclusion that reductionist moves are *nothing but* deductive moves. However, the conclusion does not follow from the premise.

If reduction were merely a form of deduction, it would follow that the original entities and those which they are reduced to are somehow the same, for the terms of the conclusion of a valid deduction must have already appreared in its premises. This implies that the replacement of the original entities by other (different) ones is only apparent and not real. The entities, concepts, and statements which are replaced in a reductionist move must be distinguishable from those which replace them. If they are not—no replacement of one entity by another (different) entity has taken place. This is not to say that no connection holds between the entities replaced and those which replace them, but only that the connection between them cannot simply be one of identity, or else a deductive one. Yet, there must be some relationship between the entities replaced and those that replace them in a reductionist move, for otherwise it would be difficult to see how the latter could replace the former. But, and this is the main point, the two must be distinguishable, for otherwise no replacement has taken place. But this cannot be the case if reduction is a species of deduction. When B is deduced from A, A does not replace B; B is simply drawn out from, because it is somehow an extension of, A. To deduce a statement from another is not to replace it by another, but only to spell out its concequences and its connection to the other. Now a reduced theory is not just an extension or consequence of the reducing theory, it is a replacement of it by something else—by something from which it cannot be deduced.

According to the concept of reduction adhered to by Feyerabend, Kuhn and Popper, reduction is viewed as a form of explication. This view is given an explicit defense by James Gaa[8]. Gaa argues that reduction is simply a kind of explicative relationship. He understands by 'explicative relationship' not a relationship that holds between two terms, the *explicandum* and the *explicans*, but a relationship hat holds between two theories, one of which explains and clarifies the other. But if this is what reduction is, then again we have no replacement of one theory by another. What we have is a clarification or an elucidation of one theory by another. However, what we do not have is a replacement of one theory by another, and thus no reduction.

As this point I shall make explicit what up till now has been implicit in my analysis. Namely, that as reduction entails replacement of one concept, or entity, or statement, or, as Gaa would claim, one theory by another, reduction is, in my view, an ontological move and not just a syntactical and/or epistemological move. What makes reductionist moves philosophically interesting is not that they are attemps to say things which have the same truth value differently, but only that they are attemps to say things which have greater (more comprehensive) truth value. What makes them philosophically interesting is that they are attempts to replace one type of things by another, such that these other things entail different world views. (The world view of someone who believes in sensations as entities in their own right is different from the world view of someone who believes that sensations are *nothing but* brain processes, i.e., simply a species of them.) That is to say, the world view of Norman Malcolm[9] is essentially different from the world view of J. J. C. Smart[10] and U. T. Place.[11] While sensations exist in Malcolm's world, they have at best a ghost-like existence in the world of Smart and Place. Now I am not claiming that there is no relationship between the syntactical, the epistemological, and the ontological moves. All I am claming is that simply to show that it is possible to make the syntactical and epistemological moves is not to show that it is also possible to make the ontological one. Of course one cannot make the ontological move without making the syntactical and epistemological move. However, just to make the syntactical and epistemological move is not to make the ontological one too. A reductionist theory does not simply clarify, elucidate, and explain another theory; it is also an attempt to present another world view. To say "X is nothing but Y" may be to claim that wherever 'X' appears we can replace it by 'Y', for 'X' and 'Y' mean the same or have the same range of truth-values. But if this is all that is asserted, then a reductionist move has not been attempted. For a reductionist move to have been attempted, one must at least imply in using the assertion "X is nothing but Y" the further claim that Xs do not exist as such, and that what we refer to as Xs are really Ys, or a species of Ys.

It could also be argued that reduction is a species of definition. For example, when behaviourists like Skinner[12] give an account of mental phenomena in behavioral terms, what they are doing appears to be describable both as reduction and as definition. Or perhaps one could say that they are reducing mental concepts to behavioral ones by definition. Jerry Fodor,[13] however, claims that the attempt to define mental words and concepts in behavioral terms is not a reductionist one. And Fodor is surely correct. That is to say, to define concepts or words from one area of discourse in terms of those from another area of discourse is not to replace the phenomena those concepts and words are used to refer to, even though it is an attempt to replace our way of talking about them. On the contrary, it is a way of saying that the so-called replaced phenomena *are* in point of fact the so-called replacing phenomena.

Rudolf Carnap[14] distinguishes between the reduction of one term to others and the definition of that term. When one term is correctly defined, the *definiendum* can always be replaced by the *definiens* in any sentence in which it appears, without changing the meaning of the sentence. That is to say, for Carnap the meaning of the *definiens* is logically equivalent to the meaning of the *definiendum*. On the other hand , I wish to claim, when one term is reduced to another, then the sentence in which the term that is reduced originally appears will not have the same meaning, if the term to which it is reduced replaces it in the original sentence. That is to say, talk about 'the sensation of pain' is not equivalent in meaning to talk about 'the brain process *qua* pain' (whatever that means). Or in other words, while a definition of an object, or term, or concept supplies us with another way of referring to it linguistically, a reduction is an attempt to replace a term that refers to, or picks out, something with a doubtful existence by a term that refers to something whose existence is not in doubt.

On one occasion I have heard the late Professor Yehoshua Bar-Hillel throw out the suggestion that reductionist moves are nothing but exercises in showing that that which is reduced and that which it is reduced to are identical. The argument, if my memory is correct, went something like this: If Xs are nothing bit Ys, therefore wherever there is an X we can write a Y and this Y is then identical to any Y. However, seriously putting forward this argument involves the mistake of thinking that Xs that are being reduced to Ys can be reduced to Ys only because they possess all—and literally all—the features of Ys. Now to state that the Morning Star is (identical with) the Evening Star, that both terms have the same object of reference, is not to make a reductionist move; for no object is being replaced by another. Rather what is being done is to state that whatever is predicated of the object referred to as the Morning Star can also be predicated of the object referred to as the Evening star and vice-versa. Now when Smart and Place claim that sensations are *nothing but* brain processes—this is not what they are claming. What they are claming is that talk about sensations is, in truth, talk about brain-processes (whatever that is), since sensations and brain-processes are numerically identical; and the licence for doing so, they claim, is that what people mistakenly think of as sensations are *nothing but* brain processes. The point is that to show things (or concepts, or terms) to be identical is not to replace one thing (or concept, or term) by another, but to show that what was previously thought to be two different things, because referred to by two different terms, is in point of fact one.

Thus far in this essay I have argued that a reductionist move must be distinguished from deduction, explication, definition and the attempt to show that two things are in point of fact identical. The point is, however, that although reductionism must be distinguished from the above it cannot really sever its ties with them, for if it did it would be difficult to see how the reduced entitiy could be reduced to the entity to which it is reduced. That is to say, X cannot be reduced to Y unless (a) the use of 'Y' has similar implications, deductive implications, that the use of 'X' has; (b) 'Y' is amenable to an explication which is similar to the explication of 'X'; (c) 'X' can be defined in terms of 'Y', and (d) there are some features of X which are indentical to some features of Y. In other words, although reduction cannot itself be reduced to either deduction, explication, definition, and the attempt to show that two things are in point of fact identical with each other, this is not to say that these moves are not part of, or do not go along with, the reductionist move. It is because they do go along with reductionism that initial plausibility is lent to the claim that reduction is *nothing but* one of them. However, those who make this claim make a similar mistake that is made by many who believe that they have made a successful reductionist move. That is to say, to show that where it is possible to talk of reduction it is also possible to talk about deduction, explication, etc., is not to show that reduction is *nothing but* deduction, explication, etc. Then again, when Smart and Place show us that wherever talk of sensations occurs it is also possible to talk of brain processes, they have not shown (or proven to) us that sensations are *nothing but* brain processes. At best they have shown us that sensation talk goes along with brain-process talk.

ENDNOTES

[1] See for example the introduction to his *The Concept of Mind* (London 1966), pp. 7–9.
[2] Nagel, E., "The Meaning of Reduction in the Natural Sciences", in: A. Danto and S. Morgenbesser (eds.), *Philosophy of Science* (Cleveland 1960), pp. 288–312.
[3] Quine, W. V., "Ontological Reduction and the World of Numbers", *Journal of Philosophy*, 61 (1964), pp. 209–16.
[4] Woodger, J. H., *Biology and Language* (Cambridge 1952).
[5] Feyerabend, P. K., "Explanation, Reduction, and Empiricism", in: H. Feigl and G. Maxwell (eds.), *Minnesota Studies in the Philosophy of Science*, Vol. 3 (Minneapolis 1962), pp. 28–97.
[6] Kuhn, T. S., *The Structure of Scientific Revolutions* (Chicago 1962).
[7] Popper, K. R., "The Aim of Science", *Ratio 1* (1957), pp. 24–35.
[8] Gaa, J., "The replacement of Scientific Theories: Reduction and Explication", *Philosophy of Science*, 42 (1975), pp. 349–370.
[9] Malcolm, N., "Wittgenstein's Philosophical Investigations", *Philosophical Review*, 63 (1954), pp. 530–559.
[10] Smart, J. J. C., "Sensations and Brain Processes", in: V. C. Chappell (ed.), *The Philosophy of the Mind* (New Jersey 1962).
[11] Place, U. T., "Is Consciousness A Brain Process?", *The British Journal of Psychology*, 47 (1956).
[12] Skinner, B. F., "Behaviourism at fifty", in: T. W. Wann (ed.), *Behaviourism and Phenomenology* (Chicago 1965), pp. 79–97.
[13] Fodor, J. A., *Psychological Explanation* (New York 1968).
[14] Carnap, R., "Testability and Meaning", *Philosophy of Science*, 3 (1936), pp. 419–471; 4 (1937), pp. 1–40.

* * *

GLAUBE, WISSEN UND DIE PRAGMATIK DES ERKLÄRENS: ZUR KRITIK DES ANSATZES VON GÄRDENFORS UND STEGMÜLLER

Michael Küttner
Freie Universität Berlin

1. Auf dem Gebiet der Explikation eines adäquaten Begriffs der wissenschaftlichen Erklärung gibt es eine relativ junge Entwicklung, die von Stegmüller als „die pragmatisch-epistemische Wende"[1] bezeichnet worden ist: Verschiedene Wissenschaftstheoretiker (unter ihnen auch Stegmüller) glauben, Erklärungen (und dann wohl auch Begründungen und Vorhersagen) ließen sich wissenschaftstheoretisch befriedigend nur spezifizieren, wenn man wesentlich auf außerlogische Aspekte zurückgreift, indem man Erklärungen versteht als Prozesse der Informationsverbesserung eines Erklärungheischenden durch sukzessiv angereicherte Wissenssituationen, deren Konsequenz eine Erhöhung des subjektiven Glaubenswertes für das Explanandum ist.

Diese neue Entwicklung ist insbesondere durch eine Arbeit von Gärdenfors[2] entscheidend vorangetrieben worden. Stegmüller hat jüngst dem Gärdenfors-Ansatz einige Verfeinerungen hinzugefügt, ihn im Kern aber unverändert vertreten.

In enger Anlehnung an Stegmüller[3] können die aus dem Ansatz resultierenden drei Begriffe der informativen Erklärung wie folgt formuliert werden:

Sei

(i) die Ausgangssituation K eine Wissenssituation von maximaler Bestimmtheit bezüglich E;

(ii) E ein singulärer Satz;

(iii) die reale Wissenssituation K_E eine Erweiterung von K;

(iv) T eine endliche Menge statistischer Sätze;

(v) C eine endliche Menge singulärer Sätze;

(vi) $T \cup C$ in K_E nicht gewußt;

(vii) die epistemische Bereicherung $K_{T \cup C}$ von K eine Wissenssituation von maximaler Bestimmtheit bezüglich E.

Dann gilt:

$T \cup C$ ist in $K_{T \cup C}$ nur dann ein Explanans für E

α) im epistemischen Minimalsinn, wenn der Glaubenswert $B_{T \cup C}(E)$ *in der epistemisch bereicherten Wissenssituation größer ist als der Glaubenswert $B(E)$* in der ursprünglichen Wissenssituation;

β) im starken probabilistischen Minimalsinn, wenn $B_{T \cup C}(E) \geqq \frac{1}{2} > B(E)$;

γ) im probabilistischen Idealsinn, wenn $B_{T \cup C}(E) \geqq 1-\varepsilon > B(E)$, ε sehr klein.

Es soll nun gezeigt werden, daß

a) keine der Bedingungen (i)−(vii) adäquat und daß β) falsch ist;

b) entgegen Stegmüllers Auffassung wissenschaftliche D-N-Erklärungen kein Grenzfall dieser informativen Erklärungen sind;

c) Antworten auf erklärungheischende Warum-Fragen geradezu nicht in Wissensverbesserungen oder Glaubenserhöhungen des Explanandum bestehen;

d) durch die Frage der Übertragbarkeit einer D-N-Modellerklärung auf faktische Explananda eine völlig andersartige Beziehung zwischen (Theorien-) Glaube und (Hintergrund-) Wissen auftritt.

2. Um zu zeigen, daß tatsächlich alle Bedingungen (i)–(vii) des Erkärungsbegriff-Tripels zumindest verbesserungsbedürftig sind, wollen wir uns zunächst auf die Grundidee der informativen Erklärung einlassen. Diese knüpft an durchaus traditionellen Vorstellungen an: Damit ein Explanandum E erklärt werden kann, muß eine Prämissenmenge aus wesentlich generellen Sätzen T und singulären Sätzen C als Explanans bereitgestellt werden. Im deduktiven Fall fordert man, daß E aus dem Explanans logisch folgt. Im induktiven (oder: probabilistischen) Fall muß das Explanans eine induktive Stütze für E liefern. Was aber als induktive Stütze gelten kann, ist anhand vieler Beispiele äußerst strittig. Der Gärdenfors-Ansatz kann am besten verstanden werden, wenn man ihn als Nachfolger eines als gescheitert zu betrachtenden Induktionsprogramms der probabilistischen Ereigniserklärung ansieht.

Wählen wir zunächst ein einfaches Illustrationsbeispiel in enger Anlehnung an Gärdenfors und Stegmüller.[4]

Die erklärungheischende Warum-Frage sei: Warum ist Frl. Ingeborg mitten im Winter sonnengebräunt? Als Explanans wird angeboten: Frl. Ingeborg hat kürzlich einen 14-tägigen Urlaub in der Karibik verbracht *(C)*. Fast alle Karibik-Urlauber kehren (nach mindestens 14 Urlaubstagen) sonnengebräunt zurück *(T)*.

Offensichtlich liegt für eine Person p_0, die zur Zeit t_0 über die Wissenssituation $K_{T \cup C}$ verfügt, welche das Wissen um das Explanans $T \cup C$ enthält, eine befriedigende Erklärung vor.

Gärdenfors und Stegmüller glauben nun allerdings, daß man sich, außer auf $K_{T \cup C}$, was wirklich trivial ist, noch auf zwei weitere Wissenssituationen K und K_E beziehen muß.[5] K ist dabei eine Wissenssituation der Person p_0, in der p_0 (noch) nicht weiß, daß E wahr ist, daß also Frl. Ingeborg sonnengebräunt ist. K_E ist jene Wissenssituation, die zu K das Wissen um die Wahrheit von E hinzufügt, ohne ein Wissen um $T \cup C$ zu erhalten. $K_{T \cup C}$ schließlich ist jene Wissenssituation, die zu K das Wissen um $T \cup C$ hinzufügt, ohne E zu enthalten.

Die so gegebene Konstruktion der drei Wissenssituationen ist nun allerdings *widersprüchlich und äußerst kontraintuitiv*.

Machen wir uns die zeitliche Folge $\{t(K), t(K_E), t(K_{T \cup C})\}$ der drei Wissenssituationen K, K_E und $K_{T \cup C}$ klar, so wird man in Anlehnung an den Vorgang des Erklärens erwarten müssen, daß gilt: $t(K) < t(K_E) < t(K_{T \cup C})$; dies weil zum einen K_E eine Folgesituation von K ist, zum anderen das Wissen um $T \cup C$ echt später als das Wissen um E vorliegen muß, damit überhaupt eine 'neue', bislang nicht vorhandene Information zum Wissen um E hinzutritt. Wenn nun $t(K_E) < t(K_{T \cup C})$, dann kann offensichtlich in $K_{T \cup C}$ das vorherige Wissen um E nicht einfach ignoriert werden.

$K_{T \cup C}$ ohne Wissen um E ist also eine *fiktive* Wissenssituation.[6] Aus zwei Gründen ist sie daher kontraintuitiv: *Historisch* betrachtet bedeutete dies, einmal erworbenes Wissen (nämlich, daß E wahr ist) in einer späteren Wissenssituation wieder zu unterdrücken. *Systematisch* betrachtet wird ein geeignetes Explanans $T \cup C$ nur relativ zu einem gegebenen und bekannten E bewußt herangezogen. E kann also in $K_{T \cup C}$ überhaupt nicht ignoriert werden.

Wir müssen uns jetzt die Frage stellen, wozu die drei Wissenssituationen denn benötigt werden. Gärdenfors und Stegmüller glauben, daß eine Erklärung nicht nur in der Bereitstellung eines geeigneten Explanans $T \cup C$ besteht, sondern daß darüberhinaus durch den Vorgang des Erklärens der *Überraschungswert* des Explanandum herabgesetzt werden muß.[7] Dies sei gleichbedeutend mit der Erhöhung des *Wertes des subjektiven Glaubens* an die Wahrheit von E.[8] Daher wird gefordert, daß die Differenz zweier subjektiver Glaubenswerte $B_1(E)$ und $B_0(E)$ im Erklärungsfall streng positiv sein müsse. Glaubensbewertungen erfolgen in Wissenssituationen. Man benötigt also mindestens je eine zu $B_1(E)$ und $B_0(E)$ gehörende Wissenssituation.

Damit die Glaubenserhöhung wirklich durch das Explanans erreicht wird, muß folglich $B_1(E) \equiv B_{T \cup C}(E)$ sein. $B_0(E)$ muß demgegenüber echt kleiner sein. Es bietet sich an, $B_0(E) \equiv B(E)$ zu setzen, also die Glaubensbewertung auf die Wissenssituation K zu beziehen, in der E nicht sicher gewußt wird. Deshalb fordern Gärdenfors und Stegmüller für eine wirksame Erklärung, daß $B_{T \cup C}(E) > B(E)$.[9]

Durch diese Bedingung wird der Erklärungsbegriff nun *völlig trivialisiert*: Wegen $t(K) <$

$t(K_E) < t(K_{T \cup C})$ und E in $T(K_{T \cup C})$ *zwangsläufig gewußt* (aufgrund obiger Erörterungen) und K so, daß E in K *nicht gewußt* wird, gilt *immer* $B_{T \cup C}(E) > B(E)$ unabhängig von der Beschaffenheit der Prämissenmenge. Weil zu jedem Zeitpunkt $t \geqq t(K_E)$ E immer gewußt wird, ist dessen Glaubenswert auch immer größer als zu einem fingierten,[10] historisch früheren Zeitpunkt $t(K)$, in dem E nicht gewußt worden ist, *sei* $T \cup C$ *wie es wolle*. Zu einem früheren Zeitpunkt $t < t(K_E)$ hingegen kann eine erklärungheischende Warum-Frage bezüglich E überhaupt noch nicht auftreten. Mithin gilt (um im Illustrationsbeispiel zu bleiben), daß der Glaubenswert von Frl. Ingeborgs Sonnenbräune *allein* durch das Wissen um diese Tatsache gestiegen ist, das Explanans also völlig überflüssig ist, und, da keine weitere Bedingung irgendeinen inhaltlichen Zusammenhang zwischen E und $T \cup C$ fordert, ein *beliebiges* Explanans herangezogen werden kann, sofern es nur mit dem Explanandum logisch verträglich ist.

Mit diesen Überlegungen ist gezeigt worden, daß die Idee der Informationsverbesserung *nicht* mit den Bedingungen (i), (iii) und (vii) in Verbindung mit dem Glaubenswertvergleich konkretisiert werden kann.

Wir wollen uns nun den weiteren, die Prämissenmenge und das Explanandum charakterisierenden Bedingungen zuwenden.

Bedingung (ii) ist *zu weit*, da tautologische Einzelfallbeschreibungen nicht ausgeschlossen werden. Tautologien sind jedoch keine geeigneten Explananda, auch nicht im Rahmen der hier kritisierten informativen Erklärungsbegriffe, da ihr Glaubenswert in jeder Wissenssituation immer maximal ist.

Bedingung (iv) ist *zu eng*. T muß im Prinzip auch strikte (also nicht-probabilistische) Sätze enthalten dürfen, nur eben nicht ausschließlich.[11]

Bedingung (v) ist aus ähnlichem Grund wie (ii) *zu weit*. Auch die sogenannten Anfangsbedingungen dürfen insgesamt nicht tautologisch sein.

Diese Schwächen sind allerdings leicht heilbar. Die noch nicht diskutierte Bedingung (vi) scheint jedoch nicht ersetzt werden zu können, ohne daß man die Grundidee preisgibt. Sie ist aber so nicht haltbar.

Die Bedingung fordert, daß man nur dann von einer Erklärung sprechen kann, wenn zum Zeitpunkt des Erklärens (genauer: zum Zeitpunkt des Auftretens der erklärungheischenden Warum-Frage) die Prämissenmenge, das mögliche Explanans, noch nicht kennt.

Wählen wir hierfür einmal ein wissenschaftliches Illustrationsbeispiel. Zu erklären sei: In der Bundesrepublik Deutschland ist 1983 die Arbeitslosenquote gestiegen. Als Explanans $T \cup C$ möge akzeptiert werden: Fast immer steigt die Arbeitslosenquote, wenn im Vorjahr eine investitionshemmende Politik betrieben wurde *(T)*. In der Bundesrepublik Deutschland ist 1982 eine investitionshemmende Politik betrieben worden *(C)*.

Wir stehen jetzt vor der unangenehmen Situation, daß dieses Explanans *nur* für denjenigen adäquat ist, der es *noch nicht gekannt* hat, also vor allem für den Laien, während ein Wissenschaftler offensichtlich mit einem bestimmten Explanans nur *genau einmal* erklären kann. In allen weiteren Fällen ist es ihm dann ja bekannt.

Auch dies ist eine (wohl äußerst unangenehme) Konsequenz der Grundidee der Informationsverbesserung durch Verringerung des Überraschungswertes.

Die immanente Kritik sei beendet mit einer kurzen Bemerkung zum durch β) gekennzeichneten zweiten Erklärungsbegriff. Die Unterscheidungen zwischen

α) Erklärungen im Minimalsinn;

β) Erklärungen im starken Sinn (Leibniz-Sinn);

γ) Erklärungen im Idealsinn;

stammen nicht von Gärdenfors. Diese hat Stegmüller selbst hinzugefügt, durchaus nicht ohne Berechtigung, im Fall β) aber in inkorrekter Weise.

β) ist ganz offensichtlich entstanden, indem zwei Bedingungen, die je für sich korrekt sind, falsch miteinander verbunden wurden. Die beiden Bedingungen sind

β_1) $B_{T \cup C}(E) > B(E)$, wie unter α)

und als verschärfende Leibniz-Bedingung[12]

β_2) $B_{T \cup C}(E) \geqq \frac{1}{2}$.

Aus β_1) und β_2) folgt aber nicht β), da *B(E) nicht kleiner $\frac{1}{2}$ sein muß*.

3. Es soll nun eine nicht-immanente Kritik[13] an der Verknüpfung des wissenschaftlichen Erklärungsbegriffs mit der Idee der Überraschungsverminderung gegeben werden.

Stegmüller glaubt, daß dieser Begriff eines der Hempelschen Probleme lösen kann. Hempel vermutete (und stritt auch dafür), daß induktiv-statistische Erklärungen als Grenzfälle deduktiv-nomologischer Erklärungen anzusehen seien. Stegmüller sieht die Lösung der Frage nach der Bezugsnähe beider Erklärungstypen völlig *entgegengesetzt*: Der Begriff der informativen Erklärung sei in seiner Allgemeinheit wesentlich nicht-deduktiv. Deduktive Erklärungen bildeten nunmehr den Grenzfall, der rein technisch so behandelt werden könne, indem alle relevanten Wahrscheinlichkeiten den Wert 1 erhielten.[14]

Man könnte sich die Kritik an dieser Auffassung Stegmüllers durch Verweis auf das bislang Diskutierte leicht machen: Ein echter Grenzfall (im Stegmüllerschen Sinne) liegt vor, wenn alle Bedingungen des Grundbegriffs erfüllt sind, und daneben noch weitere verschärfende Bedingungen gegeben werden, wie z.B.

(viii) Alle ‚relevanten‘ Wahrscheinlichkeiten nehmen den Wert 1 an; und
(ix) E folgt logisch aus $T \cup C$.

Nun haben wir aber gesehen, daß die Bedingungen des Grundbegriffs schon nicht haltbar, teilweise auch nicht verbesserungsfähig sind. Dann aber hätten wir deduktiv-nomologische Erklärungen als Grenzfall eines logisch defekten, kontraintuitiven Grundbegriffs aufzufassen. Dies wäre offensichtlich absurd.

Es findet sich aber in den Überlegungen Stegmüllers selbst ein von ihm herausgestellter Punkt, der eine weit fundamentalere Kritik gestattet.

Stegmüller schreibt (sogar kursiv): „Wenn (. . .) der Überzeugungswert von E bereits in K den Wert 1 hatte, so liefert die Hinzufügung von $T \cup C$ keine Erklärung: Der Glaubenswert des Explanandums ist ja nicht erhöht worden!“[15]

Dieser Gedanke, der die Grundidee der Informationsverbesserung konsequent anwendet, kann noch trivial verallgemeinert werden zu: Immer wenn die Hinzufügung von $T \cup C$ den Glaubenswert des Explanandum nicht erhöht, liegt keine Erklärung vor.

Ich behaupte nun, daß im Regelfall der *wissenschaftlichen* deduktiv-nomologischen Erklärung der Glaubenswert des Explanandum durch die Hinzufügung des Explanans *überhaupt nicht beeinflußt* wird, mithin auch nicht erhöht werden kann.

Überlegen wir uns das kurz am denkbar einfachsten Fall deduktiv-nomologischer Erklärungen:

T: Alles Kupfer leitet Elektrizität.
C: Das Objekt a ist aus Kupfer.
E: Das Objekt a leitet Elektrizität.

Beim Vorgang des Erklärens ist E gegeben. T und C werden (wie es Hempel schon formuliert hat) danach herangezogen. Eine wichtige Forderung an korrekte Erklärungen ist nun die *Unabhängigkeit* von E und C bzw. E und T.

Dann aber muß der Sachverhalt, daß E vorliegt, auch unabhängig von T und C festgestellt (also etwa beobachtet, gemessen) werden können.

Es ist nun nicht einzusehen, daß die Hinzuziehung von $T \cup C$ die Überzeugung einer Person, daß E wahr ist, im mindesten beeinflußt, denn diese Überzeugung hängt doch *allein* vom Vertrauen in die E feststellende *Verfahrensweise* ab.

Kehren wir noch einmal zum Karibik-Beispiel zurück. Es mag durchaus noch sinnvoll sein, (etwas salopp formuliert) zu sagen: Ich bin ganz schön überrascht, Frl. Ingeborg mitten im Winter gebräunt zu sehen. Meine Überraschung geht aber stark zurück, wenn ich danach erfahre, daß sie einen 14-tägigen Karibikurlaub verbracht hat.

Es macht aber schon viel weniger Sinn, zu sagen: Ich bin ganz schön überrascht, daß soeben auf der Straße ein Autounfall stattgefunden hat. Meine Überraschung reduziert sich aber, wenn ich danach erfahre, daß der Fahrer einen Fahrfehler begangen hat.

Überhaupt keinen Sinn macht es, zu sagen: Ich bin ganz schön überrascht, daß ein bestimmtes Objekt elektrisch leitend ist. Meine Überraschung sinkt aber, wenn ich danach erfahre, daß das Objekt aus Kupfer ist.

Die Idee der Überraschungsverringerung hat *nichts* mit der Idee der deduktiven Erklärung als wissenschaftliche Systematisierung zu tun.

Stegmüller (und auch Gärdenfors) reichern offensichtlich die Vielfalt *umgangssprachlicher* Erklärungsbegriffe um einen weiteren Begriff an.

Denken wir an Zollerklärung oder Liebeserklärung, so meinen wir eine Art von *Offenlegen*. Erklärt man uns den Blutkreislauf, so gibt man eine *Erläuterung*.

Beim Gärdenfors-Stegmüller-Typ des Erklärens wird demgegenüber so etwas wie eine Aufklärung über die einer bestimmten Person p_0 zu einer bestimmten Zeit t_0 noch nicht verfügbaren Gründe für das Auftreten eines diese Person überraschenden Ereignisses spezifiziert. Es handelt sich also um einen *Begriff der Überraschungsverminderung*.

4. Nun liegen die mit der traditionellen Auffassung vom Erklären verbundenen Intentionen nicht völlig außerhalb der Gärdenfors-Stegmüller-Intention: In beiden Fällen wird ein *Defizit* behoben bzw. gemildert.

Der traditionelle Vorgang des Erklärens ist eng verbunden mit der Idee eines Stützungsdefizits oder *Subsumtionsdefizits*. Erklärte oder erklärbare Sachverhalte liefern aufgrund ihrer Subsumierbarkeit unter eine bestimmte Theorie einen Beitrag zur Erhöhung des Vertrauens in diese Theorie. Dabei stützt sich das Vertrauen in die Theorie (etwa für prognostische Zwecke) auf die mehr oder weniger große Zahl gelungener erklärender Subsumtionen.

Es ist also genau *umgekehrt* gegenüber dem, was uns Stegmüller glauben machen möchte: Antworten auf erklärungheischende Warum-Fragen erhöhen *nicht* den Grad des Glaubens an das *Explanandum*, sondern sind potentiell geeignet, den Glauben oder das Vertrauen an bzw. in die *Theorie* zu erhöhen.

Auch das Problem der *Überraschung* tritt in geradezu entgegengesetzter Richtung auf: Überraschung entsteht, wenn Sachverhalte, die in den potentiellen Subsumtionsbereich einer Theorie fallen, tatsächlich nicht unter sie subsumiert werden können. Überraschung richtet sich also auf eine *Theorie* angesichts solcher Anomalien. Sie wird beseitigt, wenn es gelingt, die Theorie durch Modifikation auch für ehemalige Anomalien erklärungskräftig zu machen oder sie durch eine erklärungskräftigere Alternative zu ersetzen.

5. Es fällt auf, daß die Illustrationsbeispiele, die Gärdenfors und Stegmüller zur Diskussion ihres Begriffs der informativen Erklärung heranziehen, durchweg so gewählt sind, daß als Theorie eine oder höchstens zwei einfache Wenn-Dann-Hypothesen erscheinen.

Echte erfahrungswissenschaftliche Theorien sind demgegenüber viel komplexer. Und vor allem: sie liefern notwendigerweise vereinfachte und verfälschte, also *idealisierende Wirklichkeitsausschnittsbeschreibungen*.

Mit idealisierenden Theorien vorgenommene Erklärungen[16] erklären streng genommen etwas, das *faktisch so nicht existiert* (Molekülbewegungen in idealen Gasen, Gravitation von Massepunkten, Preisbildung auf Punktmärkten, usw.).

Will man solche Erklärungen auf reale Gase, masseinhomogenverteilte Planeten, Endproduktmärkte beziehen, entstehen *Angemessenheitsprobleme* gegenüber der jeweiligen Theorie:

Auf der Basis eines *Hintergrundwissens* um die bisherigen erfolgreichen wie erfolglosen Anwendungen einer Theorie ist im vorliegenden Anwendungsfall der *Glaube* (nicht an die Wahrheit der Theorie sondern) an die *Angemessenheit* zu begründen, eventuell zu rechtfertigen.

Der eigentlich pragmatische Aspekt des Erklärens liegt in dieser Angemessenheitsbegründung, nicht jedoch schon im Erklärungsbegriff, jedenfalls nicht in der (auch) von Stegmüller vertretenen Weise.

ANMERKUNGEN

[1] So wörtlich die Kapitelüberschrift in: W. Stegmüller, *Erklärung – Begründung – Kausalität* (Berlin –Heidelberg–New York 1983), S. 940.

[2] Es handelt sich um: P. Gärdenfors, "A Pragmatic Approach to Explanations", *Philosophy of Science*, 47 (1980), S. 405–423.

[3] Vgl. W. Stegmüller, a.a.O., S. 975–977.

[4] Vgl. W. Stegmüller, a.a.O., S. 987.

[5] Vgl. W. Stegmüller, a.a.O., S. 974–976.

[6] Stegmüller nennt sie „eine *hypothetische* Wissenssituation, da sie niemals realisiert worden ist, sondern nur zustandegekommen *wäre*, falls die Ausgangssituation nicht der empirischen Erweiterung (um das Wissen um E, M. K.) Platz gemacht hätte." Vgl. W. Stegmüller, a.a.O., S. 976.

[7] Vgl. W. Stegmüller, a.a.O., S. 972, sowie S. 979 und S. 986.

[8] Vgl. W. Stegmüller, a.a.O., S. 972.

[9] Vgl. W. Stegmüller, a.a.O., S. 972 und passim.

[10] Vgl. W. Stegmüller, a.a.O., S. 996: „Im Erklärungsfall wird tatsächlich fingiert, daß man sich (. . .) in der gegenüber K_E, kontrahierten' Situation K befindet."

[11] Stegmüller könnte demgegenüber allerdings einwenden, daß strikte Sätze als probabilistische Sätze mit Wahrscheinlichkeit 1 aufgefaßt werden können. Siehe hierzu W. Stegmüller, a.a.O., S. 960. Ob allerdings eine Bedeutungsgleichheit von $\wedge x(Gx)$ und $p(G, F \vee \neg F) = 1$ wirklich unterstellt werden darf, soll hier nicht diskutiert werden.

[12] Vgl. W. Stegmüller, a.a.O., S. 972. Nebenbei bemerkt müßte $\beta_2)$ $B_{T \cup C}(E) > \frac{1}{2}$ lauten, da nur hierdurch garantiert wird, daß „das Eintreten von E wahrscheinlicher wird als das Nichteintreten von E."

[13] Wegen Raumbeschränkung können nicht alle kritisierbaren Aspekte dargestellt werden.

[14] Vgl. W. Stegmüller, a.a.O., S. 991.

[15] Vgl. W. Stegmüller, a.a.O., S. 992.

[16] Siehe hierzu ausführlicher: M. Küttner, „Modell, Theorie und Erklärung in der theoretischen Ökonomik: Ein neuer Ansatz", *Epistemology and Philosophy of Science* (Proceedings of the 7th International Wittgenstein Symposium, Kirchberg 1982) (Wien 1983), S. 359–362.

* * *

ANOTHER LOOK AT CARTESIAN SCEPTICISM

Edward J. Khamara
Monash University, Melbourne

I wish to re-examine the principal arguments used by Descartes in his famous attempt to dispel scepticism and arrive at something indubitable. The basic tools to be used in my discussion will be the notions of self-refutation and self-verification, which will need to be explicated. I shall distinguish three types of self-refutation (called absolute, pragmatic, and assertive) and three parallel types of self-verification. This scheme owes much to an interesting article by the late J. L. Mackie, though the way in which I state these distinctions is quite different from his.[1]

Within this scheme, the important items for my purpose are the twin notions of *assertive* self-refutation and *assertive* self-verification. These notions are brought to bear on Descartes' sceptical and anti-sceptical reasoning in the *Meditations*, with what I take to be surprising results which are summarised at the end. I shall begin (in section I) by introducing three basic terms which are needed for explicating the various types of self-refutation and self-verification that I wish to distinguish. Section II is an elaboration of these distinctions, while the remaining three sections (III−V) are devoted to Descartes.

I. *Basic Terms*

Three basic terms I shall be using are: 'sentence', 'proposition' and 'assertion'. A proposition in my usage is that which is true or false, and bears its truth value *fixedly*. That is to say, if a proposition is true it is always true, no matter who the speaker may be or where he happens to be; and similarly if it is false. A sentence, for my purpose, is the linguistic vehicle used in expressing a proposition. On this scheme, different sentences belonging to the same language may express the same proposition. For example, the two sentences "The driver of the van had no hair" and "Tom Jones was bald" would express the same proposition if the definite description in the former sentence and the proper name in the latter sentence refer to the same person. And conversely, the same sentence may be used in different contexts to yield different propositions. I may, for example, utter the sentence "I am hungry" before having a meal to express a truth, or after the meal to express a falsehood. Then, on our scheme, I would be expressing different propositions on those two occasions and not one and the same proposition, since in our usage a proposition cannot change its truth value.[2] (I am using the term 'proposition' in the sense in which it was once fashionable, particularly in Oxford, to use 'statement'−a term which I want to avoid since it is ambiguous between what I call a proposition and what I call an assertion.)[3]

A proposition in this sense is to be sharply distinguished from the much richer notion of an assertion. As Prof. J. R. Searle once put it, "an assertion is a (very special kind of) commitment to the truth of a proposition".[4] In asserting that *p* I implicitly commit myself to the claim that I know that *p*. In making that assertion I also presume that, in the context, my remark is not pointless but worth communicating; in other words, my assertion is made in the belief that some of my hearers or readers do not already know or believe that *p*. Thus if I were to say, out of the blue, "Two and two are four", my remark would be true but pointless, and would therefore fail to make up an assertion, despite the fact that the proposition expressed by these words is perfectly true, and the sentence used perfectly meaningful.[5]

Other cases of unasserted propositions are quite easy to come by. An obvious case would be that of the antecedent or consequent of a conditional. Consider the two assertions:

(1) Sam smokes habitually.

and   (2) If Sam smokes habitually he won't live long.

The same proposition ("Sam smokes habitually") figures in both, but it is asserted only in (1). In (2) it is the entire conditional that is asserted, but not its antecedent or consequent. Other examples of unasserted propositions would be the individual disjuncts of an asserted disjunction, and propositions that figure as parts of a question, a command, or an exclamation.

II. *Self-refutation and self-verification*

Having introduced these technical terms, we are ready for our next task, that of clarifying the notion of self-refutation and its opposite, the notion of self-verification. I shall start with a fairly detailed treatment of self-refutation, of which I shall distinguish three types (absolute, pragmatic, and assertive), and then deal more briefly with the three parallel types of self-verification.

(i) We have firstly *absolute* self-refutation, which may be characterised as a special case of self-contradiction in which a proposition, however expressed, is such that if it is true it must also be false. In other words the proposition entails its own negation, so that the initial proposition must be necessarily false. Here are a two examples:

> (3) Nothing is true.
> ∴. It is true that nothing is true.
> ∴. Something is true (= negation of the initial proposition).

> (4) I know that I know nothing.
> ∴. I know nothing (i.e. I do not know any proposition to be true).
> ∴. I do not know that I know nothing (= negation of the initial proposition).

These examples bring out the peculiarity of the type of contradiction involved in absolute self-refutation. The contradiction must result from the presence of one or other of two sorts of expression that constitute propositional operators, or more precisely, proposition-forming operators upon propositions. As examples of the first kind of operator we have the expressions "It is possible that" and "It is true that". Given p, it follows that "It is possible that p"; and equally, given p, it follows that "It is true that p". Thus when this kind of operator is applied to a proposition p, the result is a complex proposition that can be inferred from the initial proposition p. The second kind of operator is exemplified by the expressions "I know that", "It is necessary that ", and "It can be proved that". When this kind of operator is applied to a proposition p, the result is a complex proposition *from which* the initial proposition p can be inferred. Thus given that "I know that p", it follows that p is true. (It should be noted that the operator "It is true that" exemplifies both kinds at once: from "It is true that p", it follows that p; but equally, from p it follows that "It is true that p".) Thus we may *define* absolute self-refutation as a case in which a proposition, however expressed, is such that if it is true it is also false, provided that the contradiction results from the presence of one or other of the two kinds of propositional operators that we have just characterised.

It should be noted that in a case of absolute self-refutation it is the proposition by itself that is self-refuting, no matter how it is expressed or who the speaker may be. Thus the contradiction involved in (4) cannot be avoided by using a different sentence to express the same proposition: e.g. by substituting a proper name for the first-person pronoun, or using a second- or third-person pronoun instead. Thus the sentences:

> (6) Jones knows that he knows nothing.
> (7) He knows that he knows nothing.
> (8) You know that you know nothing.

yield exactly the same result, and would express a proposition or propositions that are absolutely self-refuting. And since a proposition can occur unasserted, it follows that absolute self-refutation has nothing to do with assertion. Thus in the following conditional:

(9) If you know that you know nothing, then you know something.

the proposition that constitutes the antecedent is absolutely self-refuting, despite the fact that it is unasserted.

(ii) We have, secondly, a case of *pragmatic* self-refutation when the way in which a certain proposition is expressed on a certain occasion, or else the means chosen for communicating it, is incompatible with what it says, though the proposition, taken by itself, is not self-contradictory. In other words, the proposition is rendered false if one succeeds in expressing it or communicating it on that occasion. Examples are:

(10) I say by word or mouth "I am not now speaking".
(11) I write "I am not now writing".

Clearly in neither of these cases is the proposition expressed by what I actually say or write self-contradictory. That I should not be speaking now or that I should not be writing now is of course perfectly possible. The inconsistency is between what I say and the means chosen for expressing it. And the inconsistency can of course be avoided by choosing a different means of expression; thus I may avoid the inconsistency involved in (11) by asserting verbally rather than in writing that "I am not now writing".

Pragmatic self-refutation can also result from the means of *communicating* a certain proposition rather than the way in which it is expressed on a certain occasion. Consider the following example:

(12) While talking to someone on the telephone I say
     "No telephone is working at the moment".

This would again be a case of pragmatic self-refutation. If I succeed in communicating what I wanted to say I would thereby render it false, though of course it is perfectly possible that no telephone should at the moment be in working order.[6]

(iii) Neither of the two types of self-refutation so far considered is intrinsically bound up with assertion, but the third type always is: that is why I call it *assertive* self-refutation.[7] Here we have an attempt by a speaker to assert a certain proposition, but he is bound to fail because the very proposition that he is trying to assert precludes a necessary condition of his asserting it on that occasion. Consider the following remark:

(13) I know nothing.

The proposition expressed by this sentence could be true, but the speaker cannot successfully assert it, because in asserting it he would be implicitly claiming to know that it is true: which is inconsistent with what the proposition says. Yet that proposition may possibly be true. Suppose that the speaker's name is Jones: that Jones should know nothing is certainly logically possible; and the same proposition could be successfully asserted by someone else who, referring to Jones, uses the sentence "He knows nothing". Thus the utterance "I know nothing" is assertively self-refuting in that the proposition expressed precludes its successful assertion by the speaker on that occasion.[8]

Thus the utterances (4) and (13) are quite different: the former is absolutely self-refuting whereas the latter is only assertively self-refuting. Similarly the remark:

(14) I believe nothing.

110

is assertively (rather than absolutely) self-refuting; for, I want to say, anyone who asserts a certain proposition implicitly commits himself to believing that it is true. Consequently the proposition expressed in (14) precludes its assertion by the speaker, since it entails that the speaker does not believe it, which is a denial of a necessary condition of successful assertion. The point is brought out by an interesting example discussed long ago by G. E. Moore, viz.

(15) I believe he has gone out, but he has not.

Moore's remarks about this example are instructive. He writes:

> This, though absurd, is not self-contradictory; for it may quite well be true. But it is absurd, because by saying "he has not gone out" we *imply* that we do *not* believe that he has gone out, though we neither assert this nor does it follow from anything we do assert. That we *imply* it means only, I think, something which results from the fact that people, in general, do not make a positive assertion, unless they do not believe that the opposite is true . . . And it results from this general truth, that a hearer who hears me say "he has not gone out", will, in general, assume that I don't believe that he has gone out, although I have neither asserted that I don't, nor does it follow, from what I have asserted, that I don't. Since people will, in general, assume this, I may be said to *imply* it by saying "he has not gone out", since the effect of my saying so will, in general, be to make people believe it, and since I know quite well that my saying it will have this effect.[9]

Moore clearly takes "I believe that" to operate only on the first conjunct; and he could have forestalled some misunderstanding[10] by stating the conjuncts in reverse order thus:

(16) He has not gone out, but I believe that he has.

The *proposition* captured by this whole sentence is certainly not self-contradictory: the speaker may believe, but believe falsely, that X has gone out. The "absurdity" pointed out by Moore belongs, not to the proposition, but to the assertion, and amounts to saying, in our terminology, that the whole remark is assertively self-refuting. *Asserting* the first conjunct commits the speaker to believing that X has gone out, and this is inconsistent with what the second conjunct says. Thus the two conjuncts in (16) cannot be asserted at once by the same speaker; for by asserting the second conjunct he removes a necessary condition of successfully asserting the first conjunct. Note particularly the special sense in which Moore here uses the verb 'imply'. In his usage, it is always the speaker or writer who implies certain things which are conveyed indirectly through the act of asserting; but what the speaker thus implies is never directly entailed by the proposition that he asserts. In making an assertion, what the speaker *implies* (in Moore's sense) is always some condition which is standardly[11] satisfied for his assertion to be successfully made.

On the opposite side we may distinguish three parallel types of *self-verification*, with parallel labels: (i) *Absolute* self-verification is exemplified by the negation of any proposition that is absolutely self-refuting in the sense defined. Thus the negations of (3) and (4) are cases of absolute self-verification. The utterances

(17) Something is true.
and   (18) I do not know that I know nothing.

which are respectively the negations of (3) and (4), are both examples of absolute self-verification. Here, as in the parallel case of self-refutation, it is the proposition by itself that is self-verifying, no matter how it is expressed or who the speaker may be.

(ii) Secondly, we have *pragmatic* self-verification where the way in which a certain proposition is expressed, or the means employed in communicating it, guarantees its truth. Here are a few examples:

(19) I write "I am now writing".
(20) I say by word of mouth "I am now speaking".
(21) I tell someone over the telephone, "Not all telephones are out of order".

In the last example, if I succeed in communicating what I want to say over the telephone, my success would be a sufficient condition of the truth of what I say, of the proposition expressed by the words "Not all telephones are out of order".

(iii) Finally, we have *assertive* self-verification where we have a situation in which if the speaker succeeds in making the assertion that he wants to make then the proposition that he asserts must be true. Examples:

(22) I am now awake.
(23) I am not asleep.
(24) I am not dead.
(25) I am not dreaming.

The rationale of regarding all these utterances as assertively self-verifying is that in each case the *proposition* expressed by the relevant sentence specifies a necessary condition of successful assertion; hence if an assertion is successfully made the proposition that is asserted must be true.

Such remarks are usually pointless, but it would be wrong to regard them as meaningless.[12] A remark is pointless in a given context if it is too obvious to be worth communicating on that occasion. Thus if I were to say right now "I am sitting down", or "Two and two are four", I would be making pointless remarks; but these two sentences are nonetheless perfectly meaningful, and express true propositions. It would be equally wrong to equate pointlessness with what I am calling assertive self-verification; for, as the two examples just cited show, not all pointless remarks constitute cases of assertive self-verification in the sense that I have just characterised.

III. Is the c o g i t o non-inferential?

In recent years many writers, such as Prof. J. Hintikka[13] and Prof. A. J. Ayer,[14] have claimed that there is a deeper reading of Descartes according to which the *cogito* should not be taken as an inference: the certainty of "I exist" is autonomous, and is not derived by Descartes from the certainty of "I think". I do not myself believe that this interpretation has much of a textual backing. The main passage commonly relied on is the one to be found at the beginning of the *Second Meditation*, where Descartes writes: ". . . After . . . the most careful consideration, I must conclude that this proposition *I am, I exist*, is necessarily true whenever I affirm it, or apprehend it in my mind (*toutes les fois que je la prononce, ou que je la conçois en mon esprit*)."[15] This passage, I submit, is not inconsistent with the traditional reading of the *cogito* as an inference. I take it that Descartes is here using the verb *prononcer* (which I have rendered as "affirm") in the sense of making an assertion; and that the verb *concevoir* (which I have translated as "apprehend") is here used in the sense of having an experience. With this in mind, we may paraphrase the above passage as follows: "Given that I am now asserting the proposition that I exist, or that I am now actually apprehending it, it follows that I now exist. For while asserting it or actually apprehending it, I have an experience [which is what Descartes means by 'I think'], and from this fact [if it is a fact] it follows that I exist." It seems to me, then, that this passage is by no means inconsistent with the traditional inferential reading of the *cogito*.

Be that as it may, let us examine the result of this non-inferential interpretation. On our scheme, to say "I exist" is assertively self-verifying, on a par with saying "I am awake"; and conversely to say "I do not exist" is assertively self-refuting, on a par with saying "I am asleep" or "I am dreaming". The self-verifiability of "I exist" comes to this: that if the sentence is successfully used to make an assertion then necessarily the proposition that is asserted is true. And the trouble with "I do not exist" is that, if the proposition expressed by these words is true then no assertion can be successfully made. This does not mean that the sentence "I do not exist" cannot be used to express a proposition: it can be so used in a compound sentence, such as "He believes that I do not exist", where the proposition expressed by the words "I do not exist" would be false. The point is that the sentence "I do not exist" cannot be used on its own to make a true assertion; but this does not preclude it from figuring as part of a larger sentence that can be used assertively.

And now let me quote Ayer's attempt to make what I take to be substantially the same points:

> The sentence "I exist" . . . may be allowed to express a statement which like other statements is capable of being either true or false. It differs, however, from most other statements in that if it is false it cannot actually be made. Consequently, no one who uses these words intelligently and correctly can use them to make a statement which he knows to be false. If he succeeds in making the statement, it must be true.[16]

This is quite bewildering. How can the statement be capable of being false if it cannot be made when false, but can only be made when true? I think Ayer is badly in need of the distinction between assertion and proposition, and his bewilderment arises from the fact that he uses the term 'statement' to mean both an assertion and a proposition. Had he recognised this distinction he could have removed the air of paradox and put his point by saying that, although the sentence "I exist" always expresses a proposition that is either true or false, it cannot be used to make a successful assertion when the proposition is in fact false.

But let us get back to Descartes and consider the result of this interpretation of the *cogito* to which Ayer subscribes. It seems to me that such an interpretation is not as favourable to Descartes as its proponents generally assume. To see this we must realise that Descartes' aim is to secure a piece of occurrent knowledge.[17] Whether we take it inferentially or non-inferentially, the aim of the *cogito* is to attain an item expressible by the words "*I know occurrently that I exist now*", rather than "I exist now". But if so, the non-inferential interpretation clearly fails to attain that goal. It is true that if I successfully assert that I exist now then necessarily I do exist now. But what guarantee is there that I should succeed in making this assertion? And even if I do, the most I can derive is that I do exist now, *not* that *I know occurrently* that I exist now. There is, of course, an implicit epistemic commitment behind that assertion: in making it I imply (as Moore would say) that I am claiming to know the proposition to be true, or at least that I believe it to be true. But once again that would not suffice to yield the required result that Descartes needs, namely "I know occurrently that I exist now", even if I do succeed in making that assertion.

IV. *The dream argument and its scope*

We may restate the dream argument in Descartes as a *modus ponens* and articulate it as follows:[18]

1. If I do not know occurrently that I am not now dreaming then I do not know occurrently that I am now sitting by the fire.
2. I do not know occurrently that I am not now dreaming.
∴ 3. I do not know occurrently that I am now sitting by the fire.

The decisive objection to this argument is that, on our scheme, the *second* premise is assertively self-refuting, i.e. the truth of the proposition expressed by this sentence precludes its assertion by the proponent of the argument. For in asserting that proposition the sceptic claims to know it occurrently to be true, which claim is not available to him if he does not know at that time that he is not dreaming. But if the sceptic is not entitled to assert his second premiss then he is not entitled to assert his conclusion, and the argument fails for that reason.

But waiving this main objection, let us assume that the sceptic *is* entitled to assert his second premiss. What reason has he for asserting it? *How* does he know that the second premiss is true? The answer given by Descartes in the *First Meditation* is in the form of a rhetorical question: "How many times have I dreamt at night that I was in this place, dressed, by the fire, although I was quite naked in my bed?"[19] He adds that in some of these dreams the experiences he had were so similar to what he takes to be the present evidence of his senses that he was taken in by them; and he complains that "there are no sure signs or sufficiently reliable indications that would enable us to distinguish clearly between waking and sleeping",[20] i.e. signs or indications by which we could safely distinguish experiences that we have when awake from those that we have when we are dreaming.

We may restate Descartes' reason for asserting the second premiss of his dream argument as follows: (a) "I know now that I have had dreams in the past in which my experience was closely similar to what I take to be my present waking experience". But the sceptic cannot know this now unless he is awake and knows he is not now dreaming. Thus the reason (and it is the only reason) that Descartes gives for upholding the second premiss is inconsistent with what that second premiss says.

Prima facie the sceptic could escape this objection by diluting his reason for upholding the second premiss of his argument, and offering, instead of (a), the apparently weaker reason, (b) "It is logically possible that I should have exactly similar experiences to what I take to be the present evidence of my senses, and yet be dreaming". But this would not really advance his case. For in giving this as his reason he makes an assertion to the effect that the proposition expressed in (b) is true. And in asserting this proposition he is claiming to know occurrently that it is true; but he cannot have this knowledge now, given that his second premiss is true. Indeed the sceptic cannot give any reason for this second premiss; for whatever that reason may be, he would have to assert it, but he cannot successfully make that assertion if his second premiss is true.

Thus the dream argument is bound to fail. Yet the question arises: What exactly is the scope of this argument? What claims to knowledge would the dream argument impugn *if it were successful*? I take it that, as it stands, the conditional that constitutes the sceptic's first premiss is undisputable. Let us replace the inner part of its consequent by a propositional variable p, thus: "If I do not know occurrently that I am not now dreaming then I do not know occurrently that p". Our question is: What does p range over? Or more precisely: What propositions can be substituted for p so as to yield conditionals that are undoubtedly true? Descartes' answer was that p ranges over all (and only) empirical propositions, i.e. any proposition that is epistemically accessible to us only through the evidence of our senses. For he took the dream argument to show that all sensory evidence is suspect, since we cannot tell whether such sensory evidence is genuine or spurious. Non-empirical propositions, such as the propositions of logic and mathematics, are not, he thought, impugned by the dream argument; and that is why, to cast doubt upon these, he thought he had to resort to the more extravagant hypothesis of the evil demon who sees to it that we are always wrong.

It seems to me that Descartes was mistaken on this point, and that the scope of the dream argument (if successful) is as wide as that of the evil demon hypothesis. In other words, p ranges over any proposition whatever, so that: if I do not know occurrently that I am not now dreaming then I do not know occurrently any proposition at all. Descartes seems to forget that the occurrent knowledge of *any* proposition is always accompanied by an experience that the knower has at that time. And since it is always possible that any experience that we may have in waking life should have an exactly similar counterpart in a dream, it follows that we cannot clearly distinguish between the experience we may have in genuine occurrent knowledge and the experience we may have when we merely dream that we are having occurrent knowledge. My claim to know occurrently a necessary proposition, such as the proposition "$2+3 = 5$", need not involve any experience that I get through the senses; it may be based merely on the inward experience of thinking clearly about the matter at that time. But the fact that it is an inward experience does not place it outside the scope of the dream argument; for, as an inward experience, it can (if Descartes is right) have a spurious counterpart in a dream from which it cannot be distinguished. But if so, then every proposition that is a candidate for human knowledge would be impugned by the dream argument, if the latter were successful. The evil demon hypothesis was thus redundant; for contrary to what Descartes himself thought, the dream argument was just as wide in its scope.

V. *The c o g i t o as an inference*

What if we adopt the more traditional interpretation, and treat the *cogito* as an inference? On this reading Descartes claimed that his argument is sound and conclusive, because it survives the two extravagant sceptical hypotheses entertained in the *First Meditation*: namely, the hypothesis that I am now dreaming, and the supposition that there is an evil demon who sees to it that whatever I believe occurrently is false. Here again I want to show that the plausibility of Descartes' reasoning stems from the fact that he understates his conclusion. What he is after is not the proposition "I now exist" but the *stronger* epistemic proposition "I know occurrently that I now exist". And when the desired conclusion is properly stated, it is easily seen that his argument does not in fact survive the two sceptical hypotheses, and that the *cogito* as an inference fails.

First let us consider how this inferential interpretation of the *cogito* fares under the dream hypothesis. Suppose that I am now dreaming. Then I am now having an experience (or am "thinking" in the relevant Cartesian sense). It follows that, as the owner of that experience, I now exist. So far (let us say) so good. But it does *not* follow that I know occurrently that I now exist; and indeed the latter epistemic proposition is inconsistent with our initial premiss, namely the supposition that I am now dreaming.

Next let us consider the *cogito*, on this reading, under the evil demon hypothesis, about which Descartes writes:

> But there is some deceiver or other, both very powerful and very cunning, who is constantly using all his ingenuity to deceive me. Then there is no doubt that I exist, if he is deceiving me; and let him deceive me as much as he likes, he can never bring it about that I should be nothing, so long as I think I am something.[21]

Now I can think of two different ways of spelling out Descartes' reasoning in this passage: the first takes his talk of this deceiver quite literally, the second as a metaphor that needs to be cashed.

Here then is the first interpretation: "Assume that I am being literally deceived at this moment. It follows that I now exist [or, as Descartes puts it, that I am 'something' and not 'nothing']. For deceiving is a relation between a deceiver and a deceiv*ed*; and given that I am now being deceived it necessarily follows that, as the deceiv*ed*, I exist at this moment." Clearly this does not yield the desired result, that I know occurrently that I now exist, but the weaker conclusion that I now exist.

The other, more plausible way of interpreting the above passage is to replace what I take to be a metaphor by what it is intended to convey. Descartes' evil demon hypothesis is to be regarded as a picturesque way of making the assumption that I am always wrong, i.e. that whenever I believe occurrently that some proposition is true that proposition is false. So let us take this as our starting-point. Descartes' reasoning in the above passage may then be articulated as follows: "Assume that I am always wrong, so that any proposition that I occurrently believe to be true is in fact false. And assume further that I am now having certain occurrent beliefs. It follows that I am now having certain experiences, and therefore that, as the owner of those experiences, I now exist." But it does *not* follow that I know occurrently that I now exist, which is what Descartes needs. And indeed the latter epistemic proposition is incompatible with our initial premiss, namely the supposition that any proposition that I occurrently believe is false. So here again one can see that, having understated the conclusion he was after, Descartes is led to believe that he has got it when he hasn't.

I will end by summarising the main points I have made against Descartes. (i) The so-called non-inferential interpretation of the *cogito* yields a case of assertive self-verification, in that *if* the sentence "I exist " is used to make a successful assertion then what is asserted is true. But this falls short of achieving the proper goal of the *cogito*, which is to establish the epistemic proposition "I know occurrently that I now exist". (ii) The decisive objection to the sceptical argument based on dreaming is that it involves an assertively self-refuting premiss, which disqualifies the sceptic from asserting his conclusion. (iii) As an anti-sceptical argument (or inference) the *cogito* fails because it does not survive the two acid tests devised by Descartes. Its proper conclusion is the epistemic proposition just mentioned, and that is incompatible with *both* the hypothesis that I am now dreaming *and* the supposition that I am always wrong.

ENDNOTES

1 Mackie, J. L., "Self-Refutation – a Formal Analysis", *The Philosophical Quarterly*, Vol. 14 (1964), pp. 193–203. Unlike Mackie's analysis my treatment is informal, and covers cases of self-verification as well as cases of self-refutation.
2 Mackie (1964) does not make a distinction between a proposition and an assertion, and he uses the term 'proposition' differently in that he allows a proposition to change in truth value.
3 For a detailed treatment of the distinction between sentence and proposition, see E. J. Lemmon, "Sentences, Statements and Propositions", in: *British Analytical Philosophy*, ed. by B. Williams and A. Montefiore (London 1966), pp. 87–107, especially p. 97ff. Note that what I call a proposition Lemmon calls a statement (a term which I want to avoid), and what *he* calls a proposition (= the sense of a sentence) is a notion that is not used at all in this paper. I have borrowed some of Lemmon's examples.
4 Searle, John R., *Speech Acts* (Cambridge 1969), p. 29. The way in which I draw the distinction between sentence, proposition, and assertion, is exactly the same as Searle's, and I have made use of some of his examples.
5 Cf. Searle (1969), pp. 141–146.
6 Pragmatic self-refutation and self-verification are here confined to cases having to do with *linguistic* practice, with the way in which a proposition is expressed or communicated. The remark of a man who, while seated, says "I am not sitting down" would be an obvious lie, but would not constitute a case of pragmatic self-refutation in the required sense.
7 Mackie (1964) calls this type of self-refutation 'operational', a term which I find inappropriate and confusing.
8 Contrast Mackie's way of characterising this type of self-refutation, as a case in which a proposition "cannot be coherently asserted" (1964, p. 196). I want to say, rather, that the proposition expressed by, e.g., the sentence in (13) *can* be *successfully asserted*, but not by the speaker on that occasion. Mackie's characterisation runs dangerously close to the unacceptable view that such remarks are in fact senseless. For, it may be argued, the propositions which they purport to express cannot be genuine if they "cannot be coherently asserted" by any speaker on any occasion.
9 Moore, G. E., "Russell's Theory of Descriptions", reprinted in his *Philosophical Papers*, ed. by C. Lewy (London 1959), pp. 175–6.
10 See, e.g., J. Passmore, *Philosophical Reasoning* (London 1961), p. 76: "There does not seem to be any reading of the sentence which would make it both absurd and 'possibly true'."
11 The "general truth" expounded by Moore in the passage just quoted states a necessary condition of successful assertion under standard conditions. It is a pretty obvious misreading to take Moore here as making an empirical observation to the effect that *most* people believe what they assert; contrast C. K. Grant, "Pragmatic Implication", *Philosophy*, Vol. 33 (1958), p. 317; and Passmore (1961), p. 74.
12 Cf. Searle (1969), pp. 141–146. Contrast Norman Malcolm, *Dreaming* (London 1959), especially chs. 2–4, 9, and 18. According to Malcolm such remarks as (22)–(25), as well as their negations, are senseless.
13 Hintikka, J., "Cogito ergo Sum: Inference or Performance?", *The Philosophical Review*, Vol. 71 (1962), pp. 3–32; reprinted in W. Doney (ed.), *Descartes: A Collection of Critical Essays* (London 1968), pp. 108–139.
14 Ayer, A. J., "I think, therefore I am", *The Problem of Knowledge* (London 1956), pp. 45–54; reprinted in Doney (1968), pp. 80–87.

[15] Descartes, R., *Meditation II*, para. 4; see *The Philosophical Works of Descartes*, tr. by E. S. Haldane and G. R. T. Ross, Vol. I, p. 150

[16] Ayer, A. J. (1956), pp. 51–52 (= Doney, p. 85).

[17] Occurrent knowledge is here distinguished from dispositional knowledge. A man who is sound asleep and not dreaming may know a good many things *at that time*, but only dispositionally and not occurrently.

[18] I owe this formulation of the dream argument to G. E. Moore; see his paper "Certainty" in Moore (1959), p. 245; reprinted in Doney (1968), see p. 47.

[19] *Meditation I*, para. 5 (Haldane & Ross, Vol. I, pp. 145–146).

[20] Ibid. (Haldane & Ross, Vol. I, p. 146).

[21] *Meditation II*, loc. cit., note 15.

* * *

4. Philosophische Gotteslehre und Gottesbeweise

4. Philosophical Theology and Proofs for God's Existence

SOME REMARKS ON DIVINE INTENTIONALITY

Eric R. Kraemer
University of Nebraska, Lincoln

Introduction

Franz Brentano and his students have argued that intentionality is *the* mark of psychological phenomena. The importance of this claim is obvious. If there is a truly distinctive characteristic of psychological activity, then acquiring an understanding as to what this characteristic is will provide insight into what an adequate theory of mental phenomena must be like. Brentano's own characterizations of intentionality ("direction of an object", "reference to a content") are rather obscure.[1] Those of other phenomenologists are not in general any more enlightening.[2] A seemingly more promising approach to clarifying Brentano's claim has been the attempt to provide formal criteria for intentionality.[3] It is to this project that the present discussion is addressed. The question that I would like to raise is this: in assessing the various proposed criteria of intentionality, what sorts of mental creatures should we take into account?

This question may seem to have an obvious and innocent answer, namely, that we should consider all those kinds of mental beings that there are. But this response is not as clear as it might be. Should we only consider (1) just those mental beings we know for sure exist, or should we *also* include (2) other types of mental creatures whose existence is controversial? If we restrict ourselves to (1), then we face the charge of parochialism. We may also run the risk of having our proposals about the nature of intentionality shown to be inadequate. If we opt for including (2), then we encounter a second problem, namely that the most plausible candidates for criteria of intentionality proposed so far do not apply across the board. This raises the question as to whether the variety of mental beings is such that no adequate formal criterion of intentionality is to be found. Let us now turn to spelling out the problem.

I

If we consider the propositional attitudes of normal human beings (their believings, hopings, fearings, desirings, etc.) we notice that sometimes the 'object' of such attitudes exists and sometimes not. This observation has led some philosophers to propose various criteria of intentionality including, for example, the following:

> A simple declarative sentence is intentional if it uses a substantival expression—a name or a description—in such a way that neither the sentence nor its contradictory implies either that there is or that there isn't anything to which the substantival expression truly applies.[4]

This characteristic has been abandoned for being too weak, since it would allow certain non-mental phenomena to count as intentional.[5] It may be thought that this criterion is, nonetheless, an interesting necessary condition for intentionality. But it is worth remarking that the criterion is also too *strong*. For consider the beliefs of the God of the philosophical tradition. God is, among other things, necessarily omniscient. The objects of God's beliefs could not possible fail to exist. So the sentence, "God believes that Jones exists," unlike the sentence "I believe that Jones exists," implies that Jones does exist. If in searching for an adequate mark of intentionality we also consider the intentionality of God's mental states, then it is clear that the failure of existential generalization criterion is too strong. The same remarks clearly apply to other proposed marks of intentionality such as referential opacity, non-implication of imbedded clause and non-existensional occurrence.[6]

If in developing criteria of intentionality we need to take beings like God into account, then efforts up to the present to provide such criteria do not seem to have been successful. One reason for this failure is to be found in what appears to serve as the motivating principles behind these efforts. Some philosophers have referred to intentionality as "the possibility of stupidity".[7] Chisholm, for instance, has proposed criteria which, he says, are based on "the fact that men need not be rational—that a man may have contradictory beliefs and contradic-tory desires" or which are guided by "the possibility of a certain kind of error."[8] Consideration of the Divine mind shows that such motivation is not sufficiently general to encompass all types of psychological beings. For the possibility of error, stupidity, or irrationality does not apply to God.

II

If my reasoning so far is correct, then it would follow that the criteria proposed for intention-ality all run the risk of being too strong.[9] Having explicated the problem I would now like to consider some typical responses that the argument may elicit. These are of two sorts: (1) at-tempts to preserve the traditional criterial approach to characterizing intentionality, and (2) efforts to show how to avoid the problem. Let us begin with an example of the first sort. One might argue that we could salvage the criterial approach to intentionality by holding that divine intentionality should be viewed as *parasitic* upon human intentionality. The statement, "God believes that Jones exists", does entail this statement, "Someone believes that Jones exists". Since this latter statement does satisfy the proposed criteria, one might claim that for the purposes of divising criteria of intentionality we need not worry about any special features of God's beliefs. One problem with this defense is that it assumes that what is distinctive for all beliefs is to be found by considering just human beliefs alone. But this is just what the prob-lem of divine omniscience shows to be at issue. What is characteristic of the genus is, of course, to be found in each species. But we should remember that it is methodologically unsound practice to attempt to characterize a multi-specied genus in terms of just one of its species.[10]

A second series of responses to the problem of divine omniscience consists of attempts to show that one or another of the assumptions behind it is mistaken. I shall consider three such assumptions that might be challenged. Firstly, the problem assumes that God should be taken to be necessarily omniscient. Some may object that this feature does not correctly apply to God. Although such an objection is certainly controversial, it does not seriously attack the problem at hand. If God were not necessarily omniscient, one would only need to imagine some other sort of mental being who was.

This leads us to a second assumption, that the notion of necessary omniscience is unproblem-atic. There are, to be sure, very serious traditional problems associated with divine omnis-cience (such as the compatibility of Divine foreknowledge with human freedom). And it has recently been argued that there are important logical problems as well (that parallel the Liar paradox.)[11] But the difficulties that have been raised would not seem to undercut in any serious way the threat that a suitably reconstructed notion of necessary omniscience would still pose for providing an enlightening criterion of intentionality.

A third assumption that may be challenged is that it is important to consider divine inten-tionality if we are to provide an adequate account of the intentionality of human beings. Some may object that, since human mental states are so very different from those mental states ascribed to the Deity, we may content ourselves with intentionality criteria derived from a study of human mentality alone. What I find problemtic about this response is that criteria so derived, though useful indications of symptoms of intentionality in human beings, do not provide an insight into the general phenomenon of intentionality. If intentionality is an important feature of our mental life, we should not rest content with anything less than a truly general understanding of it.

It is instructive to remember a complaint that is often lodged against defenders of the identity-theory of the mind-body relation. It has become common to object that it is a mistake to identify mental states as being nothing but brain-states as there might be creatures (such as Martians) who possess mental states but lack brain states.[12] The point of this complaint is that the identity theory is too narrow, that an adequate account of mental phenomena must be sufficiently broad to apply to different sorts of mental beings.[13] I am suggesting that informative criteria of intentionality also need to be similarly general.

It should not be concluded that the criteria so far proposed for intentionality are without any significance. They can still be used to perform an instructive corrective function with respect to the various general theories of mental phenomena that have been proposed[14]. For if such a theory is to be adequate, it needs to be consistent whith the propositional attitudes of humans displaying those features that the intentionality criteria so far discussed have emphasized. One conclusion which should be drawn from this discussion is this: it is a mistake to hold that one has gained an insight into intentionality if one's theory of the mental can only accomodate these criteria. It has been maintained that mental phenomena are too varied to all fall under some set of formal criteria of intentionality.[15] The point of the present discussion is to suggest that a second sort of variety, namely, the variety of types of mental beings, also poses a serious problem for the criterial strategy.

————————

ENDNOTES

1 Brentano, F., *Psychology from an Empirical Standpoint* (trans. L. McAlister) (New York 1973), p. 88f.

2 Heidegger, M., for example, speaks of the "structure" of "comportments . . . of directing-oneself-toward, of being-directed-toward", in: *The Basic Problems of Phenomenology* (trans. A. Hofstadter) (Bloomington, Indiana 1982), p. 58f.

3 See, for example, R. M. Chisholm, *Perceiving* (Ithaca 1957), p. 170f.; G. E. M. Anscombe, "The Intentionality of Sensation", the *Analytic Philosophy* II, ed. R. J. Butler (Oxford 1965), 158–180; R. M. Chisholm, "Intentionality", in: P. Edwards (ed.) *The Encyclopedia of Philosophy* (New York 1967), Vol. 4, p. 201f.; A. Marras (ed.) *Intentionality, Mind and Language* (Urbana 1972), Section I.; and A. Marras, "Intentionality Revisited", *Philosophia*, Vol. 12 (1982), 21–35.

4 Chisholm, R. M. (1957), p. 170f.

5 Chisholm (1967: p. 203) points out that the non-mental sentence, "New Zealand is devoid of unicorns," satisfies this criterion.

6 For a discussion of similar problems for recent, complicated criteria proposed by Chisholm, see E. R. Kraemer, "Divine Omniscience and Criteria of Intentionality", *Philosophy and Phenomenological Research* Vol. 45 (1984). The problem of accounting for Divine omniscience is also faced by George Bealer's recent attempt (in *Quality and Concept* (Oxford 1982), section 48) to characterize intentionality in terms of 'contingent connections'. A similar difficulty arises for Chisholm's attempt to define the notion of a 'mental attribute' in "On the Nature of the Psychological", *Philosophical Studies*, Vol. 43 (1983), 155–164.

7 Sober, E., in "Why must Homunculi be so stupid?" *Mind* Vol. 91 (1982), p. 420, approvingly attributes this remark to Dennis Stampe.

8 Chisholm, R. M., "Psychological Concepts", in: H. N. Castañeda (ed.), *Intentionality, Minds and Perception* (Detroit 1966), 11–35, p. 12.

9 It should be noted that G. E. M. Anscombe's criterion (1965: p. 161f.) based on the possible *indeterminacy* of the object ("I can think of a man without thinking of a man of any particular height; I cannot hit a man without hitting a man of some particular height . . .") does seem to apply to God. It is open to question, however, whether this criterion is sufficiently general. For it would not seem to apply, for example, to thoughts about abstract objects such as numbers.

[10] For further discussion of this point see E. R. Kraemer (1984). Compare H. Morick's remark, "that an object in fact exists doesn't alter the character of the way in which we are directed upon it", in: "Intentionality, Intensionality and the Psychological", *Analysis*, Vol. 32 (1971), 39–44, p. 41.

[11] Grim, P., "Some Neglected Problems of Omniscience", *American Philosophical Quarterly*, Vol. 20 (1983), 265–276.

[12] Putnam, H., "The Nature of Mental States", in: *Mind, Language and Reality* (London 1975), 429–440.

[13] For a similar complaint see D. M. Armstrong who, in: *A Materialist Theory of the Mind* (London 1968), argues that behaviorism is inadequate for not being compatible with the existence of disembodied minds.

[14] See, e.g., K. V. Wilkes, *Physicalism* (Atlantic Highlands, New Jersey 1978), Ch. IV; W. Lycan, "Form, Function and Feel", *Journal of Philosophy*, Vol. 78 (1981); F. Dretske, *Knowledge and the Flow of Information* (Cambridge, Mass., 1979), Ch. 7.

[15] Kim, J., "Materialism and the Criteria of the Mental", *Synthese*, Vol. 22 (1971), 323–345, p. 329.

* * *

KNOWLEDGE AND BELIEF IN ST. ANSELM'S PROOF

A. Zvie Bar-On
The Hebrew University, Jerusalem

The proof referred to in this paper* is St. Anselm's Ontological Argument for the Existence of God. I submit that the text of the argument in question is contained in chapters 2, 3 and 4 of St. Anselm's *Proslogion*. I shall refer to these three chapters as to one textual unit and shall consider every single sentence in them as a part of St. Anselm's Argument.

The autor calls the inquiry presented in this text "unum argumentum", and rightly so. Still, the term 'argument' received in later usage a slightly narrower connotation, according to which we would distinguish more than one argument within St. Anselm's chain of reasoning. To avoid misunderstanding I shall bow to the later usage, calling the whole piece 'the Proof' and its separate phases 'Arguments'.

As I read it, the Proof can be divided into the following eight parts:

Part I, the Opening Prayer, in which the position of the author as that of a believer is depicted and the purpose of the Proof stated;

Part II, the Preliminaries, where the position of the Fool of the Psalms as that of a non-believer is presented, the key-concept of the Proof, namely the concept of that-than-which-not-hing-greater-can-be-thought, is put forward as at least meaningful even for the Fool, and the basic distinction between possible and actual existence is explained and examplified;

Part III, where the First Argument is developed, in which that-than-which-nothing-greater-can-be-thought is shown to exist in reality;

Part IV, in which the Second Argument is delineated, showing that that-than-which-nothing-greater-can-be-thought exists necessarily;

Part V, in which the Third Argument is construed to show that God is that-than-which-not-hing-greater-can-be-thought;

Part VI, where the Fourth Argument is presented, to show that God is not only that-than-which-nothing-greater-can-be-thought, but also that-to-which-nothing-equal-can-be-thought, i.e. that He is the greatest of all being;

Part VII, the clarification of the Puzzle of the Fool who had allegedly thought the unthinkable; and finally

Part VIII, the Concluding Prayer in which the result of the Proof is summarized.[1]

On a closer inspection we may specify these eight parts as follows: Parts III, IV, V and VI, which contain four separate arguments, give us the core of the Proof, its central chain of reasoning; Parts I and VIII will be considered as the 'external framework' of the Proof, while Parts II and VII as its 'internal framework'.

Both of these frames are naturally of a meta-theoretical character. While the first one is construed as a dialogue between the author and God, the second one turns out to be a dialogue, or a controversy, or even better—an intellectual transaction between the author and the Fool of the Psalms.

In recent discussions on St. Anselm's Proof, conducted largely as logical or para-logical exercices, relatively little attention has been paid to these two frames. For our investigation of the Proof, however, they are of paramount importance. Let me quote the wording of the external frame and then comment on it. Here is the first section of the frame, the Opening Prayer: "Well then, Lord, You who give understanding to faith, grant me that I may understand, as much as You see fit, that You exist, as we believe You to exist, and that You are what we believe You to be".[2] And now the second section: "I give thanks, good Lord, I give thanks to You, since what I believed before through your free gift I now so understand through your illumination, that if I did not want to *believe* that You existed, I should neverthe-less be unable not to understand it".[3]

It is quite clear that the topic of the external frame is the relationship between belief and understanding which in this context, as will become obvious later, is synonymous with know-ledge. In the Opening Prayer the dependence of knowledge on belief is alluded to in the follo-wing items:

1) The *very act* of applying to God marks the author's belief in God's existence. However, from the content of the prayer we gather that it is *only* belief, not knowledge.

2) The *reason* for this appeal to God gives evidence of another belief of St. Anselm's, one concerning God's essence. What the author seeks is the understanding of what he believes, or in other words, he seeks knowledge of both, God's existence and certain aspects of His essence. And he appeals to God who, as he believes, "gives understanding to faith", or as we would say it, 'enables the believer to transform his belief into knowledge' with a request that this ability be given to him.

Thus, in the author's case, as we would interpret it, the dependence of knowledge on belief has two aspects: (1) without belief he would not seek God's assistance for gaining knowledge; and (2) without belief he would not have any chance of getting this assistance, so that he would not after all gain any knowledge.

The situation, however, has changed significantly in the other section of the first frame. The impression here is that knowledge has become independent: ". . . if I did not want to believe, I should nevertheless be unable not to understand . . ."

Now this astonishing transition to independence of knowledge from belief gains consolida-tion within the internal frame of the Proof: the dialogue of the author with the Fool of the Psalms. Here the starting point is the very opposite to that of the external frame; it is the lack of belief in the existence of God: "the Fool has said in his heart there is no God".[4] All the same, the Fool of the Psalms is supposed to be a rational being and as such he must follow where a logical argument leads. Eventually, with St. Anselm's help, he will arrive to the con-clusion identical *in content* to the belief in God's existence, but by rational means alone. The reliance on belief will no longer be needed. To see this let us join the two on their intellectual journey.

In the part which we have called 'the Preliminaries' the Fool of the Psalms, who said in his heart there is no God, turns out to be also a man who can grasp the concept of that-than-which-nothing-greater-can-be-thought as meaningful, and the distinction between existence in thought and that in reality as legitimate. For that the religious belief is apparently not needed.

Now begins the proper chain of reasoning. The proof follows the lines of a *reductio ad impossibile*.[5] What escaped the attention of many analysts, however, is that the *reductio* pre-mise is nothing but a reformulation of the Fool's dictum in terms of the Preliminaries, as men-tioned above:

1) That-than-which-nothing-greater-can-be-thought exists in mind alone (*not* in rea-lity).

But it is out of the question for a rational being to abide with proposition (1)—or the *reduc-tio* premise—together with two other propositions listed in *Proslogion* 2:

2) If that-than-which-nothing-greater-can-be-thought exists in the mind, it can *at least* be thought to exist in reality.
3) Existence in reality is greater than existence in the mind only.

As a rational being the Fool cannot possibly object to these two propositions. But as such he cannot also help seeing that the three above propositions together entail a formidable contra-dictory assertion:

4) That (hypothetical) being than which nothing greater can be thought is a being of which something greater *can* be thought.

Again, for a rational being this is a pitfall from which an escape must be found. Since the contradiction derives from the logical product of propositions (1), (2) and (3), to escape it it will be sufficient to deny any one of them. Which of the three is to be discarded? It is again a matter of elimination on rational grounds: St. Anselm appears to have no doubt that the Fool won't object to accepting propositions (2) and (3) as absolutely sure knowledge. Thus the only proposition that can be eliminated is (1). The negation of it gives us the next proposition:

5) Both in mind and in reality there is something than which nothing greater can be thought.

So far the First Argument. The second one proceeds on parallel lines. We have proved with the Fool's full consent that that-than-which-nothing-greater-can-be-thought exists in reality. Suppose, however, that

6) The existence of that-than-which-nothing-greater-can-be-thought is contingent (or in St. Anselm's *cum* the Fool's language, it is something that although existing can be thought not to exist).

If he abided with this proposition, the Fool would be again caught in a contradiction. To see that he must only add to (6) the two unexceptionable following propositions:

7) If that-than-which-nothing-greater-can-be-thought exists contingently, it can at least be thought to exist necessarily; and
8) Necessary existence is greater than contingent existence.[6]

From (6), (7) and (8) together follows the same contradictory proposition (4) which followed also from (1), (2) and (3). The same purely rational procedure is used and the result here too is the negation of the contradictory proposition, which will give us

9) that-than-which-nothing-greater-can-be-thought exists necessarily, i.e. its non-existence is unthinkable.

We have reached a crucial point in the Proof. As far as the text is concerned, we are in the middle of Chapter 3 of the *Proslogion*. The author is satisfied to have proved, with full collaboration of the rational Fool, that that-than-which-nothing-greater-can-be-thought exists, first—in the mind, second—in reality, and third—of complete necessity. It has not yet been proved that it is *God* we are talking about, that God is that-than-which-nothing-greater-can-be-thought.

Curiously enough, what was perfectly clear to the Fool of the Psalms escaped the attention of many commentators.[7] Most of them simply ignored the second part of the third chapter, considering it as outside of the Proof proper. Still, however few and insignificant these lines may look, they contain no less than *two* arguments without which, according to my reading, the whole proof would be essentially defective, as far as St. Anselm's intentions are concerned.

The first of these two arguments proposes to show that *God* is that-than-which-nothing-greater-can-be-thought, while the second one adds that God is that-to-which-nothing-equal-can-be-thought, i.e. that He is the greatest of all.

The first of these two steps is again construed in the form of a *reductio ad impossible* argument, the *reductio* premise being the proposition:

127

10) Some intelligence (maybe the Fool) thinks of something greater than God.

It follows that

11) The creature puts itself above its creator and judges him;

which according to St. Anselm is completely absurd. We have to deny the *reductio* premise and accept the proposition that anything greater than God is unthinkable, i.e.

12) God is that-than-which-nothing-greater-can-be-thought.

Well, nothing greater than God can be thought. But is anything equal to Him thinkable? If this was allowed, all that was achieved up to now would be outmatched. The God whose existence was proved would not be the God of the believer at all, certainly not of the monotheistic believer. The rational Fool would not perhaps mind, but St. Anselm could not possibly allow it. It would mean for him that the reason's *tour de force* did not reach its ultimate target. It was therefore necessary to show that God is the greatest of all. The argument runs as follows:

13) God is unthinkable as non-existent;

however,

14) Anything else *can* be thought not to exist, i.e. everything else exists (if it does at all) contingently.

From (13) and (14) taken together we obtain

15) God is the only one whose non-existence is unthinkable;

and since whatever cannot be thought not to exist is greater than that which can be thought not to exist (Proposition (8)),

16) God is the greatest of all.

With this we have come to the end of Chapter 3 and of the central core of the Proof. St. Anselm successfully brought the Fool *qua* rational being to the very point he was meant to achieve.

But this is not yet the end of the story. When St. Anselm looks back at the route he had travelled together with the Fool, a puzzle crops up. How was it possible for the Fool to think at the beginning what turned out to be unthinkable at the end?

Chapter 4 of the *Proslogion* proposes a solution to this puzzle, certain aspects of which are of a special interest to us. On the face of it St. Anselm's solution focusses upon the equivocal nature of the concept of thinking. But when inspected closer the issue turns out to concentrate on the distinction between thinking and understanding, which at least in one of its aspects can be considered as the distinction between belief and knowledge.

Already the allegedly first critic of St. Anselm's Proof, the monk Gaunilo de Marmoutier, arguing as it were "on behalf of the Fool" made use of the difficulties arising from this subtle distinction. Referring to what we have labelled 'the Second Argument', Gaunilo urges that instead of concluding that the Supreme Being cannot be thought of as non-existent, we should say that He cannot be *understood* (in the sense of 'known') as non-existent, and this for the following reason: things which do not exist cannot be *understood* as existent, although they can be *thought* (conceived, imagined, believed) to exist. This is the way in which the Fool thinks of God as non-existent. To strengthen his case Gaunilo added the following remarkable consideration:

Don't I *know* with complete certainty that I exist? But cannot I think of myself as non-existent, while I know for certain that I do exist? This confrontation of my knowledge of myself as existent with my thinking of myself as non-existent makes me face a dilemma: if I can think of myself as non-existent, why shouldn't I be able to think the same of other things of which I know with complete certainty that they exist, and first and foremost of God? And if I can *not* think of myself as non-existent, why should it be strange that I cannot think of God as non-existent?[8]

St. Anselm replies to this criticism by sharpening the distinction between thinking and understanding, which will now involve a more systematic statement of the distinction between several senses of 'thinking', as well as an elaboration of the distinction between contingent and necessary existence. I shall present St. Anselm's analysis in a somewhat free rendering.[9]

Consider two entities, a and b. Suppose a exists contingently, while b exists necessarily. Now if someone, say S, understands (i.e. knows) that a exists, the situation is such that in one sense S can not think (I shall label it 'think$_1$') of a as non-existent, while in another sense (think$_2$) he can do so. He can not think$_1$ of a as non-existent in the sense that he is not entitled to say: 'I understand (know) that a exists, but I think (believe) that a does not exist'. If S said so, he would contradict himself, since 'I understand (know) that so-and-so' entails 'I think (believe) that so-and-so' (although not *vice versa*, but this is of no concern to us at the moment).

However, S can think$_2$ of a as non-existent, meaning that he is entitled to assume the *possibility of a's non-existence* (since a, as we have assumed, exists contingently, it could not have come into existence and it could also cease to exist).

It is different with entity b. If S understands (knows) that b exists and *how* it exists (i.e. necessarily), he cannot think$_1$ of b as non-existent for the same reason that he could not think$_1$ of a as non-existent. But neither is S entitled to think$_2$ of b as non-existent, since there is no point in assuming the possibility of b's non-existence. There is no such possibility, b existing necessarily by assumption.

We may conclude that as far as thinking$_1$ is concerned, there is no difference between the entities a and b, but they differ from each other with respect to thinking$_2$, and because of this difference *thinking$_1$ and understanding are not interchangeable*.

St. Anselm considers himself (as, according to him, everyone should) as existing contingently. He therefore can not think$_1$ of himself as non-existent, but he can certainly think$_2$ so. He is quite able to think (or believe), for example, that he is going to die tomorrow.

Thus Gaunilo's dilemma is dissolved: it is true that I can think of myself as non-existent, in spite of the fact that I *know* with absolute certainty that I exist. But there is no way of deriving from this my ability to think of God as non-existent. My existence is contingent, His is necessary, and that makes all the difference.

So far so good. However, the Fool's puzzle remains still unsolved.

Let us go back to the stage where we have pointed out that although the statement 'S understandt (knows) that so-and-so' entails the parallel statement 'S thinks that so-and-so', the converse does not hold: 'S thinks (believes) that so-and-so' does not entail 'S understands that so-and-so'. Thinking or believing alone does not entail understanding or knowledge. That is to say, S can think of something as existing without understanding (knowing) that it actually exists.

We shall now employ again the difference between contingent and necessary being. If a is a contingent entity, S can think of a as non-existent, whether he understands that a exists or not. But if b is a necessary entity, S can think of it as non-existent *only if* he does not know that b exists and how it exists. If he knows that, he can not think the non-existence of b.

This was precisely the situation of the Fool before he had entered the intellectual transaction with St. Anselm. Even if he accepted that 'God' meant that-than-which-nothing-greater-can-be-thought, it does not follow that he had understood what this entails regarding the existence and the mode of existence of God, and so it was still possible for him to think of God as non-existent. He may be a fool or a villain, so long as he had heard the words and grasped their meaning, but did not see what results from them by way of orderly reasoning, he could think of God as non-existent. As soon as he understood it, he would not be able to do so any longer.

With this the puzzle of the Fool's conduct was solved and the Proof completed. But another, probably unintended result was achieved: knowledge, including religious knowledge, emerged as independent of belief, meaning religious belief.

ENDNOTES

* I am indebted to the editor of this volume for his critical remarks which enabled me to improve my exposition.
1 For comparable divisions of St. Anselm's Proof see John Hick and Arthur C. McGill (eds.), *The Many-Faced Argument: Recent Studies in the Ontological Argument for the Existence of God* (1967), p. 4ff.; D. P. Henry, *Medieval Logic and Metaphysics: A Modern Introduction* (1972), p. 102ff. Henry's division would be highly recommendable, were it not for two shortcomings: (i) It leaves out Ch. 4 altogether, thereby obliterating the remarkable symmetry between parts I and II on one hand, and parts VII and VIII on the other; (ii) it fails to display the logical relations within the second half of Ch. 3.
2 St. Anselm, *Opera omnia*, ed. by F. S. Schmitt, Vol. I, p. 101 (quoted here from Charlsworth's translation, as in St. Anselm's *Proslogion*, 1965, p. 117).
3 *Opera omnia*, Vol. I, p. 104 (Charlsworth's translation, p. 121).
4 *ibid.*, quoted there from the Psalms, 14:1 and 53:2.
5 To reconstruct thus St. Anselm's reasoning is by now almost a commonplace among logicians dealing with it. Still, it is also quite common to make the *reductio* pattern dependent upon the assumption that St. Anselm "defines" God as that-than-which-nothing-greater-can-be-thought, which is, as I see it, a misinterpretation of the text.
6 Here I opt for the already traditional rendering of (6)−(8) and against Henry's version, according to which (*Medieval Logic* etc., p. 109ff.) we have to ascribe to St. Anselm a difference in meaning between "not possible to be thought not to be" and "to be necessarily". Cf. Norman Malcolm, "Anselm's Ontological Arguments", *The Philosophical Review*, 69 (1960), pp. 41−62 (Also in *The Many-Faced Argument*, pp. 301−320); Robert M. Adams, "The Logical Structure of St. Anselm's Arguments", *The Philosophical Review*, 80 (1971), pp. 28−54.
7 A noteworthy exception is Anselm Stolz. Cf. "Zur Theologie Anselms in Proslogion", *Catholica*, 2 (1933), pp. 1−21 (English translation in *The Many-Faced Argument*, pp. 183−206).
8 *Opera omnia*, Vol. I, p. 129.
9 *ibid.*, p. 133ff.

* * *

THE KIEFER ARGUMENT

Mylan R. Engel Jr. − Wolfgang L. Gombocz
University of Arizona, Tucson − Karl-Franzens-Universität, Graz

Theistic arguments from design have been thought by some to be quite convincing, but by others to be rather unconvincing. There is, however, one type of design argument which "has a peculiarly rational twist and which has, moreover, been hardly more than dimly perceived by most of those who have considered this subject"[1]. This sophisticated version of a teleological argument is to be attributed to James Kiefer and will accordingly be called the "Kiefer Argument". The main thrust of this argument lies in its asserting that *all people*, whether they know it or not, believe that their senses were *arranged* and *designed*. After pointing out this necessarily commonly held belief, the argument goes on to claim that this designer is God.

Since generally we think we know what we believe, one may be wondering how the Kiefer Argument can claim that we all believe the senses were designed, *whether we know it or not*. Admittedly, this claim seems *prima facie* counter-intuitive, but since "the idea we want to develop here is not easy to grasp without misunderstanding"[2], it is urged that one hold these intuitions in abeyance for the moment. In order to prevent such misunderstanding, one of Taylor's examples will now be presented as a means of setting the stage for the Kiefer Argument.

Suppose a stone were unearthed, and in addition to being almost perfectly rectangular, it was covered with cuts and scrapes. Suppose further that the cuts and scrapes remarkably resembled a rather primitive alphabet[3]. Now, one must admit that the scratches could have come about in a purely natural way without the aid of any ancient recorder's hand or chisel, e.g. they could have arisen as a result of glaciation. Even so, an archaeologist might be able to translate these scratches into a meaningful message, e.g. KIMON THE GREAT DIED HERE ON THE WAY TO ATHENS. If one were to believe that Kimon died here on the way to Athens *solely* on the basis of the stone, then one could not *consistently* believe that the marks on the stone arose naturally as a result of glaciation. The reason for this is: *If* one believes the marks convey a message about Kimon, then one *must* also believe that someone *made* the marks intending to convey a message about Kimon. Of course, it is certainly possible that the seemingly purposeful scratches did arise wholly accidentally, because "surely the mere fact that something has an interesting or striking shape or pattern and thus *seems* purposefully arranged is no proof that it is"[4]; but in the event that the scratches did arise accidentally, they could not count as *evidence* of Kimon's death or of anything else not related to themselves. They may serve as evidence of the glaciation which caused them, but they cannot count as evidence of anything wholly independent of themselves or their origins. The point of this example is: To count the scratches as a message is *ipso facto* to believe in a purposeful message-giver which intended to convey a message about Kimon.

According to the Kiefer Argument, this interesting feature of messages and the signs used to convey them is also applicable to the messages of the senses. Just as the scratches must have an arranger if they are to count as *evidence* of any true message not concerning themselves or their origins, so too must the senses have an arranger if they are to count as *evidence* of any true messages about the world. Of course, it is possible that the senses never convey any true messages, in which case no arranger or designer need be presupposed, but if one believes that the messages of the senses are true, one must also believe that *the senses were arranged* in such a way as to convey those messages. If one believes the senses were arranged, one must also believe they had an arranger. And if one believes in an arranger of the senses, then *a fortiori* one must believe that that arranger is capable of so arranging the senses. To arrange scratches on a stone is one thing; to arrange senses is quite another. Scratches can be arranged by human beings, but if the senses are arranged, they seem to require a higher being as their arranger. Thus, it seems natural to believe that a higher being *is* the arranger, given that one trusts the senses.

Of course, one does not have to believe the senses were arranged, any more than one has to believe the scratches were intentionally cut into the stone. It is indeed possible that the senses arose in an impersonal, nonpurposeful, wholly naturalistic manner, just as the scratches may have resulted from glaciation. But if one does believe that the senses arose accidentally in a purely naturalistic way, then one cannot consistently and/or rationally believe that the messages the senses give are true. However, if

> we do assume that they [the senses] are guides to some truths having nothing to do with themselves, then it is difficult to see how we can, consistently with that supposition, believe them to have arisen by accident, or by the ordinary workings of purposeless forces, even over ages of time[5] (brackets and their contents added).

The important point to be stressed now is that we do not simply marvel at the fact that the senses' messages are intelligible, but rather we *rely* on the senses as our *sole evidence* for discovering truths about the world which are wholly independent of the senses themselves. Since "it would be irrational for one to say *both* that his sensory and cognitive faculties had a natural, nonpurposeful origin and *also* that they reveal some truth with respect to something other than themselves"[6], and since we all hold that at least sometimes the senses are trustworthy and do reveal some truths with respect to things other than themselves, then if we are to be rational, we must believe, *whether we are aware of it or not*, that the senses arose in a non-natural, purposive manner, i.e. they were purposefully arranged by a very powerful arranger.

Presently one begins to feel the strength of the Kiefer Argument. Certainly, all of us on a large variety of occasions trust our senses to give us truths which are not related to the senses *per se*. Yet, this fact alone does not seem like it should be sufficient to compel us to believe in *God* as arranger. However, given our finding that we do presuppose a message-giver whenever we take something to be a truth-conveying message, how can we reconcile our taking the messages that the senses give to be true, while simultaneously denying that there is a sense arranger? This puzzle is what concerns the remainder of this paper, and unless it can be solved, one *must* accept the Kiefer conclusion which states that since we *rely* on the senses to give us true messages, we must *ipso facto* believe that God (or some mighty arranger) designed them.

Where the fallacy in the Kiefer Argument is (if there is one) is not immediately apparent. However, one point of contention is the presupposition that there is only one kind of message. The message of the scratches is a linguistic message, and consequently, the only reason it has any meaning at all is because it fits into a pre-established set of conventional rules, signs, and symbols. Suppose that the primitive alphabet had never been established. If this were the case, the stone would have failed to convey a message. It is only in light of a pre-existing primitive alphabet that the scratches have any meaning apart from themselves. We can refer to messages conveyed through languages as *conventional messages* and to the signs of these languages as *conventional signs*.

There are, however, clearly other kinds of signs besides conventional signs, e.g. *natural signs*. Suppose one is tracking a deer which one has wounded while hunting. The drops of blood on the ground are a rather reliable indicator that the wounded deer was where the drops are now. The deer does not *intend* to leave signs whereby the tracker can track it down. Rather, the signs are one-sided in that they can be interpreted by an interpreter, but were *not* given intentionally by a sign-giver. So, an essential difference between conventional signs and natural signs is that the former require a sign giver and, to be successful, a sign receiver, as well; while the latter only require a sign receiver or interpreter.

Does the finding of another type of sign defeat the Kiefer Argument? No, the Kiefer Argument obviously allows for the existence of natural signs. If the scratches were taken to be the result of glaciation, then by dating the stone a geologist could establish that glaciers moved through such and such a place at such and such a time. Thus, the stone would be a natural sign of glaciation. Note that natural signs never give any message unconnected with themselves or their origins. To view the stone as a natural sign of glaciation is to interpret something about the origin of its scratches. However, if the scratches are to tell us anything independent of themselves, they must be arranged, i.e. conventional signs. This is the point of the Kiefer Argument, and discovering that natural signs exist does not alone undermine it.

However, if the senses are more like natural signs than conventional signs, then this would undermine the Kiefer Argument. It is difficult to determine what kind of sign the senses are. They do seem to tell us truths which are wholly independent of themselves and their origins, e.g. that there is a dirty yellow wall in front of me, which while true, seems to be completely independent of my eyes (as organs) and of their origin (however it is that humans came to have eyes). So, *prima facie* it seems the senses function more like conventional signs in that they do give messages independent of themselves and their origins, and this only supports the Kiefer Argument so much more.

There does seem to be one clear difference between the marks on the stone and the senses. The senses are *directly* affected by those external things about which they supposedly give us true messages, e.g. my eyes are directly affected by the beautiful flower in front of them. The marks on the stone, on the other hand, are only *indirectly* affected by those things which they give us messages about. They are not directly affected by Kimon at all. They are only indirectly affected by Kimon through *direct* intervention by people *intending* to convey a truth about Kimon. More precisely, for the scratches to give a true message about Kimon, there must be an arranger truthfully connecting the message with what it is about. For the senses to give a true message, they must be directly affected by that about which they give the message. The senses as such give no messages. They only relay, i.e. pass along, how they are being affected. For my senses to give me a message about the dirty yellow wall in front of me, there must be a dirty yellow wall in front of me affecting my senses in a certain way (bracketing the hallucination case). But if the scratches give a message about themselves, e.g. "These scratches are in slate", they give that message, *not* because they are in slate, but because someone has arranged them to give that message. The scratches are *not* affected by their "being in slateness", whereas the senses are affected by the wall's "dirty yellowness". Although there is a difference here, it is not clear that this difference greatly weakens the Kiefer Argument.

Consider the scratches again. For the scratches to give a true message about Kimon, something, namely an arranger, must *tie* the scratches and Kimon together in a certain way. Are the senses so different? If the senses give a true message about a dirty yellow wall, is not something required to tie the senses to the wall? To simply say that the wall so affects the senses will not suffice without begging the question. In fact, this again might support the Kiefer Argument further, since merely affecting the senses gives no more *truth* to their messages than rain's affecting the stone does to the stone's message. The next move of Kiefer is to claim that if you believe the senses give *true* messages, then you must believe a mighty arranger arranged the senses to be affected in certain ways, *since without arrangement there are no true messages*.

This last move of the Kiefer arguer may be unjustified. Why this is the case will become apparent as the last and most plausible attack on the Kiefer Argument is made. Upon close reflection, it becomes apparent that the Kiefer Argument depends for its strength on the premise that the senses are *signs* of truths about the world. From whence comes the natural tendency to view senses as signs? This tendency comes from the fact that both senses and signs can be said to "convey messages". However, there are at least *two* ways to convey messages, and unsurprisingly, recognizing these ways helps distinguish signs and senses. Signs convey messages by being a direct source of the message. However, there is another way to convey a message, namely, to transmit or carry a message from one place to another. For example, a telephone can be said to convey messages from one person to another. The truth of the message is not affected by the telephone, but rather the message (one person speaking) affects the telephone in a certain way (it causes the phone to have certain electrical firings). Note: Although telephones definitely convey messages, they are in no way signs of any kind.

The senses seem to convey messages in a way much more similar to telephones than to scratches. The senses carry (transmit) messages only after something external has affected them. Signs, on the other hand, are *not* affected by what they convey a message about, but can be said to be the source of a message once they are interpreted. Senses, however, are not the source of any messages, but rather the messages affect the senses in a certain way (certain electrical firings, etc.). It is simply this process of *affecting* the senses which results in message transmission (message conveyance).

A Kiefer-type response might be that since telephones need designing so do the senses. However, that response greatly weakens the Kiefer Argument in two ways. First of all, it is to admit that there are at least two senses of the phrase 'convey a message' and thereby to admit that the senses are not signs, which is a premise necessary for the success of the Kiefer Argument. Secondly, not all sign and message processors are designed. For example, if a person puts a message in a bottle and casts it to sea, and it is found by someone else, then the sea "conveys the message" (carries the message) from one person to another; and to claim the sea is designed is a *petitio principii*. Another example of a natural message conveyer is air, which is the medium through which all our auditory messages are conveyed.

Having found the equivocation with regard to 'convey a message' may not completely defeat the Kiefer Argument, and neither may the discovery that the senses are not signs, but these two findings do provide a starting point for the eventual destruction of the Kiefer Argument. More work is needed to conclusively undermine the Kiefer Argument, and until this is done, the Kiefer Argument will remain a source of paradox which cuts deeply.

ENDNOTES

[1] Taylor, Richard, *Metaphysics* (Englewood Cliffs, New Jersey ³1983), p. 100. — This very first quote is given here in the wording of the second edition (1974), p. 114. All other quotations are from the third edition.
[2] Taylor (1983), p. 100.
[3] Taylor (1983), pp. 101–102.
[4] Taylor (1983), p. 101.
[5] Taylor (1983), p. 104.
[6] Taylor (1983), p. 104.

* * *

EVOLUTION UND SCHÖPFUNG: URSPRUNG DES UNIVERSUMS

Werner Leinfellner
University of Nebraska, Lincoln

1. Die evolutionäre Wende in der Physik

Die evolutionäre Wende in der Physik spielt sich heute in drei neuen „revolutionären" Theorien dieser ältesten europäischen Disziplin ab: 1. in den großen vereinheitlichenden Theorien der physikalischen Kräfte (Grand Unification Theories oder GUT), die die evolutionäre Entwicklung der vier heute existierenden Kräfte (Gravitation, Elektromagnetismus, starke und schwache Kräfte) aus einer einzigen, am Anfang des Universums existierenden Urkraft erklären; 2. in der Quantenchromodynamik (Quarktheorie), die den Aufbau aller Materien aus u- und d-Quarks und den Leptonen (z.B. Elektronen), sowie deren Transmutation ineinander (z.B.: Hadronen in Elektronen, vice versa) erklärt; und 3. in einer neuen evolutionären Kosmologie, die lückenlos darstellt, wie aus Energie die Quarks, die Kernpartikel, die Helium- und Wasserstoffatome, und aus diesen durch Kernfusion im Inneren der ersten Sterngeneration die Elemente bis Eisen entstanden. Nicht nur das, sie kann auch erklären, wie die Fusion der Elemente bis Uran in den Nova- und Supernovaexplosionen vor sich ging und wie aus dem ins All geschleuderten interstellaren Staub die zweite Sterngenerationen mit Planetensystemen, wie unser solares System, sich entwickelten, auf denen dann die biologische Evolution starten konnte, die bis zu den menschlichen Kulturen sich weiterfortsetzte (siehe Übersichtstafel 1). Was Mystiker von Pythagoras bis zu den heutigen, der indisch-chinesischen Mystik zugewandten Physikern[1] intuitiv erschauten, ist heute ein systematischer Zusammenhang von wissenschaftlichen Theorien gigantischen Ausmaßes geworden, der, auf die kürzeste Formel gebracht, besagt, daß, um die kleinsten uranfänglichen Einheiten des Mikrokosmos zu verstehen, man das Universum als Ganzes, den Makrokosmos, verstehen muß, vice versa.

Die evolutionäre Wende in der Physik ist also eine geschichtliche Erklärung einer Selbstschöpfung, die das erste Mal lückenlos eine theoretische Begründung bringt, wie das Universum aus einem anfänglichen Gleichgewichtszustand höchster Symmetrie sich in das höchst komplexe, asymmetrische Universum von heute durch periodenweisen Zusammenbruch der ursprünglichen Symmetrie der Strukturen entwickelte. In diesem Artikel wird nun versucht, die Grundprinzipien der GUT-Theorien, der Quantenchromodynamik und der evolutionären Kosmologie zusammenzufassen und mit den Grundprinzipien der biologischen Evolution zu vergleichen. Evolution als eine komplexe Funktion f, die auf der Einwirkung von Zufallsereignissen der Ekosysteme E auf die evolvierenden Systeme S beruht, besteht aus zeitabhängigen Trajektorien (evolutionäre Entwicklung der Systeme), $\dot{S} = f(S,E)$. Im Gegensatz zur traditionellen Ansicht soll aber die Entwicklung g der Ekosysteme $\dot{E}$ nicht nur von den zeitlich vorangehenden Zuständen E der Ekosysteme abhängen, $\dot{E} = g (E)$, sondern, wie Lewontin richtig bemerkte,[2] soll eine gegenseitige funktionale Abhängigkeit g von S und E die Entwicklung der Ekosysteme selbst steuern, d.h., $\dot{E} = g (S,E)$ soll gelten. Evolvierende Systeme S und die Ekosysteme beeinflussen sich gegenseitig im Verlaufe der Evolution und zwar so, daß die Schöpfung von neuen „Materienarten" eine zeitlich ablaufende Realisation (f) von unter bestimmten Umweltbedingungen E_i, während einer Zeitperiode Δt_i, evolutionär stabilen Systemen ist. Ändern sich die Umweltbedingungen von z.B. E_i zu E_j (siehe Tabelle 1), dann ändert sich auch die Stabilität der evolvierenden Systeme, d.h. eine ganz neue Art von Materie entsteht (S_j), unter dem Selektionsdruck der neuen Umwelt (E_j), eine Art, die besser angepaßt, d.h. evolutionär stabil unter E_j ist. Besser angepaßt heißt in der frühen Evolution des Kosmos: im thermodynamischen Gleichgewicht mit der veränderten Umwelt (E_j) befindlich.

Ein Beispiel, wie vom Makrokosmos her der Mikrokosmos verstanden werden kann, ist das Quarkparadox. Darunter versteht man einfach, daß es heute nicht (mehr) möglich ist, die Existenz von Quarks nachzuweisen. Kann man also von etwas behaupten, daß es existiert, wenn man seine Existenz nicht nachweisen kann? Das Paradox löste sich auf, als man herausfand, daß die Quarks nur unter den hochenergetischen Umweltsbedingungen der ersten drei Epochen $E_1 \rightarrow E_3$ als freie Teilchen existierten oder, wie man sagt, evolutionär stabil waren, diese evolutionäre Stabilität aber beim Abkühlen des Kosmos, der Ekosysteme, unter $10^{13°}$ C verloren. Doch erlangten sie bis heute eine neue geschützte „Lebensform", eine Nische „eingefroren in den Kernpartikeln", den Hadronen (Neutronen, Protonen und den Mesonen). Nach Salam, Weinberg, Fritzsch, Trefil[3] erzwangen die selektiven Umweltveränderungen (Temperaturabfall und Expansion) des frühen Universums eine neue Existenzform der Quarks „in der Gefangenschaft der Kernpartikel", wo sie ähnliche Bedingungen wie im freien Zustand vor der Periode 3 fanden. Man kann hier von der „ökologischen Nische" und dem „Sterben" der Quarks als freie Teilchen in Analogie zur biologischen Evolution sprechen, in der Arten aussterben und dem Überleben von neuen, besser angepaßten Arten Platz machen. Die Quarks „überlebten" in den Kernteilchen durch eine Art unzertrennlicher Kooperation, die erklärt, warum sie nicht mehr frei existieren, und zugleich auch, warum die aus u- und d-Quarks bestehende Materie so stabil ist. Ähnlich wie Flüssigkeitsmoleküle beim Auskristallisieren ihre Bewegungsfreiheit verlieren, so sind die Quarks ab der dritten Periode (E_3) durch die starken Kernkräfte in einem Gleichgewicht innerhalb der Kernpartikel gehalten, gehören zu einer Kategorie von Mikropartikeln, die ganz und gar nicht den Atomen ähneln, sondern vielmehr den Zellbestandteilen oder den menschlichen Organen. Auch diese waren in frühen Stadien der Evolution frei existierend, verloren ihre Freiheit aber zu Gunsten einer Kooperation innerhalb von neuen Supersystemen, wie Zelle, Organismus, innerhalb derer sie nun weiterexistieren − aber nicht mehr im freien Zustand, (Vergleiche hiezu auch die Darstellungen der Rolle von kompetitiven und kooperativen Stadien der biologischen Evolution bei Leinfellner 1983[4].)

Ganz ähnlich liegen die Verhältnisse bei der evolutionären Isolierung und Aufspaltung der kosmischen Urkraft in die heute vorhandenen vier Kräfte, Gravitation, Elektromagnetismus, starke und schwache Kräfte durch plötzliche Symmetriebrüche nach der 1., 2. und 3. Periode (siehe Tabelle 1). Trotz des schwer verständlichen mathematischen Apparates aller dieser Theorien haben sie durch die Verschmelzung von Makro- und Mikrotheorien und durch ihre strukturalistische Natur, d.h. durch Behandlung von allgemeinsten Strukturen der Energie und der Materie, ihres fließenden Gleichgewichtes, ihrer Symmetriesprünge und evolutionären Trajektorien einen Begriffsapparat geschaffen, der auch den Nichtphysiker zu einem geistigen Überschauen der geschichtlichen Abläufe verhilft, die eigentlich unsere Geschichte ist. Die Funktion dieser Theorien wird damit wieder THEORIA (θεωρία), eine Weltansicht und ein Überschauen einer Entwicklung, die uns erklärt, warum wir hier in diesem Universum sind.

2. Wiederholung der Schöpfung und Retrodiktion

Die nächste Frage, die sich hier unwillkürlich aufdrängt, ist die der empirischen Bestätigbarkeit von geschichtlichen Vorgängen 15 Milliarden Jahren vorher. Wer hat denn die Umwandlung von Quarks in Leptonen (z.B. Elektronen) − so könnte man naiv fragen − je beobachtet? Nun kann man aber heute in den Riesenbeschleunigern energetische Zustände, wie sie einst z.B. nach der Periode 3 existierten, wieder erstehen lassen, verwirklichen. Man kann also die Umwelt, die damals herrschte, sozusagen in Miniatur wiederholen und die Reaktionen, wie sie damals abliefen, experimentell beobachten. Diese technische Realisierung z.B. von Partikelerzeugung wie von W und Z Vektor-Bosonen, die ja Elektromagnetismus und schwache Kräfte zu einer Kraft reduzieren, ist einfach die Realisation von kosmischen Umweltsbedingungen und ihrer „selektiven Auslese", wie sie einmal in E_3 geherrscht hatten. Sie ist nicht eine Nachschöpfung oder Simulation, sondern einfach Schöpfung „en miniature". So war die Erzeugung von W und Z Bosons (Teilchen) in Genfs CERN-Beschleuniger durch eine Energie von 540 GeV die Schöpfung von Reaktionen, wie sie $10^{-10}-10^{-5}$ Sekunden nach dem Urknall herrschten. Es bedarf natürlich heute dieser gigantischen Energiebeschleuniger, um Partikel zu erzeugen, die diese Energie in einer Umwelt, angeheizt auf 10^{13} °C, auf natürliche Weise besaßen. Nur unter diesen Umständen konnte der empirische Nachweis erbracht werden, daß elektromagnetische und schwache Kräfte eins waren, denn man kann „künstlich", experimentell heute beobachten, wie durch die intermediären Vektorbosonen W,Z — die eigentlich „erschaffenen", bzw. entdeckten Teilchen — sich Elektronen aus der Leptonenfamilie in Quarks und elementare Kernpartikel umwandelten, vice versa. Es ist für die Plausibilität und Durchschlagskraft der neuen Kosmologie unerläßlich und unbedingt wichtig, daß sie experimentell wiederholt werden kann. Man muß hier trotz des so rasanten Fortschritt der „Schöpfungsmaschinen" die Schwierigkeiten berücksichtigen, dem Punkte 0 der Schöpfung immer näher und näher zu kommen. Das Fermilab in Chicago wird Partikel bis zu 1000 GeV, das Soviet-Synchroton bis zu 6 Billionen EV und das geplante Desotron in den USA bis zu 20 Billionen EV erzeugen können. Allerdings müßte ein Beschleuniger, der Partikel der Planckzeit wieder ins Leben ruft ($0-10^{-43}$ Sekunden) von der Erde bis zum nächsten Fixstern, α-Centauri, reichen, wenn nicht neuartigere Methoden zur Erzeugung hochenergetischer Zustände erfunden werden. Der Griff zurück und damit die Plausibilität, sowie der Glaube an die neue evolutionäre Kosmologie werden außerdem durch Riesenteleskope und Radioastronomie, die bereits 18 Milliarden Jahre „zurücksehen", erhärtet, und die Tatsache, daß die von A. Penzias und R. Wilson entdeckte Hintergrundstrahlung von 7.37 cm und einer Energie von nur 0.00002 EV tatsächlich sozusagen das Echo des Urknalls ist (für dessen Entdeckung sie den Nobelpreis erhielten), macht die neue Kosmologie zum ersten Male empirisch bestätigbar. Es sind die empirischen Bestätigungen der evolutionären Theorien des Kosmos, die sie im Bewußtsein der Menschen zu weit mehr als nur zu einem neuen wissenschaftlichen Schöpfungsmythos von morgen machen, der nach und nach alle anderen zu verdrängen scheint.

3. Vom Urknall zum Zerfall: Endlichkeit des Universums

Was Fritzsch, Weinberg, Trefil und die Mehrheit der neuen evolutionären Kosmologen vertreten, ist eine neue Kosmologie, die im Begriffe ist, die heutige theologische christliche Kosmologie abzulösen. Die wissenschaftlich empirischen Argumente sind überwältigend und haben einen noch nie dagewesenen Einfluß auf die Kultur unserer Zeit. Dazu kommt, daß die Widersprüche der Big-Bang Theorie Gamovs von der neuen „Inflationären Evolutionstheorie" aufgelöst wurden. Die alte Urknalltheorie, basierend auf Hubbles Gesetz der Expansion des Universums, gestattete einesteils, den Film der Expansion theoretisch zurückzudrehen; was aber empirisch in den ersten Bruchteilen von Nanosekunden sich ereignete, blieb ein Mysterium. Mit der neuen „Inflationären Theorie" wurde eine brillante Kosmologie geboren, nach der in den ersten Bruchteilen von Nanosekunden das Universum durch eine sehr kurze, aber äußerst schnelle Ausdehnungsperiode ging, in der unter dem Einfluß von Zufallsfaktoren sozusagen die Weichen für die spätere Evolution gestellt wurden und in der die Naturkonstanten entstanden, die auch den heutigen Kosmos charakterisieren. Erst danach wurde die Ausdehnungsrate konstant und erreichte die Hubble'schen Werte. Die Theorie der ersten inflationären Phase führte zu überraschenden Ergebnissen der neuen Kosmologie. Infolge der Rauminflation und durch den selektiven Einfluß der Umwelt, d.h. durch das einfrierende Absinken der Temperatur bzw. der heute zur Beschreibung des Energiehaushaltes übliche Giga-Elektronen-Volt (siehe Tabelle 1) entwickelten sich die vier heutigen Kräfte aus einer einzigen kosmischen Urkraft. Nur diese unglaublich kurze Instabilitätsperiode, vergleichbar mit einer rapide um sich greifenden Mutation, kann die spätere Galaxienbildung und die heutige Komplexität des Kosmos erklären. Ob nun 1. das Universum offen, d.h. die Evolution aus einem einzigen unwiederholbaren Urknall erfolgte, oder, ob es 2. oszilliert und nach ca. 20 Milliarden Jahren sich zusammenzieht, oder ob 3. die Kosmologie der schwarzen Löcher, nach der der Zerfall in den zentralen schwarzen Löchern der Galaxien bereits begonnen hat, die richtige Theorie ist, alles das ändert nichts an der Finitheit dieses Universums, in dem es keine Unsterblichkeit gibt. Auch Protonen leben nur 10^{31} Jahre, Atome besitzen ebenfalls nur eine evolutionäre Stabilität, sie haben nur eine relative Lebensdauer bezüglich bestimmter Umweltsbedingungen. Die Evolution in einem offenen Universum (Fall 1, Tab. 1, 12), das bisher als unendlich angesehen wurde, führt aber auch unweigerlich zu einem Ende, zu einem immer kälter werdenden Universum, erfüllt schließlich nur noch mit strahlender Energie, Photonen. Was für ein Fall nun tatsächlich zutreffen wird, hängt von der genaueren Bestimmung der kritischen Masse des Universums ab.

Neuere Schätzungen der Neutronenmassen über 50 EV und unter Einbeziehung der dunklen Massen der schwarzen Löcher ergeben eine kritische Massendichte, die tatsächlich zur Bremsung der heutigen Expansion des Kosmos führen würde. In diesem (Fall 2, Tab. 1, 11) des geschlossenen Universums würde es nach ca. 10^{12} Jahren nach dem Urknall zu einem Zusammenfall der Galaxien kommen und alle Epochen der kosmischen Entwicklung würden dann umgekehrt durchlaufen werden. Wiederum werden dann die letzten 10^{-43} Sekunden entscheidend werden. Zieht sich das ganze Universum auf eine Singularität zusammen, in der Raum, Zeit und Materie nicht mehr existieren, die Evolution sozusagen stille steht, oder bildet sich ein neuer Zyklus mit einem Überschuß von Quarks in der 3. Periode unter $10^{28°}$ C, der dann zur nochmaligen Bildung von Atomen, Sternen, Galaxien und Leben führt, das alles bleibt offen, übrig bleibt nur noch die Finitheit des Universums, in dem wir leben.

Fest steht damit auch die Endlichkeit, die evolutionär bedingte relative Lebensdauer von allen noch so stabil und für die Ewigkeit geschaffen zu scheinenden Strukturen und Systemen.

4. Die kosmische Evolution und die Rolle der evolutionären Stabilität

Versteht man unter Evolution eine sich selbst verbessernde Anpassung an jeweilige Ekosysteme E mit dem Resultat, die Stabilität der angepaßten Systeme S zu optimieren, als auch eventuell zu Veränderungen des Ekosystems selbst zu führen, $\dot{S} = f(S,E)$ und $\dot{E} = g(S,E)$, dann gibt es eine physikalische Evolution für Quarks, Kernpartikel, Atomkerne, Atome, Sterne, Galaxien. Symmetriebrüche führen von einfachen zu komplexeren Systemen im Falle des Abkühlens des Universums, und von komplexeren zu einfacheren im Falle der Erhitzung des Unversums, Betachtet man die an die Umgebung, Ekosystem E_j sich anpassende Produktion von evolutionär invarianten oder stabilen, einfachen Systemen S_i zu immer komplexeren, an das Ekosystem E_j sich anpassenden Systemen S_j, wobei die S_i-Systeme „aussterben" oder in „Nischen", d.h. in stabilen Partial-Ekosystemen (PS) weiterexistieren, dann kommt man zu einem hierarchischen Aufbau des Kosmos als eine in finiter Zeit durchlaufende Evolution. Die Aussonderung der starken Kräfte aus der kosmischen Urkraft als Anpassung an das sich neu bildende Ekosystem E_2, die Separierung der schwachen Kräfte durch die Veränderung des Ekosystems E_2 zum kosmischen Ekosystem 3 und schließlich die Ausscheidung und das Einfrieren der elektro-magnetischen Kräfte durch Änderung von E_3 zu E_4 sind solche evolutionär-selektive Anpassungen. Man darf aber nicht vergessen, daß durch die Schöpfung (Evolution) neuer Systeme (S_i zu S_j) auch die Umgebungssysteme sich ändern (E_i zu E_j), gemäß den Trajektorengleichungen: $\dot{S} = f(S,E)$ und $\dot{E} = g(S,E)$.

Die ab E_5 erfolgende Evolution der Materie beginnt mit weiterer Anpassung an sinkende Temperatur und abnehmende Energie der Partikel. Einfrieren der Quarks in einer Nische, den elementaren Partikeln, erfolgt dadurch, daß die starken Kräfte, die die Quarks in Hadronen und Mesonen zusammenhalten, sich selektiv unter Veränderung des kosmischen Ekosystems von E_4 zu E_5 bilden. In dieser Form, im „Nukleonengefängnis", erweisen sie sich evolutionär stabil, aber nicht mehr als freie Quarks, wie sie noch in E_4 existieren konnten. Das Quarksterben, wie es in der kosmophysikalischen Literatur genannt wird, ist nur mit dem Aussterben z.B. von freien Zellbestandteilen (Mitochondrien, Nuclei, Ribosomen, Chloroplasten) als freie Teilchen und ihrem Fortbestehen in der Symbiose der Zelle vergleichbar, ein Zusammenschluß, aus dem die vielleicht wichtigste Einheit des Lebens, die Zelle, entstand.

Das Ausfrieren der Materie – im Übergang von E_4 zu E_5 – geht evolutionär weiter, wenn Nukleonen entstehen und stabil in E_5 bleiben. Man sieht hier deutlich, daß „evolutionär stabil" bedeutet, daß ein System S_i stabil nur innerhalb des Ekosystems E_i ist. Solange die Bedingungen des Ekosystems E_i existieren, solange bleibt auch S_i stabil. Der Übergang von E_6 zu E_7 löst die Schöpfung von Helium und Wasserstoff aus, macht das Universum lichtdurchlässig, und die Formierung von Sternen der ersten Generation kann beginnen. Die heutigen Kräfte, die die Materie zusammenhalten, bestehen sozusagen ab E_4 nur in Nischen oder Partial-Ekosystemen getrennt weiter; die Quarks werden von den starken Kräften in den Hadronen und Mesonen zusammengehalten, haben dort ihre Nische gefunden; die elektromagnetischen Kräfte binden die Quarks und die Elektronen in den Atomen zusammen, und die schwachen und die Gravitationskräfte, die für alle Teilchen relevant sind, haben sich ebenfalls genau so evolutionär entwickelt, wie die Materie, die aus u- und d-Quarks sich selektiv entwickelt hat. Quarks, Nukleonen (Proton, Neutron), Atomkerne, Atome, Sterne, Moloküle, Galaxien und schließlich und endlch die lebendigen Systeme sind die in den verschiedenen Epochen sich evolutionär entwickelnden invarianten oder evolutionär stabilen makroskopischen Strukturen von immer größerem Komplexitätsgrad. Aber: evolutionär stabil sind auch die in bestimmten geschützten Ekosystemen lange Zeit überlebenden (stabilen) Strukturen. Nur in einem relativ erkalteten Universum konnten sich evolutionäre, komplexe makroskopische Strukturen (Systeme) entwickeln, wie Galaxien, Planetensysteme und lebendige, sich selbst vermehrende, evolutionär stabile Arten. Evolutionär stabil oder invariant heißt nicht für alle Ewigkeit stabil, sondern in bestimmten Ekosystemen und unter deren speziellen Bedingungen stabil. So wird heute auch das Proton als evolutionär stabil angesehen, denn es „lebt" nicht ewig, trotz des für uns eine Ewigkeit bedeutenden Alters von 10^{31} Jahren.

Wenn man fragt, wieso und warum die Entwicklungsphasen so und nicht anders verlaufen sind, warum z.B. die Evolution der Atome nicht beim Wasserstoff und Helium stehen blieb, sondern sich durch Ausbrennen in den Sternen der 1. Generation bis zum Element Eisen weiterentwickelten, oder warum ausgerechnet Nova- und Supernova-Explosionen die Schöpfung der Elemente bis zum Uran weiterforttrieben, aus denen allein die zweite Sterngeneration mit Planeten und Leben sich entwickeln konnten, oder warum ein Überschuß von Materie über Antimaterie existiert, dann muß man heute zu den Zufallsentwicklungen des allerjüngsten Universums, das erst 10^{-35} Sekunden alt war, zurückgreifen, d.h. also zu einer Periode, als das Einfrieren und die Separierung der fundamentalen Kräfte begann. In der frühen inflationistischen Periode spielten Zufallsabweichungen die Rolle einer Art von Mutationen. Die ersten Ansätze zur Bildung von Galaxien durch magnetische Monopole, d.h. von Partikeln, die das Äquivalent eines isolierten Nord- oder Südpoles sind, eine schwere Masse von 10^{16} GeV besitzen, und in der Lage sind, Leptonen in Quarks zu verwandeln, erfolgten hier, Punkt –, kettenförmige und raumartige Anordnungen von Mikropartikeln, Zufallsabweichungen von der Homogenität der expandierenden Masse bilden die Kondensationskerne für die Formierung von Galaxien 500.000 Jahre später.[6] Defekte dieser Art sind Ansätze zu neuen Strukturen, wenn und nur wenn der Selektionsdruck des neuen kosmischen Ekosystems ihre Entwicklung gestattet. Man muß sich aber sofort fragen, woher diese Zufallseinwirkungen denn tatsächlich kamen. Die Beantwortung dieser Frage führt zum nächsten Punkt, 5.

5. Allzusammenhangsthese als Konsequenz der neuen Kosmologie?

Kurz ausgedrückt besagt sie, daß in jedem Zustand des Universums, in jeder Epoche ein Allzusammenhang alles Geschehens, der sich entwickelnden Systeme und der Ekosysteme besteht. Nichts kann außerhalb dieses Zusammenhanges liegen, es gibt keine „externen" Kräfte mehr. In der Relativitätstheorie ist dies Prinzip klar damit ausgedrückt, daß, wo Materie, Raum und Zeit sind nichts außerhalb ist. In biologischen Evolutionstheorien ist es der gegenseitige Einfluß von sich entwickelndem System und Ekosystem, z.B. der Allzusammenhang alles Lebens im System Erde, vice versa. Dieser Allzusammenhang ist nun nichts anderes als das allem Geschehen zugrundeliegende dynamisch fluktuierende statistische Kausalfeld, bzw. -netz (siehe Leinfellner 1978, 1982).[7] Jedes Ereignis gehört einem lokalen, dieses einem globalen, letzteres einem planetaren Netzwerk etc. an, d.h. ist von unzähligen Partialursachen des Feldes mit verschiedenen Gewichten verursacht. Infolge der Unschärferelation ist es nun unmöglich, alle Partialursachen einzeln in einem deterministischen Sinne zu erfassen oder anzuführen. Es ist in indeterministischen Theorien, die z.B. nur ein Gruppenverhalten, aber nicht ein ein-deutiges Verhalten von Einzelindividuen vorhersagen, auch garnicht notwendig, alle Partialursachen im Detail anzugeben. Jede dieser Partialursachen fluktuiert in ihrem Gewicht, d.h. in ihrem Wahrscheinlichkeitsmaß. Jedes, von unzähligen Partialursachen bedingte Ereignis, von dem man weder die Gewichtung infolge seiner Fluktuation, d.h. Abhängigkeit von Partial-Partialursachen angeben kann, noch eine vollständige Liste derselben, ist ein Zufallsereignis. Das einfachste Beispiel ist Würfeln. Jederzeit kann nun z.B. eine Partialursache ihr Gewicht verändern, stärker, schwächer werden, sie kann wie eine Mutation dem Selektionsdruck unterliegen oder ihn optimal ausschalten. Zufallsereignisse sind undenkbar ohne das zugrundeliegende Kausalfeld, dessen Aktivität direkt proportional der Temperatur einer Periode, bzw. dem Energiegehalt der Teilchen einer Anfangsperiode ist.

Man kann daher auch die hier benutzte holistisch ontologische Definition von Zufallsereignissen als eine Variante des Bellschen Theorems ansehen, oder kann das zugrundeliegende Kausalfeld als das Spannungsfeld zwischen Exergie und Energie auffassen,[9] oder zwischen entropischen Ekosystemen und negentropischen Evolutionssystemen. Zwischen Chaos und absoluter Ordnung liegt aber das Produkt beider, die invarianten oder evolutionär stabilen Systeme.

Die Evolution des Kosmos ist daher der immerwährende selektive Einfluß eines entropischen, allumfassenden kosmischen Ekosystems auf relativ geordnete, d.h. evolutionär stabile Strukturen von Systemen komplexer höherer Entwicklungsstufe. Diese können den störenden Einfluß des fluktuierenden Kausalfeldes und seiner Zufallsereignisse paralysieren, aber nicht stoppen. Evolutionär stabile Strukturen können z.B. durch die in den SU(5) oder SU(10) festgelegten Symmetriebedingungen definiert werden, die bei etwa 10^{15} GeV den Unterschied zwischen Leptonen und Quarks durch die X-Teilchenwechselwirkung aufheben. Erhaltungsgesetze für Ladung etc., Oktettformation in Molekülen legen evolutionär stabile Strukturen in bestimmten Umwelts-, bzw. Ekosystemen etc. fest, die eine relative Stabilität oder invariantes Verhalten von Systemen in bestimmten Ekosystemen E_i definieren. Es ist damit klar geworden, daß die Allzusammenhangsthese, genau so wie Bells Theorem aus der Quantentheorie, hier aus der Evolutionstheorie folgen muß.

6. Relative Existenz als Folge der evolutionären Kosmologie

Die Produkte jedes evolutionären Prozesses sind relativ stabile, eine bestimmte Zeitdauer invariant bleibende und für eine bestimmte Nische, Ekosystem E_i optimal angepaßte Strukturen S_i. Die für ein Ekosystem E_i stabilen Strukturen S_i entsprechen in der Darwinschen Theorie genau dem "survival of the fitting". Da aber das fluktuierende zugrundeliegende Kausalfeld niemals zur Ruhe kommt, schon wegen des immer vorhandenen Entropie-Anstieges, "zerbrechen" die vormals stabilen Strukturen, es kommt nach Trefil zu "symmetry breaks" und neue, durch den Temperaturabstieg verursachte, evolutionär stabile Systeme, bzw. Strukturen treten auf. Die Gesamtheit der Veränderungen und der Zufallseinwirkung stellt den Evolutionsgenerator dar. Evolutionär invariant heißt nur, daß über einen gewissen Zeitraum hinsichtlich eines Ekosystems oder Nische relativ unveränderliche dynamische Strukturen existieren oder, wie in lebendigen Species, sich relativ invariant reproduzieren. "Relativ" bedeutet hier z.B.: trotz einer durch Mutationen hervorgerufenen minimalen Fehlerquote von $1:10^{11}$ in der menschlichen Zellreproduktion. Relativ oder evolutionär stabil sind z.B. die Symmetriebedingungen der Quantenchromodynamik (SU(5) und SU(10) Symmetrie), die seit Weyl "Invarianztheorien" genannt werden, weil gewisse Symmetriebedingungen bei der Schaffung von Elementarteilchen, unter Erhaltung von Energie, als invariant bezeichnet werden können. Erhaltungsgesetze, wie das TCP-Theorem sind Invarianzen für bestimmte Systeme S_i in bestimmten Ekosystemen E_i. Eventuell auftretende Verletzung der Erhaltung der Energie kann infolge der Unschärferelation nur sehr sehr kurz, unter 10^{-23} Sekunden sein. Weitere Invarianzen (evolutionäre Stabilitäten) sind der Durchmesser des Elektrons = 10^{-7} cm), Farblosigkeit der u-, d-Quarks in den Mesonen, Baryonen. In der SU(5)-Theorie Howards, Georgis und Sheldons Glashows, für die letzterer den Nobelpreis 1979 erhielt, kann man die invariante Symmetrie zwischen Leptonen und Quarks einfach darstellen:

Tabelle 2 $\qquad v e = u_r \, u_g \, u_B$

$\qquad\qquad\qquad \bar{e} = d_r \, d_g \, d_b \, ,$

wobei r, g, b, für rot, grün und blau steht. Für diese acht Teilchen besteht folgende Invarianz: die Summe aller elektrischen Ladungen der „Familie" Lepton-Quark verschwindet:

$$0 \qquad 2/3 \qquad 2/3 \qquad 2/3$$

$$-1 \qquad -1/3 \qquad -1/3 \qquad -1/3.$$

Die Summe der Ladungen ist null, weil die Leptonen und Quarks durch ein invariantes Symmetrieprinzip miteinander verwandt sind. Sie sind in der SU(5)-Theorie nun nichts anderes als verschiedene Manifestationen desselben Urbestandteiles, d.h. desselben einzigen Urteilchens unter der Ekobedingung von 10^{15} GeV und einem Abstand von 10^{-29} cm. Unter diesen Bedingungen sind keine Unterschiede zwischen der Farbkraft und der elektromagnetischen mehr vorhanden (siehe Periode 3). Diese Wechselwirkung oder Umwandlung von Quarks in Elektronen d.h. das Verschwinden des Unterschieds zwischen Elektromagnetismus und den schwachen Kräften geht durch Austausch eines X-Teilchens vor sich. Da diese Umwandlung erst bei einer Teilchenmenge von 10^{15} EeV, die heute noch nicht in den Schöpfungsmaschinen, den Beschleunigern, erreicht werden kann, erfolgt, so haben notgedrungen die Physiker nach einer anderen, „indirekten" Bestätigung der SU(5)- und auch der SU(10) − Theorie gesucht. Da das Proton- bis jetzt als ein mit unendlicher Lebensdauer angesehenes Teilchen − aus drei Quarks besteht, so könnten sich diese einmal infolge der Unschärfe, d.h. von Zufallsstreuung, gefährlich nahe kommen. Normalerweise haben sie im Proton einen Abstand von 10^{-14} cm. Bringt aber der Zufall sie doch einmal auf 10^{-29} cm zusammen, dann müßte eines der Quarks „mutieren", d.h. sich in ein Positron, Mitglied der Leptonfamilie, verwandeln und damit auch die Existenz des Quarks und des Protons beenden. Die Wahrscheinlichkeit dieses Ereignisses liegt bei $1:10^{31}$, und daher kann das Proton, das man bis jetzt als „ewigen" Grundbaustein der Materie ansah, auch nur eine Lebensdauer von 10^{31} Jahren besitzen. Daraus folgt, daß in einer Masse von 17 Tonnen Wasser, die 10^{31} Protonen enthalten, man einen Zerfall pro Jahr beobachten könnte. Dieser Protonenzerfall, $p \rightarrow e^+ + \pi^o$ (p = Proton, e^+ = Positron, π^o = o−Pion), den Physiker und Astronomen seit Jahren in USA, Deutschland, Sowjet-Union, Frankreich nachjagen, wird ein Experimentum Crucis für die Ehe von Partikelphysik und neuer Kosmologie werden. Sein experimenteller Nachweis würde erweisen, daß Protonen und damit alle Atomkerne, kurz, die Materie, nicht ewig, daß auch sie nur evolutionär stabil oder evolutionär invariant sind. Auch Protonen „sterben", wie 90% aller Arten, die einst die Erde bevölkerten, die einen früher, die anderen später ausgestorben sind. Sterben sie, dann wurden sie auch einmal geboren und damit ist die physikalische Evolution Hauptidee der neuen Kosmologie geworden.

Chemische Moleküle (Strukturen) bilden keine Ausnahme, nur sind ihre Lebenszeiten, wenn sie nicht in künstlich stabilen Ekosystemen aufbewahrt werden, ungleich kürzer. Die berühmten Oktettformationen chemischer Elemente und Moleküle zeichnen sich durch evolutionäre Stabilität aus, die natürlich wie alle evolutionäre Stabilität statistischen Charakters ist. Schließlich und endlich sind lebendige, sich selbst vermehrende Lebewesen Art-invariant, oder, wie die Biologen es bezeichnen, evolutionär stabil. Die von Maynard-Smith eingeführte evolutionäre Stabilität der Arten gegenüber Mutanten in kleiner Zahl und relativ kleinen Änderungen des Ekosystems, d.h. der selektiven Einwirkung des Ekosystems, beruht auf der Annahme, daß evolutionär stabile Systeme das komplexe Produkt der Interaktion zwischen Ekosystemen und den Systemen, gemäß $g = E.E + 2ES + S.S$ oder $E^2 + 2ES + S^2$ sind, d.h. die Summe der Veränderungen innerhalb des Ekosystems $= E^2 +$ der Interaktion ES und SE plus der internen Änderungen $= S^2$.

Eine eingehende Darstellung der statistischen Invarianzthese für die Erkenntnistheorie, Wissenschaftstheorie, Semantik und Systemtheorie, die eine Verallgemeinerung der hier benützten evolutionären Stabilität ist, findet sich bei Leinfellner E. und Leinfellner W. (1978).[8]

7. Informationsthese.

Eng verbunden mit der Invarianzthese ist die Informationsthese. Wenn ein System evolutionär stabil wird, dann kann dieser Zustand als eine Art Informationsspeicherung der optimalen Strukturen S_i bezüglich E_i ($S_i \varepsilon E_i$) angesehen werden. Evolutionär stabil heißt: über eine gewisse Zeitspanne $\triangle t$ und hinsichtlich eines bestimmten Ekosystems E_i stabil. Informationsspeicherung und evolutionäre Stabilität sind natürlich keine anthropomorphen Kategorien; sie haben nichts mit Bewußtsein zu tun, man kann aber einfach sagen, daß ein Partikel der SU(5)-Familie die physikalische Möglichkeit besitzt, sich in ein anderes, in der Tabelle 2 angeführtes Partikel, gegeben die Umstände in E_i, zu verwandeln. Man kann aber nicht sagen, daß ein Photon in einem Stern-Gerlach-Zerfall sich an das andere Photon erinnert, wie dies heute öfters ausgedrückt wird. Information ist auf dieser Stufe nichts anderes, als die Möglichkeit zu besitzen, auf bestimmte invariante oder evolutionär stabile Art zu reagieren. Wenn man Invarianz sprachlich mathematisch ausdrückt, kommt natürlich sofort der durch Erkenntnis gewonnene, präzisierte Informationsinhalt uns ins Bewußtsein. Doch dies ist nur die anthropomorphe Seite der Information, objektiv realistisch ist sie invariante Struktur, Möglichkeit, in einer bestimmten statistisch invarianten Art und Weise zu reagieren. Chemische Systeme im Gleichgewicht oder auch ein Pseudogleichgewicht, das sich immer wieder einspielt, ceteris paribus, sind wirkliche Informationsträger für uns, Informationsträger eines evolutionär stabilen Ablaufs. Als sich in der Schöpfungsphase 2 aus reiner Energie die ersten elementaren Teilchen formten, existierten Quarks nur in der relativ kurzen Zeitperiode von 10^{-43} bis 10^{-33} Sekunden in der Form von freien Teilchen. Beim Übergang $E_3 \rightarrow E_4$ änderten sie ihre freie Stabilität zu einer evolutionär gebundenen, die sie bis heute bewahrt haben. Man kann daher den ganzen kosmischen und natürlich auch den biologischen evolutionären Prozeß als Informations-Strukturspeicherung invarianter evolutionär stabiler Konfigurationen ansehen, d.h. als einen die Ordnung bewahrenden Prozeß. In Leinfellner 1983 ist der biologische Speicherungsprozeß von z.B. evolutionär stabilem Verhalten in den Genen eingehend beschrieben und mit der Speicherung von Informationen im menschlichen Gehirn (Gedächtnis) und in der menschlichen Kultur verglichen worden.[4]

8. Religionen und die Rechtfertigung kosmologischer Modelle und Weltanschauungen.

Die Endlichkeits-Konsequenz der evolutionären neuen Kosmologie ist einfach auszudrücken: Nichts ist in diesem Universum für die Ewigkeit geschaffen. Zwar „leben" Protonen 10^{31}

Jahre und die langlebendsten Strukturen, die schwarzen Löcher, sogar 10^{100} Jahre. Verglichen mit der Lebensdauer der Erde mit ca. 12×10^9 Jahre scheint ihr Alter, angenommen das Universum ist offen, zwar unbegreiflich länger zu sein; aber unsterbliches Leben, ewige Dauer gibt es im jetzigen Universum nicht, das, wenn offen (Fall 1), 10^{100} Jahre alt wird und, wenn geschlossen, 20×10^9 Jahre expandiert (Fall 2). Von der Unmöglichkeit der Ewigkeit ist auch Poppers Dritte Welt der Kultur und des Geistes betroffen, sie kann nicht losgelöst vom Kosmos existieren. Die Konzeption eines absolut unendlichen Raumes fiel schon mit der Relativitätstheorie; in der neuen Kosmologie entsteht der Raum mit dem expandierenden All und vergeht auch wieder, wenn das Universum in sich zusammenfällt. Nirgendwo in diesem Universum findet sich ein Platz für Unsterblichkeit, für eine unsterbliche Seele, für ein ewiges Leben nach dem Tode, für einen ewigen Geist der dieses Universum aus dem Nichts erschaffen hat, es sei denn in unserem spekulativen Bewußtsein, in unserer Vorstellung, Kultur, Religion. Dies ist vielleicht der Grund, warum so viele Physiker und Kosmologen sich den Religionen zuwenden, die wie Hinduismus, Buddhismus, Zen-Buddhismus, Jainismus, Taoismus und die japanische Shinto-Religion keinen „westlichen" Schöpfergott besitzen, sondern für die der Kosmos mit allen seinen zeitlichen Entwicklungen und seiner Geschichte das Gegebene ist. Sie alle teilen einen historischen Realismus mit den evolutionären Physikern, für die die Evolution identisch mit Geschichte ist. Daher wendet sich die evolutionäre Kosmologie im Grunde garnicht gegen die Religion per se oder gegen Religiosität, Kult und Glauben, sondern gegen die judäo-christliche Kosmologie des Schöpfergottes, der den Kosmos aus einem absoluten Nichts erschaffen hat. Es war sicherlich eine Kosmologie, die nicht mehr zur heute so wichtigen sozial-ethischen, kulturellen Funktion der Religion gehört, wie es immer deutlicher in gegenwärtigen Interpretationen des Neuen Testaments zu finden ist. Überdies scheint die Schöpfungsgeschichte (Kosmologie I) des alten Testaments mehr eine des Planeten Erde zu sein als die des Universums. Es ist nun vielleicht nützlich die drei Haupttypen von Schöpfungsparadigmen, das der Schöpfung aus dem Nichts (I), das Demiurg-Paradigma (II) und das Evolutionsparadigma (III) auf ihre Gemeinsamkeiten zu untersuchen. Das erste Paradigma (I) ist das der Weltschöpfung aus dem Nichts (creatio ex nihilo), nach der die Welt, bzw. der Kosmos in seiner Gesamtheit das Produkt eines göttlichen geistigen Willens ist. Creatio ex nihilo war die abendländische Kurzformel dieser nicht nur christlichen Kosmologie. Das zweite Paradigma (II) soll nach Plato das Demiurg-Paradigma genannt werden. Nach ihm erschafft ein göttliches Wesen − analog einem Künstler, Techniker − die Welt aus einem als vorhanden gedachten, nicht erschaffenen Stoff. Er schafft aus formloser Materie, bei Plato nach dem Plan, bzw. den Urbildern, den Ideen, die geordneten Formen der Welt. Timaios, das meistgelesenste Werk der Antike, und das alte Testament, das aber zweifellos mehr die Erschaffung des Planeten Erde als die des Universums behandelt, sind Beispiele für II. Das dritte Paradigma der Evolution (III) behauptet, daß ein nicht notwendigerweise als ewig angenommener Stoff (Materie oder, heute, Energie) aus sich heraus durch die selbstorganisierenden Kräfte eines zusammenhängenden dynamischen Ganzen sich zur heutigen Welt entwickelte. Paradigma I und III werden meist als unversöhnliche Gegensätze angesehen; das ist aber keinesfalls immer der Fall. Erstens können alle drei Paradigmata im Mittelpunkt von Religionen stehen, z.B. die Evolution des Guten im Kampf gegen das Böse im Zoroasters Religion. Zweitens basieren alle drei auf der Geschichtlichkeit der Welt und der Kulturen, d.h. auf der relativ selbständigen Entwicklung der Menschen, in die Gott in I und II korrigierend, bzw. strafend, in III die Selektion von Zeit zu Zeit eingreifen. Es wird also in I, II und III die Beantwortung der Frage nach dem Sinn des Universums mit dem Sinn der menschlich sozialen Entwicklung verknüpft. Nun hat die gegenwärtige Verwissenschaftlichung des Paradigmas III durch gigantische neue Theorien zum Ausbau einer Weltansicht geführt, die, genau so wie einst die Kosmologien I und II, auch Antworten auf die Sinnfrage, warum wir hier sind, einfach dadurch geben konnte, daß sie die kosmische mit der biologisch-kulturellen Evolution verknüpfte. Dies hat die kuturelle Bedeutung der evolutionären Kosmologie (III) grundlegend geändert, sie ist damit zur universalen Geschichte geworden. Stand im Galileo-Konflikt eine Einzelwissenschaft dem umfassenden Weltbild (aus Paradigma I und II bestehend) gegenüber, das, weil es lückenlose Antworten auf die Frage nach dem Sinn des Kosmos geben konnte, damals nicht aufgegeben wurde, so — sollte es wiederum zu einer unglücklichen Konfrontation, etwa der Kreationismus-Kosmologie (I) mit der nun wissenschaftlich untermauerten Evolutionskosmologie (III) kommen, so sieht die Situation heute völlig anders aus. Die wissenschaftlich physikalische, neue Kosmologie ist nicht nur unlösbar mit der stärksten Wissenschaft unserer Kultur, der Physik, verbunden, sondern hat sich auch Technologie, Schöpfungsmaschinen, Radioastronomie etc. einverleibt, kurz, sie ist die einheitliche Theorie der kosmischen, biologischen und der kulturellen Entwicklung geworden. Molekulare Biologie, Entschlüsselung des genetischen Codes, Genetechnologie, Genetik, Soziobiologie, Evolutionäre Anthropologie und Evolutionäre Geschichte der animalischen und menschlichen Intelligenz, die Schaffung mathematischer Evolutionstheorien (z.B. Populationsgenetik, Theorie der dynamischen differentiellen Spiele) haben aus dem Evolutionsparadigma eine faszinierende, nicht nur geistige Eliten, sondern auch die Massen anziehende Weltanschauung und Kosmologie gemacht, die die letzten Fragen, wie Sinn des Kosmos, der Welt, des Menschen ebenso beantworten kann, wie früher die Kosmologien I und II. Doch die Philosophie, die bis ins zwanzigste Jahrhundert im Banne der Ontotheologie stand, wie es Heidegger ausdrückte, d.h. der Kosmologie I und II, ist noch kaum von dieser Wende ergriffen. Sie befindet sich vielmehr seit Hegel in einem Dilemma zwischen dem Paradigma der Schöpfung und dem der Evolution.

Während Kosmologien der Type I und II in der Philosophie zu einem Panentheismus führten, nach dem das Weltall in Gott ruht und eine Erscheinungsweise Gottes ist (Spinoza, Idelismus, Goethe, Einstein), ist im Typ III die Welt eine Erscheinungsweise einer niemals ruhenden Energie, deren Evolution die historischen Veränderungen des ganzen Universums sind, verursacht durch die gegenseitig sich wenigstens in einem Teil des Universums selbstorganisierenden Teilkräfte. Die dynamischen Teilkräfte erzeugen, wie in diesem Artikel im Detail beschrieben worden ist, die universale Geschichte und die evolutionär stabilen Systeme von immer komplexerer Struktur und Ordnung und schließlich und endlich als Endprodukt unsere Kultur.

9. Das Dilemma der Philosophie

Die Frage ist: Hat die Philosophie mit dieser Entwicklung Schritt gehalten? Hat sie selbstorganisierende, Geschichte erzeugende Systeme je studiert? Es scheint vielmehr, daß sie seit Hegel sich weder für noch gegen den Evolutionismus entscheiden konnte oder wollte. Ein Musterbeispiel dafür ist Hegels Begründung seiner Philosophie, die er selbst als Abstraktion christlich religiöser Ideen ansah. Doch hat er seine Philosophie sozusagen zweifach fundiert: einerseits auf der Kosmologie I und andererseits auf der Geschichtlichkeit, der Entwicklung zur Kultur. Er verwendete das Paradigma II, wenn er seine Logik als Plan der Welt im Geiste Gottes vor ihrer Erschaffung ansah, wenn er seine Naturphilosophie als die Beschreibung der Verwirklichung (Schöpfung) dieses Plans in der materiellen Welt betrachtete und schließlich und endlich, wenn er in der Phänomenologie des Geistes das Bewußtwerden des Schöpfungsvorganges im menschlichen Geiste, in seiner Wissenschaft und Kultur als Rechtfertigung desselben ansah. Andererseits tritt das Paradigma III in der Tatsache der historischen Entfaltung menschlicher Kultur hervor, in der wegen der nichtwegzuleugnenden Freiheit des menschlichen Willens auf eine mechanistische, automatische und deterministische Verwirklichung des Planes Gottes verzichtet werden muß. D.h., daß wir Endpunkt einer langen Entwicklung sind, die wir auch ohne Zuhilfenahme äußerer externer Kräfte mehr oder minder erklären müssen, macht die Geschichte autonom, kurz evolutionär. Der Rechtfertigung, daß wir hier sind, im Glauben an die Verwirklichung eines göttlichen Plans oder aus einem göttlichen Willen, steht die Selbstorganisation des Planes entlang den Trajektorien, die unsere universale Geschichte sind, gegenüber. Das Dilemma der Philosophie besteht darin, daß sie unentschieden bleibt zwischen theologischer Schöpfung und dem Konzept der Evolution als sich selbst aufbauende, organisierende universale Geschichte eines dynamischen Kosmos, dessen Evolution nicht mehr durch externe Kräfte gelenkt oder beeinflußt werden kann, einfach weil nichts außerhalb des zusammenhängenden sich selbst organisierenden Ganzen liegen kann.

ANMERKUNGEN

[1] Zukav, G., *The Dancing Wu Li Masters*, (New York 1979), Talbot, M., *Mysticism and the New Physics* (New York 1980); Capra, F., *The Tao of Physics* (Berkeley 1975).

[2] Lewontin, R. C., "Gene, Organism and Environment", in: Bendall, D. S., (Hrsg.), *Evolution from Molecules to Men* (Cambridge 1983), S. 282f.

[3] Weinberg, S., *Die ersten drei Minuten* (München 1977); Fritzsch, H., *Vom Urknall zum Zerfall* (München 1983); Trefil, J. S., *The Moment of Creation* (New York 1983).

[4] Leinfellner, W., "Das Konzept der Kausalität und der Spiele in der Evolutionstheorie", in: Lorenz, K., Wuketits, F. M., *Die Evolution des Denkens* (München 1983), S. 232–238.

[5] Trefil, J. S., *The Moment of Creation* (New York 1983), S. 127–28.

[6] Trefil, J. S., "The Moment of Creation (New York 1983), S. 277

[7] Leinfellner, W. „Kausalität in den Sozialwissenschaften", in: G. Posch (Hrsg.) *Kausalität: neue Texte* (Stuttgart 1981), S. 231f.; Leinfellner (1983), Siehe 4, S. 218ff.

[8] Leinfellner, E. und Leinfellner, W. Ontologie, Systemtheorie und Semantik (Berlin 1978), S. 160f., 168.; Leinfellner W. "Grundtypen der Ontologie", in: R. Haller, W. Grassl *Sprache, Logik und Philosophie*, (Wien 1980), S. 125.

[9] Erikson, K. E., Kamal-Islam, S., „Der erste Tag", in: *Bild der Wissenschaft*, Vol. 20/2 (1983), S. 114.

[10] Fritzsch, H., *Vom Urknall zum Zerfall* (München 1983), S. 194f.

[11] Leinfellner (1983), siehe 8.

* * *

TABELLE 1: SCHEMATISCHE ÜBERSICHT ÜBER DIE EVOLUTION DES KOSMOS (Stand 1983)

ZEITLICHER VERLAUF DER EVOLUTION DES KOSMOS

ZEITLICHER VERLAUF DER EVOLUTION

ZUKUNFT — GEGENWART

1. PLANCK ZEIT — 0–10^{-43} sec — $t > 10^{32}$ °C
- Ein Superpartikel, (Masse 16 GeV) im Thermodynamischen Gleichgewicht Boson = Fermion
- Eine einzige Urkraft gemäß der GUT
- Stabilisierung (Ausfrieren) der Gravitationskraft

2. PROTOMATERIE AERA — 10^{-43}–10^{-33} sec — 10^{28} °C
- Quarks Antiquarks, Leptonen, Neutrinos, X-Teilchen, Gluonen mit Quarküberschuß über Antiquarks im thermodynamischen Gleichgewicht
- Zwei Urkräfte: Gravitation, Stark-schwache Elektro-Kräfte
- Stabilisierung (Ausfrieren) der starken Kraft

3. ELEKTROSCHWACHE A. — 10^{-33}–10^{-10} sec — 10^{14} °C
- 3 Urkräfte: Gravitation, starke und elektroschwache Kräfte
- Stabilisierung der schwachen Kraft

4. QUARK AERA — 10^{-10}–10^{-5} sec — 10^{12} °C
- Freie Quarks sterben durch Nukleonen-bildung aus
- 4 Kräfte: Gravitation, starke, schwache und elektromagnetische Kräfte
- Ausfrieren (Stabilisierung) der Quarks in Nukleonen

5. NUKLEONEN AERA — 10^{-5}–10^{-3} sec — 10^{9} °C
- Bildung von 25% Neutronen, 75% Protonen, Vernichtung von Elektronen-Positronen Paaren
- Lichterfüllung des Universums und Entkopplung der Neutrinos
- Stabilisierung (Einfangen) der Elektronen

6. ES „WERDE LICHT" AERA — 10^{-3}–30 min. — 9×10^{6} °C
- Helium, Wasserstoff Stabilisierung

7. Wasserstoff-Helium-Aera — 30 min.–5×10^{6} Jahre
- Erzeugung von 77% Wasserstoff und 23% Helium, als Ausgangs-Atome: Lithium bis bzw. Uratome
- Helium, Wasserstoff Stabilisierung

8. Aera der 1. Sterngeneration — 10^{6}–10^{9} Jahre
- Erzeugung durch Fusion (Ausbrennen) im Sterninneren der Atome: Lithium bis Eisen

9. Aera der schweren Atome — 10^{9}–20×10^{9} Jahre
- Supernovaexplosion von Sternen 3.5 × Sonnenmasse
- Galaxienbildung
- Novaexplosionen von Sternen 1.5–3.5 × Sonnenmasse
- Kosmischer Abfall: schwarze Zwergsterne

10. Aera der 2. Sterngeneration, Beginn des Lebens
- Neutronensterne, Pulsare, Quasars, Schwarze Löcher
- Bildung aus interstellarer Materie, enthaltend alle Atome der 2. Sterngeneration z.B. der Erde, ab 17×10⁹ Jahre: Leben Kosmischer Abfall: schwarze Zwerge

11. GESCHLOSSENES OSZILLIERENDES UNIVERSUM
- Wenn Massendichte über 10^{-29} g/cm³: nach 40×10^{9} Jahren Kollaps des Universums durch einen immer heißer werdenden Zerfall und Zurückkehr zum Ausgangspunkt 0 und der Planck Zeit (1)

oder ENDE:

12. OFFENES UNIVERSUM
- Wenn Massendichte unter 10^{-29} g/cm³: Protonensterben nach 10^{31} Jahren, Verdampfen der Zwergsterne nach 10^{60} Jahren und der schwarzen Löcher nach 10^{100} Jahren. Ende: immer kälter werdendes, mit elektromagnetischer Strahlung (Energie) erfülltes Universum.

DIE KONTROVERSE „EVOLUTION UND SCHÖPFUNG" IN DER BIOLOGIE

Franz M. Wuketits
Universität Wien

Im Jahre 1642 will der damalige Vizekanzler der Universität Cambridge, John Lightfood, das genaue Datum der Schöpfung errechnet haben: Demnach soll die Welt um 9 Uhr am Morgen des 17. Septembers 3928 v. Chr. entstanden sein.[1] So präzise arbeiten die heutigen Evolutionstheorien freilich nicht, aber sie liefern Beschreibungs- und Erklärungsmodelle für die Entwicklung des Kosmos, der Erde und der Lebewesen auf *rationaler* Grundlage unter Berücksichtigung eines sehr umfangreich gewordenen *empirischen* Materials. Zwar sind unter diesen Voraussetzungen viele einst rätselhafte Erscheinungen längst außerhalb jedes Mythos erklärbar, aber die Kontroverse „Evolution oder Schöpfung?" ist uns erhalten geblieben. Gerade in neuerer Zeit sind in den USA wieder die Stimmen der *creationists* laut geworden,[2] nicht minder haben aber auch in Mitteleuropa jüngst sogar einige Naturwissenschaftler gegen die Erklärugsansprüche der Evolutionstheorie ihre Stimme erhoben.[3] Mag sich die Zahl jener Naturwissenschaftler, die ein Bekenntnis zur Schöpfungslehre ablegen, auch in Grenzen halten, so ist es notwendig, sich mit ihren Argumenten auseinanderzusetzen, um die auch erkenntnistheoretisch gegebenen Widersprüche zwischen Evolutionstheorie und Schöpfungsglauben deutlich zu machen. Beschränken wir uns hierbei auf den Bereich der *biologischen* Evolutionstheorie, muß zunächst klar gemacht werden, daß Evolution und Schöpfung (Evolutionstheorie und Schöpfungslehre) prinzipiell *unvereinbar* sind und der Versuch einer Synthese nicht von Erfolg gekrönt sein kann. Und diejenigen, die sich als Evolutionsgegner deklarieren, bezeugen im übrigen meist eine profunde Unkenntnis der biologischen Evolutionstheorie und ihrer Grundlagen. Einige klärende Bemerkungen sind hier vonnöten.

Die (biologische) Evolutionstheorie hat prinzipiell drei Fragen zu beantworten und somit drei Hauptaufgaben zu erfüllen:[4]

1. Haben sich die Organismenarten in der Zeit gewandelt? – Diese Frage ist heute eindeutig mit „ja" zu beantworten. Aus praktisch sämtlichen biologischen Teildisziplinen (von der Morphologie bis zur Molekularbiologie) liegen empirische Belege dafür vor, daß die Arten nicht konstant, sondern variabel sind.
2. Wie verlief die Evolution der Organismen? – Hierbei hat die Evolutionstheorie die Aufgabe zu erfüllen, den Ablauf der Stammesentwicklung einzelner Arten und schließlich des gesamten Organismenbereichs zu rekonstruieren; diese Rekonstruktion findet z.B. in sog. Stammbäumen ihren Niederschlag, die nach Maßgabe der biologischen Theorienbildung und des jeweils zur Verfügung stehenden empirischen Materials ständig verbessert werden.
3. Was sind Mechanismen, die Triebkräfte der Evolution? – Das ist die schwierigste Frage der Evolutionsforschung; diese Frage steht auch heute noch im Brennpunkt evolutionstheoretischer Untersuchungen. Eine über das Konzept Darwins hinausgehende Theorie trägt dabei sowohl den externen (Selektion durch die Umwelt) als auch den internen (Binnenmilieu des Lebewesens) Faktoren Rechnung und läßt die Evolution als komplexes Wechselspiel zwischen Organismus und Außenwelt erscheinen.[5]

Die Beantwortung der dritten Frage nimmt jedoch keinen Einfluß auf die Tatsache der Evolution selbst. Sofern in diesem Punkt noch erhebliche Schwierigkeiten bestehen und die Beurteilung der Evolutionsmechanismen nicht einheitlich erfolgt, bedeutet das nicht – wie so manche Kritiker bzw. Gegner der Evolutionstheorie irrtümlich annehmen −, daß die Evolutionstheorie insgesamt falsch wäre. Die Evolution, der Wandel der Organismenarten in Gestalt und Lebensweise, bleibt für die Biologie ein *Faktum*. Zumindest die überwiegende Mehrzahl heutiger Biologen sieht in diesem Zusammenhang keine Schwierigkeiten. Wenn das eine oder das andere Evolutionskonzept auch von Biologen kritisiert wird, dann heißt das nicht, daß man am Evolutionsgedanken zweifelt, sondern nur, daß die Mechanismen der Evolution noch nicht hinreichend bekannt sind und die Evolution *kausal* noch nicht hinreichend *erklärt* ist.

Die meisten Kritiken erfuhr in den letzten Jahrzehnten die Evolutionstheorie Darwins, die mit dem Mechanismus der natürlichen Auslese operiert. In dieser Theorie überleben bekanntlich nur diejenigen Lebewesen, die die relativ beste *Anpassung* an die jeweiligen Umweltbedingungen zeigen. Es ist absolut nicht gerechtfertigt, heute zu sagen, die Theorie Darwins wäre grundsätzlich falsch, weil dieses *survial of the fittest* logisch eine tautologische Struktur aufweist. Darwin hat die Mechanismen der Evolution − nach dem Stand des biologischen Wissens um die Mitte des 19. Jahrhunderts − durchaus richtig beurteilt, doch ist sein Konzept mittlerweile selbstverständlich wesentlich ergänzt und im Detail modifiziert worden. Dem Vorwurf der Tautologie kann man heute dadurch begegnen, daß man die erwähnten Wechselbeziehungen zwischen Organismus und Umwelt besser herausarbeitet. Richtig bemerkt dazu Hull:

> The principle of the survival of the fittest is officially a tautology in certain operationally oriented versions of evolutionary theory, and these versions suffer accordingly. It is not a tautology in those versions of evolutionary theory which recognize the key role played in evolution by the organism-environment relation[6]

Indem dieser Relation Organismus-Umwelt gebührend Rechnung getragen wird, erweitert sich die Evolutionstheorie zu einer umfassenden *Systemtheorie der Evolution*, die auf den Prämissen Darwins und seiner Epigonen beruht, diese jedoch übersteigt.[7]

Der Evolutionsgedanke aber ist wesentlich älter als Darwins epochemachendes Werk.[8] Es ging dabei zunächst darum, überhaupt die Veränderbarkeit der Lebewesen zu erkennen und sich von dem Gedanken an eine *einmalige* Schöpfung alles Lebenden zu befreien. Die folgenden Erkenntnisvoraussetzungen waren dafür von überragender Bedeutung:[9]

1. Die Loslösung von statischen Weltbildern und die Erkenntnis der Dynamik allen Naturgeschehens (*Dynamisierung* des Weltbildes).
2. Die Entwicklung einer Vorstellung großer Zeiträume (*Temporalisierung* des Weltbildes).
3. Die Überwindung der Vorstellung einer Einheit des Lebenden im Sinne der romantischen Naturphilosophie und die Erkenntnis, daß aus wenigen Ursprungsarten sich stets weitere Arten entwickelt haben, wodurch erst (in einem kontinuierlichen Prozeß der *Diversifikation*) die Mannigfaltigkeit des Lebendigen als reale Verwandtschaft aller Arten miteinander gedeutet werden kann.
4. Die Erkenntnis in der Geschichte *einheitlich* wirkender Faktoren. Diese Erkenntnis wurde zunächst in den Erdwissenschaften (Hutton, Lyell) ausgesprochen (*Uniformitarismus*) und auf die Biologie übertragen.
5. Die Loslösung von der Vorstellung eines einmaligen Schöpfungsaktes, dem alle Lebewesen als unveränderbare Geschöpfe entsprungen sind und die Entwicklung von Vorstellungen eines *realen Artenwandels* in der Zeit.

Diese Erkenntnisse sind selbstverständlich eng miteinander verknüpft und ergeben erst in ihrer Synthese eine Evolutionstheorie in weiterem Sinne.

Da das Festhalten am Schöpfungsglauben gerade eines der Hindernisse für die Erkenntnis der Evolution war, ist es allerdings − auf erkenntnistheoretischer Ebene − nicht möglich, die Schöpfungslehre mit der Evolutionstheorie zu vereinen. Unter Berücksichtigung der Geschichte der Evolutionstheorie muß somit deutlich gemacht werden, daß Schöpfung und

Evolution einander widersprechen. Es mag sein, daß der Mensch aus anderen als rationalen Gründen („Geborgenheitsgefühl" in der Schöpfung) sich zum Schöpfungsglauben bekennen will, auf naturwissenschaftlicher Ebene widerspricht dieser Glaube jedoch sowohl den empirischen Tatsachen als auch den daraus gezogenen Schlußfolgerungen.

Zu den philosophisch höchst relevanten Schlußfolgerungen der Evolutionstheorie zählt einmal, daß die Entstehung des Lebens auf der Erde (vor etwa 3,5 bis 4 Jahrmilliarden) als Prozeß der *materiellen Selbstorganisation* gesehen wird.[10] Demnach liegen die Bedingungen der Lebensentstehung in der Materie, der Rückgriff auf übernatürliche Faktoren ist nicht mehr nötig. Zum zweiten ist die Evolutionstheorie von entsprechender Tragweite in bezug auf eine Interpretation des Menschen und seiner Position im Kosmos. Es kann als eine ausgemachte Sache gelten, daß der Mensch in die Evolution alles Lebenden eingefügt ist und daß seine Evolution den gleichen Prinzipien folgte wie die Entwicklung anderer Lebewesen:

> Als *biologische* Spezies ist der Mensch zuallererst als ein Produkt der Evolution zu betrachten; und niemand kann heute ernsthaft daran zweifeln, daß der Mensch wie alle übrigen Organismen unseres Planeten der Evolution entsprungen ist . . . [Und] wollen wir uns ernsthaft bemühen, unsere Position in der Natur zu begreifen, dann vermittelt die Biologie uns eine denkbar breite Basis.[11]

Dabei geht es allerdings nicht allein um eine Klärung der Evolution des Menschen unter anatomisch-physiologischen Gesichtspunkten, sondern die − im vergangenen Jahrhundert schon vorgezeichnete (Darwin, Spencer) − evolutionäre Perspektive in der Betrachtung der *geistigen* Phänomene öffnet unseren Blick auch für die stammesgeschichtlichen Voraussetzungen des Erkennens und Denkens.[12] Keineswegs wird dabei geleugnet, daß die geistige Eigenschaften unserer Gattung etwas spezifisch Menschliches sind; ebensowenig ist daran zu zweifeln, daß diese Eigenschaften auf einer kategorial höheren Stufe stehen als die organischen Phänomene, daß also „das geistige Leben des Menschen eine neue Art von Leben sei".[13] Aber auch dieses „geistige Leben" muß auf die Evolution zurückgeführt werden, muß seine Wurzeln in der Evolution des Lebendigen haben. Daß sich hinter diesem Postulat kein ontologischer Reduktionismus verbirgt, wird man verstehen, wenn man die Evolution insgesamt als einen Prozeß begreift, in dem fortgesetzt *Neues* entstanden ist. In diesem Prozeß war der Mensch zwar kein *notwendiges* Ergebnis, aber allein, daß ein Wesen mit der Fähigkeit der Selbstreflexion auftreten konnte, zeugt von der Unermeßlichkeit der Evolution.

Es könnte sogar sein, daß jenes Geborgenheitsgefühl, das vielen Menschen der Schöpfungsglaube vermittelt hat, auch in einer umfassend verstandenen Evolution wiedergefunden werden kann, vorausgesetzt, man identifiziert sich mit der Natur, mit dem organischen Werden und Gewordensein. Dies jedoch sind psychologische Momente, über die uns eine strikt naturwissenschaftlich verstandene Evolutionstheorie keine befriedigende Auskunft mehr zu geben vermag. Andererseits sollte man die Evolutionstheorie in dieser Richtung auch nicht überstrapazieren, da sie sonst wiederum mit antiquierten Schöpfungsmythen vermengt werden könnte. Wichtig ist jedenfalls, zwischen Schöpfungslehre und Evolutionstheorie zu unterscheiden, da beide auf unterschiedlichen Erkenntnisvoraussetzungen beruhen. Die moderne Biologie klammert den Schöpfungsgedanken weitgehend aus − dies ist denn auch eine wichtige *methodische* Prämisse, da der Glaube an eine außernatürliche Schöpfergewalt naturwissenschaftlich keinen Erkenntniswert hat. Letzten Endes bleibt für den Naturwissenschaftler hinsichtlich der oft so genannten „letzten Fragen" nur der Standpunkt des *Agnostizismus*.

ANMERKUNGEN

1 Zit. nach Dunbar (1070).
2 So z.B. in Arkansas; vgl. Dickson (1981).
3 Vgl. z.B. Illies (1979).
4 Vgl. z.B. Wuketits (1982).
5 Hierzu hat Riedl (1975) eine Theorie der Systembedingungen der Evolution vorgelegt.
6 Hull (1974), S. 69.
7 Vgl. Riedl (1975); Wuketits (1982).
8 Vgl. Darwin (1859).
9 Vgl. Wuketits (1982, 1983a).
10 Vgl. Eigen und Winkler (1975).
11 Wuketits (1983a), S. 223.
12 Vgl. Lorenz (1973); Lorenz und Wuketits (1983); Riedl (1980); Vollmer (1975); Wuketits (1981, 1983b).
13 Lorenz (1973), S. 229; im Original kursiv.

LITERATUR

Darwin, Ch., *On the Origin of Species by Means of Natural Selection* (London 1859).
Dickson, D., „Creationism again an issue in Arkansas", *Nature* 291 (1981).
Dunbar, C. O., *Die Erde* (Lausanne 1970).
Eigen, M. und R. Winkler, *Das Spiel. Naturgesetze steuern den Zufall* (München—Zürich 1975).
Hull, D., *Philosophy of Biological Science* (Englewood Cliffs 1974).
Illies, J., *Schöpfung oder Evolution* (Zürich 1979).
Lorenz, K., *Die Rückseite des Spiegels. Versuch einer Naturgeschichte menschlichen Erkennens* (München—Zürich 1973).
Lorenz, K. und Wuketits, F. M. (Hrsg.), *Die Evolution des Denkens* (München—Zürich 1983).
Riedl, R., *Die Ordnung des Lebendigen* (Hamburg—Berlin 1975).
Riedl, R., *Biologie der Erkenntnis* (Berlin—Hamburg 1980).
Vollmer, G., *Evolutionäre Erkenntnistheorie* (Stuttgart 1975).
Wuketits, F. M., *Biologie und Kausalität* (Berlin—Hamburg 1981).
Wuketits, F. M., *Grundriß der Evolutionstheorie* (Darmstadt 1982).
Wuketits, F. M., *Biologische Erkenntnis: Grundlagen und Probleme* (Stuttgart 1983a).
Wuketits, F. M. (Hrsg.), *Concepts and Approaches in Evolutionary Epistemology* (Dordrecht—Boston—Lancaster 1983b).

* * *

5. Religion, Religionsphilosophie und Wittgenstein

5. Religion, Philosophy of Relgion, and Wittgenstein

WITTGENSTEIN AND CHRISTIANITY

William Young
University of Rhode Island, Kingston

Wittgenstein was born into a family in which the father was Protestant and the mother Roman Catholic. He was baptized and brought up in the faith of his mother. By the time in which he studied under Russell at Cambridge he appears to have reacted against his religious training. Russell states that Wittgenstein was decidedly anti-Christian at that period of his life.[1] In a letter to Lady Ottoline Morrell, March 17, 1912, Russell writes of Wittgenstein as more terrible with Christians than himself and recounts his fierce attack on an undergraduate monk at tea time. On May 30, however, Russell expresses his surprise at Wittgenstein saying how he admired the text, "what shall it profit a man if he gain the whole world and lose his own soul," and going on to say how few there are who don't lose their soul.

The turning-point in Wittgenstein's religious outlook occurred during his military service in the First World War. In the town of Tarnov in Galicia he visited a book shop which contained only one book, Tolstoy on the Gospels. He bought it and read it and re-read it, and carried it with him even when under fire. To his friend, Ludwig von Ficker, he wrote, July 24, 1915, that this book had kept him in life. Wittgenstein did not confine himself to reading Tolstoy's truncated version of the Gospels. In a letter to Paul Engelmann, Sept. 4, 1917, he requested a Bible in a small-size, but still legible edition. When Wittgenstein read the Gospels in prison he discovered much that Tolstoy has omitted. F. Parak, one of Wittgenstein's fellow prisoners at Monte Cassino (Oct. 1918 to 1919) informs us that Wittgenstein quoted II Corinthians V, 17 and claimed that this had been his own experience.[2] Russell writes Lady Ottoline, Dec. 20, 1919, after discussing the *Tractatus* with Wittgenstein at the Hague, that he reads people like Kierkegaard and Angelus Silesius. Russell also mentions the influence of James' *Varieties of Religious Experience* during the winter Wittgenstein spent alone in Norway before the war.

From these biographical data we may gather that during the time of the composition of the 1914—16 *Notebooks* and the *Tractatus* Wittgenstein had adopted a positive attitude toward religion in general and Christianity in particular, quite divergent from a positivistic repudiation of them as nonsensical. Some entries in the *Tractatus* at first sight might appear to point in the opposite direction. "The totality of true propositions is the entire Natural Science." (4.11) Moreover "God does not reveal himself in the world." (6.432) It would follow that there is no factual revelation of God in the Bible or elsewhere in the world. Natural and revealed religion are alike denied propositional content. Language can only depict facts, but sentences purporting to be about God cannot be regarded as pictures of facts. Facts are contingent. (1.21) There are not even necessary causal connections linking them together. (5.136; 5.1361; 6.37) This rules out necessarily true statements about God. The only necessarily true statements, or rather pseudo-statements are the tautologies of formal logic. (6.1; 6.11)

As well known, the *Tractatus* resolves the apparent difficulty for religion by identifying its sphere with the Mystical. "There is, indeed, that which is inexpressible. It *shows* itself; it is the Mystical." (6.522) But the mystical cannot provide a propositional revelation, such as historic Christianity has claimed to possess in the Bible. Scripture contains propositions expressed in language that can be understood and that have been judged to be true or false. The mystical, on the contrary, is inexpressible and dispenses with propositions and with such linguistic forms as imperatives as well. Over the entrance to the temple of mystical religion is inscribed the closing aphorism of the *Tractatus*: "whereof one cannot speak thereof one must keep silence," (7) Such religion can hardly be the religion of the Bible, for the religion of the

Bible is the religion of the Word. Yet we have seen that when Wittgenstein was completing the *Tractatus*, he was reading the Bible with serious interest.

On the one hand, it should be clear that Wittgenstein is not propounding the Positivist thesis that, since only scientific statements make sense, religion and ethics are to be relegated with metaphysics to the Limbo of outdated superstitions. Superstition in fact is identified with belief in the causal maxim, 5.1361. Wittgenstein meant seriously the delcaration made to Fikker that the point (Sinn) of the *Tractatus* was ethical.[3] On the other hand, the religious outlook expressed in the book cannot be regarded as specifically Christian. It is not even unambiguously theistic. The temporal immortality of the soul is rejected at 6.4312. There are suggestions of pantheistic mysticism, possibly reflecting Angelus Silesius' *Cherubinischer Wandersmann*, more pronounced in the *Notebooks* than in the *Tractatus*. Entries of June 11, 1916 identify God with the meaning of life, of the world, and reduce prayer to thought about the meaning of life. The personality of God appears to be dissolved in the metaphor of God as Father. An entry of July 8 reads: "God would be in this sense simply fate or, what is the same thing: the world independent of our will." There follows the cryptic aphorism: „There are two deities (Gottheiten): The world and my independent Ego." The references to a strange will on which I appear dependent need not imply divine personality if Wittgenstein like Schopenhauer has an impersonal will in view. The entry of Aug. 1, upon first reading, has a pronounced pantheistic ring: "How everything stands in God. God is how everything stands." This sounds like a simple indentification of God with the world considered as the totality of facts. Yet this entry, retained in the *Proto-Tractatus*[4] but not in the *Tractatus* seems to conflict with Tractatus 6.41, which develops an entry of June 11, 1916 that the meaning of the world must lie outside the world. A possible solution, developed by Eddy Zemach,[5] would take "how things stand" not to be the contingent facts, but the logical form of the facts, suggested by 4.5 "The general form of the proposition is: This is how things stand." Since the general form of the proposition is the essence of the proposition and of the world, (5.471; 5.4711) the identification of this form with the meaning of the world is plausible. Nevertheless, this refinement of the pantheistic view does not readily harmonize with "not in the world, but outside it."

Even after due recognition of the omission of pantheistic sounding Notebook entries and the resulting accentuation of the element of transcendence in the *Tractatus* Wittgenstein's religious outlook cannot be said to unambiguously theistic and certainly must be denied to be specifically Christian. The issue is not that some particular Christian doctrines are called into question, but that the Tractatus standpoint rules out all religious doctrine considered as making truth claims and leaves only a mystical experience that does not admit of expression in language.

In his later years, Wittgenstein's concern with Christianity continued and even became acute at times, while his anti-intellectualist view of religion was sharpened and its implications for Christianity developed. In 1937 he writes,[6] "Christianity is no doctrine, I mean, no theory about what has happened and will happen with the human soul but a description of an actual occurrence, and likewise despair and deliverance through faith. Those who speak of this (like Bunyan) simply describe what happened to them, whatever anyone might say about it."

This entry is significant in its trenchant expression of the paradoxical position in which the characteristic features of Pauline, Augustinian or Evangelical Christian experience are esteemed, while the doctrinal content presupposed, if the experience is to have objective validity, is dismissed as unessential. The anti-theoretical theory of religion betrays a pronounced kinship with the subjective existential thinking of Sören Kierkegaard.

There is a cluster of 1937 manuscript entries which strike the same note. One speaks of the tyranny of dogma with a reference to the Catholic church. (*VB*, p. 60) Another, reflecting on the allegory of Bunyan's *Pilgrim's Progress*, speaks of rules of life clothed in pictures. These pictures describe a course of conduct, but do not provide a foundation for it. Religion says: Do this, think this way. When it attempts to give a ground, a valid opposite ground is to be found. (*VB*, p. 61f.) In this connection, the first of several entries on Predestination appears: "Election of grace: One is allowed to write this, only under the most fearful suffering—and then it means something entirely different . . . It just isn't a theory. Or also: if this is truth, then it is not what appears at first sight to be expressed by it. It is a sigh or a cry rather than a theory ." (*VB*, p. 63)

Wittgenstein disclaimed understanding Kierkegaard's *Concluding Unscientific Postscript.* Yet he also spoke of the Danish thinker as the greatest philosopher of the 19th century. An entry of Oct. 22, 1937 opens with a quotation from Kierkegaard and continues with remarks on indirect communication in Scripture. The message of the Gospels is held not to allow of communication through the best and most accurate historian. On Dec. 8 Wittgenstein writes: "Christianity is not based on a historical truth, but it gives us a (historical) account, and says: Now believe! . . . *Here you have an account—do not relate yourself to it as you do to another historical account!* Let it take an altogether different place in your life." (*VB*, p. 67) The following day he writes that faith would lose nothing, should the historical reports in the gospel be demonstrably false. It is not that faith concerns universal truth of reason, but that historical proof, the historical proof game, does not concern faith at all. (*VB*, p. 68)

The last entry relating to Christianity at this time contains some striking reflections. Wittgenstein finds himself unable to call Jesus "Lord", because he does not believe that Jesus will come to judge him. This would make sense only if he led an entirely different life. Yet he feels inclined to believe in the resurrection of Christ. We cannot be satisfied with wisdom and speculation. Only *love* can believe in the resurrection. (*VB*, p. 68f.)

As for Kierkegaard and Jaspers the absolute certainty of faith is not theoretical but existential, so for Wittgenstein, his soul with its passions, not his abstract mind needs redemption. (*VB*, p. 69) The mystical has given place to the existential. There remains a tension in the later religious outlook between the experience of sin and grace on the one hand and the ethical demands of moral responsibility on the other. A 1947 entry in which life is compared to a path on a slippery mountain edge explains the meaning of the denial of free-will. (*VB* p. 121) In 1948 and 1949 important discussions of predestination suggest that Wittgenstein was deeply exercised with respect to his own eternal destiny in the face of an oppressive sense of guilt.[7] Some months before his death, Wittgenstein had two conversations on God and the soul with a Dominican priest in Oxford. This furnished the basis for the giving of conditional absolution by the priest while Wittgenstein was in a coma on his death bed. From this arose the legend that Wittgenstein returned to this childhood faith before his death.

Wittgenstein's renewed concern with the question of the existence of God in his last years appears in an entry on "The essence of God guarantees his existence." Characteristically, the continuation consists of an exercise in conceptual analysis. It is not a matter of existence at all. Could one also say, the essence of a color guarantees its existence? We could describe what it would be like if there were gods on Olympus, but not what it would be like if there were God. (*VB*, p. 155) Another entry points out that one does not come to believe in the existence of God through such proofs. Their role is indicated in terms similar to the Augustinian and Anselmic *CREDO UT INTELLIGAM*. Life can educate to belief in God. Experiences of life, not visions or other sensory impressions, but suffering of various sorts may force upon us the concept 'God'. Wittgenstein suggests an analogy with the concept 'Object'. (*VB*, p. 161f.)

In spite of these late approaches to a rational theology, there is an aphorism of 1949 in the style of Kierkegaard: "If Christianity is the truth, then all philosophy about it is false." (*VB*, p. 157)[8]

ENDNOTES

[1] Russell, B., "Ludwig Wittgenstein", in: *Mind*, 60. No. 239 (1951).
[2] Parak, F., "Ludwig Wittgensteins Verhältnis zum Christentum", in: *Proceedings of the 2nd International Wittgenstein Symposium* (1978), p. 9.
[3] *Briefe an Ludwig von Ficker* (Salzburg 1969), p. 35.
[4] p. 238, an unnumbered remark.
[5] Zemach, E., "Wittgenstein's Philosophy of the Mystical", in: *Review of Metaphysics* 18 (1964), 39—57.
[6] *Vermischte Bemerkungen*, p. 59, Translations are my own.
[7] For a discussion of Wittgenstein's reflections on this subject, see my paper "Wittgenstein and Predestination", in: *Proceedings of the 2nd International Wittgenstein Symposium*, pp. 513—516.
[8] Portions of Russell's letters to Lady Ottoline Morrell were made available by the Bertrand Russell Archives, McMaster University, Hamilton, Ontario, Canada.

* * *

WITTGENSTEIN AND RELIGIOUS BELIEF

Jerome Balmuth
Colgate University, Hamilton, New York

I

One of the most significant remarks for understanding Wittgenstein's later views of religious belief is the question and observation in 508/509 on "On Certainty".

> "What can I rely on?/I really want to say that a language game is only possible if one trusts something (I did not say 'can trust something')."

This is part of his general reflection on the bases of knowledge and justification, when, as he says

> "giving grounds . . . justifying the evidence, comes to an end . . . not [in] a kind of seeing . . ., [but in] our acting" (204)

Such a "ground", he adds, "is not *true*, nor yet false" (205)

The question of "trust" or reliance is elsewhere linked in O. C. to the idea of a "system" of beliefs, as in 603. In justifying the appeal, say, to the certainty that water boils at circa 100° c (599), Wittgenstein remarks that experimental confirmation is not sought; and if it is, it is significant only as it is "surrounded" by others which combine to form a "system". While such a "trust [has] also proved itself", still "I rely on these experiences, or on the reports of them" even initially, and "I feel no scruples about ordering my own activities in accordance with them".

This account of trust and its connection with a system of beliefs and activities are clearly illuminating suggestions about how religious beliefs work for a person and in a community. Wittgenstein remarks (144) on how a child "learns to believe a host of things. I.e. it learns to act according to these beliefs [and so] forms a system of what is believed . . .". Such an account fits accurately the way religious beliefs are taught and supported in religious communities. The central narratives of Exodus, of the ministry of Jesus, as well as of Genesis, for example, are intended to provide the Hebrew and Christian communities with a workable picture of the world as a whole. They review the past while explaining the critical significance of certain remembered events for the founding of those communities. These accounts serve, in effect, as communal testimony to the continuing meanings of certain special events. Seen from outside, however, these are puzzling and tendentious accounts; but from within the community they are extraordinary: revealing expressions of a giving and loving God manifesting His power and presence in human events. Those "events", for religious persons, are in Wittgenstein's terms, anchors which "stand fast"—"unshakeably fast" (144), and so are not liable as others "to shift". They serve as grounds or "principles" (124) for testing subsequent accounts and judgments—and so form part of a system of beliefs which gives vitality or force to arguments about the occurence and significance of other events. What Wittgenstein says about beliefs, generally, applies then to systems of religious beliefs.

> "All testing, all confirmation and disconfirmation of a hypothesis takes place already within a system. And this system is not a more or less arbitrary and doubtful point of departure for all our arguments: no, it belongs to the essence of what we call an argument. The system is not so much the point of departure, as the element in which arguments have their life" (105, O.C., Pg. 16e).

One might point out, by extension, that the vitality of present-day philosophical discussions of say, causality and freedom, depend on certain pre-philosophical, theological viewpoints about the world and its workings under God and human choice.

What are some of the consequences of this view of religious beliefs?

First, religious beliefs do not function the way we like to view the workings of ordinary empirical claims. There is not that cognitive posture of studied, in principled, indifference to the truth of falsity of particular propositions that characterizes the ideally disengaged investigator or empirical matters. (This, of course, is a caricature as well.) Propositions within religious systems are not allowed easily to be confronted or even challenged by empirical matters; rather empirical matters are more likely to be tested or viewed under their rubric. Thus, if the Hebrews escaped from the Egyptians by somehow (you wouldn't believe how!) successfully negotiating the Red (reed) Sea, while their pursuers were dramatically engulfed, the empirical oddity of these conjuctions is less problem of their truth for the community, than a confirmation of their singular importance. It is *just because* the Hebrews knew of the natural movements of bodies of water—seas or lakes—that their escape by this route was so much more significant—a unique untoward event—a "miracle", if you will, and not accountable under normal explanations.

In this tendency to protect basic beliefs, Wittgenstein is saying, religious communities and persons are no more defensive or superstitious or ignorant or psychologically deranged than non-religious communities which take ordinary and common scientific experience as providing acceptable accounts of natural events. It is against the ordinary explanation that the Hebrews make the claim that the events they encountered must count as special and unique evidence of God's action. Again, it is because ordinary accounts fail to explain certain facts, viz. the Hebrews' remarkable survival as a freed community, that an explanation of a different kind is required.

Secondly, it does not follow, nor is it the case that religious beliefs are invariably impervious to empirical matters: that there is never, for the person or community, conflict, and alternative candidates for contradictory readings of these events. Two examples which cut different ways suggest how this has worked.

a) Despite the promise of a new land, and the fulfillment, at least partially, of the promise of freedom from the Egyptians, the Hebrews find themselves suffering and doubting the authenticity of the original promise. Their doubts reach a climax whan, according to the Exodus story itself, they proceed to make a golden calf: an act in direct and dramatic conflict with the injunctions earlier laid on them, and to which they nominally subscribed. The biblical significance of the golden calf is its depiction of the persistent strains on the (religious) commitment to sustain trust in the promise of God, through the test of hard reality and suffering. The full narrative insists, however, on seeing a pattern of trust on God's part and betrayal on the part of the community; these challenges are resolved, however, as occasions for renewed commitment, and of reassurance in God's faithfulness.

b) But this result, renewed commitment, is *not* invariable nor assured and as the biblical stories imply, not always the case. For example, for contemporary Hebrews, and indeed for religious persons everywhere, the event of the Nazi Holocaust is the single most challenging test to confront religious sensibility and forms of life. Here, for many, is a final crisis of faith, and in fact not all believers can accept it, as a careful reading of contemporary religious literature will show.

The results, then, are not as predictable as those who construe religious belief as "dogma" or "superstition" are inclined to assume. In fact, we underestimate the dynamic and revitalizing nature of religious forms of life because we fail to see that such forms are not collections of independent and insulated beliefs, but a complicated way of viewing the world through a system or network—the metaphor being the same one Wittgenstein earlier used about Newtonian physics. The vitality of a system of belief is just its capacity to confront all aspects of the world in a special interpretation for the community that employs its distinctive language game. This, in turn, is tied to many other beliefs not distinctive to the religious community. It is this last which allows the religious community continuity, on different levels, with the larger non-religious community. It allows it to seem and indeed be part, if not wholly one, with the larger *form of life,* while maintaining, for its followers, its own unique forms. So religious persons may be scientists, technicians, military officers, and politicians, even philosophers—apparently without essential conflict. Although Wittgenstein often talks about religious beliefs as if they are the beliefs of individuals, in fact, as his appeal to "system" shows, he is talking about a community of believers for whom the one distinctive language-game may be expressive of a unique way of life, without denying the claims of other language-games.

II

Norman Malcolm, in his 1975 paper "The Groundlessness of Belief"[1] is very impressed with one particular line of Wittgenstein's thought. He begins with the remark from *On Certainty*: "The difficulty is to realize the groundlessness of our believing," (166) and adds that Wittgenstein was "here thinking of how much mere acceptance, on the basis of no evidence, forms our lives." Malcolm then argues the very strong claim that "the lives of educated sophisticated adults are also formed by groundless beliefs", an unquestioned framework, accepted trustingly, without reflection or decision. To demand grounds, Malcolm argues, is pathologically futile and question-begging, like attempts to ground memory beliefs, or to explain intentions by mental state counterparts, or to justify a practice by appealing to memory samples or internalized rules, etc. All such moves are either circular because the putative ground is not identifiable independently of what it is supposed to ground, or regressive, since it suffers from the same disability of requiring a grounding. It appears to me here, however, that Malcolm has treated a feature of particular language games, as an essential feature of the whole practice of language, and this is misleading in a fundamental way.

Notice first that the quotation from Wittgenstein "The difficulty is to realize the groundlessness of our believing" (166) does not, by itself, warrant "the groundlessness of belief" nor the more ambitious claim that "religion is groundless." If our believing — using, as Wittgenstein does, the gerund — is groundless, this implies no more than that the believer may have and require no grounds; it does not imply that what the believer would term "grounds," "evidence," or "justification" is not available nor able to be produced if sought. Of course an attempt to provide grounds presumes other beliefs which, in respect to those being examined, may be said to be "groundless" (see 519)—and this may be all that Malcolm means. But I believe his way of putting it is unfortunate for three reasons which I cannot expand on here. (1) It tends needlessly to reinforce the suspicions of the anti-religious theorists that religious beliefs are finally non-rational if not irrational irrespective of Malcolm's attempt to show "groundlessness" to be a common feature of all systematic discourse including science and (2) it suggests that a religious community's beliefs are simply arbitrary—(non-grounded) when in fact they are sought to be justified historically. (See for example the urgency with which the Mormon's claim a grounding in the common witness for the Book of Mormon), and (3) it misrepresents the logic of faith, and its continuing crisis of confidence in the face of reality: a basic belief can lose its ground or credibility.

Contrary to Malcolm I am inclined to summarize Wittgenstein's view as holding that fundamental beliefs are neither grounded nor groundless since they are not subject to a language game in which they require justification. But this is only a remark about the (possibly temporary) status of some beliefs or other and not about any particular beliefs for an individual or community. It is thus a *grammatical* remark about what it means to be a fundamental belief: it does not imply that there must be certain absolute or groundless beliefs for a person or community, any more than there is one absolute and universal language game. Any belief which is fundamental for one system of language *may* become fair game for justification in another i.e., it may become controversial and unsettled, even if, in fact, it never does. This is what happens when someone loses religious faith.

I think Wittgenstein showed great sensitivity to this ambivalent status of beliefs, particularly religious beliefs, and that this remains a continuing thread in his work.

––––––––––

ENDNOTE

1 Reason and Religion, ed. S. C. Brown (Cornell 1977).

* * *

WITTGENSTEIN AND THE MIRACULOUS

Terence J. McKnight
New University of Ulster, Coleraine

In the 'Lecture on Ethics',[1] Wittgenstein commented on the topic of miracle in the following fashion:

> . . . we all know what in ordinary life would be called a miracle. It obviously is simply an event the like of which we have never yet seen. Now suppose such an event happened. Take the case that one of you suddenly grew a lion's head and began to roar. Certainly that would be as extraordinary a thing as I can imagine. Now whenever we should have recovered from our surprise, what I would suggest would be to fetch a doctor and have the case scientifically investigated and if it were not for hurting him I would have him vivisected. And where would the miracle have got to? For it is clear that when we look at it in this way everything miraculous has disappeared; unless what we mean by this term is merely that a fact has not yet been explained by science which again means that we have hitherto failed to group this fact with others in a scientific system. This shows that it is absurd to say 'Science has proved that there are no miracles'. The truth is that the scientific way of looking at a fact is not the way to look at it as a miracle. For imagine whatever fact you may, it is not in itself miraculous in the absolute sense of that term. For we see now that we have been using the word 'miracle' in a relative and an absolute sense.[2]

For Wittgenstein, it seems, to view an extraordinary event, claimed as a miracle, from the standpoint of science is to completely miss what constitutes its miraculous nature. The scientific and the religious points of view cannot complement each other, rather they must be contrasted. But is this viewpoint really tenable when we are examining events considered to be miracles? Miracles, within the Christian religious tradition, are not merely extraordinary events; they are rather events which seem to violate, break known natural laws. As D. Hume stated, "A miracle is a violation of the laws of nature."[3]

It seems that before we can even begin to identify an event as a miracle, we must have a knowledge of the natural law or laws which it is supposed to violate. And this, as Hume has reminded us, is no gratuitous requirement; it is, rather, demanded by the very definition of the term 'miracle'. At the very least, a necessary condition for judging an extraordinary event to be a miracle is a knowledge of the particular natural laws with which it is in conflict. Without a scientific or natural understanding of the world, as a background, the concept of miracle could have no application.

Now, while it may be conceded that the above comments are highly important, it may also be felt that they do less than justice to the analysis Wittgenstein was offering. What, in particular, appeared to alarm Wittgenstein was *not* the requirement that a knowledge of scientific laws is a necessary condition for identifying an event as a miracle, but rather the possibility that a scientific investigation of a miraculous happening could serve to elucidate its *miraculous status*. If such an investigation were to be carried out, Wittgenstein was of the opinion that 'everything miraculous about the event would disappear' because 'the scientific way of looking at a fact is not the way to look at it as a miracle'. I believe Wittgenstein's fears are justified here and to illustrate this I want, first of all, to offer a brief account of an incoherence implicit in the term 'miracle' and, secondly, to elucidate the task of the scientist faced with an extraordinary event which seems to violate natural law or laws.

To assert that a miracle has occurred is to claim that a law of nature has been violated whilst simultaneously remaining a true law of nature. But of course, from a scientific point of view, genuine counter-instances to a law of nature do not violate it, but rather falsify it. And if a law

161

of nature has been falsified it is no longer possible to talk of it as a law of nature. In short, it simply does not make sense to talk of miracles as constituting genuine counter-instances to a *true* law of nature.

But what then is the task or role of the scientist when he discovers that a particular law of nature has been falsified? It would seem that the scientist is committed to try to discover and formulate a new law, which must replace the now discredited old law.

The particular difficulty which the scientist's approach poses here for the religious person, who believes miracles occur, is that it renders it impossible to draw a distinction which, for the religious person, is crucial. When such a person says a miracle has taken place, he means that an event has occurred which is scientifically or naturally inexplicable *in principle*. The inexplicability in principle is derived from a belief that *no possible* scientific or natural explanation is, or could ever be, available to account for the occurrence of the event. From a scientific point of view, however, an event identified as scientifically inexplicable can only be classified as inexplicable when contrasted with *presently available knowledge* of scientific laws, and is thus an event which, as Wittgenstein would have said, we 'have hitherto failed to group . . . with others in a scientific system'.

It does look as if Wittgenstein's worst fears are justified, because the inexplicability in principle that the religious person claims for miraculous occurrences cannot be arrived at from a *legitimate* scientific standpoint. In using the word 'miracle' in a 'relative sense' one can never approach the 'absolute sense' of that term. It is not that 'science has proved that there are no miracles' but, more simply, science must necessarily eschew the use of such a concept. The word 'miracle', used in a relative sense, represents, as Wittgenstein would say, a mere interest in facts, qua facts.[4] However, if the term is used in an 'absolute sense', one displays, Wittgenstein claimed, a concern with value and "although all judgments of relative value can be shown to be mere statements of facts, no statement of fact can ever be, or imply, a judgment of absolute value."[5] And yet, for Wittgenstein, some facts can "seem to have supernatural value."[6] Miracles, it seems, are events which are facts, and yet at the same time retain an absolute or supernatural value.

To fully appreciate this line of thought, I think we must turn and examine some comments Aquinas made on the topic of miracles in the *Summa Contra Gentiles*.[7] There, Aquinas, very generally, described miracles as being "done by God outside the order usually observed in things."[8] For Aquinas, miracles can be classified into three degrees.

Miracles of the first and second degree involve violations by God of the natural order or natural laws. They are events which go beyond nature: events which nature, unaided, could not produce. However, a miracle of the third degree is well within the capacity of nature only, according to Aquinas, there are occasions when effects are produced which have a supernatural cause. On such occasions, God acts to bring about certain effects, even though nature unaided could produce the *same* effects.

A miracle, properly understood, is a direct act of God in the world. Thus, in Wittgenstein's 'absolute sense of the term', a miracle is not a *mere* fact or event in the world; it is a direct *act* of God in the world—this is what *constitutes* its supernatural or absolute value, and is the basis of its scientific inexplicability *in principle*. With this understanding at hand, we can now even see the confusion implicit in Hume's approach to the miraculous. Hume, in demanding violation of natural law as a necessary condition for identifying a miraculous event, confused a *secular* epistemological necessary condition with the religious understanding of the term. The error, in the 'scientific approach', is a failure to separate epistemological and intelligibility considerations.

It may be felt that, when miracles are viewed as direct acts of God in the world, many of the recalcitrant philosophical problems, generated by the concept, can be solved. However, it seems to me that if one gives this account of the nature of the miraculous one focuses attention on what is perhaps *the* core philosophical problem: that of trying to give an account of what it could mean to say that God, conceived as He is in the Christian tradition, acts in the world. God, within the mainstream Christian tradition, is an eternal, i.e. timeless, transcendent, incorporeal person who acts intentionally in the world, His creation. Is the concept of such an individual, conceived as acting, coherent?

Now, of course, the above assertions do not amount to any kind of proof that the concept is incoherent. I have only suggested that there is a major philosophical problem here. However, I feel I must agree with A. Kenny when he stated, "I know of no successful treatment of the philosophical problems involved in conceiving a non-embodied mind active throughout the universe: it is indeed rare to find among theistic philosophers even an attempt to solve the problems."[9] Surely it must behoove any philosopher, concerned to illustrate the coherence of the concept of miracle, to take this problem and challenge seriously, because, in a very important sense, the issues and the problem raised here constitute the *most fundamental* consideration? Unless one can have a coherent concept of a transcendent, incorporeal agent, the concept of miracle can, under no circumstances, be applied.

It looks very much as if Wittgenstein, in stressing the importance of 'using the word "miracle" in an absolute sense', has drawn our attention to *the* fundamental problem facing the religious person. While with the 'relative sense of the term', it was not possible to transcend scientific considerations and interests, nor indeed affirm a religiously adequate conception of the miraculous, it seems that, when one employs the 'absolute sense of the term', the resultant concept could well be radically incoherent.

In saying this, I am really not adding anything to M. Hesse's percipient remark, made in a short contribution to a Cambridge Seminar on Miracles:

> And even more difficult to understand ... is theological talk about the special acts of a transcendent God. The offence of particularity is still with us, whether these special acts violate or conform with the laws of nature. The fundamental problem is not about miracle, but about transcendence.[10]

And she was right.

One final point: I have not been primarily concerned with a straight exegesis of Wittgenstein's ideas. My main concern has been with the concept of miracle; and I have utilised Wittgenstein's comments, in a particular fashion, in order to gain some insight into the nature and difficulties of that concept.

ENDNOTES

[1] Rhees, R., "Wittgenstein's Lecture on Ethics", *Philosophical Review* Vol. 74 (1965), pp. 3–12.
[2] Rhees (1965), pp. 10–11.
[3] Hume, D., *Enquiries Concerning the Human Understanding* (Glasgow-New York ²1902), p. 114.
[4] Rhees (1965), p. 6.
[5] Rhees (1965), p. 6.
[6] Rhees (1965), p. 10.
[7] Pegis, A. C., (ed.), St. Thomas Aquinas, *Basic Writings* (New York 1945).
[8] Pegis (1945), *Summa Contra Gentiles* Bk. III, Chp. 101.
[9] Kenny, A., *God and the Philosophers* (Oxford-London 1979), p. 127.
[10] Hesse, M., "Miracles and the Laws of Nature", in C. F. D. Moule (ed.), *Miracles* (London 1965), pp. 41–42

* * *

TOLSTOIS *KURZE AUSLEGUNG DES EVANGELIUMS* UND WITTGENSTEINS *TRACTATUS LOGICO-PHILOSOPHICUS*

Heinz Hellerer
Universität München

Obwohl die Interpreten des *Tractatus logico-philosophicus* bisher zahlreiche Versuche unternommen haben, seine wenigen darin enthaltenen Aussagen über das Lebensproblem oder das Mystische auszulegen, blieb im Zusammenhang damit jedoch die Frage, von welchen Vorbegriffen Wittgenstein ausging und durch welche Vorstellungen sein Bild von Religion und vom Lebensproblem geprägt war, weitgehend unbeantwortet. Diese Quellen seines Denkens sollen im folgenden ein wenig beleuchtet werden.

Ein interessanter Hinweis in diese Richtung ergibt sich aus einem von Wittgenstein selbst geschriebenen Brief an Ludwig von Ficker, der sich offenbar damals in einem psychisch desolaten Zustand befand:

> Sie leben sozusagen im Dunkel dahin und haben das erlösende Wort nicht gefunden. Und wenn ich, der so grund verschieden von Ihnen bin, etwas raten will, so scheint das vielleicht eine Eselei. Ich wage es aber trotzdem. Kennen Sie die „Kurze Erläuterung des Evangeliums" von Tolstoi? Dieses Buch hat mich seinerzeit geradezu am Leben erhalten. Würden Sie sich dieses Buch kaufen und es lesen? Wenn Sie es nicht kennen, so können Sie sich auch nicht denken, wie es auf den Menschen wirken kann. (*Briefe*, S. 72f).

Wittgenstein bescheinigt damit also einem Werk von Tolstoi eine außerordentliche Wirkung auf sich selbst; worum handelt es sich nun dabei?

Vom März 1880 bis zum Juli 1881 arbeitete Tolstoi an einem monströsen dreibändigen Werk über die Evangelien, das erstmals 1892 in Genf unter dem Titel *„Réunion, traduction et examen des quatre Évangiles"* erschien;[1] da die religiös-moralischen Schriften Tolstois in Rußland selbst verboten waren, mußten sie im Ausland erscheinen. In diesem Oeuvre wird jede Perikope der Bibel zuerst auf griechisch angeführt, dann auf russisch nach der Übersetzung der Synodalausgabe. Jeder Perikope ist zudem persönliche Auslegung Tolstois beigefügt, an zahlreichen Stellen auch eine tiefergehende Analyse und Diskussion des Textes. Nach der Fertigstellung dieses Werkes erkannte Tolstoi jedoch, daß ein solch monumentales Werk mit seinem eigenwilligen exegetischen Anspruch der Masse der Leser verschlossen bleiben würde, und beschloß deshalb, zusätzlich eine kleinere Ausgabe – quasi eine Art Einleitung – zu der *„Réunion"* zu publizieren. Diese Einleitung erschien 1890 wiederum in Genf unter dem Titel *„Abrégé de l'Évangile"*, fünfzehn Jahre später in England (Christchurch 1905) und 1918 schließlich auch auf russisch in Moskau.[2]

Ein Jahr nach der Genfer Ausgabe von 1890 kam diese *„Abrégé"* auch in deutscher Übersetzung auf den Markt, und zwar unter dem Titel *„Kurze Auslegung des Evangeliums"* im Steinitz-Verlag in Berlin (1891), und kurz darauf, 1892, bei Reclam in Leipzig unter der Überschrift *„Kurze Darlegung des Evangeliums"* mit einem Vorwort von Arthur Luther. Diese Reclam-Ausgabe der Evangelienschrift Tolstois schenkte Wittgenstein 1923 seinem Freund Heinrich Postl, der sie dann wiederum der Wittgenstein-Dokumentation in Kirchberg/NÖ zur Verfügung stellte; ob diese dort vorliegende Ausgabe tatsächlich diejenige ist, die Wittgenstein den ganzen 1. Weltkrieg über mit sich führte,[3] läßt sich heute nicht mehr mit letzter Sicherheit feststellen.

Drei Gründe sprechen nunmehr dafür, daß Wittgensteins Vorstellung von Religion, wie er sie im Tractatus darlegt, tatsächlich durch die Evangelienschrift wesentlich beeinflußt wurde:

1. Die *„Kurze Auslegung des Evangeliums"* bezeichnet Wittgenstein selbst, auch wenn er

den Titel offensichtlich falsch zitiert, als für sich relevant. Da keine weitere Schrift Tolstois über die Evangelien existiert, die einen ähnlichen Titel tragen würde, und außerdem beide Ausgaben der „Kurzen Auslegung" im Taschenbuchformat erschienen sind, konnte er nur dieses Werk von Tolstoi den ganzen Krieg über mit sich führen.

2. Weder Wittgensteins Briefen, noch den Berichten seiner Zeitgenossen und Bekannten läßt sich entnehmen, daß er sich bereits vor dem Kauf der Evangelienschrift mit religiösem Schrifttum auseinandergesetzt hätte; ihr Einfluß auf seine Begrifflichkeit und seine Vorstellungen zum Thema Religion und Mystik ist daher umso höher zu veranschlagen.

3. Eine Reihe von inhaltlichen Parallelen zum Tractatus; sie müssen noch etwas beleuchtet werden:

Nach Tolstoi liegt die ärgste Fehlinterpretation des kirchlich überlieferten Gottesbildes in der Trennung von Gott und Leben; für ihn ist Gott zwar einerseits der „endlose Urquell der Dinge",[4] doch andererseits eine rein geistige Erscheinung. Die Annäherung an diesen Gott kann daher nicht durch äußerliche Tätigkeiten wie Kult, Liturgie oder Sakrament erreicht werden, sondern ausschließlich durch die Versenkung in das eigene Innere und die Absage an das „fleischliche" Leben. Nachdem im Tractatus ja immerhin der lapidare Satz steht: „Gott offenbart sich nicht in der Welt." (TLP 6.432), möchte man nun zunächst annehmen, daß von diesem Konstrukt eines geistigen Gottes keinerlei Brücke zu Wittgenstein geschlagen werden kann; auf der anderen Seite aber läßt sich Wittgensteins Tagebüchern entnehmen, daß er sich mit der Gottesfrage intensiv auseinandergesetzt hat und keineswegs einen dezidiert atheistischen Standpunkt einnimmt.[5] Diese auf den ersten Blick so widersprüchliche Einstellung wird jedoch einsichtig, sofern man zugesteht, daß hier die tolstoianische Gottesvorstellung als operanter Mechanismus fungiert: Tolstoi lehnt – ebenso wie Wittgenstein – den Gedanken an eine direkte göttliche Offenbarung in der Welt zwar ab, dennoch aber bleibt für ihn ein „Geist-Gott" die Grundlage alles Geschehens und aller Dinge. Dieser göttliche Urquell wird in der äußeren Welt nicht manifest und kann nur im Inneren des Menschen entdeckt werden. Trotz einer gänzlich anderen Terminologie wird die strukturelle Ähnlichkeit des TLP zum Denken Tolstois in dieser Beziehung deutlich greifbar: Nach Wittgensteins Abbildtheorie der Sprache können nur Tatsachen in der Welt ausgedrückt werden, von diesen ist jedoch – wie bei Tolstoi – keine Lösung grundlegender Probleme zu erwarten (TLP 6.4321); die Abbildtheorie verwehrt Wittgenstein nun zwar auch die direkte Benennung des Grundes aller Tatsachen, das transzendente Verständnis der Tatsachengesamtheit wird im TLP aber dennoch manifest: „Nicht wie die Welt ist, ist das Mystische, sondern daß sie ist." (TLP 6.44).

Noch deutlicher wird die Parallele zwischen Wittgenstein und Tolstoi bei den Ausführungen über das „Leben außerhalb der Zeit": Nach Tolstoi ist der Mensch da, wo er in der Einheit mit dem Willen des „Geist-Gottes" lebt, dem linearen Zeitlauf enthoben – er lebt in einem ewigen Jetzt, im „wahren Leben außerhalb der Zeit",[6] das gleichzeitig auch außerhalb der Persönlichkeit stattfindet. Das wahre Leben ist damit ebenso überzeitlich wie überindividuell. Die Möglichkeit einer Loslösung von der Verhaftung an die Zeit hat indessen auch Wittgenstein ernsthaft in Betracht gezogen; er löst die Unsterblichkeitsfrage ganz gleich wie Tolstoi, indem er als Ewigkeit nicht die Perpetuierung des Daseins in einer linear verstandenen Zeit sieht, sondern als die Beendigung der Zeit in einem Leben in der Gegenwart (TLP 6.4311). Dabei ist nach Wittgenstein dieses Leben außerhalb der Zeit genau wie das Gesichtsfeld zwar objektiv begrenzt, aber subjektiv unendlich und daher ewig. Eng verbunden mit der Frage nach dem Leben außerhalb der Zeit stellt sich für Wittgenstein ebenso wie für Tolstoi das Problem des richtigen und glücklichen Lebens dar. Aus Wittgensteins Tagebüchern läßt sich ablesen, daß ihn zunächst vor allem der Gedanke an ein harmonisches Dasein beschäftigte:

> Das glückliche Leben scheint in irgendeinem Sinne harmonischer zu sein als das unglückliche. In welchem aber?
> Was ist das objektive Merkmal des glücklichen, harmonischen Lebens? Da ist es wieder klar, daß es kein solches Merkmal, das sich beschreiben ließe, geben kann.
> Dies Merkmal kann kein psychisches, sondern nur ein metaphysisches, ein transzendentes sein. (Tagebücher 1914–1916, S. 171).

Wittgenstein nimmt hier den Grundgedanken Tolstois, daß das gute und glückliche Leben in einer Harmonisierung besteht (bei Tolstoi in der Harmonisierung des Subjekts mit dem göttlichen Willen), zwar auf, vermag aber nicht anzugeben, womit dieses Leben harmonisiert werden soll, da ein objektives Merkmal in der Tatsachenwelt nicht vorhanden ist. Das glückliche Leben ist daher ein sich selbst rechtfertigendes harmonisches Dasein, doch das Womit der Harmonie ist nicht abbildbar und nicht sprachlich faßbar. Vor diesem Hintergrund wird z.B. der folgende opake Satz des Tractatus verständlich: „Die Lösung des Rätsels des Lebens in Raum und Zeit liegt außerhalb von Raum und Zeit. (Nicht Probleme der Naturwissenschaft sind ja zu lösen.)" (*TLP* 6.4312) Bei aller Ähnlichkeit zwischen Tolstoi und Wittgenstein bleibt damit zwischen den beiden Denkern doch die Differenz bestehen, daß es für Wittgenstein keine Verschmelzung mit einem Lebensurgrund, keine *unio mystica* im Sinne Tolstois gibt, wohl aber eine mögliche Beantwortung der entscheidenden Lebensfragen.

Vor dem Hintergrund der tolstoianischen Evangelienschrift zeichnet sich nunmehr ein Transzendenzverständnis des frühen Wittgenstein ab, das durch die folgenden drei Komponenten beschrieben werden kann:

1. Die Grundlage dieses Transzendenzverständnisses bildet die christliche Religion, wenn sie auch hier in einer ganz bestimmten, mystisch verklärten Form aufscheint, die mit den orthodoxen Formen des Christentums nichts gemein hat.

2. Aufgrund seiner Sprachphilosophie kann Wittgenstein eine transzendente Grundlage der Tatsachenwelt nicht als eine solche benennen, da eine solche sich in der Tatsachenwelt gerade nicht manifestiert. Aus den wenigen Äußerungen des *TLP* zu diesem Thema darf man indessen schließen, daß Wittgenstein sehr wohl eine solche Grundlage annimmt.

3. Wittgenstein hat hier eine Möglichkeit eröffnet, wie das rational ausgerichtete, naturwissenschaftliche Denken und die Religion miteinander vereinbart werden könnten − nicht in der Kommunikation beider Bereiche, wohl aber im existentiellen Vollzug des Einzelnen.

ANMERKUNGEN

[1] Nach: N. Weisbein, Vorwort zu: L. Tolstoi, *Abrégé de l'Évangile*, (Paris 1969), S. VII.
[2] A. a. O.
[3] Laut einer brieflichen Mitteilung B. Russells an Lady Ottoline vom 20. Dezember 1919 führte Wittgenstein die Evangelienschrift Tolstois den ganzen Krieg über bei jeder Gelegenheit mit sich. In: L. Wittgenstein, *Briefe*, S. 101.
[4] Tolstoi, L., *Kurze Auslegung des Evangeliums*, (Berlin 1891), S. 51.
[5] Vgl. dazu insbesondere L. Wittgenstein, *Tagebücher 1914−1916*, S. 165−168, sowie L. Wittgenstein, *Prototractatus*, S. 238.
[6] Tolstoi (1891), S. 6.

* * *

PRIVATE LANGUAGE AND RELIGIOUS EXPERIENCE

Reijo J. Työrinoja
University of Helsinki

Religious experience has commonly been considered the most personal and individual experience which a man can posses. Especially within the idealistic Protestant tradition man's relation to God has been thought to be founded on such a personal and private experience that nobody else can ever know the substance of that experience but the person himself. This conception of immediate and private religious experience includes however the specific idea of the relation between religious experience and language. Accordingly a person identifies and names his private inner experience immediately and privately in his own mind. The conception of the logical privacy of experiences presupposes that a person has his own inner private language by means of which he is able to pick up and identify his different experiences in the stream of his inner mental events.

Wittgenstein's remarks on private experience and private language throw an interesting light on this question of the nature of religious experience. He writes: " 'You can't hear God speak to someone else, you can hear him only if you are being addressed'. – That is a grammatical remark." (*Z.* § 717). The remark under consideration is thus a remark on the logical grammar of the expression "to hear God speaking", or a remark on its peculiar *use* in the religious language-game. We can say "I hear John speaking to Mary", but not "I hear God speaking to Mary". Wittgenstein defines private language as a language in which the words "are to refer to what can only be known to the person speaking; to his immediate private sensations. So another person cannot understand the language." (*PI.* § 243). In a logically private language it is essential that the words refer to something which can be *known* only to the person himself. It presupposes that a person could also give *private meanings* to the words expressing his private sensations and experiences. The words of a private language acquire their meanings on the basis of what a private person experiences *immediately* in his own mind. This criticism of "the immediately known" is an important feature in Wittgenstein's so called 'private language argument.'

What if a private language is thought of as a language in itself? It has to give a person the method by means of which he is able to identify his inner experience. When a person has some experience he has to name it, impress it on himself, carry it in his mind, and identify it correctly in some other situation in the future. A person makes rules and conventions for himself and commits himself them. He is able to make sure that he has followed the rule correctly and has correctly used the same sign for the same inner experience. But how can he be sure that he has used the sign of a certain experience in the right way? How can a person discern the right way from the wrong way? How can he decide and commit himself to using the *same* sign for the *same* experience in his mind? What does the word "same" mean here? It seems as if a person does not need any criterion in order to make sure of the right usage of the sign. He is always able to remember right the connexion between the sign and the experience. Now, according to Wittgenstein, we can no longer talk about 'right'. (*PI.* § 258). "If everything can be made out to accord with the rule, then it can also be made out to conflict with it. And so there would be neither accord nor conflict here." (*PI.* § 201). If the use of the word "rule" is to be meaningful, one has to be able to act according to the rule and contrary to the rule, to obey it and to disobey it. If this is not possible, the consequence is that one can no longer talk about "a rule" or "to obey a rule". To follow a rule and to obey a rule are customs, uses and institutions; they are practices, not something which only one man can do. (*PI.* §§ 199, 202)

The idea of the private experience and the private language leads to the fact that one cannot meaningfully speak about the *object* of an experience. It is this that Wittgenstein wants to to show by his argument of "a beetle in the box." If the word "beetle" is to mean something which each person sees only in his own box, or in his own mind, then the thing itself called beetle has no role in the language-game played with the word "beetle." If people cannot even in principle compare the contents of their "boxes" with each other, it does not matter what they have in their boxes. If the contents of sensation or experience is regarded as a private object present only to the single mind, and its logical grammar is construed on the model of 'object and designation,' then "the object drops out of consideration as irrelevant." (*PI*. § 293). By criticizing the possession of of a private language Wittgenstein wants to save "our commonsense notion about what we should commonly call the objects of our experience." (*BB*. p. 44). The idea of the private object of an experience destroys the notion about the object the experience. The concept of the object of the experience has no use if the meaning of a private experience rests only on what each one sees or experiences in his mind and what is logically independent of other users of language.

Wittgenstein applies the private language argument also to religious language in his *Lectures on Religious Belief*, when he discusses the meaning of the word "death" and the possibility of giving it a private meaning. The word "death" is, like every word, a public instrument of language "which has a whole technique of usage." (*LC*. pp. 68–69). If a person uses the word "death" while he means something private by it, then one can ask what connects the private meaning of the word "death" with that which we call death? If his idea of death is something completely private, there is no ground to call it an "idea of death" unless it is something we connect with death. If the private meaning of "death" has nothing to do with that which other people call death, then "it does not belong on the game played with 'death', which we all know and understand." (*LC*. p. 69). No rules can connect the private meaning of "death" with that which is called death, because there is no language-game where the word "death" could be used. In such a case the rules only hang in the air; "for the institution of their use is lacking." (*PI*. § 380). Therefore, if that which someone calls idea of death "is to become relevant, it must become part of our game." (*LC*. p. 69).

It is not possible to let the meaning of religious language depend on private immediate experiences, if one still wants to speak meaningfully about the object of religious experiences. An experience of something is logically dependent on the description of that experience in language. The "substratum" of an experience is "the mastery of a technique." "It is only if someone *can do*, has learnt, is master of, such-and-such, that it makes sense to say he has had *this* experience." (*PI*. II, pp. 208–209). Religious language is a part of the public game played by means of language. Although the meanings of its expressions cannot be private, they actually *refer* to private experiences. Wittgenstein says that "the essential thing about private experience is really not that each person possesses his own exemplar, but that nobody knows whether other people also have *this* or something else." (*PI*. § 272). Experiences are private in the sense that of course nobody else can have *my* experiences. This is not anyway a factual or metaphysical statement concerning inner experiences. The sentence "inner experiences are private" is the grammatical picture which describes the logical grammar of those words referring to our personal experiences. But it does not say that those words have the twofold meaning; the meaning that they have for everybody, and in addition, the private meaning that holds for only one person (*PI*. § 273).

The word "experience" does not derive its meaning from private mental events. One should not presuppose at all that the word "experience" has only one and exact use and meaning in our language-games. The concept of 'experience' goes as far as the different examples of its use go, and it can be explained only by means of examples. 'Experience' is not a concept with definite boundaries. (Cf. *PG*. p. 112). The different uses of the word "experience" form its meaning and thus our concept of 'experience'. (Cf. *PI*. § 532). The different but related uses of "experience" form rather "a family". The concept of 'experience' is "family resemblance," because the word experience has more than one use and meaning, in fact "a family of meanings." (*PI*. §§ 67, 77). The concept of experience is modified by the language-game in which the word "experience" is used. Particularly, the experience of God is the experience of the living person, because the word "God" is used as the word representing a person. The expressions "God sees," "God hears," "God loves," etc. are legitimate moves in the religious language-game. However, according to Wittgenstein, "only of a living human being and what resembles (behaves like) a living human being can one say: "it has sensations; it sees; is blind; hears; is deaf; is conscious or unconscious." (*PI.* § 281). The use of the words "to see", "to hear", "to love" have their paradigms in the first place in human behaviour, in the way in which living human beings react in certain situations. For that reason the religious use of language presupposes the mastering and understanding of the non-religious use of language. Here also "family resemblances" are in question. A blind and deaf person cannot understand the meaning of the expressions "God sees" and "God hears", because the paradigms of their normal use are inadequate for him.

An experience is a definite experience only in the language-game. Only the person who masters already the religious language-game can have *religious* experiences. He has to know the paradigm situations of the religious use of certain words. The religious use of words are still related in many different ways to their non-religious use. One can say that they belong to the same "family of cases". (Cf. *PI.* § 164). A colour blind person is incapable of using certain words, because he cannot learn their paradigms. But this colour blind person is not only *colour* blind, but *meaning* blind too. "The person who cannot play *this* game does not have *this* concept." (*RoC.* III, § 115). Can one talk about 'meaning blindness' also in regard to the religious meaning of certain word, for example "God", in the same manner as one talks of the meaning blindness involved in colour blindness? Are there some paradigms of religious use of language the lack of which implies that a person is unable to play this particular language-game? (Cf. *PI.* § 57). Wittgenstein himself suggests this possibility when he says: "What must the man be called, who cannot understand the concept 'God', cannot see how a reasonable man may use this word seriously? Are we to say he suffers from some *blindness*?" (*RPP.*, I, § 213).

* * *

WITTGENSTEIN ON PRIMITIVE RELIGION

Norman Lillegard
University of Nebraska, Omaha

Frazer tells the story of the King of the Wood at Nemi in a way that evokes what is strange, dreadful and tragic in it.[1] He seems to have thought that if he could determine what sort of views or thinking was behind this and other customs, then he would also understand what was strange or impressive in them. Wittgenstein has two main objections to Frazer's way of dealing with the data. First, he holds that either Frazer's account does not help us to understand what is impressive in these customs, or if it sometimes does it is not for the reasons Frazer supposes. Secondly, he argues that Frazer is mistaken to begin with in supposing that primitive customs and rituals are based upon views or ways of thinking (opinions). I will not expound or discuss the first of these objections. It has recently been discussed and illustrated in an interesting way by Frank Cioffi and I have nothing to add to his remarks.[2]

Frazer thought that primitive beliefs and practices arose from primitive scientific thinking. Thus he claimed that various rituals involved the application of "laws" such as the law of similarity (like produces like). This law is applied in rain ceremonies in which clouds or thunder are *mimicked*, for example. Belief in such laws is, according to Frazer, very like belief in scientific laws. These laws are thought to explain the course of events in nature and to be perfectly exceptionless and beyond the reach of any kind of personal agency. Believing in them is a matter of having an opinion or view about how nature works.[3] Wittgenstein regards all of this as utterly misguided. He denies that attempts to explain something, opinions, or views, give rise to primitive rituals and beliefs. ". . . the characteristic feature of primitive man is that he does not act from opinions" (BFGB 71).

Frazer's kind of account and Wittgenstein's objections can be profitably discussed in the light of a distinction between rituals which are simply or primarily expressive or symbolic, on the one hand, and rituals which are "magical" in the sense that they involve specific routines aimed at producing extraneous effects. For example, in Bulgaria and among the Bosnian Turks a woman will adopt a child by pushing him through her skirts (GB 15). Frazer counts this as a clear case of homeopathic magic, but surely Wittgenstein is justified in objecting that it is insane to suppose that the woman mistakenly believes that the child has actually been born to her (BFGB 66). Rather this appears to be a symbolic or expressive gesture, an example of the first type of ritual. The second type is illustrated by the following; the natives of southeastern Australia sometimes stick sharp pieces of bone, etc. into an enemy's footprints as if to lame him (GB 44). Frazer counts this as a clear case of contagious magic. Wittgenstein objects to such an interpretation on several grounds, two of which are as follows. First, the same savage who does this ". . . really builds his hut out of wood and carves his arrows skillfully and not in effigy" (BFGB 64). This fact is taken by Wittgenstein to indicate that in stabbing the footprint the primitive is not employing a technique to get a result. His *techniques* are generally quite sensible. Secondly Wittgenstein points out that there are many similar practices among civilized people, such as burning someone in effigy or kissing the picture of a loved one (BFGB 64). These actions come more or less naturally. They are *instinctive*. We simply act in these ways ". . . and then we feel satisfied" (BFGB 64). No elaborate explanation seems necessary in our case. Why should one be needed for an understanding of the primitive's behaviour? Moreover, bringing such phenomena into connection with instincts which we possess *is* the explanation of them which we want (BFGB 72). (This last claim is, I think, meant to be supported by the kinds of considerations discussed by Cioffi in the essay mentioned above).

170

No doubt many rituals are primarily expressive or include a very large expressive or symbolic component. It does not follow that none of them involve pseudoscientific beliefs, as Wittgenstein seems to claim. Some anthropologists distinguish the first type of ritual from the second by pointing out that the second type (which is very common) involves magic while the first does not.[4] Yet magic seems to typically involve erroneous opinions. Primitives mistakenly believe that the garden made with magic will flourish, the cargo cult will bring cargo, etc. How can Wittgenstein deny this, unless he has generalized from the first type of ritual to all types, thus concluding that *all* ritual is purely expressive?

Before we attribute an egregious *non seguitur* to Wittgenstein, we should remember that he does not deny that an opinion might enter into a ritual (BFGB 80), that a religious belief might develop into a sort of (mistaken) theory, (BFGB 62), that a deified king might be fool enough to opine that he has powers which he plainly does not have (BFGB 73).Primitive religion is not necessarily more immune to corruption and confusion than are others forms of life. What he *does* deny is that it *arises out of* a theory or is the result of a way of thinking. Rather it arises out of instinctive reactions and actions. However, he does not claim that this fact distinguishes religious or magical practices from other activities, for in his view every form of life or language game arises out of primitive instinctive actions and reactions.[5] What is meant by 'primitive' in this connection? Wittgenstein answers: "Surely that this way of behaving is prelinguistic; that a language game is based on it, that it is the prototype of a way of thinking and not the result of a way of thinking" (Z 541). According to Wittgenstein magic is distinguished from science by the fact that ". . . in science there is progress, but in magic there isn't. Magic has no tendency to develop" (BFGB 74). I take him to mean that magical rituals do not usually develop much beyond the primitive reactions which give rise to them, whereas the primitive reactions which give rise to causal notions (reactions to being pushed, for instance) are left far behind in the elaboration of causal notions in science. But what reasons are there for believing that magic should be characterised in this way?

The sense of an action is a function of context (a move is *what* it is only *in a game*). *What* is the primitive doing when he stabs a footprint with a bone? According to Frazer he is doing a kind of applied science. That is the sense his action has so to grasp it we must understand the background of theorizing which gives it this sense. Wittgenstein on the other hand avers that the primitive is doing something like what we do when we burn someone in effigy. Now it is clear that when we do such a thing we are not doing applied science. This can be seen from the attitude towards evidence and experiment which goes with such an action. If someone were to propose a test to determine whether or not burning in effigy is efficacious, we would think he was joking, or insane. This background fact gives a sense to the action in question different from that possessed by actions which are the application of scientific or technical knowledge. However it is possible to grant this point while still maintaining that what *we* are doing when we burn someone in effigy bears only a *prima facie* resemblance to what the primitive is doing when he, for example, stabs a footprint, precisely on the grounds that he does take seriously evidence for and against the value of such practices. Evidence that this is so can be found in anthropological literature. For instance, the Puluwat Islanders observed many taboos and rituals relating to seafaring. Christian missionary priests did not insist that they give up these beliefs and practices, but did stress that they were not efficacious. That did not by itself lead to an abandonment of the old ways, but eventually one of the great Puluwat navigators decided that the priests might be right and set out on a voyage without observing any of the taboos or performing the necessary rituals. He returned unscathed and, according to Gladwin, shortly thereafter these rituals and taboos were entirely abandoned.[5]

This looks like a straightforward case of giving up a practice in the light of falsifying evidence. Yet there are reasons to think that this sort of case does not tell as decisively against Wittgenstein's account as we may be tempted to suppose. Large scale changes in belief and practice can seldom be appropriately described as simply the rejection of particular beliefs in the light of falsifying evidence, comparable, say, to the rejection of the corpuscular theory of light in the wake of Foucault's experiments. I cannot take space here to attempt a full account of what is required for a good description of such changes, but a few facts and conceptual points apropos this particular case deserve to be at least mentioned.

We need to keep in mind that the change which Gladwin describes was gradual. Long before anyone dared to test certain of the old ways, missionaries had already undermined many related beliefs and practices. Perhaps more importantly, they had brought a utilitarian perspective to bear on these practices in the very act of denying that they were *efficacious* (they did not condemn these practices as *impious*, according to Gladwin). It is possible that in doing this the missionaries directed the attention of the islanders to a non-essential aspect of their rituals and thereby increased or produced a preoccupation with that aspect. The point is that certain kinds of criticism and analysis can alter the sense that people have of their own practices or forms of life, and at the same time cause them to be impressed by features of the world and their lives that had hithero gone unnoticed or carried little weight. A fascination with technological success might come to replace concerns with ways of coming to grips with the unavoidable contingencies of existence. The result might be that a person comes to see his old way of life as superstitious or in some other way inconsequential.

The notion that a person might be tutored or coaxed into a kind of blindness to his own life is not, I think, farfetched. But some people might not even need tutoring. Coulton tells of a medieval peasant who kept the communion host tucked under her tongue all the way home from church, then removed it, broke it up, and spread it on her garden.[7] No doubt she had been taught that the host had lifegiving power. But we might also say that she had succumbed to the temptation to see this fact in a way that might be turned to her immediate worldly advantage, and this is something which deeper attention to the inner character of the eucharist would have discouraged. Is it not possible that a whole community, as well as individuals, might become corrupted in similar ways, out of similar motives? Wittgenstein says, "New language games come into existence, others become obsolete and forgotten." (PI 23) Many become *corrupt* in the course of becoming obsolete.

I have tried to indicate some lines along which one might argue in trying to show that what we are tempted to call "the abandonment of a ritual or belief in the light of falsifying evidence" may not be what we take it to be, namely itself evidence (grammatical evidence) that the ritual in question is a crude kind of science. But if a ritual is not crude science it does not follow that it is merely expressive, or that it has more than a *prima facie* resemblance to some ritual of our own. It might be neither like our science nor our rituals, in important respects. Explanation in anthropology may require a search for illuminating analogies from our own experience (that is what Wittgenstein gives us) but no analogy is perfect. There is no reason to believe that Wittgenstein could not accept this point, and there is evidence in his remarks that he does accept it. Thus there is no need to force his remarks into the procrustean bed of emotivism or some other kind of noncognitivism. Primitive religion is neither crude science nor merely expressive behaviour, on Wittgenstein's view.

ENDNOTES

1 Cf. Ludwig Wittgenstein, "Remarks on Frazer's Golden Bough," trans. John Beversluis, in *Wittgenstein: Sources and Perspectives*, C. G. Luckhardt, ed. (Ithaca 1979), p. 63. This work will henceforth be referred to in my text as 'BFGB,' followed by the page numbers from this volume.
2 Cioffi, Frank, "Wittgenstein and the Fire Festivals," in Irving Block, ed. *Perspectives on the Philosophy of Wittgenstein* (Oxford 1981), p. 232.
3 Frazer, James, *The Golden Bough* (New York 1942), p. 11. This work will henceforth be referred to in my text as 'GB,' followed by page numbers from this edition.
4 Cf. Bronislaw Malinowski, *Magic, Science and Religion* (New York 1948), pp. 37−38.
5 Cf. Wittgenstein, *Culture and Value* trans. Peter Winch (Oxford 1980), p. 31.
6 Gladwin, Thomas, *East is a Big Bird* (Cambridge 1970), pp. 17−20.
7 Coulton, C. G., *Life in the Middle Ages* (Cambridge 1967), p. 72.

* * *

WITTGENSTEIN, RELIGION, ATHEISM

Stanislav Hubík
Czechoslovak Academy of Sciences, Brno

When going through Wittgenstein's works roughly from the beginning of the 30's it can be stated that he asigns an important role to religion, although on the other hand we are told that it is just the religion that cannot be discussed. This fact misleads some interpreters to conclusions about Wittgenstein's religious mysticism (quote at least J. A. Passmore according to whom Wittgenstein stops in his *Tractatus* at the point where R. Otto starts). Let us have a closer look at the statement "it cannot be discussed" and at his so much emphasized mysticism.

Tractatus informs us that the most important matters cannot be discussed in a language based on the existing type of rationality which is in its essence mathematizing. Wittgenstein arrived at this finding under manifold temporal influences as was convincingly shown by A. Janik and S. Toulmin. Especially K. Kraus and F. Mauthner shaped the views of the young Wittgenstein who was endowed with a remarkable ability for logical analysis. And not only Kraus or Mauthner but other Viennese thinkers, too were leading a sharp fight with the phenomenon called the *phrase*.

Here I do not mean "the phrase" in the literary or journalistic sense of the word which would be only one aspect of the problem. This aspect was intensively and critically treated by, for example Kraus who wrote: "Journalism concentrates chiefly on the fact how to polish again and again the glaze of corruption. The more it escalates usury with spiritual and material wealth, the higher is the need for making the veil of bad intentions more attractive." Kraus observed the phrase as "a form that serves as a mere cover of content itself, a mere guise for the body and not the body for spirit".[1] The phrase of spiritual corruption was concerned here, "the terrible development" of linguistic and intellectual forms was dealt with—as was declared by Kraus in connection with his evaluation of H. Heine's role in this process.

Philosophical efforts of the young Wittgenstein are being considered in the same way as a specific attack against the phrase in the widest sense of the term. Nevertheless, Wittgenstein's criticism of the phrase differs from the ironical method of Kraus. He did not identify himself with Krausian *sprachcritical* mysticism ("I rule over the language of the others. My language holds rule over me as it pleases."[2]), on the contrary, he intensively created formally logical and logically philosophical tools of linguistic catharsis. In my opinion, Wittgenstein went on further than Kraus. He found out that the entire intellectual situation of the period not only journalism was saturated with the phrase, that rationality was sinking deeper and deeper into the traps of phraseology depriving the language of its meaning—or better to say, the phrase itself was becoming the meaning. He came to the conclusion that "the glaze of corruption" is polished also by philosophy, ethics, the existing language of religion, atheism, etc. And thus, finally it is not important what is written but what is not written.[3]

Although Wittgenstein considers Mauthner's Sprachkritik as negative in *Tractatus* (*TLP* 4.0031), still it seems that he was inspired by Mauthner more than he was willing to admit. Mauthner is also a critic of the phrase in the wide sense of the term: ". . . it is theology that is hidden in our entire thinking and talking, (. . .) words are mere gods."[4] Not the phrase but the action—such is the *ideational* polarity of Mauthner's *sprachcritical* position. Both sides—that means Kraus' criticism of the phrase and Mauthner's criticism of the linguistic fetishism--found their expressions in Wittgenstein's delimitation of the meaningful "so to say from the inside". Once in *Tractatus*, for the second time—and more intensively—in this later writings and lectures.

The question is what has it to do with the theme given in the title of my paper (Wittgenstein, Religion, Atheism)?

Moral, religious, atheistic or simply world-view positions represent doubtlessly what cannot be discussed according to the young Wittgenstein. These matters pass beyond all possibilities of being grasped in a language, that is a language saturated with the phrase. These problems can only be "pointed at" (shown). I assume that Wittgenstein gave up the possibility of a sensible discussion of religious, atheistic, moral, etc. problems not only for logical reasons but because of Kraus's and Mauthner's arguments, too. The early Wittgenstein shifts the statements of religion (atheism. ethics, etc.) beyond the borders of meaningful language not only because they oppose the demands put on a meaningful statement (syntactic and semantic claims) but because the language of religion (primarily of Christianity) is saturated with the phrase and the same applies to the language of atheism (especially of philosophically critical atheism), too. The language of religion and atheism "polishes the glaze of corruption" and "escalates the usury" (Kraus) of various kinds. Such a language can either be critized or one can keep silent. The early Wittgenstein has chosen the latter path.

And this is the very point which a Marxist theoretician finds the most remarkable, especially in the light of the whole Wittgenstein's philosophical work.

When K. Marx and F. Engels were dealing with critical analysis of young-Hegelian philosophical thinking they were evaluating the young-Hegelian radical criticism of religion, too. In this connection they wrote among other things: ". . . the demand to change consciousness leads finally into the demand to interpret in different ways what exists that means to accept it on the basis of another interpretation. In spite of their would-be world-destructive phrases young-Hegelian ideologists are extremely conservative. The youngest ones from among them found a correct expression for their activity when claiming they fight only against *phrases*. But they forget that they confront these phrases with new ones and they do not fight with the real contemporary world at all when fighting only against phrases of this world".[5] Marx and Engels rejected the theory saturated with the phrase, they refused linguistic fetishism and hypercriticism of the young-Hegelianists. They drew attention to the fact that "one of the most difficult tasks of philosophers is to descend from the world of ideas into the real world ... . It would suffice if philosophers changed their language into a common one out of which their language is abstracted; they would realize that it was a truncated language of the real world and furthermore, they would come to the conclusion that neither ideas nor language are special isolated spheres just by themselves; they are but *manifestations* of real life."[6]

The young Wittgenstein was also convinced that the functions of language free from "phrases" were guaranteed by "an everyday language" (*TLP* 5.5563). In the early 30's he fully concentrated on this subject and he saw a barrier against phrases in the common language (in its "everyday use" − *PI*, § 133).

The early Wittgenstein's philosophy can be considered as criticism of the phrase (the fact that it was not criticism of metaphysics was proved by others, for example by Fann). As for religion, atheism, ethics and some other principal world-view positions the early Wittgenstein's philosophy is not an unanimous rejection of religion or atheism, it is but a rejection of the religious, atheistic, ethical, etc. phrase. Wittgenstein's statement: "God does not appear in this world" (*TLP* 6.432) can be understood in this way, in the same manner can be understood Wittgenstein's division of the world into "the world of the facts, not of the things" (*TLP* 1.1) and "my world" (*TLP* 5.62). And in such a way his explication about the misuse of language in the case of religious reflections (*A Lecture on Ethics*) can be understood.

It can be stated that Wittgenstein avoided the philosophical interpretation of religion critically treated by Marx and Engels in the above-given context. Marx and Engels drew the conclusion that the question of philosophical criticism is in fact of secondary importance because "the weapon of criticism cannot substitute for the criticism of weapons". The fight against "the phrase" must remain *practical*. Naturally, the early Wittgenstein could no reach any similar idea for many reasons. Nevertheless, the way he was treating the given problem suggests that the early Wittgenstein, in my opinion, already knew that "manifestations of real life" cannot be studied as "the phrases" but they must be grasped practically.

The standpoint of practical materialism was characterized by Marx for example in *The Theses on Feuerbach*. Here he emphasized a new approach to relations between the subject and the object out of which arises a new conception of truth.[7] Some signs of practical materialism are to be found also in the late Wittgenstein. His entire conception of the language-games, of the forms of life seems to develop an active approach to language in a sense of practical materialism. It is especially evident when Wittgenstein is reasoning about the socially-practical conditioning of manipulation by linguistic expressions, about the conditioning of linguistic activities by real interests (*PI*, § 570). The full development of this active, practical aspect gives rise to a new attitude of philosophy toward religion, atheism and other basical world-view standpoints in the late Wittgenstein's philosophy.

The problem of religion, atheism, etc. becomes according to the late Wittgenstein a practical one, that is the problem of form of life. Not the language of the phrase, but the form of life is "the house of being" for religion or atheism. Marx and Engels have shown that criticism of the phrase is but a mere phrase of criticism; whereas the problem of religion and atheism is practical,[8] although only abstraction will matter during the first phase in the development of communist atheism.[9]

The late Wittgenstein similarly shows that the sharing of religious faith, atheistic or any other principal world-view attitude does not mean an agreement in opinion but "in the form of life" (*PI*, § 241) and the form of life is known to be "the given", "the bustle of all human activities" (*Z*, § 567). Can this remarkable philosophical parallel be developed further?

I presume it cannot. It must be admitted that the late Wittgenstein leads his rejection of the phrase into socially practical consequencies (he proceeds further than for example young-Hegelians) but here he stops. The form of life is for him "the protophenomenon" (*PI*, p. 226) that resists the language of the phrase and that cannot be made clear. "The given" can be transfered into a hermeneutic problem but this is not point.

This fact stands out even more clearly when considering the whole self-destructive character of the late Wittgenstein's philosophy. The self-negation can be again taken as the rejection of the phrase—but this time of an eventual Wittgenstein's own phrase. But what this aspect underlines even more is the entirely practical character of the problem of religion, atheism and other principal world-view standpoints.

Marx did not suppose that the form of life could resist a theoretical analysis. He came to know that it cannot be a philosophical analysis falling into the traps of the metaphysical phrase but an analysis drawn from materialistic dialectics, an analysis of real social circumstances in which economic relations of the given social phrase of development are being enforced as dominant. (Marx does not absolutely approve this thesis, he considered political economy not to be the principal science in the post-capitalist society.) However, Marx called his attention to the fact that investigating the form of life "starts post festum, that is it issues from the finished results of an evolutionary process. Forms (...) are keeping already their stability as natural forms of social life long before people have been trying to understand for the first time not the historical character of these forms which on the contrary seem to them to be unchangeable, but their content".[10]

Marx noted in this very connection that even the form of life, "the given" can become clear not only through practice but through theoretical analysis, too. I suppose it is not incidental that he pronounced this thesis in the context of his account on goods fetishism and religion.[11]

Of course, we cannot speak about the parallel between Marx's and Wittgenstein's approach any more. Marx was putting into practice his intention to analyse theoretically real social conditions, Wittgenstein was not. Furthermore, Marx aims at a socially political revolutionary change of social conditions. (Naturally, we are aware of the lapse of time between the thinkings of both philosophers and we realize other analogical facts, too.)

The relation of Wittgenstein's philosophy to religion, atheism and other principal world-view standpoints is marked—similarly as in the case of Marx and Engels—by his critical rejection of the speculative phrase (as well as critical) by the refusal to build "another interpretation" of the given. Wittgenstein's philosophy transfers the question of religion, atheism and other principal world-view standpoints from the level of philosophical speculation (the phrase) to the level of practice (the form of life). And this is the moment where Wittgenstein's philosophy stop's for many reasons wellknown to our assembly. And this is the starting point for Marx.

ENDNOTES

1 "Und nichts ist dem Journalismus wichtiger, als die Glasur der Korruption immer wieder auf den Glanz herzurichten. In dem Maße, als er den Wucher an dem geistigen und materiellen Wohlstand steigert, wächst auch sein Bedürfnis, die Hülle der schlechten Absicht gefällig zu machen." Kraus, K., *Untergang der Welt durch schwarze Magie* (München 1960), p. 192.
2 "Ich beherrsche nur die Sprache der andern. Die meinige macht mit mir, was sie will."
   Kraus, K., *Beim Wort genommen* (München 1955), p. 326
3 Wittgenstein, L., *Briefe an Ludwig von Ficker* (Salzburg 1969), p. 35−6.
4 Mauthner, F., *Beiträge zu einer Kritik der Sprache*, Vol. 1 (Leipzig 1923), p. 170.
5 "Diese Forderung, das Bewußtsein zu verändern, läuft auf die Forderung hinaus, das Bestehende anders zu interpretieren, d.h. es vermittelt einer anderen Interpretation anzuerkennen. Die junghegelschen Ideologen sind trotz ihrer angeblich 'welterschütternden' Phrasen die größten Konservativen. Die jüngsten von ihnen haben den richtigen Ausdruck für ihre Tätigkeit gefunden, wenn sie behaupten, nut gegen '*Phrasen*' zu kämpfen. Sie vergessen nur, daß sie diesen Phrasen selbst nichts als Phrasen entgegensetzen, und daß sie die wirkliche bestehende Welt keineswegs bekämpfen, wenn sie nur die Phrasen dieser Welt bekämpfen." Marx, K., Engels, F., *Werke*, Vol. 3 (Berlin 1969), p. 20.
6 "Für die Philosophen ist es eine der schwierigsten Aufgaben, aus der Welt des Gedankens in die wirkliche Welt herabzusteigen. (. . .) Die Philosophen hätten ihre Sprache nur in die gewöhnliche Sprache, aus der sie abstrahiert ist, aufzulösen, um sie als die verdrehte Sprache der wirklichen Welt zu erkennen und einzusehen, daß weder der Gedanken noch die Sprache für sich ein eigenes Reich bilden; daß sie nur *Äußerungen* des wirklichen Lebens sind."
   Marx, K., Engels, F., *Werke*, Vol. 3 (Berlin 1969), p. 432−3.
7 Marx, K., Engels, F., *Werke*, Vol. 3 (Berlin 1969), p. 5.
8 "Alles gesellschaftliche Leben ist wesentlich *praktisch*."−"Die wirkliche, praktische Auflösung dieser Phrasen, die Beseitigung dieser Vorstellungen aus dem Bewußtsein der Menschen wird, wie schon gesagt, durch veränderte Umstände, nicht durch theoretische Deduktionen bewerkstelligt."
   Marx, K., Engels, F., *Werke*, Vol. 3 (Berlin 1969), pp. 7, 40.
9 "Die Philantropie des Atheismus ist daher zuerst nur eine *philosophische* abstrakte Philantropie, die des Kommunismus sogleich reel und unmittelbar zur *Wirkung* gespannt."
   Marx, K., Engels, F., *Gesamtausgabe*, Vol. 3 (Berlin 1932), p. 115.
10 "Es beginnt post festum und daher mit den fertigen Resultaten des Entwicklungsprozesses. Die Formen (. . .) besitzen bereits die Festigkeit von Naturformen des gesellschaftlichen Lebens, bevor die Menschen sich Rechenschaft zu geben suchen, nicht über den historischen Charakter dieser Formen, die ihnen vielmehr bereits als unwandelbar gelten, sondern über deren Gehalt."
   Marx, K., Engels, F., *Werke*, Vol. 23 (*Das Kapital*) (Berlin 1962), p. 89−90.
11 "Der religiöse Widerschein der wirklichen Welt kann überhaupt nur verschwinden, sobald die Verhältnisse des praktischen Werkeltagslebens den Menschen tagtäglich durchsichtig vernünftige Beziehungen zueinander und zur Natur darstellen."
   Marx, k., Engels, F., *Werke*, Vol. 23 (*Das Kapital*) (Berlin 1962), p. 94.

* * *

6. Religion und (religiöse) Praxis

6. Religion and (Religious) Practice

RELIGIOUS IDEALS AS REASONS FOR ACTION

Shyli Karin-Frank
Tel-Aviv University, Ramat Aviv

1.

A religious ideal is a model of perfection which has no existence in reality and which is connected with a belief in God and a system of prescribed actions. The problem discussed in this paper is whether one can regulate and judge one's life in the light of religious perfection, or is the attempt to justify one's behaviour, by pointing toward ideals, a fallacy that expresses a mere psychological illusion? I will argue that ideals are essential to all religions, yet it is logically impossible to act upon them, therefore being religious is, to some degree, aiming at the impossible, in a way that religious practice is misleading. For the sake of the argument, the present discussion necessarily withdraws from radical scepticism.

2.

Religious ideals constitute two different groups: ideals which express the absurd and ideals which express the moral ought.

A) Ideals in which the absurd is built into their meaning are those which display unification with God either through love or true knowledge. These ideals do not address themselves to the individual's conceptual reason, but rather to the heart, the core of true personality. The model of the kingdom of Heaven expresses an unsolved paradox as it is the conjunction of a constant and eternal presence of unification with the Divine with a constant demand to overcome the infinite gap between the human individual and God. The ideal of True Knowledge implies the suspension of human reason because it is inadequate for obtaining truth; the latter is immediate by nature. The ideal of Absolute Obedience to God posits the absurd as the content of religious belief and it permits, even glorifies an obedience to contradictory demands. It is impossible to consider these ideals as reasons for action: One cannot plan actions based upon an absurd or upon a belief in contradictions. Different religions suggest and recommend different types of activities as necessary conditions to attain perfection. Yet all religious activities are external to ideals not only because they are not included in their content, but also because there is no path from human efforts to the absurd. Even if by means of revelation one gains access to the irrational content of such ideals, one still lacks adequate means to apply or to imitate these ideals. It seems that the only way to relate to such ideals is by a religious "leap". Yet a "leap" or a series of "leaps" are conditioned by God's grace which is external and unpredictable. Therefore it cannot be considered as a case of human planning; the latter requires intention and some factual knowledge. If a belief in such ideals does influence one's daily life, it is in the psychological sense only: It functions to motivate one's efforts to practice religious demands.

B) Ideals which display the perfection of human conduct are those which maintain the dichotomy between God and man's soul. The ideals of Justice, Love, Mercy, are very much like secular ideals of morality: In both cases the contents of the ideals do not necessarily imply absurdity and irrationality.

179

a) The denial of regulative ideals on the basis of sceptical rationality. 1. It is possible to plan one's life in the light of goals if those are not a-priori prints but rather ad-hoc ends. 2. A-priori models of perfection are not cognitively apprehended and even if they were, it would not be possible to reach a common consent about their content, furthermore, even if such consent were achieved one could never find means to apply ideals, with the result that acting upon them could lead to an opposite effect from that desired.

The sceptical denial of regulative ideals is not satisfactory: 1. The considerations raised by this conception exclude, from the beginning, all religious activities as lacking direction, because they are based on a belief in God, which inflicts the whole system with its irrationality. 2. If the aim is to illuminate the unique nature of ideals, the sceptical approach is not relevant because it rejects, without distinction, ideals as well as a-priori principles. 3. The sceptical criticism can be met with counterarguments which are based on a totally different conception of rationality, and which affirms truth, certainty and a-priori ends.

b) The affirmation of regulative ideals on the grounds of dialectical historical considerations: 1. It would appear that a theoretical view which argues that ideals are being realized through the course of history necessarily affirms the possibility to act upon ideals. If all actions are necessarily guided by an ideal, then it is possible to aim at that ideal. 2. Dialectical historical versions of idealism state the existence of a gap between the ideal and the real, yet they do not hold this gap to be infinite. Other metaphysical suppositions about the ontological monism, the a-priori end of historical process, and the dialectical relations between reason and reality, entail the conclusion that the essence of history is the overcoming of oppositions toward the final realization of the ideal; it is the negation of the gap between the ideal and reality. 3. It also follows that each historical stage is a greater realization of the ideal and a better one, relative to the previous phase.

The dialectical point of view shows some defects, apart from the fact that it assumes a large stock of metaphysical suppositions: 1. The nature of historical realization of ideals is not individualistic, and true human goals are universal. Thus conflicts with the common view of religions which stresses the personal value of human actions as well as human duties and responsibilities. It also conflicts with the immediate and personal relation between man and God. 2. The dialectical conception does not, and cannot, distinguish between ideals or applying positivistic rules or acting arbitrarily and unconsciously: All actions—positive or negative—are determined by history and strive to realize the ideal. This conflicts with the religious view which denies the possibility to act upon ideals in an immoral way. 3. The historical realization of ideals contradicts the religious status of the ideal, in the sense that its transcendental nature is negated at the last phase of history. Although it does express the humanistic aspirations of traditional dialectical idealism, which puts man in God's place, it is inadequate for religious intentions.

c) The conception which I wish to put forward is the denial of regulative ideals on the basis of logical considerations: 1. There exists a linguistical or metaphysical gap between ideal and reality in the sense that they are infinitely opposite to each other. From the ideal's point of view whatever is not ideal is bad. Therefore it is not possible to realize ideals—partially or fully—or to imitate them, as all these attempts will, on principle, lack an ideal character. As ideals and reality exclude each other "acting upon ideals" is an apparent contradiction. 2. It follows that it is impossible to describe ideals apart from their constitutive principles, as every description includes contingent elements which contradict the definition of the ideal. 3. In reality people sometimes sincerely wish to imitate ideals, but apart from its psychological function, this fact does not give empirical activities any religio-ideal nature, nor does it ensure that the individual has approached closer to the ideal. 4. If improvement is at all possible, one can only testify to such improvement on the basis of some criteria. If the criterion is subjective sense of improvement it may be considered to be misleading by its very nature. If an objective measurement of improvement is possible in relation to a previous situation, it does not follow that one can ascribe causal qualities to ideals. The reason for improvement can lie elsewhere or can be merely arbitrary.

3.

Given the opposition between reality and ideal it is of interest to inquire into the status of ideals in a religious system, and of intentions to act upon them:

a) From the religion's point of view, the system is closed and constitutive. It defines, by and for itself, its truths and ends, in a way that implies definitive actions which are essential to religious life.

b) From the religion's point of view, an ideal is an indispensible element. All religions stress the necessity of models of perfection, without which other religious principles as well as human life lack a full religious sense.

c) Religious life does not tolerate pluralistic principles and rules. Part of the meaning of being religious is based on the commitment to value perfection and to strive for it.

4.

What could be the meaning of human commitment to ideals?

a) One could argue that ideals define the boundaries of the right conduct as well as the full extention of evil, apart from its empirical sense. In this case an ideal is a boundary concept which is necessary to religious life both ontologically and epistemologically even though it is unattainable.

b) One could argue that acting upon ideals means to believe and to value a perfection without being able to judge one's life is coherent with that perfection. The individual holds some ideals related to his belief in God, and as cognition is irrelevant to the nature of religious belief, the only way one knows that one is moving in the right direction is through the grace of God.: It gives him a glimps of the long path that will get him closer to that ideal. This confidence he cannot share with others nor can he prove the rightness of his course of actions.

c) One may consider religious ideals as ultimate standards with the function of presenting the individual as sinful and defective. Although ideals cannot serve as standards of constructive criticism—because all judgements in the name of perfection are totally negative—they sharpen one's awarness of one's human condition.

5.

It follows that it is impossible to aim at ideals, in spite of their being necessary and obligatory:

a) Religious system excludes pluralism of values and activities: One cannot ignore ideals and remain religious at the same time, as there are no alternatives to lead religious life. Religion implies absolute and ultimate demands, thus being religious entails acting upon prescribed ideals, or acting in a way that is logically impossible.

b) The result is that apart from the irrational belief in God and in some given truths, religion obligates religiously impossible conduct. If the discussion started with the assumption that religious activities may be rational to a degree, the conclusion is that at least parts of religious practice are completely irrational. The existence of activities that are considered religious because they are related to a religious institution, and the fact that people state their religious attitudes, do not entail a full and coherent religious meaning of these activities. In this sense, some religious practices may be considered as misleading: while actions are prescribed by their ideal ends, nevertheless there is still no way that these actions could be judged according to these ideals.

6.

Three more conclusions are of interest:

a) Acting upon ideals puts the individual in an immediate relation to God and in isolation from others, in the same manner as in the experience of revelation. The result is that communal life, which is part of the religious institution is no more than the external conjunction of individual attempts to practice religious demands. Their uniting principle is the transcendental God.

b) A commitment to religious life means, among other things, to be the agent of isolated and sporadic actions which do not constitute a coherent behaviour that can be justified or criticized publicly.

c) In spite of, and as a result of, the ultimate and non−pluralistic nature of religion, acting upon ideals entails anarchy, exactly in the same way as expressed by radical scepticism, because it is not possible to validly choose one alternative over the other, as more representative of the ideal.

* * *

A WITTGENSTEINIAN ANALYSIS OF THE DEPTH GRAMMAR OF RELIGIOUS BELIEF AND PRACTICE

Thomas T. Tominaga
University of Nevada, Las Vegas

One may argue that implied in the diversity and multiplicity of religious beliefs is the basis for validating and relativizing the truth of every religious belief adhered to and practiced by any primitive, traditional, or contemporary religion. Furthermore, one may also argue that a Wittgensteinian view of religious belief would seem to imply a similar validation[1] and relativization[2] of the truth of religious beliefs, since it recognizes a plurality of religious forms of life which must be accepted as the givens.[3] However, whether or not a Wittgensteinian view of religious belief does imply the alleged validation and relativization is an issue that depends largely on our understanding and discovering of some significant aspects of the depth grammar indicative of a particular religious belief. Whether the religious belief in question is Buddhist, Christian, Confucian, Hindu, Jewish, Samoan, or Taoist, we need to make and support a Wittgensteinian analysis of some significant aspects of the depth grammar of religious beliefs in practice so that we can place in perspective and eliminate the alleged wholesale validation and relativization.

With this objective in mind, I will first make clear what is meant by the 'depth grammar' of religious belief and what the nature of religious belief consists of. Second, I will explain why the alleged validation and relativization is misleading and unsound. Third, I will show why our emerging Wittgensteinian view is not susceptible to the alleged wholesale validation and relativization of religious beliefs. And finally I will state and discuss some key reasons why our Wittgensteinian view is defensible without validating and relativizing many different religious beliefs.

In order to understand what is meant by the 'depth grammar' of religious belief, it is helpful to relate the 'depth grammar'[4] of religious belief to its 'surface grammar'.[5] By the surface grammar of religious belief, we mean the recognizable way in which a constructed or uttered sentence, expressive of a religious belief, looks like in written language or sounds like in spoken language. By the depth grammar of religious belief we mean the particular use made of a picture projected by an accepted religious belief in conjunction with certain circumstances and surroundings. What people want to picture with their religious beliefs are new ways of life and new attitudes toward this life and the life after death, all of which will require a new language and new ways of communicating.[6] Unlike the surface grammar of religious belief, the depth grammar is shown by a personal commitment to a way of acting that is characterized by the willingness to live by one's convictions without the fear of death. Moreover, unlike the surface grammar of religious belief, the depth grammar requires not only linguistic and speech acts. It also requires, if not more so, pragmatic acts that can bring about the intended effects pictured by the accepted religious beliefs.

From a Wittgensteinian perspective, we would fail to understand the depth grammar of religious belief if we are predisposed to explain religious beliefs as 'testable hypotheses'.[7] This is because testable hypotheses, unlike religious beliefs, can become true or false if they can be substantiated or refuted by empirical or scientific evidence. One defensible way of avoiding such a misunderstanding is to view our religious beliefs as 'unshakeable convictions'[8] whose acceptance need not be based on testing for their truth or plausibility. Viewed as unshakeable convictions, our religious beliefs can and do change, regulate, and guide a person's whole life, even to the point of risking everything including his life.[9] We can see that it is part of the depth grammar of our religious beliefs that they become demonstrable as unshakeable convictions which have the potential to guide, change, and regulate our lives daily. Consequently the view that reduces our religious beliefs to testable hypotheses is conceptually incompatible with the depth grammar of our religious beliefs.

One may now argue that what we have done is to have implied and endorsed the validation and relativization of religious beliefs. On the one hand, we have done so by recognizing the existence and legitimacy of each religious belief by virtue of its status as an unshakeable conviction and not as a testable hypothesis. On the other hand, we have done so by recognizing the diversity and multiplicity of religious beliefs in a manner comparable to allowing many different religious language-games to co-exist with their own rules. Although this argument appears to be valid, it is unsond and misleading because it has failed to have a clear understanding of the depth grammar of religious beliefs. Moreover, it has also failed to realize and take into account some significant aspects of the depth grammar of religious beliefs that would prevent them from being susceptible to being trivially validated and unnecessarily relativized.

In order to make these two failures explicit, let us discuss briefly at least four significant aspects crucial to understanding the depth grammar of religious beliefs in practice. Given that the depth grammar of religious beliefs is shown by an accepted practice in connection with particular circumstances and surroundings, it is an essential and integral part of the depth grammar of religious beliefs that: (a) they are not meaningfully amenable to being contradicted;[10] (b) they are neither reasonable nor unreasonable in the perjorative sense of ignoring the standards of rationality;[11] (c) they rest on no rational or ordinary grounds beyond an ungrounded action or accepted form of life which each religious believer may make manifest in the daily conduct of his or her life without the presumption of indubitability or high scientifically calculable probability;[12] and (d) they picture or project new spiritual attitudes and new ways of life which necessitate a new language which can be learned and used as part of a shareable practice.[13]

Let us elaborate briefly on each of these four aspects. Concerning the first aspect, religious beliefs in practice are not propositions which we can contradict by affirming or denying the opposite.[14] By virtue of their non-contradictory status, religious beliefs cannot be justifiably viewed as testable hypotheses whose truth can be affirmed and/or denied, since neither their truth nor their falsity is in question. Religious beliefs cannot be contradicted because people, be they religious believers or not, tend to think in entirely different ways[15] which are appropriate within an accepted framework. Moreover, the many different ways in which people think may and can prevent them from having the thoughts that are normally associated with certain religious beliefs.

Concerning the second aspect, we do not mean to imply that our religious beliefs are lacking in reasonability or are opposed to acceptable standards of rationality. What we mean to convey is that the connections and pictures depicted by our religious beliefs are imaginable and realizable in a non-reasonable, flexible, dynamic mode of operating that is not amenable or limited to the reasonable-unreasonable dichotomy.

Concerning the third aspect, we are reminded that the demonstration of religious beliefs through commitment and action is not contingent on some supporting grounds with the guarantee of epistemological certainty or high probability. Rather our religious beliefs become exemplified in the ungrounded way we do act and live our lives daily. What this aspect shows is a non-epistemological dimension implicit in our unshakeable convictions[16] beyond which there are no further grounds to which we can meaningfully appeal for an endless justification of our religious beliefs.

And concerning the fourth aspect, we have in mind the picturing of new spiritual attitudes and new ways of life, all of which are describable and showable through learning and using a new language in connection with possible ungrounded ways of acting for believers to change and fulfill their lives under specific circumstances. With this aspect, our religious beliefs are equipped with a future-oriented dimension which points to the possibility of adopting new religious beliefs that would project new attitudes, new values, and new lifestyles.

On the basis of the preceding discussion, I believe that our analysis has disclosed three key reasons that would make our Wittgensteinian view defensible. The first reason comes from the observation that one helpful way of understanding the nature of religious belief is to observe and learn how people use certain picturable ways of acting and living under specific circumstances and surroundings to express the depth grammar of their accepted religious beliefs. Although there is an element of contingency present in the selection of a picture appropriate to each religious belief, such a contingency does not significantly contribute to the validation and relativization of religious beliefs. For, the question as to which picture is appropriate to a particular religious belief is answerable only by the specific challenge and concrete change which each believer goes through in his or her life under some relevant circumstances.

The second reason comes from the recognition that when religious beliefs are viewed depth-grammatically as unshakeable convictions which can guide, change, and regulate a believer's entire life, the issue of the alleged wholesale validation and relativization of religious beliefs can be seen to be artificial and misguided. What is revealing is that the alleged wholesale validation and relativization is predicated on the mistaken premise that religious beliefs and shareable practices are testable hypotheses which should be explained, verified, and justified. The error here is due to the failure to recognize that it is against the depth grammar of religious beliefs to be treated as testable hypotheses, since religious beliefs cannot be contradicted by virtue of their being there as part of the believer's life as it were, but not by virtue of their being true *a priori*, or by rational justification, or by scientific verification.

And the third reason comes from the discovery that the methodology applicable to religious beliefs viewed as unshakeable convictions is quite different from that applicable to religious beliefs viewed as testable hypotheses. In the former, the appropriate methodology is one of phenomenological description[17] of religious beliefs and practices for their own self-worth or for whatever they appear to be. In the latter, the appropriate methodology is one of hypothetical explanation of and terminal justification for the origin and existence of religious beliefs and practices.

Given these reasons, the overall conclusion is that our Wittgensteinian view is defensible in two ways. Stated positively, it is defensible provided that religious beliefs are viewed depth-grammatically as unshakeable convictions with the potential to bring about some describable life-changing actions and life-fulfilling effects on the part of believers. Stated negatively, it is defensible when religious beliefs are not viewed as testable hypotheses whose truth and status cannot be countered or contradicted with an opposite verdict. This negative way of making our Wittgensteinian view defensible seems to show a phenomenological suspension of what may be called the dialectical or normative stance in our Wittgensteinian view of religious beliefs. Accordingly, instead of imposing hypothetical explanations and terminal justifications, religious beliefs are to be acknowledged and described for their meaning and value as they are embodied and shown in each believer's practice and way of acting and living. Although our Wittgensteinian view may be only partly but not fully defensible, it is significant to observe two complementary consequences. On the one hand, the alleged wholesale validation and relativization is due largely to viewing our religious beliefs as testable hypotheses, which consequence can be eliminated by viewing depth-grammatically religious beliefs as unshakeable convictions which give rise to non-contradictory, non-reasonable, ungrounded ways of acting and living. On the other hand, the descriptive emphasis of our Wittgensteinian view is made methodologically compatible with the undeniable diversity and multiplicity of religious beliefs by curtailing any attempt to subject one-sidely to an indiscriminate scrutiny or ethnocentric speculation the life-changing and life-fulfilling potential of other people's religious beliefs, rituals, and practices, in which case no counter-judgment or normative assessment is appropriate and called for.

ENDNOTES

1 Gellner, Ernest, *Words and Things* (Boston 1959), p. 222.
2 Glebe-Møller, Jens, "Marx and Wittgenstein on Religion and the Study of Religion," in E. Leinfell-ner, W. Leinfellner, A. Hübner, and H. Berghel (eds.), *Wittgenstein and His Impact on Contemporary Thought* (Vienna 1978), pp. 526-527.
3 Wittgenstein, L., *Philosophical Investigations*, tr. G. E. M. Anscombe (New York 1968), p. 226e.
4 Wittgenstein (1968), § 30, p. 14e and § 664, p. 168e. Cf. Ludwig Wittgenstein, *Lectures and Conversations on Aesthetics, Psychology and Religious Belief*, ed. Cyril Barrett (Berkeley and Los Angeles 1967), p. 56, p. 63.
5 Wittgenstein (1968), § 664, p. 168e.
6 Engelmann, Paul, *Letters from Ludwig Wittgenstein with a Memoir*, tr. L. Furtmuller (Oxford 1967), p. 135.
7 Wittgenstein (1967), p. 56, p. 60. Cf. Henry LeRoy Finch, *Wittgenstein—The Later Philosophy* (Atlantic Highlands, New Jersey 1977), p. 202.
8 Wittgenstein (1967), p. 54. Cf. Ludwig Wittgenstein, *On Certainty*, tr. Denis Paul and G. E. M. Anscombe (Evanston, Illinois and New York 1969), § 103, p. 16e.
9 Wittgenstein (1967), p. 54.
10 Wittgenstein (1967), p. 54, p. 55.
11 Wittgenstein (1967), p. 58.
12 Wittgenstein (1967), p. 54, p. 57. Cf. Wittgenstein (1969), § 110, p. 17e. Norman Malcolm, *Ludwig Wittgenstein: A Memoir* (London 1966), p. 72.
13 Engelmann (1967), p. 135.
14 Wittgenstein (1967), p. 53.
15 Wittgenstein (1967), p. 55.
16 Wittgenstein (1967), p. 54.
17 Wittgenstein, Ludwig, "Remarks on Frazer's *Golden Bough*," tr. John Beversluis, in C. G. Luck-hardt (ed.), *Wittgenstein: Sources and Perspectives* (Ithaca, New York 1979), pp. 62−63.

* * *

WITTGENSTEINS WIEDERHOLUNG DER EINSICHT KIERKEGAARDS IN DIE PARADOXALITÄT DES BEGRIFFS DES ETHISCHEN UND DES RELIGIÖSEN

Reiner Wimmer
Universität Konstanz

Verschiedenartige Quellen bezeugen Wittgensteins Kenntnis und Hochschätzung von Kierkegaards Person und Teilen seines schriftstellerischen Werkes. So berichtet Drury von folgendem Ausspruch Wittgensteins: „Kierkegaard was by far the most profound thinker of the last century. Kierkegaard was a saint".[1] Die frühesten Zeugnisse einer Beschäftigung Wittgensteins mit Kierkegaard verweisen auf das Jahr 1929. Bei einem Gespräch im Hause Schlicks am 30. Dezember 1929 spricht Wittgenstein von dem „Trieb" des Menschen, „gegen die Grenzen der Sprache anzurennen," den auch Kierkegaard gesehen und „sogar ganz ähnlich (als Anrennen gegen das Paradoxon) bezeichnet" habe.[2] In einem Vortrag über Ethik und Religion, der nur noch in einer englischen Fassung existiert und den Wittgenstein nach Ausweis seines Herausgebers, Rush Rhees, zwischen September 1929 und Dezember 1930 in Cambridge vortrug, greift Wittgenstein den Kierkegaardschen Begriff des Paradoxen an zentraler Stelle auf und formuliert: „It is the paradox that an experience, a fact should seem to have supernatural value".[3] In Wittgensteins Nachlaß, soweit er bisher veröffentlicht ist, wird Kierkegaard, wenn ich recht sehe, viermal erwähnt.[4] Die Stellen stammen aus den Jahren 1937, 1940 und 1946. Es gibt keinen Hinweis darauf, daß Wittgenstein mit Teilen von Kierkegaards Werk oder speziell mit seinem Begriff des Paradoxen schon zur Zeit der Abfassung des *Tractatus* vertraut gewesen wäre. Um so erstaunlicher und bedeutsamer ist trotz mannigfaltiger methodischer und konzeptioneller Unterschiede die schon von Wittgenstein selbst beobachtete Übereinstimmung zwischen ihm und Kierkegaard in bestimmten ethischen und religionsphilosophischen Grundüberzeugungen, wie sie Kierkegaard systematisch vor allem in der *Abschließenden Unwissenschaftlichen Nachschrift* zu den *Philosophischen Brocken* und Wittgenstein im *Tractatus*, in Tagebuchaufzeichnungen des Jahres 1916 und in seiner Ethikvorlesung zum Ausdruck gebracht hat.

So sprechen Wittgenstein wie Kierkegaard von einem relativen und einem absoluten Gebrauch der Ausdrücke ‚Wert' bzw. ‚Zweck' oder ‚gut'.[5] Nur der absolute Gebrauch ist für beide der eigentlich ethische bzw. ethisch-religiöse. Er bezieht sich auf Wert, Zweck oder Sinn des menschlichen Daseins im ganzen. ‚Absolut' besagt, daß das Verständnis der genannten Ausdrücke keinen Maßstab oder Bezugspunkt voraussetzt. Daß es eine solche absolute Verwendung gibt, die nicht leerläuft, sucht Wittgenstein mit dem Hinweis auf eigene Erfahrungen zu belegen. Er spricht 1. von dem Staunen über das Dasein der Welt, der Erfahrung der Welt als eines Wunders, 2. von der Erfahrung, sich absolut sicher, geborgen zu fühlen, was auch immer geschehen mag, und 3. von der Erfahrung moralischer Schuld.[6] Er selbst erhebt jedoch einen gewichtigen Einwand gegen sein auf der Erfahrung unbedingten Sinns gegründetes Verständnis des Ethischen und Religiösen. Dieser Einwand hat mit der Schwierigkeit zu tun, daß nicht begreiflich erscheint, wie etwas *in* der Welt, *im* Leben den Sinn der Welt, des Lebens im *ganzen* zeigen kann. Er spitzt das Problem noch dadurch zu, daß er von den erwähnten drei Grund-Erfahrungen sagt, sie selber besäßen „in some sense an intrinsic, absolute value". Andererseits seien sie jedoch nur Tatsachen *im* Leben. Deshalb müsse er zugeben, daß es „nonsense" sei zu sagen, sie seien von absolutem Wert. Wittgensteins Erörterung kulminiert in dem schon zitierten Satz: „It is the paradox that an experience, a fact should seem to have supernatural value".[7] Dieser Satz erinnert mitsamt dem Kontext an die Thematik der *Philosophischen Brocken* und der *Nachschrift*: Kann ein Augenblick im Leben absolute Bedeutung haben? Kann es einen geschichtlichen Ausgangspunkt für ein ewiges Bewußtsein geben?

Wittgensteins Erörterung der Erfahrung des Ethischen und Religiösen ist aporetisch: Einerseits läßt sich die Erfahrung absoluten Sinns nicht leugnen; Wittgenstein steht selbst für sie ein und bezeugt sie. Andererseits scheint es eine solche Erfahrung nicht geben zu können: Der Sinn des Lebens kann sich nicht im Leben zeigen. Wie stellt sich Wittgenstein dieser Situation? Offenbar hält er *beide* Seiten des Paradoxons fest und erfüllt damit den Begriff dessen, was Kierkegaard ‚Glauben' nennt, und zwar Glauben im allgemein religiösen Sinne (Religiosität A), noch nicht Glauben im christlichen Sinne (Religiosität B), der sich auf das „Paradox sensu strictissimo" bezieht, nämlich Gottes Menschwerdung.[8]

Die Wurzel des Paradoxes — sowohl im allgemein religiösen wie im christlichen Sinne verstanden — besteht für Kierkegaard in der eigentümlichen Verfassung des Menschen, nämlich eine Synthese von Ewigem und Zeitlichem, Unendlichem und Endlichem darzustellen, wie er vor allem zu Beginn von *Die Krankheit zum Tode* fast lehrsatzartig kundgibt. Erst indem der Mensch sich zu dieser Synthese, die er selbst ist, verhält, *existiert* er im Kierkegaardschen emphatischen Sinn des Wortes; erst dann geht es ihm um sich selbst, bejahend oder verneinend. Insofern der Mensch sich nicht selbst verdankt, sondern durch ein Drittes gesetzt ist, verhält er sich in seinem Existenzverhältnis nicht nur zu sich selbst, sondern auch zum Grund seiner selbst, und auch hier wieder bejahend oder verneinend.

Wollten wir Kierkegaard fragen, woher er wisse, daß es sich so mit dem Menschen wesentlich und eigentlich verhalte, würde er vielleicht antworten, daß er das nicht wisse und auch nicht wissen könne, sondern daß er es glaube, zu glauben versuche. Der Anschein zu wissen entstehe in einem philosophischen Werk wie dem der *Nachschrift* fast unvermeidlich, obwohl das Nichtwissenkönnen sein Hauptthema sei, etwa in der Gegnerschaft zur Hegelschen Spekulation. Schon mit der Überschrift des Werkes habe er darauf aufmerksam machen wollen; des weiteren habe er es unter einem Pseudonym (Johannes Climacus) herausgegeben und es schließlich mit einem Widerruf versehen: „Also, das Buch ist überflüssig, darum mache sich auch keiner die Mühe, sich darauf zu berufen; denn wer sich darauf beruft, hat es eo ipso mißverstanden. [...] so enthält, was ich schreibe, gleichzeitig eine Mitteilung dessen, daß alles so zu verstehen ist, daß es widerrufen ist".[9] Auch Wittgenstein widerruft den *Tractatus* an seinem Schluß. Bei Wittgenstein wie bei Kierkegaard geschieht dieser Widerruf aus ähnlichen Gründen. Wer das Werk verstanden hat, bedarf aber des Widerrufs eigentlich nicht mehr; denn er hat erfaßt, daß sich das, von dem die Rede ist, rechtens nicht objektivieren und beschreiben läßt, weil es kein Objekt unserer Anschauung, unserer Erfahrung darstellt, sofern sie gegenstandsbezogen ist. Nur ein Sprechen, das über seine Beschreibungsfunktion hinaus durchsichtig, offen ist für das Ganze des Daseins und seinen Sinn, fügt der un- oder auch übergegenständlichen Erfahrung des Ethischen und Religiösen keine Gewalt zu. Sowohl Kierkegaard als auch Wittgenstein haben diese Möglichkeit des Sprechens vor allem der Dichtung vorbehalten.

Unsere gegenstandsbezogene Alltags- und Wissenschaftssprache anerkennt und erfaßt nur gegenstandsbezogene, oder allgemeiner und weniger mißverständlich formuliert: sachverhaltsbezogene Erfahrungen. Wittgenstein — und auch Kierkegaard, sofern er die sokratische Anamnesis der ewigen Bestimmung des Menschen ausdrücklich als menschliche Möglichkeit anerkennt — etabliert einen zweiten Erfahrungsbegriff. Erfahrung in diesem Sinne ist un- bzw. übergegenständlich, weil auf das Ganze der Gegenstandswelt, des Lebens bezogen; sie ist un-, oder besser: übervernünftig, weil sie rein sachverhaltsbezogene Sprache und Vernunft transzendiert und deshalb auch nicht objektiv (wie ein Sachverhalt, der in der Welt, im Leben besteht) festgestellt, als vorhanden oder nicht vorhanden bewiesen werden kann. Von hierher wird auch Kierkegaards die gesamte *Nachschrift* durchziehende und häufig zu subjektivistischen Mißverständnissen Anlaß gebende Sprechweise von der „Subjektivität", der „Innerlichkeit" der Wahrheit der Existenz verständlich. Ähnlich spricht Wittgenstein.[10]

Das Paradoxe dieser Erfahrung aber bleibt: Das Umfassende zeigt sich, aber in den Grenzen der Zeit, des Menschen und seines Horizonts. Hier setzt der Zweifel, die Skepsis der Vernunft ein. Ihr tritt der Glaube als das Festhalten am Unbedingten der Erfahrung des Ethischen und Religiösen entgegen, von Kierkegaard als „absolute" oder „unendliche Leidenschaft" bezeichnet – eine Bestimmung des Glaubens, die von Wittgenstein 1946/47 aufgenommen wird.[11]

In den *Vermischten Bemerkungen* findet sich nun aber eine Stelle aus dem Jahre 1937, an der Wittgenstein die Rede vom Paradox zuurückzuweisen scheint. Er schreibt: „Das Christentum gründet sich nicht auf eine historische Wahrheit, sondern es gibt uns eine (historische) Nachricht und sagt: jetzt glaube! Aber nicht, glaube diese Nachricht mit dem Glauben, der zu einer geschichtlichen Nachricht gehört, – sondern: glaube, durch dick und dünn und das kannst Du nur als Resultat eines Lebens. *Hier hast Du eine Nachricht, – verhalte Dich zu ihr nicht, wie zu einer anderen historischen Nachricht!* Laß sie eine *ganz andere* Stelle in Deinem Leben einnehmen. – Daran ist nichts *Paradoxes!*"[12] Wittgenstein nimmt hier Kierkegaards Problem vor allem der *Philosophischen Brocken* auf. Mir scheint aber, daß er weder dem Glaubensbegriff Kierkegaards noch seinem eigenen religiös-ethischen Erfahrungsbegriff gerecht wird. Beide Begriffe sind geformt an der Einsicht in die Unfähigkeit der menschlichen Vernunft, absoluten Sinn zu erfassen, und der gleichzeitigen Einsicht in das Unerlaubte, ihn fallen zu lassen, jedenfalls für den, der ihn erfahren hat.

ANMERKUNGEN

[1] Drury, M.O'C., „Some Notes on Conversations with Wittgenstein", R. Rhees (Hrsg.), *Ludwig Wittgenstein: Personal Recollections* (Oxford 1981), S. 102; vgl. N. Malcolm, *Ludwig Wittgenstein: A Memoir* (London, Oxford, New York 1958), S. 71, 75.
[2] Wittgenstein, L., *Schriften 3: Wittgenstein und der Wiener Kreis. Gespräche*, aufgezeichnet von F. Waismann (Frankfurt 1967), S. 68.
[3] „Wittgenstein's Lecture on Ethics", *Philosophical Review*" Bd. 74 (1965), S. 10.
[4] Wittgenstein, L., *Vermischte Bemerkungen* (Frankfurt 1977), S. 65, 66, 78, 102.
[5] „Wittgenstein's Lecture on Ethics", S. 8; S. Kierkegaard, *Abschließende Unwissenschaftliche Nachschrift*, Zweiter Teil, Zweiter Abschnitt, Kapitel IV, Sectio II, Teil A, § 1.
[6] „Wittgenstein's Lecture on Ethics", S. 8, 10.
[7] Vgl. Anm. 3.
[8] Vgl. *Nachschrift*, Zweiter Teil, Zweiter Abschnitt, Kapitel II.
[9] *Nachschrift*, Anhang: Das Einverständnis mit dem Leser.
[10] Vgl. *Schriften 3*, S. 117, Z. 4–8.
[11] Vgl. *Vermischte Bemerkungen*, S. 102, 108.
[12] *Vermischte Bemerkungen*, S. 67. (Die Satzzeichen sind die des gedruckten Textes.)

* * *

WITTGENSTEIN AND JASPERS – HOW TO LIVE IN BORDERLANDS

Stig Nystrand
University of Lund, Sweden

There are many paradoxes connected with the philosophy of Ludwig Wittgenstein. The man who in *Tractatus* had the courage to declare that he had silenced all questions, at the same time let loose an endless stream of questions, and with his sayings *about* the work made it into the big mysterious Question. This Question later exploded into the hundreds of questions in PI, but the one overwhelming question about the meaning of world and life remained, though now incorporated into his view of philosophy as something of an almost organic nature.[1]

Some of the Wittgensteinian questions may find an answer, a beginning to a fruitful answer in a comparison between his philosophy and parts of the philosophy of Karl Jaspers, e.g. his concepts 'Grenzsituation', 'mögliche Existenz', 'das Umgreifende', 'Scheitern', 'Erhellung', 'Einstellung', 'existentielle Kommunikation'. The similarities between these two philosophers are sometimes striking. Even if they moved in different circles, their aims and goals are surprisingly similar. In order not to press the comparison into a literal one, I would like to call it morphological.

Jaspers too, asked many questions, many large and encompassing questions. The most intensive of all was his demand on the existential communication, the one involving two persons in the same attitude of understanding, having the same Einstellung to the world and to life in that situation of nearness Jaspers called 'liebender Kampf'.[2] And like Wittgenstein he was not afraid to ask questions coming out of loneliness and despair. And what is more, to be alone (einsam), was a necessary condition, even if not the sole or sufficient one in order to communicate yourself to someone else. The paradox is: no real self without the other and no self without being alone. The answer is: the necessary thing is not to be *with* somebody but *for* somebody.

The feeling out of which one human being communicates with another is the feeling of being given to another (Geschenktwerden), at least being given to the situation where communication is made possible. It could be fruitful to compare this positive term of Jaspers' with Heidegger's 'geworfen'. To be thrown out into the world certainly sounds to be a negative situation. And yet—it is out of this that the despair arises, which is the foundation of all conscious existence. And as is known[3] Wittgenstein took a positive attitude to this concept of Heidegger's—even though he might have been a little provocative in front of the Vienna circle when this was being uttered. It may be though, that there isn't much of an opposition between Jaspers and Heidegger/Wittgenstein—in this now mentioned respect. Jaspers certainly acknowledged the precarious situation of man as one of being pushed into the void. By the 'Geschenktwerden' I think he meant, that by realising how this 'Geworfensein' is *common* to all human beings, we can see a possibility to reach every one, and every one individually, in his despair. This is a gift.

It may seem a gift also because through the act of existential communication a human being becomes conscious of himself as an individual, and he discovers his personal integrity.—The "running up against the limits of language" Wittgenstein talks about e.g. to Waisman[3] bears in fact a resemblance to the existential communication of Jaspers—which cannot be put into a straightforward linguistic expression. Language is a limit, but it shows that there is something beyond.

But Jaspers was a lonely thinker. He says: "Ist nicht mein Philosophieren der Kommunikation von allen modernen Bemühungen der einsamste?" This he wrote in his great three-part

Philosophie in 1932.[4] The loneliness that might arise out of efforts to give yourself, the inner-most self, in communication, was nothing strange to Wittgenstein. Already in 1914 he said: "Am leichtesten verliert man sich selbst, wenn man sich anderen Leuten schenken will."[5] — And the author of Tractatus, though he claimed to have solved the problem of truth, was a troubled mind. In the Forword (*TLP*, pp. 4—5) he asserts that *thoughts* are there expressed — thoughts, not philosphy, but also that these thoughts show how little is achieved when all the problems of truth are solved. Because, as we can see now, these problems were for him of small importance seen from the viewpoint of *life*, the terrible, anguish-filled life.

Wittgenstein and Jaspers also had in common a firm belief that their guiding ideas came to them early in life and stayed with them ever after. This also implies that they thought them worthy of sticking to. Wittgenstein hinted at this several times and expressed it explicitly to O'Drury.[6] For Jaspers' part we can e.g. consult his autobiography to find expressions of the same kind.[7]

You can also see that these basic ideas for both Wittgenstein and Jaspers belonged to the idea of philosophy as something that was not identical with science, and something demanding different sorts of language games. Another common conception running through their thinking was the necessity of concepts like Weltanschauung, Weltbild, Lebensform. — Their relation to the times they were living through were coloured by the same kind of pessimism. But their thinking in and of history, of philosophy of history and of history of philosophy, showed marked differences. Wittgenstein travels criss-cross through life, *making* up its history as he goes along. Jaspers is living *in* history, freely moving through the ages without a fixed chronology, making intellectual history present. But both are traditionalists. "Ich bringe keine neue Philosophie", Jaspers exclaims.[8] This stands comparison with Wittgenstein's famous claim that he is only a reproductive philosopher (*VB*, p 43).

The important concepts Weltanschauung and Weltbild could perhaps be illustrated as follows. A Weltbild, 'picture-of-the-world', consists of everything you *know* (through your intuitive certainties and sensitiveness and your intellectual theory of knowledge), also that which you ought to know, but are not conscious of — and the psychological factors connecting all the abovementioned. A Weltbild is, in a broad sense, objective. — A Weltanschauung, 'worldview', has a Weltbild as a basis, is also an awareness of *having one*, but is also more than this. Having a part in certainties of the kind Wittgenstein talks about, the Vorwissen, belongs to a Weltanschauung. So does my world of values, my feeling of responsibility for myself and for the world I try to make mine, or at least try to be a member of. It is a subjective appraisal of the world *I* accept. Experiencing myself as an Existenz in those situations Jaspers talks about as Grenzsituationen is an essential part of a Weltanschauung. — This way of looking at Weltbild and Weltanschauung will, I think, argree with what can be gathered from Jaspers' writings

It is not quite consistent with what you can sort out from the manifold Wittgenstein-utterances on the subject. It may be that a Weltbild for Wittgenstein would consist of the Vorwissen also — but not only of that, not even if the Vorwissen is taken as that which constitutes the intellectual foundations of a culture. This last-mentioned aspect on Weltbild seems to be held by von Wright.[9] — A Weltbild, in Wittgenstein's sense, could perhaps be taken as the Vorwissen + all the areas of life where language-games can be applied. That would exclude the attitude, in a Weltanschauung-sense, you have to life as something that has to be *lived*, not intellectually contemplated on. The way I describe Weltbild and Weltanschauung they both *together* would probably constitute what Wittgenstein would call Lebensformen, forms of life.

What is essential to a Lebensform, and a Weltanschauung, cannot be comprehended with scientific methods, or with the ideas of a so called scientific philosophy alone. But the Weltbild can be apprehended with science. And that is quite *necessary*, in order to get a proper picture, according to Jaspers. What is correct in science is important to philosophy, the foundations of philosophy. But philosophy cannot, Jaspers means, be a science, neither can philosophy say anything about what is correct or not in science. But the meaning (the Sinn) of science is dependent on philosophy. You can find expressions to this end e.g. in Jaspers' autobiographical sketch.[10]—The same *kind* of opinion was held by Wittgenstein, as can be seen from sayings dating from the thirties.[11]

A central work in Jaspers' production is *Die grossen Philosophen*. It is not only a personal account of (certain parts of) the history of philosophy, it is also a projection into the past of Jaspers' own thinking. In the introductory part[12] he writes about how the philosopher's personality shows itself in his work, philosophy, in contrast to science, has never achieved plain truth. On the contrary: "Zur Wahrheit des Werkes gehört die Wahrheit des Menschen, der es denkt. Im Werk selbst ist er erkennbar." Doesn't this sound much like one of Karl Kraus' expressions?! That it does so, is doubly interesting since we now know the extent of Wittgenstein's debt to Kraus and his followers.

The Weltbild we have depends on the knowledge we have, a. of facts, b. of the social games, whether of a linguistic nature or not, which constitute our social surroundings.—The Weltanschauung we have got and which we want to take part in, the fact that we *will* the world, does not necessarily depend on factual grounds, but is always impregnated with values. And these are values which we acknowledge in society and/or which we invent.

All his life Wittgenstein seems to have put the aspect of Weltanschauung ahead of the Weltbild-one. But we know that he was in doubt about the possibility of expressing in language anything concerning it. Even later in life he talked about the wall we bump into, when trying to express the innermost meaning of the world.[13] Earlier though, in the times of the Notebook and Tractatus, it is wellknown that he thought it necessary to trace out the world of knowledge and logical necessities, to show the edges of the world of facts. All this in order to point out how little is achieved in doing so. Because what makes us human beings lies outside of this world, Wittgenstein thought.

The boundaries he ran into, that which could but be shown, were part of a situation in which you *had to* show your cards. Do you accept the inexpressible as part of your life?, was the question Wittgenstein asked himself first and then *showed* others how to take up. He *expressed* thoughts, as he said in the Forword to Tractatus. I even think that his early philosophy is a conscious attempt at creating an impossible situation, an existential situation in which *being sure* means being sure of stepping on boundaries. And Wittgenstein probably also thought that he knew *why*—nobody could really have *that* knowledge claimed in Tractatus. That was the first inexpressible! He was in a Grenzsituation, in Jaspers' sense of the word, i.e. a situation where your awareness makes you into a possible Existenz. For Jaspers all that was impossible could be an object of choice in that you become aware of yourself as *being* in the world when confronted by a boundary. On the other hand, Wittgenstein's message was, I think: choose among all the possible worlds the only one not possible.

This "impossible world", which implied solutions of all the problems of knowledge, at the same time implied that this situation cannot be expressed in language—which in turn means that I am alone in my world, that it is *my* world and that I am responsible for it. The metaphysical subject doesn't count facts *in* the world. It rests in the encompassing, das Umgreifende, on the other side of the borderlines drawn by your living self. The despair Wittgenstein felt was in part a despair of not being *with* the metaphysical subject. In spite of that, it was *necessary* to create this boundary-situation, the opposite of the world of facts and values, otherwise the boundaries themselves wouldn't be noticed. The rules of logic were in that way transmuted into rules of morals. Ethics and logic, ethics and the world, are one, Wittgenstein thought with Weininger—as is now well known and accepted. At least he thought so then.

The players of the game of knowledge would get applause from the spectators in the value-world, who couldn't get in through the fence of logic and empirical rules. "A good thing", Russell and the logical empiricists thought. "An unimportant thing", the author of Tractatus thought, the players are anyway just playing, the spectators are out there in the world. Wittgenstein's greatest despair was to know his own great competence as one of the players but to feel inadequate as a citizen in the world of values.—This all created a longing comparable to homesickness. In this connection I often think of Joseph Roth and his novel Radetzkymarsch, where it is said about a person that he "glich einem Manne, der nicht nur seine Heimat verloren hatte, sondern auch das Heimweh nach dieser Heimat." There are other resemblances to Wittgenstein and the Tractatus-world to be found in the bock also.[14]

The concept 'Grenzsituationen' used by Jaspers so often, meant many things. Situations, according to Jaspers, cannot be handled without relating them to a definite meaning, they are a "sinnbezogene Wirklichkeit". The meaning (Sinn) a boundary-situation has, is then a feeling of having come to an end, signified by suffering, death, guilt, but the Grenzsituation also moves into our lives when we are struck by the insight that we always are at some particular boundary, we are bound to social and physical, also psychical, surroundings. Perhaps we feel stuck with a particular Lebensform and cannot see how to do anything about it in *this* world. We know that there are *certain* boundaries we *never* can pass, e.g. in language, in the use of language. This last situation is probably the one actualized in Wittgenstein's early thinking. We can increase our knowledge, but in a certain *important* way that may be a blind alley. We use up our funds of language and still we don't get a full view of life.

The stress Jaspers put on silence and on being alone within yourself is of course a key to his interest in the Tractatus-world.[15] Jaspers seems to mean that we tend to express more than we really *are*—and perhaps more than our concept of reality allow us to. Therefore silence, the withdrawing of direct, descriptive speech, is necessary. At least as a therapeutic means. The failure in reaching another person, a person representing human and spiritual nearness, can lead to the failure of my life in an existential sense. To 'Scheitern', as Jaspers calls it.

The silence of Scheitern is not altogether negative. The Scheitern can be a sign of somebody having *tried*. The crack-ups, the rifts, in the world, or in the experienced world of a person, are signs of there having been life.—In art, a rough and torn, an unfinished work, like one of Leonardos paintings or designs, is often considered aesthetically more valuable than a smooth, finished work. That could be *one* way of looking at aesthetics and ethics as one. There are numerous examples in Wittgenstein's texts from the earlier period (Notebooks from summer 1916, Tractatus from 6,37 onwards) that illustrate a skidding along the fences, a Scheitern in not getting through the barrier of language, the barrier, the construction of which Wittgenstein changed later in life.—The importance of 'nonsense' in Wittgenstein's early and middle philosophy can easily be compared to Jaspers' Scheitern. This is especially clear in the end-passage of the Lecture on ethics.[16]

In a saying from the end of the thirties you can see that Wittgenstein no longer thought of truth as something you had to look for on both sides of a border—if possible—but as something that belonged to your whole life, and dependeing on your personal integrity (*VB*, p. 73).—In a conversation with O'Drury (1949)[17] Wittgenstein uttered: "Every sentence in the Tractatus should be seen as the heading of a chapter needing further exposition." Thus, he not only questioned th truth of Tractatus, but he also wanted to split up the form, the parts, of the Tractatus-world. He thought it needed to wax. *Its* form of life wasn't *his* any longer—the boundary-situation he created with the closed sentences and the hinted-at inexpressibles of Tractatus was no longer necessary for his life and philosophy. He was looking for other forms.

I have tried to point out how Wittgenstein attempted to use the field of knowledge, not only in his search for truth, but also as a means of tracing the boundaries of meaning in human life. But we have lot of evidence from Wittgenstein's life of how he sought out situations and problems that put him in Grenzsituationen, to use Jaspers' terminology, where "die Welt gerät in die Schwebe". One such was considering suicide, as we can gather from the Notebooks of 1916, from letters to Engelmann and Russell. He even said that he volunteered for service in the First world war in order to get killed. The fact that he in spite of that fought very bravely, probably in order to survive, could be seen as an interesting parallel to what Allan Janik says about Otto Weininger's influence on Wittgenstein. An influence that even included views on suicide.[18]—Wittgenstein believed with Weininger that man was alone and lonely in the universe and to say yes to this was what morality was about. "On this account of the human condition, says Janik, suicide is clearly the elementary sin."

The 'confessions' which Fania Pascal and Rush Rhees tell us about and comment on[19] can be understood as (unconscious?) existential acts. As can his ambivalent attitudes to Jewishness, which were a search for identity—in his case it may have been quite unconscious.—Hannah Arendt has said[20] "only a pariah could affirm his or her Jewish identity and seek politically a place for Jews to live without compromising their identity." A "pariah" in Arendt's words was a Jew who didn't want to assimilate, who refused to give in to demands from the oppressing community.—Interesting to note is that Karl Jaspers, who was Arendt's friend and teacher, in Die großen Philosophen used the term 'pariahs' of philosophers in general.[21] Was it as such a pariah Wittgenstein would have liked to live? Was it his incapability, personal and cultural, to do so that lay at the root of his confessions in the thirties?

To be a real Existenz, Jaspers says, demands that a possible Existenz makes himself 'offenbar' in communication with another possible Existenz. The term 'offenbar', as used by Jaspers, is here to be understood in two of its meanings. 1. As something made clear, manifest, that is clarity arising out of being aware of the encompassing, das Umgreifende. 2. As something *revealed*. You want to reveal that which is really you, your inner attitude to life, your personal self.—This last-mentioned meaning of course has a touch of 'Offenbarung'—a miracle. It seems to me that Wittgenstein demanded nothing less than that from his friends in life, his contemporaries in philosophy. And he got disappointed. He probably felt a kindred feeling expressed in the writings of Kierkegaard—but also a striving towards the miraculous which made Wittgenstein call him a saint.[22]

The making manifest (offenbar) demands an attitude of honesty, integrity, on part of those participating in the communication, a getting into the other person's life-situation. Perhaps we could call it a deep understanding of a Lebensform. Wittgenstein anticipated in the Tractatus-forword, as also later in the forword to Philosophische Bemerkungen, that he would be understood only by those who already thought as he did. That is—you know, have to know, how to play the game before you even know the rules. And precisely that is the essence of Jaspers' existential communication. That is why I would like to call this communication a language game which touches the foundations of human life.

The founding, primitive language-games which Wittgenstein describes in the beginning of Philosophical Investigations (*PI*, p. 2ff) seem to be very static, graphic, devoid of feeling. But if you infuse this primitive communication of ordering and obeying with love, Liebender Kampf, with a reaching out—then I think you get quite close to the game of existential communication. Spiritual gestures, instead of physical.

The existential communication, like Wittgenstein's showing (Zeigen), goes beyond words, but the meaning of the process depends on *there being* a language, any language. It could be the private language Wittgenstein talks about in the Investigations—the language so much misunderstood. Why not consider the *understanding* of this kind of 'private language' in itself an expression of a primitive language-game? Then you shall see that it is never a question of whether we understand the pain, or feelings, or love, or hate. With the stuff of Jaspers' 'liebender' understanding we can "divide through" where the beetle in the box is supposed to be or not to be. That isn't the question then.

Just a last comparative remark. The existential communication advocated by Jaspers is supposed to be all-consuming. A successful one adds to the world of the performers—a failure, a Scheitern, may put up walls, the world gets smaller. So the world of the happy waxes, the world of the unhappy wanes. (Cpr *TLP*, 6.43). And to notice this we need, not the magnifying-glass of science, but the signifying-glass of human understanding.

———

ENDNOTES

[1] See especially Ludwig Wittgenstein: The Yellow Book, in Alice Ambrose (ed), *Wittgenstein's Lectures Cambridge 1932–35* (Oxford 1979), p. 43. Here philosophy is said to be organic in Schopenhauer's sense, which means e.g. that a book on philosophy with a beginning and an end is an impossibility. Philosophical problems are compared to roads you have to walk, one at a time, perhaps the same one several times, before you get a hunch of how the roads connect.

[2] See e.g. Karl Jaspers: *Philosophie* (Berlin-Göttingen-Heidelberg 1948, first ed. 1932), p. 351ff.

[3] Waismann, Friedrich, *Witgenstein and the Vienna circle* (Oxford 1979), p. 68.

[4] Jaspers 1948, p. XXXIX

[5] Quoted from Rush Rhees (ed): *Ludwig Wittgenstein. Personal recollections* (Oxford 1981), p. 216.

[6] Rhees (ed) (1981), p. 171.

[7] Jaspers, Karl, Philosophische Autobiographie, in *Philosophie und Welt* (München 1958), p. 386. There he says: "Blicke ich auf meine geistige Entwicklung, so meine ich etwas von Kindheit an Gleichbleibendes zu sehen ... es hat niemals Wandlungen der Überzeugungen gegeben, keinen Bruch, keine Krise und Wiedergeburt."

[8] Saner, Hans, *Karl Jaspers in Selbstzeugnissen und Bilddokumenten* (Reinbek bei Hamburg 1970), p. 152.

[9] Wright, G.H. von, Wittgenstein on certainty, in *Wittgenstein* (Oxford 1982), p. 176.

[10] Jaspers (1958), p. 372. "Mit dem philosophischen Denken geschieht ein Durchbruch durch die Rationalität aber mit rationalen Mitteln–über den Verstand hinaus, ohne den Verstand zu verlieren."

[11] Lee, Desmond, *Wittgenstein's Lectures Cambridge 1930–32* (Oxford 1980), pp. 24, 26. There you can find syings like these: "Thought is not something hidden; it lies open to us. What we find out in philosophy is trivial; it does not teach us new facts, only science does that. But the proper synopsis of these trivialities is enormously difficult, and has immense importance. Philosophy is in fact the synopsis of trivialities."

[12] Jaspers, Karl, *Die großen Philosophen* (München 1957), pp. 75–76.

[13] Quoted from Adolf Hübner & Kurt Wuchterl: *Ludwig Wittgenstein* (Reinbek bei Hamburg 1979), p. 120, VB p. 38.

[14] e.g. Wittgenstein and his philosophy could be compared to baron von Trotta's uncompromising passion for truth, even the faintest leaning towards falsity would disturb his personal integrity–no matter if the falsity was to his advantage or not.

[15] Jaspers, Karl, *Von der Wahrheit* (München 1947), pp. 463–64, and *Provokationen. Gespräche und Interviews* (München 1969) pp. 19–21–where he gives credit to Wittgenstein, saying e.g. "der Antrieb bei ihm ist, das worüber man schweigen muß, keineswegs dem Chaos anzuliefern, sondern es für seine Person, vielleicht an der Grenze der Verzweiflung ... so zu behandeln, daß, was zu diesem Zeitalter mit ihm selber in seiner Logik wirklich wird als ganzes nichtig ist."–Jaspers also reminds himself that he, when writing about the Indian philosopher Nagarjuna thought of Wittgenstein. Jaspers' writings on Nagarjuna is in Jaspers (1967), especially pp. 934–36, 944, 953.

[16] Wittgenstein, Ludwig, Lecture on ethics, *Philosophical Review* vol 74 (1965), pp. 3–12.

[17] Rhees (ed) (1981), p. 173.

[18] Janik, Allan, Wittgenstein and Weininger, in Elisabeth Leinfellner et al (eds): *Wittgenstein and his impact on contemporary philosophy. Proceedings of the 2nd International Wittgenstein symposium* (Vienna 1978), pp. 25–30.

[19] Rhees (ed) (1981), 48–49, 51–52, 192, 195ff.

[20] Quotation from Elisabeth Young-Bruehl: *Hannah Arendt, for Love of the World* (New Haven 1982), p. 121.

[21] Jaspers (1957), p. 84.

[22] Rhees (ed) (1981), pp. 102–3.

* * *

DAS (NEUE) ÖKO-SYSTEMISCHE DENKEN UND DIE FLUCHT (?) IN DIE (ALTE) RELIGIOSITÄT

Wulf Hübner
Universität Hamburg

In den Disziplinen, die sich der wissenschaftlichen Bestimmung unseres, des Menschen, Verhältnisses zur Natur bzw. zu uns selbst, gewidmet heben (Ökologie, Anthropologie, Psychotherapie), wird der Ruf nach einem neuen, „ganzheitlichen" oder systemischen Denken immer populärer. Dabei spielen überraschenderweise Religiosität und Glaube eine ausgezeichnete Rolle: wollen die Menschen die Basis für eine menschenwürdige Existenz nicht überhaupt zerstören, müssen sie, so heißt es, zu einem „wie immer begründeten religiösen Verhältnis zur Natur"[1] finden, müssen sie zu einer „theologischen Betrachtung der Natur"[2] kommen, die es „dem Menschen verbietet, die Natur lediglich funktional auf ihre, der Menschen Bedürfnisse hin zu interpretieren"[3] und sie mittels instrumenteller Strategien beherrschen zu wollen, eine Betrachtung, die den Menschen lehrt, „den Reichtum des Lebendigen als einen Wert an sich zu respektieren".[4] Und, allgemeiner noch: es ist die Theologie − von Bateson am Beispiel der Theologie der anonymen Alkoholiker (AA) dargestellt − die „einer Erkenntnistheorie der Kybernetik sehr nahe kommt."[5]

Im folgenden möchte ich zeigen, wie Religiosität und Glaube beidemal dazu dienen, ein Dilemma zu verdecken, um mit konstruktiven Bemerkungen zum selben Thema abzuschließen.

Zunächst zum Mensch-Natur-Verhältnis. An die Stelle des anthropozentrischen Funktionalismus soll eine „nichtfunktionale Ethik der dreifachen Ehrfurcht vor dem, was über uns, was unseres gleichen und was unter uns ist"[6], treten. Wie erlangt man Ehrfurcht? Die Absage an eine Bezugnahme auf menschliche Bedürfnisse überhaupt bedeutet, daß der Respekt vor dem Eigenwert des Reichtums des Lebendigen (was ist mit dem Unlebendigen?) in keinem Sinn als eine menschliche Regung oder als eines unserer eigentlichen Bedürfnisse eingesehen werden kann. Entsprechend der klassischen Dichotomie von Leidenschaften und (moralischen) Pflichten bleibt als Grundlegung für die dreifache Ehrfurcht nur die Pflicht zu dem, bereits zitierten, wie immer begründeten religiösen Verhältnis zur Natur. Wie aber soll eine Pflicht zur Ehrfurcht gedacht werden können? Diese kann doch nur erfahren, nicht aber geboten werden. In diesem Zusammenhang fungiert Religiosität als Büßer für die durch verschwundenen Bezug auf menschliche Bedürfnisse entstandene Lücke. Diese ist zunächst durch Bedürfniskritik und nicht durch Glaube zu schließen. Ich komme darauf zurück.

Nun zur Bestimmung unseres Verhältnisses zu uns selbst und zur Theologie der AA, bzw. deren therapeutischem Weg. Der erste der berühmten 12 Schritte auf diesem Weg verlangt, „daß der Alkoholiker zugibt, gegenüber dem Alkohol machtlos zu sein."[7] Im zweiten Schritt artikulieren die AA die Überzeugung, „daß eine Macht, die größer ist als wir selbst, uns wieder gesund machen könnte."[8] Diese Überzeugung findet ihren Ausdruck im Gebet der AA, in dem sie um diese Beziehung, also um Demut etwa, bitten.

Bateson nun reklamiert dieses praktisch-therapeutische Vorgehen der AA als empirischen Beleg für seine theoretische, systemische Auffassung, daß der Begriff ‚Selbst' wie das ganze Repertoire der Handlungssprache − ‚Akteur', ‚Zweck', ‚Handlungsobjekt', ‚zweckgerichtete Handlung' etc. − einer unkorrekten Erkenntnistheorie angehören. Die Einsicht der AA, daß der Alkoholiker den Kampf gegen die Flasche nicht gewinnen kann, weil er, wie die Formulierung anzeigt, seine Sucht als etwas ihm oder seinem Selbst Äußerliches ansieht und erlebt, diese Einsicht faßt Bateson auf als Bestätigung seiner Maxime, die Relation von Mensch und Umgebung, Teil und Ganzem müsse überhaupt als Beziehung des Einzelnen zu einer Macht

196

begriffen werden, die größer ist als der/das Einzelne. Die symmetrische Relation Teil versus Ganzes ist durch eine komplementäre zu ersetzen.

Das Dilemma der systemischen Sichtweite liegt, in diesem Zusammenhang, in Folgendem. Sie ist auf das strikte Einhalten einer Beobachterperspektive verpflichtet und reduziert. Nur aus dieser kann die Charakterisierung der Relation Alkoholiker − Alkoholismus durch den Satz erfolgen ‚Alkoholismus ist eine Macht, die größer ist als das Selbst‘, oder retrospektiv, wie es die AA tatsächlich tun: „Wir geben zu, daß wir . . . machtlos waren.“[9] Aus der Ich- oder Teilnehmerperspektive gesprochen ist der Satz schlicht das Bekenntnis „Ich bin Alkoholiker“ und damit der Ausdruck einer geistigen Erfahrung, der nämlich, „von der Flasche besiegt zu werden und es zu wissen“.[10] Weil damit der erste Schritt getan, weil diese Erfahrung der erste Schritt zur Heilung ist, ist, wer diesen Satz aufrichtig äußert, kein Alkoholiker mehr! Der Alkoholiker gibt mit dieser Erfahrung nicht sein Selbst auf, höchstens sein „altes“, er verleugnet nicht länger, was er doch war, ein Alkoholiker, der nun auf dem Weg ist, es nicht mehr zu sein. Eine fatale Selbst-Bestimmung und -erfahrung ist einer angemesseneren gewichen. Bei Einhaltung der systemischen Sicht ist diese − selbstreflexive − Erfahrung nicht einmal formulierbar. Dieses theoretische Dilemma wird durch den Hinweis auf die praktisch-therapeutische Effizienz der AA bzw. ihrer Theologie nicht behebbar.

Abschließend die konstruktiven Bemerkungen. Am Beispiel des Gebets will ich das mir für eine alternative Sichtweise Wesentliche verdeutlichen.

Die AA bitten, betend, um Demut. Wenigstens psychologisch ist ausgeschlossen, daß man, um Demut betend, zugleich hochmütig sein kann. „Ist das Gebet ehrlich“, so schreibt Bateson, „kann Gott nichts anderes als die Bitte zu erfüllen.“[11] Das heißt, die Aufrichtigkeit der Bitte um Demut zeigt sich in der Demut des Betenden. Gebet und Demut stehen zueinander nicht in der Relation von Mittel und Zweck. Obwohl Beten als absichtsvolle, bewußte und zielgerichtete Handlung unternommen wird, ist doch das Ziel, auf das sie gerichtet ist, gänzlich unverfügbar. Weil Beten, formalpragmatisch gesehen, einen Adressaten erfordert, der das Gebet erhört, die Bitte erfüllt, das Erhoffte schenkt, gibt es „Gott“ oder „das Ganze“. Die Relation Teil − Ganzes steht für Mensch und Gott. Aber sie verdunkelt mehr als daß sie Klarheit schafft. Sie verdunkelt nämlich den Umstand, daß wir Demut, Ehrfurcht und Gelassenheit deshalb als etwas betrachten, das wir nur als Geschenk erlangen können, weil wir diese Haltungen nicht handelnd herbeiführen, sondern sie nur erfahren können. Demut und Ehrfurcht sind wie Trauer und Glück, Verzweiflung, Gewißheit und Liebe Widerfahrnisse, die wir nur erleiden können (wenn wir dazu bereit sind). Die metaphorische Redeweise von Teil und Ganzem erhält dann diesen Sinn: solange wir nur einen Teil unserer Affekte und Leidenschaften, unseres Selbst, kennen, sind wir denen, die wir nicht kennen, die aber unser Denken, Handeln und Reden ebenso prägen, ausgeliefert. Kennten wir sie alle, so kennten wir uns selbst ganz, wären wir ganz, i.S. von heil. So ist, denke ich, der alte Rat der Theologie zu verstehen, wir müßten Gott in uns finden.

In einem letzten Schritt möchte ich das am Beispiel Veranschaulichte verallgemeinern. Die Kritik am anthropozentrischen Funktionalismus ist angemessen, weil wir beim Denken in Mittel-Zweck-Relationen der Illusion aufsitzen, wir könnten durch die Ergebnisse unseres Handelns, das sind die aus der naturwissenschaftlich angeleiteten Bearbeitung der Natur hervorgegangenen Güter, Befriedigung „machen“, Mängellosigkeit des Mängelwesens, als das der Mensch von der Anthropologie unheilvollerweise bestimmt wurde, zweckrational herbeiführen. Dieser Kampf gegen die Mängel kennt keinen Sieger. So wie die Affekte, die den Alkoholsüchtigen zur Flasche greifen lassen, mächtiger sind als er, weil er sie nicht kennt, sie aber sein Handeln bestimmen, so sind unsere Leidenschaften und Affekte stärker, als daß sie durch den Ge- und Verbrauch von Gütern sich still stellen ließen. Genauer noch: auf diese Weise können sie gar nicht erfahren werden. Auf diese Weise können wir uns selbst, unsere Menschlichkeit, nicht erkennen, und eben auch nicht, was wir als unsere wahren Bedürfnisse doch unbedingt erfahren möchten(?).

Damit ist das neue Denken als eine Variante des alten erkannt. Neben der Sollensethik, die seit Kant immer wieder mit dem Ziel ausgearbeitet worden ist, den Menschen vor dem

Menschlichen, seinen Leidenschaften und Affekten, die ihn blind machen für die Erfordernisse der (Zweck-)Rationalität, zu schützen, indem er Prinzipien an die Hand bekomme, an denen er sich soll orientieren können, neben der Pflichtethik also, spielen Religiosität und Glaube eine ausgezeichnete Rolle, nämlich jene, die in der sokratisch-platonischen Tradition mit den Worten ‚Gelassenheit‘, ‚Ruhe der Seele‘ oder ‚Eudämonia‘ umschrieben wurde. Die Handlungsweise, auf die wir uns festlegen müssen, um unsere Existenz als menschenwürdig erfahren/gestalten zu können, kann so gekennzeichnet werden: Handle stets so, daß du die Gelassenheit, die du brauchst, um dich ganz (d.h. alle menschlichen Leidenschaften und Affekte) erfahren zu können, nicht gefährdest. Dies ist die Umformulierung der Version des kantischen Imperativs, die mit der Blindheit, mit der er gegenüber der sokratischen Tradition geschlagen war, versöhnen mag: „Handle stets so, daß du würdig wirst glückselig zu sein“ lautete seine Formulierung.

Die Erkenntnis, daß die Menschen selbst die Adressaten ihrer Bitten und Gebete um Gelassenheit, Demut und Ehrfurcht sind, diese alte Erkenntnis können wir von der Theologie lernen.

ANMERKUNGEN

[1] Spaemann, R., „Technische Eingriffe in die Natur als Problem der politischen Ethik“, in D. Birnbacher (Hrsg.), *Ökologie und Ethik* (Stutgart 1980), S. 198.
[2] Rock, M., „Theologie der Natur und ihre anthropologisch-ethischen Konsequenzen“, in Birnbacher (1980), S. 101.
[3] ebd.
[4] Spaemann ebd.
[5] Bateson, G., „Die Kybernetik des Selbst: Eine Theorie des Alkoholismus“, in ders., *Ökologie des Geistes* (Frankfurt a. M. 1981), S. 400.
[6] Spaemann ebd.
[7] Bateson (1981), S. 404.
[8] Bateson ebd.
[9] Bateson ebd.
[10] Bateson (1981), S 405.
[11] Bateson (1981), S. 432.

* * *

ÜBER VERNUNFTGEMÄSSES HANDELN – ZUR ANTHROPOLOGIE DER EUROPÄISCHEN TRADITION, „VERANTWORTUNG DER WISSENSCHAFT" ZU DENKEN

Peter Klein
Universität Hamburg

„Instrumentelle Vernunft", d.h. methodische, rationale Erkenntnis der Welt und deren Auswertung in der technischen Gestaltung der Welt, ist ein Charakteristikum europäischen Denkens. Ihre Tendenz, Menschen und Dinge dabei ausbeuterisch in Dienst zu nehmen und sie dadurch zu zerstören, hat sowohl eine „Umweltkrise" als auch eine spezifische „Innenwelt-krise" der Orientierungslosigkeit der Menschen bewirkt. Obwohl diese Auffassung weithin angenommen ist, ist es bisher nicht gelungen, vernünftige Alternativen des Selbstverständnis-ses und Verantwortung realisierende Handlungsziele für diese Gesellschaft abzuleiten und verbindlich zu machen. Skepsis gegenüber den (Natur-) Wissenschaften und Rückgriff auf außereuropäische Denktraditionen können nicht als solche Alternativen gelten, da die erste das Fundament für mögliche Auswege, die zweite den besonderen anthropologischen Rang des europäischen Denkens beseitigte.

Demgegenüber soll hier darauf verwiesen werden, daß die Gefährdung durch sich selbst dem europäischen Denken seit alters vertraut ist und daß es in ihm – obwohl mißverstandene und verschüttete – grundlegende Denkfiguren besonders an seinen maßgeblichen histori-schen und systematischen Knotenpunkten gibt, gerade auf der Basis wissenschaftlicher Erkenntnis zu verantwortlichem Handeln sich selbst und der Welt gegenüber zu gelangen, so daß erst dann von „vernünftigem" Handeln gesprochen werden kann. Die zwei dargestellten Beispiele repräsentieren zugleich die beiden wesentlichen Typen solcher Reflexion,

1. den der „religiösen Weltauslegung", in der Wissenschaft als im Dienste der Wahrheit zum Heil des Menschen,

2. den der „ästhetischen Reflexion", in der Welt- und Selbstangemessenheit des Handelns als Postulate der Vernunft selbst gedacht zu werden.

Zu 1. Die weiträumig und grundlegend zerstörerische Instrumentalisierung der Wissen-schaft wurde erst möglich in ihrer von Galilei grundgelegten neuzeitlichen Gestalt. Sie traf daher sogleich auf den Widerstand eines Denkens, das – als „Religion" per definitionem – die verantwortliche Auslegung des Ganzen der Welt zum Heil des Menschen zum Ziel hat und in diesem Rahmen die Reichweite der Ansprüche der Wissenschaft zu prüfen hat. Mit dieser Aufgabe ist durch gesellschaftlichen Konsens eine „Kirche" betraut und hat ihr in insti-tutionellen, sachgemäßen Formen zu entsprechen. Im Falle Galileis bewegte sich die Prüfung auf drei Ebenen:

– Bei der „Anhörung" 1616 stand im Mittelpunkt die seit den Griechen bekannte – und der Galilei-Zeit gut vertraute, schlicht schulgerechte – Unterscheidung der Wissenschaft von den Gegenständen der äußeren Welt in „mathematica", die systematisierte Beschreibung der Erscheinungen in „Hypothesen", u.a. mit der Absicht ihrer gezielten Benutzung im Handeln (der „mechaniké techné"), und „physica", der Erkenntnis der Welt in ihrem Wesen und aus ihren Gründen mithilfe der in ihr wirkenden Kräfte.

Die von der Kirche bestellten Qualifikatoren der Indexkongregation bestritten nicht die „mathematische" Nützlichkeit des kopernikanischen Weltsystems zur Beschreibung der Erscheinungen, waren aber der Meinung, daß bloße auf die Erscheinungen passende Beschreibung noch kein Kriterium der Wahrheit gerade dieser Beschreibung sei, eine heute elementaren Schulstoff darstellende, aber eben auch damals elementare Auffassung (die aber die moderne Naturwissenschaft dazu mißbraucht, guten Gewissens nur mathematica zu betreiben und zur Handlungsgrundlage zu machen; s. 2).

Die für die Zwecke der physica gelegentlich eingesetzte pythagoreisch – platonische Denkfigur, die mathematische Gestalt der astronomischen Gesetze als Beleg ihrer göttlichen Herkunft und mithin als Wahrheit anzusehen, mußte mit dem Vorliegen zweier alternativer Systeme ergänzt werden um Betrachtung der wirkenden Kräfte, also eine Himmelsdynamik, die eine Entscheidung zwischen den Alternativen herbeizuführen hatte. Keplers Arbeiten hierzu lagen zu jener Zeit erst z.T. vor und waren von beiden Seiten kaum rezipiert; Galileis Argumente für die Wahrheit des kopernikanischen Systems waren dagegen stets kinematischer Art oder falsch.

– Die Qualifikatoren kamen weiterhin zu dem Schluß, daß das kopernikanische System im Widerspruch zu gewissen Stellen der Hl. Schrift und ihrer Auslegung durch die Kirchenväter stehe, was seine Interpretation nicht als mathematische Hypothese, wohl aber als physikalische Wahrheit verbot. Doch ist die Auffassung falsch, daß durch diese Qualifikation der theologischen Schriftauslegung ein Primat gegenüber der Wissenschaft eingeräumt werde, vielmehr mache umgekehrt, so der Vorsitzende, Kardinal Bellarmin, ein wissenschaftlicher Wahrheitsbeweis eine ihm scheinbar widersprechende Schriftstelle zum Rätsel (diese, als inspiriertes Wort Gottes, natürlich nicht falsch!). Wissenschaft vermag somit im Gegenteil Beiträge zu der dem Lehramt der Kirche stets abverlangten Schriftauslegung zu leisten, kann aber einen grundlegenden Wandel der Auslegung erst herbeiführen, wenn tatsächlich ein wissenschaftlicher Wahrheitsbeweis geführt wurde, was ja aber bei Galilei nicht der Fall war, „und im Zweifelsfall soll man die Schrift, wie sie von den heiligen Vätern ausgelegt wurde, nicht verlassen", weil die Schrift eine ganzheitliche Halt und Orientierung gebende Weltauslegung vermitteln soll.

– Das Inquisitionsverfahren 1632/33 behandelte die von Galilei nur verfälschend befolgte Auflage, das Argument des Papstes Urban VIII gebührend zu berücksichtigen, daß wir wegen der Allmacht Gottes niemals sicher sein können, die wahren Wege Gottes erkannt zu haben. Dieser sog. „theologische Vorbehalt" ist durchaus mehr als eine Caprice oder eine Rückzugsposition der Kirche vor den Ansprüchen der Wissenschaft; er ist vielmehr konstitutiv für den Glauben und formuliert die Vertrauens- und Glaubensbedürftigkeit eines endlichen Wesens auf die sich uns schenkende Gnade Gottes, eines Wesens, das sich der Beschränktheit seiner Erkenntnis, der wissenschaftlichen wie der auf die Schrift sich stützenden, bewußt ist. Mit ihrer Kritik an der Mißachtung dieses Vorbehalts bezeichnete die Kirche mithin den Kern eines sich überhebenden, weil seine menschlichen Grenzen nicht beachtenden wissenschaftlichen Denkens.

Zu 2. Im 17. und 18. Jh. stellte die Vernunft des europäischen Menschen sich zunehmend, unter Verzicht auf eine überirdische Orientierung und die Erinnerung an ihre Endlichkeit, auf sich selbst. Kant zeigte in der „Kritik der reinen Vernunft" (KrV), daß dabei der theologische Vorbehalt säkularisiert als „kritizistischer Vorbehalt" wiederkehrt: Die empirische Analyse des Erkenntnisvorgangs, systematisiert zur begrifflichen Zergliederung der erkennenden Vernunft, zeigt, daß an keiner Stelle dieses Vorgangs die Gegenstände der Erkenntnis uns als sie selbst zugänglich werden, sondern stets nur gemäß den Verfahrensweisen der erkenntnisvermittelnden Mechanismen. Demzufolge kann Wissenschaft nie sicher sein, die Wahrheit über die Welt erkannt zu haben, da uns die Welt nur den Verfahrensweisen unserer Erkenntnis entsprechend zugänglich wird. Das bedeutet zunächst, daß die Absicht der physica, Erkenntnis der Welt in ihrem Wesen und aus ihren Gründen zu erbringen, prinzipiell unmöglich ist. Neuzeitliche Naturwissenschaft hat ihr Selbstverständnis zurecht auf mathematica, Beschreibung von Erscheinungen, reduziert.

Damit aber würde sie a fortiori der Auslegungskriterien auf Verantwortung vor der Welt im Ganzen hin bedürftig. Verweigert die Vernunft einer Kirche das Recht, diese zu geben, so müßte sie sich selbst solche Kriterien geben. Kant zeigt, daß dies für die faktisch vorfindliche Vernunft, verschärft man sie zu einem Begriff von Vernunft überhaupt, der Fall ist; das ist der Inhalt der „Kritik der praktischen Vernunft" (KpV), *wie* dies geschieht, der der „Kritik der Urteilskraft" (KdU).

Die erkennende Vernunft nimmt an unserer Vernunft, soweit sie Handeln beabsichtigt, Postulate praktischen Handelns wahr, die als unbedingte Postulate das Handeln steuern. Es sind dies die Postulate von Freiheit, Gott und Unsterblichkeit, die auf Handeln hin im „kategorischen Imperativ" zusammenwirken. Diese Postulate sind nicht so zu verstehen, als werde, gegen die KrV, das Dasein ihres Inhalts behauptet (dann wären sie Gegenstand der KrV, und dort führt die Daseinsbehauptung zu transzendentalem Schein), sondern es wird von Kant lediglich die Wirksamkeit des Postulats des Daseins jener drei im praktischen Handeln wahrgenommen und dies auch nur konstatiert für den Fall, daß in der Tat nach Vernunftprinzipien gehandelt werden soll (und nicht, wie es im Alltäglichen die Regel ist, nach Neigung, Opportunität usw.).

Weiterhin wäre es verfehlt anzunehmen, daß mit den Postulaten der praktischen Vernunft eine „Ethik" in dem Sinne gegeben sei, daß auf ihrer Basis nunmehr prinzipiengeleitetes Handeln möglich sei. Denn es bleiben die Postulate wie ihr oberster Grundsatz, der kategorische Imperativ, erstens formal: der Wille hat weder ein Objekt noch ein Ziel, deren er als menschlicher Wille aber bedarf; zweitens haben sie ihren Ort in einer Welt außerhalb der Erfahrung, während sich Handeln in der Welt der Erfahrung vollzieht.

Die Vernunft bedarf mithin der Brückenprinzipien, mit deren Hilfe die als Erscheinung erkannte Welt im Lichte der unbedingten praktischen Postulate, und umgekehrt diese im Lichte jener „beurteilt" werden. Dies leistet die Urteilskraft; sie muß, um die bezeichnete Brücke bilden zu können, der Handlung beabsichtigenden Vernunft leitende Ideen bieten und zwar
- ein Bild vom Ganzen der Welt (das kritizistische Korrelat zur „naiven" Absicht der physica: Erkenntnis der Welt im Ganzen und in ihrem Wesen);
- ein Bild von der angemessenen Befindlichkeit des Menschen in der Welt (das kritizistische Korrelat zur „naiven" Absicht einer Religion: der transzendierenden Weltauslegung zum ewigen Heil des Menschen).

Beide Bilder, die wiederum zwar von Erkenntnis geleitet und bereichert, aber nicht selbst Erkenntnis sind, stehen unter der übergreifenden Idee der „Zweckmäßigkeit". Das meint hinsichtlich des Objekts des Handelns: daß das konkrete Objekt so zu behandeln sei, daß es, als Teil einer zweckmäßig geordneten Welt empfunden, diese Zweckmäßigkeit befördere; es meint hinsichtlich des Subjekts des Handelns: daß das Subjekt durch die Beziehung seiner Handlungsprinzipien auf das Handlungsobjekt sein Handeln als sich selbst und der Welt im Ganzen angemessen weiß. Durch die Reflexion auf die gegenseitige Angemessenheit von Subjekt und Objekt im Lichte unbedingter Postulate wird das Handeln „schön" und sittlich — schönes Handeln dem Menschen wie der Welt gerecht. Genauso beschreibt aber auch gegenwärtiges „ökologisches" Denken sein Ziel; die drei kantischen Kritiken können daher als formales Fundament einer ökologischen Ethik gelten, welche damit zugleich als „vernunftgemäß" zu bezeichnen ist.

Die Inhalte der ästhetischen Reflexion beziehen wir einerseits von der Wissenschaft, andererseits von sowohl evolutionär wie kulturell vermittelten Postulaten und Beurteilungsmustern moralanaloger und ästhetischer Art. Insofern evolutionäre wie kulturelle (auf quasievolutionäre Weise entstandene) Wertungsmuster auf die einzige dem Menschen mögliche Weise hinsichtlich ihrer Passung auf die hypothetische „Welt an sich" geprüft sind, kann „vernunftgemäßes" als „verantwortliches" Handeln gelten.[1]

ANMERKUNG

[1] Die ausgearbeitete Langfassung des vorstehenden Beitrags erscheint in einem Aufsatzsammelband unter dem gegenwärtigen Arbeitstitel „Bausteine zur Anthropologie der Wissenschaft".

* * *

VOM HIMMLISCHEN MANDAT ZUM FATUM – ASPEKTE DER CHINESISCHEN RELIGIOSITÄT

Thaddäus T. C. Hang
Nationaluniversität Chengchi, Taipei, Taiwan
Republik China

Wir werden den schicksalhaften Sinnwandel des Schlüsselwortes „Ming" während der dreitausend Jahre der chinesischen Geschichte verfolgen, um den entsprechenden Wandel des religiösen Bewußtseins zu beobachten.

I. Ursprünglicher und abgeleiteter Sinn des Wortes „Ming"

Die ersten chinesischen Schriftzeichen wurden in Tierknochen und Schildkrötenschalen eingeritzt. Sie waren Orakelinschriften. Viele Zehntausende solcher Orakelinschriften wurden Anfang dieses Jahrhunderts in Anyang in der heutigen Provinz Honan gefunden. Die Schriftzeichen sind vereinfachte Bilder, die heute als „Schalen-und-Knochen-Schriften" bekannt sind. Etwas später wurde die gleiche Bildschrift auch in Bronzegefäße eingeritzt und deshalb Metallschrift genannt. Aus diesem Material erhält man ein genaues Bild von den chinesischen Schriftzeichen des Altertums, nämlich von der Ying-Dynastie bis zum Beginn der Chou-Dynastie (etwa 1400–1112 v.Chr.). Es ergibt sich, daß vor dem Jahr 1001 v.Chr., in dem König Mo zu herrschen begann, das Schriftzeichen „Ming" gar nicht existierte. Statt dessen gab es das Zeichen „Ling", welches eindeutig einen kniebeugenden Menschen darstellte, und das entweder Befehl vom Shang-ti (hoher Kaiser = Gott) oder von einem König bedeutete. Dieses Zeichen ist in heutiger, vereinfachter Form noch immer sehr geläufig und hat dieselbe Bedeutung („Befehl"). Etwa in der Zeit des 10. bis 9. Jahrhunderts v.Chr. war ein Mund an der linken Seite desselben Zeichens hinzugekommen, offensichtlich deshalb, weil der Befehl gewöhnlich durch den Mund erteilt wurde. Diese neue Form wurde zunächst neben der alten unterschiedslos gebraucht. Beide Formen waren wahrscheinlich Varianten eines einzigen Zeichens. Aber in späterer Zeit, etwa im Buch der Oden, wurde die neuere Form dieses Zeichens mehr gebraucht. Dieses neue Zeichen „Ming" hat ursprünglich dieselbe Bedeutung, nämlich die des Befehls oder Mandats vom Shang-ti oder von einem König.

Bald entwickelte sich ein neuer Gebrauch des Zeichens „Ming", u.zw. im Sinne von „Schicksal eines Einzelnen" oder „eines Reiches", das sich durch den Willen Gottes ergab. Zwei Schicksalsarten sind im Buch der Oden und im Buch der Geschichte (Shu-king) zu erkennen: die erste kam durch den absoluten göttlichen Befehl zustande ohne menschliches Zutun, und kann deshalb als unbedingter „Ming" bezeichnet werden; die andere kam zwar auch durch den göttlichen Befehl zustande, doch nur in Abhängigkeit von verschiedenen Bedingungen, durch deren Erfüllung bzw. Nicht-Erfüllung es realisiert würde. Diese zweite Schicksalsart mag deshalb „bedingter Ming" heißen. Am öftesten sprach man von dieser Art „Ming", wenn von göttlicher Belohnung oder Bestrafung die Rede war. Konfuzius und Menzius jedoch hüteten sich sehr, von solchem bedingten „Ming" zu sprechen; sie vermieden Aussagen über göttliche Belohnung oder Strafe. Beide hielten sich streng an den unbedingten „Ming", insbesondere im ursprünglichen Sinn des göttlichen Befehls oder des himmlischen Mandats, dem es mit Ehrfurcht zu gehorchen galt. Daß die Chinesen seit mehr als dreitausend Jahren bis zu Konfuzius und Menzius an einen Gott als Person glaubten, ist von keinem ernstzunehmenden Gelehrten in Zweifel gezogen worden. So erklärten z.B. Fung Yu-lan und Ch'ien Mo Konfuzius für gottgläubig, obwohl sie selbst es nicht waren. Auch hinsichtlich Menzius sprechen die Originaltexte eine unzweideutige Sprache. Die Benennung von Shang-ti wurde bald mit jener von „T'ien" (Himmel) unterschiedslos gebraucht. Schließlich war der

Name „T'ien" fast allein im Umlauf, im besonderen zur Zeit von Konfuzius und Menzius (6.–5. Jahrhundert v.Chr.).

II. Wandel des religiösen Bewußtseins durch Taoismus u. Spät-Konfuzianismus

Der Glaube an einen höchsten, persönlichen Gott wurde im Altertum Chinas durch die naive Vorstellung charakterisiert, daß gute und üble Taten durch ihn vergolten werden, und zwar schon in dieser Welt. Während der Zeit der Frühling-und-Herbst-Annalen (722–481) und mehr noch in der unmittelbar folgenden Zeit der streitenden Reiche (480–221) wurde die genannte Gottesvorstellung vielfach erschüttert, weil offensichtlich gute und üble Taten regelmäßig unvergolten blieben. Der Druck solch unerklärlicher Tatsachen trieb Laotze und seine Schule in die sichere Zuflucht zum beständigen Walten des kosmischen Weges (Tao). Wie die Geschichte der Han-Dynastie (Han-shu: Yi-wen-tzu) mit Recht bemerkte, entstand die taoistische Schule aus Kreisen von Geschichtsbeamten (Shih-kuan). Wie schon Shih-ma Ch'ien in seinem berühmten Geschichtswerk notierte, war Laotze ein Archivar des Chou-Reiches. Nach der eben zitierten Geschichte der Han-Dynastie beobachteten Laotze und sein Gefolge „die alten und jetzigen Wege des Erfolges und Mißerfolges, des Lebens und Sterbens, des Glücks und Unglücks" der geschichtlichen Geschehnisse. Sie kamen schließlich zu der Schlußfolgerung, daß der Tao als alleinige Kraft in Gestalt von Yin und Yang im ganzen Kosmos waltete, und er allein für alle Erfolge und Mißerfolge, ja für alle Geschehnisse der Welt verantwortlich wäre.

Laotze, der größte Metaphysiker Chinas, erhielt also die Inspiration und Impulse seiner philosophischen Spekulation über „Tao" aus sehr konkreten Situationen der Existenz. Allem Anschein nach war diese taoistische Denkweise zur Lebenszeit von Konfuzius bereits im Umlauf. Viele gewichtige Gründe aber sprechen dafür, daß das Buch „Tao-te-king" erst in der Zeit der streitenden Reiche (480–221 v.Chr.) entstanden ist. Das Buch muß damals wie ein Donnerschlag gewirkt haben. Viele, sogar Mitglieder konfuzianischer Schulen, verloren dadurch ihren altehrwürdigen Glauben an einen vergeltenden Shang-ti. Aus diesem Grund war es auch erklärlich, daß Motze (501–416) den Konfuzianern seiner Zeit den Vorwurf machte, daß sie den „T'ien" für nicht-einsichtig (pu-ming) hielten. Doch dachte Motze, ein glühender Theist und Aktivist für allgemeine Bruderliebe, gar nicht daran, die taoistischen Einwände zu erwidern; vielmehr deutete er „T'ien" als allgemeinen Vergelter; dies führte zu dem Resultat, daß die chinesische Intelligenz von einer theistischen Religiosität endgültig Abschied nahm. Später behauptete Wang Ch'ung (27–100), ein derartiger Glaube gehörte nur noch „dem dummen Volk".

Hsüntze, der um das Jahr 313 v.Chr. geboren wurde, teilte die politischen und moralischen Ansichten des Konfuzius; er war ein echter Schüler konfuzianischer Lehre. Allerdings adoptierte er die Metaphysik des Tao, ohne aber die Konsequenzen der taoistischen Schule zu ziehen. Die Schüler Laotzes folgerten daraus die praktische Konsequenz des passiven Nichts-Tuns, vor allem auf dem Gebiet der Politik und der Moral. Obwohl Hsüntze nur an den „beständigen Weg" des „himmlischen Geschehens" glaubte, anstatt an einen theistischen Shang-ti, dachte er nicht daran, alle diesem „Weg" zu überlassen. Vielmehr lehrte er, das beständige Walten des Tao zu „kontrollieren und benützen". Wenn der Himmel trotz seines allgemein waltenden Gesetzes und seiner Erzeugungskraft die gezeugten Dinge nicht „unterscheiden" und regieren kann, dann bleibt nichts übrig, als daß es die edlen Menschen tun. „T'ien und Ti erzeugen den edlen Menschen; der edle Mensch gibt T'ien und Ti Ordnung . . . Ohne edle Menschen gibt es keine Ordnung in T'ien und Ti." Damit ist eine höchst originelle Synthese zwischen konfuzianischem Betätigungsdrang und Verantwortungsbewußtsein der Welt gegenüber einerseits und taoistischer Metaphysik andererseits gelungen. Diese Synthese dauert bis in unsere Zeit an.

In gewissem Sinne wurde diese Synthese durch Tung Chung-shu (176–93 v.Chr.) vollendet. Nach Hsüntze besitzt der Himmel kein Unterscheidungsvermögen, er scheint aber absichtlich zu handeln, indem er die Regierenden um des Volkes willen einsetzt. Tung Chung-shu ging einen Schritt weiter: Sein Himmel und seine Erde waren Naturerscheinungen; gleichzeitig besaßen sie unendliche Güte und moralischen Willen. Die viel später hinzukommenden Sung- und Ming-Konfuzianer (960–1279 und 1368–1644) lehrten im Grunde das Gleiche. Diese Tatsache, die von ausländischen Forschern oft als „kosmologischer Abgrund zwischen China und dem Westen" empfunden wird, ist dadurch erklärbar, daß die Synthese zwischen Konfuzianismus und Taoismus nicht vollständig geglückt war.

III. Radikal-Taoistischer „Ming" im Sinne eines blinden Fatums

Bereits Hsüntze gebrauchte den Begriff „T'ien-ming" im Sinne eines beständigen Naturgesetzes. Das war möglich, da die Taoistische Schule schon vor ihm den Begriff „Ming" wesentlich geändert hatte. Ursprünglich nur Befehl oder Mandat bedeutend, umfaßte der Begriff später (im abgeleiteten Sinne) auch die Geschehnisse oder das Menschenschicksal als Folge des göttlichen Befehls. Da für Taoisten an die Stelle Gottes der Tao oder der kosmische Weg getreten war, ist es verständlich, daß in den Augen des „Tao-te-king" dieser kosmische Weg alle Dinge hervorbringt und von allen verehrt wird, denn alles kommt „beständig und spontan ohne Befehl von Jemandem". Chuangtze kam ein Stück weiter, indem er die Idee eines „spontanen Ming" aufnahm. Damit war der Tao gemeint. Ein anderer (bereits oben zitierter) Denker, Wang Ch'ung, entwickelte die radikale Lehre vom „Ming" im Sinne des blinden Fatums, das die Menschen vom ersten Moment der Geburt zum Glück oder Unglück bestimme. Daher sei guter „Ming" mit der Übeltat verträglich; umgekehrt auch schlechter „Ming" mit guter Tat. Denn nach ihm beherrscht das Weltall keine Zweckmäßigkeit, der Mensch komme ebenso wenig zweckmäßig in die Welt, wie die Läuse auf den Menschenkörper. Nach Kuo Hsiang, der im Jahre 312 starb, ereigne sich alles durch den „Ming": Alles was geschehen ist, hätte unmöglich nicht geschehen können. Alles ist notwendig und unvermeidlich.

IV. Sinndeutung des „Ming" durch Volksbuddhismus und durch die Taoistische Religion

Wahrscheinlich kam der Buddhismus im Jahre 68 A.D. nach China. Er wurde wie eine Erlösung empfunden, im besonderen zu einer Zeit, in der alles sinnlos erschien. Allerdings fand der Gelehrtenbuddhismus (nach der Lehre der Sutras) keine Verbreitung im chinesischen Volk. Dagegen verbreitete sich rasch jene Form des Volksbuddhismus, die von der Tang-Zeit (618–907) an bis heute die meisten Chinesen für sich gewonnen hatte; in der Vorstellungswelt dieser Form von Buddhismus haftet jedem sein voriges Karma als Schicksal oder „Ming" an. Um ein gutes oder besseres Karma für die nächste Transmigration zu sichern, bemüht sich ein Buddhist, das Gute zu tun und den Buddha Amida zu verehren. In der Praxis wird der Buddha Amida wie eine Art buddhistischer Gott verehrt, denn es wird angenommen, daß er seine Verehrer im westlichen Paradies wiedergeboren werden lasse.

Die taoistische Religion wurde etwa in der zweiten Hälfte des 2. Jhdts. begründet. Der Taoismus als Religion glaubt an unzählige Geister und Götter, die über gute und üble Taten des Menschen wachen. Oberhalb dieser Götter nahmen die Taoisten einen höchsten Gott an. Insoweit es den Begriff von „Ming" betrifft, ist die Auffassung der taoistischen Religion vom Volksbuddhismus übernommen worden.

Epilog

Wenn wir auf dreitausend Jahre des „Ming"-Begriffes und des chinesischen religiösen Bewußtseins zurückblicken, dann muß uns auffallen, daß von der Erweiterung oder Verengung der Sinndeutung des „Ming"-Begriffes das weitere und engere religiöse Bewußtsein abhing. Das göttliche oder himmlische Mandat hat mit der Kultivation der allgemeinen Güte zu tun, während das blinde Fatum oder das rein individuelle Schicksal den Blick des Menschen auf das eigene Interesse verengt. Es müsste also die naive Vorstellung Gottes einmal durch den ihr gegensätzlichen Tao-Gedanken verfeinert bzw. ergänzt werden.

* * *

7. Religion, Wissenschaft, Weltbild

7. Religion, Science, World Models

ORGANIZING IMAGES AND SCIENTIFIC IDEALS: DUAL SOURCES FOR CONTEMPORARY RELIGIOUS WORLD MODELS

Frederick Ferré
University of Georgia, Athens, USA

My aim here is to draw attention to a particular form of metaphorical imagery—I shall call it the "religious world model" (RWM)—which I believe to be immensely influential but inadequately noticed by philosophers of religion. These models hold vital sway over the consciousness of any age, including our own supposedly "secular" one. I shall argue that they arise from various sources, not only from well recognized religions like Christianity but also (very importantly for our civilization) from such vigorous expressions of creative imagination[1] as the sciences.

I. What are RWMs?

I define the religious world model in terms of three necessary conditions: (1) a *representational* (i.e., referential) *capacity*, (2) a *comprehensive* (i.e., world-inclusive) *scope*, and (3) an intensely *valuational* (i.e., religious) *potency*. Any image suggesting how *all things fundamentally should be thought,* which also *expresses or evokes profound value responses*, will be considered an RWM for the purposes of this paper.

My basic thesis is that RWMs function profoundly in the ordering of society itself. It is clear that we are deeply influenced, today as always, by value-laden conceptions of what the world is like. More and more people are becoming conscious of the degree to which our relations to each other and to the environment have been shaped by a vision of nature and man's place in it that is not the only one possible for human beings to adopt.[2] It is tragic that such awareness of the presence of RWMs in the background of social and environmental practices has had to wait so long. The further pity is that vast numbers of people are still unaware of the conceptual and religious roots of the crisis-time into which we have entered. They are half-blind, therefore, to their own participation in the problem and to their own potential role in its outworking.

II. Where Do RWMs Come From?

It would be fascinating to speculate about the origin of RWMs in the two hemispheres of the brain: whether in some cases our RWMs are more readily traceable to our right-hemisphere engagement with patterns, while in other cases they may be better interpreted as extensions from our left-brain hunger for linear explanation.[3] Since the burden of this paper is to suggest that RWMs arise both from myth and from science, the suggestion is attractive, but it cannot be pursued here.

Instead, I shall be content to trace the parallel and contrasting ways in which traditional mythic metaphors, on the one hand, and central scientific ideals, on the other, become potent RWMs that deeply influence our daily lives today. RWMs come by different paths from more than one source and one of these sources for our society is science. Science, therefore, is even more significant in our culture than is normally recognized, because science contributes vitally not only to our knowledge and technology but also to our ultimate vision of things. Religion, likewise, is even more pervasive and influential in our civilization than modernity's brash secular front mitht suggest, because RWMs shape not only our formal worship and our official ethical codes but also the basic attitudes and real policies with which we approach each other and the world in which we live.

A) Traditional Religious World Models (RWMs)

Human beings are myth-making animals. By "myth" in this context, I do not of course mean to imply anything false or outmoded. I mean, rather, to refer to the network of stories which provides a framework of intelligible order and moral guidance for the originating, story-telling community (and for others who may make them their own).[4]

I believe that these images, which may be called "organizing images" because of the role they play in organizing the perceptions and values of those who dwell on them, may become in the full sense models for the understanding of the world if, in addition to their several value roles, they are also taken seriously for *critical thought*.

As an *organizing image*, a metaphor's power of stirring values is vested in its vivid concreteness as it captures attention and consent. As a *model*, a religious world model, the metaphor's function is to suggest general respects in which the profoundly real may be critically thought to resemble features of the familiar and treasured. In this way the image becomes a model and the model gives rise to theory, i.e., to a structured and logically disciplined effort to conceptualize the unknown out of the materials of the known.

Religious theory, on this view, is always derivative from the value-drenched imagery that constitutes its heuristic metaphor. The highest flights of theological construction, no matter how coherent and adequate they may be intellectually, return for their religious authority to earth again in poetry, whence they were launched. One can see this with especial clarity in connection with doctrines about God that spring from the key Christian metaphor of God as Father. The image is vital to the Christian RWM: it is dramatized in such parables as the Prodigal Son; it is reinforced in Christian liturgy with the constant repetition of the Lord's Prayer beginning, "Our Father,..." God is not literally a father at all, of course, and yet the metaphor has great point both for the stirring of potent feeling (as organizing image) and also (as model) for the stimulating of profound thought, e.g. about Creation, Moral Theology, Providence, Ecclesiology, and Soteriology. As we shall note, it has an important social impact, as well.

B) Science-generated Religious World Models (RWMs)

It is less often noticed that RWMs spring also from modern science. Science seeks to explain as well as to control the world we live in. But explanation is an inherently open ended process. The principles used for explanation are subject, themselves, to a demand for explanation. Once this is supplied, by invoking further principles, these, too, will be subject to still more explaining. The quest for understanding would seem in principle forever unattainable. Scientists, however, do not give up their efforts in despair over the logical truth that every explanation remains unexplained as long as the whole hierarchy of explanations remains without a theoretical anchor. Instead, working scientists take for granted certain principles[5] as not requiring explanation, as being understandable "straight off", as it were, on their own credentials. These principles, which Stephen Toulmin calls "ideals of the natural order",[6] seem simply to "stand to reason". When one gets to one of these ideals of the natural order, one has reached a satisfying bottom deck in the quest for understanding.

In Newtonian physics, for example, a body will continue in uniform motion in a straight line (or remain at rest) as long as no forces are acting on it. Changes in motion−starting, stopping, speeding up, slowing down−need explanation, but in the absence of such changes, uniform straight line motion just "stands to reason".

That this readiness to accept some bottom deck to the otherwise infinite regress of explanation is not without its historical risks is shown by the fact that ideals of the natural order are subject to historical displacement. This happens with difficulty, for reasons that will become apparent, but it happens. For example, prior to the Newtonian ideal of unaccelerated *straight-line* motion as "standing to reason", astronomers such as Copernicus and even Galileo took as wholly natural and without need for explanation the ideal of uniform *circular* motion.

Thinking of circular motion as "natural" is of course vastly different theoretically from taking a similar view of straight-line motion. Beyond theory, however, ideals of the natural order are intimately related to still broader value-laden assumptions drawn from the cultural context out of which they arise. The Copernican ideal of natural circular motions, for example, did not by any means originate with him. On the contrary, it was a pre-Ptolemaic, pre-Aristotelian ideal of astronomical explanation set by Plato[7] as a challenge to his successors: to account, by appealing to none but "perfect" uniform motions, for the complex appearances of the heavens. Behind Plato's challenge was a deeply value-laden motive. First, only the perfect forms are fully intelligible; and, second, the heavens, being divine, would be desecrated by being thought in any terms short of perfect motions. Still earlier than Plato's views lay another great tradition, that of Pythagoras, who had earlier taught his followers to think of the real as identical with the perfect intelligibilities of number. Second, enfolding much of Greek thought and perception, was the cultural premise that the better, more admirable forms were the closed or limited ones. Why is a circle more "perfect" than a zig-zag or an endless straight line? To the culture that built the Parthenon, with its firmly limited lines and graceful, closed proportions, the answer was obvious. In the context of ethical thought stressing the avoidance of the *hubris* of excess, preference for the limited above the unlimited, for the self-contained circle above the alarming craziness of erratic motion—all these were too plain to require argument. Behind the explanatory ideals of Copernicus and Galileo, therefore, and far below the conscious surface of the scientific specifics being investigated, were profound visions of the nature of the world, and visions shot through with intuitions of basic value.

On the other side, with Newton and the ideal of straight-line motion, equally deep implications for ultimate reality and value can be seen. True, theoretical specifics were the immediate reasons for Newton's shift in ideals; he was interested in explaining a wider range of data in one set of principles than could have been done without penetrating below the ideal of uniform circular motion.[8] But with his scientific revolution came also a revolution in underlying philosophical and religious world-views. The image of the straight line, without beginning or end, as the ideal form of motion, had its own value implications. No longer ideally bounded by the sedate limits of form, space had to be assumed to be infinite in the Newtonian scheme;[9] and bolstered by Newton's prestige, the concept of infinity itself could be embraced as something good and attractive rather than unthinkable and threatening. Here we see a value-universe that is open-ended, not curved in upon itself. Thus the religion of *progress*, faith in human culture ascending forever on the endless inclined plane of historical development, would soon follow the Newtonian shift from the bounded to the boundless ideal of the natural order.

III. How Do Religions World Models Matter?

Identifying our key motivational images allows us to because more self-aware about why we have become as we are and where we may be headed.

A) Patriarchalism

One of the traditional organizing images that we had occasion to notice in a previous section is that of Fatherhood. The paternal values are profoundly part of human experience, and were functioning to organize families, villages, and nations long before our biblical tradition incorporated and modified such father-imagery into what we think of today as the Fatherhood of God. From Sky God to Zeus, from Jehovah to the Father in Heaven, the high concepts of rule and responsibility, moral principle and generativity, the brotherhood of Man under the cosmic Father, and similar values, were expressed and reinforced by traditional organizing imagery centering around the phenomenon of paternity.

It would be difficult to overstate the pervasive influence of this RWM, older than Christianity but strongly supported in Christendom by the theology, the liturgy, and the spirituality of Christian faith. The language of prayers and hymns, despite feminist attempts at reform, seems ineradicably masculine. Our taken-for-granted political structures are deeply hierarchical in structure. So are the structures of our economic and academic institutions. So, indeed, are the conceptions we internalize about ourselves, in a world of rules and authorities and father-figures.

More and more frequently the charge is made that our stress on *hierarchy* leaves *community* underattended, that our emphasis on *rules* leaves *insight* undernourished, and that aggressive, competitive, masculine values lead to conflict, exploitation (of persons and of nature) and to the horrors of war.[10]

This charge is a serious one, and must be attended by those who are concerned for the spiritual health and future course of civilization. Have our traditional RWMs overemphasized the masculine values at the cost of the feminine? Should there be more recognition of the phenomenon of Motherhood, and all that this stands for, in our society's institutions? Has a traditional RWM led us astray toward the rape of the earth and the brink of nuclear destruction?

These questions cannot be answered lightly, and it will need to be enough to ask them at this time. But if the question is whether and how RWMs "matter," the simple putting of these questions provides a start towards an answer.

B) Progressivism

Another characteristic of our civilization is its trust in the future. Unlike most human cultures, the modern world has operated with an open-ended sense of possibility and without much consciousness of limits. Led by the dynamic example of science, with its endless vistas for refinement and cognitive growth, and driven by the industrial power of science-led technology, our modern civilization—socialist as well as capitalist—has assaulted the future with aggressive confidence in its destiny.

Behind all this, allowing it and encouraging it, is the vision of the universe as likewise open-ended. As we saw earlier, the Newtonian revolution was not only a change in theoretical dynamics but also a shift in sensibility: space itself becomes homogeneous and infinite so that the straight line of endless motion can become the ideal of natural order, replacing the closed figure of the circle not only in theoretical principle but also at the center of modern consciousness.

Again, only recently, we have begun to question the values generated by this science-based RWM. The classical faith in Progress began to fade, of course, at the beginning of this century, with the tragedy of the First World War, but it has taken until the present to absorb the more fundamental shocks to our culture's mythic faith in growth.[11] Can we continue our patterns of exponential growth without destroying the earth and ourselves, either by pollution or overcrowding or exhaustion of natural resources? Has the heady image of limitless motion along an endless line proven, as an RWM, to be dangerously delusive? Was it applicable only to an unusual era of ample resources and empty spaces? Will its influence destroy our biosphere, and us with it, unless alternative RWMs can be found to guide our basic perceptions and practices in the building of a post-modern civilization that can live more gently on the earth?

It is not necessary to attempt an answer to these pressing questions here in order to see how enormously important they are to our daily lives and to our future.

C) Organicism

Are there then emergent RWMs that may give us some ground for fresh hope in a world battered and torn by the old? One possibility that I glimpse is of an emergent organicism in thought and value that may be (in part at least) generated by the new science of ecology. Not since the Newtonian revolution at the start of the modern age has the valuational overtones of a science so captured the imagination of so large a segment of society.

The religious world metaphors that arise from ecology as a pioneer post-modern science guide thought and feeling toward mutuality rather than hierarchy and toward cycles rather than open-ended lines. The model of infinitely complex interaction among symbiotic organisms replaces the picture of kingly rule. The internal evolution of richly supportive *modi vivendi* contrasts with the external enforcement of decrees. The political consequences of such revolutionary changes in basic ideals are difficult to anticipate in detail; but it is clear that if ecology-generated RWMs become typical of a future civilization, these consequences will be profound.

Imagine also the difference to our economic life that would be made by substituting the RWM of the *circle* for the progressive, infinitely extensible line. Nature *will* close the cycles that man attempts to force open with his progressive, dominating ways. The question is whether we shall cooperate with the wisdom of nature or be crushed.[12] Newton's infinite line may be an ideal of the natural order for pre-Einsteinian cosmological theory, but it is no viable ideal for a world grown aware of ecology. Sufficiency, balance, equilibrium, fulfillment within limits—these are the new ideals from ecology that may be in the process of replacing the progressivist RWMs of the modern era.[13]

In this way, by drawing attention to the ultimate values implicit in the great, global metaphors-in-conflict that surround us, philosophy of religion may broaden our awareness of the ultimately religious dimensions of contemporary "secular" society. In addition, philosophy of religion can bring its critical tools to bear upon these various contending religious ideals and help put them into the context of traditional, recognized religions, like Christianty, so that the current clash of faiths may be subjected to the scrutiny of reason.

ENDNOTES

[1] For an eloquent expansion of this theme, see J. Bronowski, *Science and Human Values* (N.Y. 1965).
[2] Lynn White, Jr., suggests a switch to the imagery of St. Francis in his influential "The Historical Roots of Our Ecologic Crisis" *Science*, 155, 10 March, 1967, pp. 1203–1207. Theodore Roszak offers "the Old Gnosis" in: *Where the Wasteland Ends: Politics and Transcendence in Postindustrial Society* (Garden City, N.Y. 1973). I discuss "polymythic organicism" in my *Shaping the Future* (N.Y. 1976). Many other alternatives are available.
[3] For an illuminating and authoritative account, see Roger W. Sperry, "The Great Cerebral Commissure", *Scientific American*, 210, 1964. Also see *Idem*, "Hemisphere Deconnection and Unity in Conscious Awareness", *American Psychologist*, 23 (1968), pp. 723–733.
[4] For a thoughtful discussion of an allied viewpoint, see Wolfhart Pannenberg, "The Later Dimensions of Myth in Biblical and Christian Tradition", in: *Basic Questions in Theology*, (originally from *Terror und Spiel. Probleme der Mythenrezeption* (1971)) translated by R. A. Wilson (London 1973).
[5] This includes principles and also practices, methods, standard instrumentation, aims—all that goes into what T. S. Kuhn calls the "paradigm" for normal science. See his *The Structure of Scientific Revolutions*, second edition (Chicago 1970), especially Section II. For our purposes, the key principles and implicit or explicit imagery or beliefs of the scientific community at any given time (what Kuhn calls "metaphysical paradigms" and "values" in his Postscript to the second edition, *Ibid.* are of primary interest.
[6] Toulmin, Stephen, *Foresight and Understanding* (Bloomington 1961).
[7] See Plato's *Timaeus*, trans. by F. M. Cornford (Indianapolis 1959), and T. S. Kuhn's discussion in *The Copernican Revolution: Planetary Astronomy in the Development of Western Thought* (N. Y. 1957), pp. 28ff. Another good treatment is provided in Stephen Toulmin and June Goodfield. *The Fabric of the Heavens: The Development of Astronomy and Dynamics* (N. Y. 1961), especially Chapter 2.

8 Toulmin and Goodfield, op. cit., especially Chapter 9.
9 For an excellent discussion of the radical shift in the concept of space, and its loss of "place" in the Newtonian world view, see Joseph J. Kockelmans, "Reflections on the Interaction between Science and Religion," *The Challenge of Religion*, ed. by Frederick Ferré, Joseph Kockelmans, and John E. Smith (N. Y. 1982), pp. 296–316.
10 For some ground-breaking literature, see Mary Daly, *Beyond God the Father* (Boston 1973); Carol Ochs, *Behind the Sex of God* (Boston 1977); and Elizabeth Dodson Gray, *Patriarchy as a Conceptual Trap* (Wellesley, Massachusetts 1982).
11 See the literature of limits—pro and con—represented in part by Jay W. Forrester, *World Dynamics* (Cambridge-Massachusetts 1971); D. H. Meadows, *et. al., The Limits to Growth* (N. Y. 1972); H. S. D. Cole, *et. al., Models of Doom* (N. Y. 1973); E. F. Schumacher, *Small is Beautiful* (N. Y. 1973); M. Mesarovic and E. Pestel, *Mankind at the Turning Point* (N. Y. 1974); William Ophuls, *Ecology and the Politics of Scarcity* (San Francisco 1977); and my own *Shaping the Future*, op. cit.
12 Commoner, Barry, *The Closing Circle* (N. Y. 1971). See especially pp. 298–299.
13 I have recently attempted to draw attention to this possibility in my "Religious World Modelling and Postmodern Science". *Journal of Religion*, 62 (1982), pp. 261–271.

* * *

ÜBER DIE NOTWENDIGKEIT DES GLAUBENS FÜR DAS WISSEN

Harald R. Wohlrapp
Universität Aachen

Die heute selbstverständliche Trennung des wissenschaftlichen Forschens vom religiösen Glauben ist bekanntlich dadurch zustande gekommen, daß die neuzeitliche Wissenschaft sich bei ihrer Entstehung gegen die Religion durchsetzen mußte. Insofern es aber natürlich auch vorher Wissenschaft gab, haben wir Anlaß, unser vom Glauben getrenntes Wissen als eine Form von Wissen aufzufassen. Mit Wilhelm Kamlah nenne ich sie „profan".[1] Die Aufhebung der Trennung zwischen Religion und Wissenschaft wäre auf der Seite der Wissenschaft das Abstreifen der profanen Form. Im hier formulierten Gedankengang wird dazu die erste Hälfte skizziert, die zweite angedeutet. Die Skizze bringt eine pragmatische Akzentverschiebung im Wissensbegriff, welche dann eine Revision der Profanität nach sich zieht: Es zeigt sich, daß zum wissenschaftlichen Forschen ein wahrhaft unerschütterliches Vertrauen nötig ist. Weil uns solches Vertrauen bislang nur in religiöser Form geläufig ist, habe ich die These im Titel in die etwas paradoxe Formulierung einer Notwendigkeit des Glaubens für das Wissen gesetzt. Nun zur Sache.

‚Wissenschaftliches Wissen' steht hier nicht einfach für Kenntnisse z.B. über die Zusammenhänge zwischen Druck und Volumen bei Gasen. Sondern es wird der dynamische Aspekt herausgehoben; wie das ja seit der Kuhnschen Wende weitgehend akzeptiert ist. Es geht also um den Prozeß, in dem solche Kenntnisse entstehen und vergehen bzw. sich als unfertig oder irrig erweisen. Im Kontrast zu den seit Kuhn geläufigen Darstellungen wird dieser Prozeß aber nicht als eine bloß theoretische Entwicklung, sondern grundsätzlich pragmatisch angesehen. Das soll hier heißen: Theorien werden als „Orientierungen" in unserer Lebensgestaltung aufgefaßt. Damit ist der Gang der Wissenschaft ein prominenter, aber keineswegs eigendynamischer Teil der Entwicklung unserer Orientierungen.

Weil diese Sichtweise bei weitem nicht so geläufig ist, wie die dynamische,[2] versuche ich eine kurze systematische Einführung. Dazu vergegenwärtige man sich, in welcher Weise wir im Alltag orientiert sind: Unser Verhalten ist nicht amorph, sondern hat Regelmäßigkeiten dadurch, daß wir beim Handeln gewisse Gesichtspunkte berücksichtigen. (Zweifelhafte) Weisheiten wie ‚Jeder ist sich selbst der Nächste' oder ‚Ehrlichkeit macht sich bezahlt' gehören ebenso dazu wie zwangsbewehrte oder erwünschte Normen, z.B. zur Sicherung des Eigentums oder der Grenzen des Alkoholkonsums. Auch einfache Theorien aus Physik, Medizin, Biologie usw. sind dabei; wie z.B. daß die Häufigkeit des Einschaltens die Lebensdauer einer Glühbirne bedingt, daß Lesen bei Kunstlicht die Augen stärker beansprucht, daß auch Zimmerpflanzen einen Tagesrhythmus haben usw. Wie kommen wir an unsere Orientierungen? Manche übernehmen wir, manche bilden wir selber, indem wir bemerkte Erfahrungsregelmäßigkeiten formulieren oder Gewünschtes als verbindlich setzen. Von den meisten wissen wir es nicht. Sie gehen irgendwie aus den Erlebnissen, Interaktionen und Gesprächen hervor. Um die Ausbildung von Orientierungen ein bißchen zu verstehen, unterscheiden wir zwei Phasen. In der ersten sind uns mehrere, z. T. konträre Orientierungen möglich, wir sind im Handeln und Verhalten unsicher, unschlüssig, eben nicht orientiert. In der zweiten sind wir, wie auch immer, zu einer Orientierung gelangt. Das muß nicht *eine* Ansicht sein, es kann eine Kombination mehrerer sein, vielleicht gar konträrer. Wichtig ist, daß wir das jetzt zusammenbekommen haben und uns in bestimmter Weise verhalten können. Die wissenschaftliche Bildung von Orientierungen ist sodann eine reflektierte Verschärfung der alltäglichen: Für die Vereinheitlichung sind bewährte Standards des Forschens und Argumentierens vorhanden, nach denen wir von vielen vorhandenen Vorschlägen zur Annahme „eines" –

insofern als richtig geltenden – Vorschlags zu gelangen versuchen. Und da dieser Vorschlag jedenfalls die weitere Sicht der Sache strukturiert, möglicherweise auch in technischem Handeln angewendet wird, ist er eben eine „Orientierung". Von wissenschaftlichen Orientierungen wissen wir also, wie sie zustande kommen; nicht insofern wir immer sagen könnten wie die Festlegung auf sie faktisch vollzogen wurde, sondern insofern wir diese Festlegung stets systematisch reproduzieren können, indem wir sie nämlich „begründen". Soviel hier zur Pragmatik des Wissens.

Aus der Kombination der dynamischen Betrachtungsweise mit diesem pragmatischen Aspekt ergibt sich, daß Wissenschaft eine höchst riskante Sache ist. Denn einerseits müssen wir uns eingestehen, daß Wissen im Hinblick auf eine Geschichtlichkeit vorläufig ist. Andererseits ist es mit Rücksicht darauf, daß es uns orientiert, also unsere Welt gestaltet, jeweils endgültig: hier kann nichts rückgängig gemacht werden. Gerade wenn unerwünschte Phänomene auftreten, lassen sich Korrekturen nur durch Weitergehen erreichen. Dafür ein Beispiel: Als Carl Röntgen 1895 die Emissionen der Kathodenröhre untersuchte, fand er jene Strahlung, die dichtes Material durchdringt, insbesondere den menschlichen Körper. Dies Resultat wurde erst der Fachwelt, dann zunehmend einer breiten Öffentlichkeit vorgestellt und dabei der Effekt an der durchleuchteten Hand eines Assistenten, manchnal nachmittagelang, demonstriert. Die betreffenden Personen bekamen eigenartige Krankheiten und deren Erklärung gab weitere Aufschlüsse über die Röntgenstrahlung und über Strahlungen überhaupt: daß das aggressive Vorgänge sein können. Bitte verstehen Sie diese Darstellung nicht als eine Rechtfertigung nach dem Muster, der Fortschritt habe eben seinen Preis. Zwei Punkte sollen daran deutlich werden. Erstens daß sich die weltgestaltende Funktion des Wissens schon vor einer bewußten Anwendung in Techniken geltend macht; und wir nicht genau bestimmen können wie. Derart bittere Belehrungen lassen sich bei mehr Zurückhaltung im Umgang mit Forschungsresultaten vielleicht oft abmildern. Prinzipiell vermeiden lassen sie sich nicht. Dies ist der zweite Punkt: Unser jeweiliges Wissen ist nicht nur begrenzt durch Unklarheiten, die uns bewußt sind und vor denen wir uns zu hüten versuchen können. Sondern es ist darüber hinaus durchsetzt mit Nichtwissen, von dem wir nichts wissen (am erwähnten Beispiel der Sachverhalt, daß Strahlen nicht immer so etwas Freundliches wie Licht sind). Um diese „Verknotung" des Nichtwissens zu lösen, dazu sind wir auf dessen Verwirklichung angewiesen. Es ergibt sich, daß die Wissensbildung ein nicht voll kalkulierbarer Prozeß ist, daß wir sehr böse Überraschungen erleben können und Korrekturen nur über ein Weitergehen erreichbar sind, welches wiederum nicht voll kalkulierbar ist. Dies ist die Begründung der These, daß für das Wissen Glauben nötig sei.

Die alltägliche Risikobereitschaft, die wir angeblich schon aufbringen, wenn wir uns z.B. in ein Auto setzen, reicht nicht aus, denn die bezieht sich auf die Stabilität der Normalsituation unseres Lebens. Gerade die wird aber durch den Gang der Wissenschaft beseitigt. Hierfür bringen wir also ein viel grundsätzlicheres Vertrauen auf, das sich als Fortschrittsoptimismus überschwenglich äußerte und deshalb als profane Variante des religiösen Heilsglaubens aufgefaßt worden ist. Der auch stets artikulierte Pessimismus wäre dann ein ebenso quasireligiöser Zweifel, gegen den aber bislang das Vertrauen überwogen hat. Möglich war das, weil die angesprochene Auflösung der Knoten des Nichtwissens sich nicht notwendig in bitteren Belehrungen vollzieht. Häufig genug hat die Verwirklichung des Wissens ja zu ganz neuen Möglichkeiten geführt und einen zunächst unabsehbaren Nutzen gebracht. Als z.B. Guericke und Pascal den Luftdruck untersuchten, hätten sie sich sicherlich nichts von luftgepolsterter Fahrzeugbereifung träumen lassen. Derartige Fälle sind ja die Demonstrationsbeispiele für den Fortschrittsglauben. Er hat sie aber nicht nur, sondern braucht sie auch unbedingt. Bleiben sie aus oder stellt sich der Eindruck ein, daß die bitteren Belehrungen überwiegen, dann ist er am Ende.

Diese Labilität des benötigten Vertrauens unterscheidet die profane Wissenschaft von der in die Religion eingebettete. Aber eine bewußte Rückkehr zur Religion muß nach der Aufklärung wohl hauptsächlich als verbrämtes Eingeständnis, die Verantwortung nicht mehr tragen zu können, gewertet werden. Vielleicht geht es ja auch anders: Indem wir unsere Begriffe von

Wissenschaft und von Vertrauen so weiterbilden, daß das Vertrauen der Wissenschaft nicht mehr äußerlich ist und gleichsam in der Luft hängt, sondern durch das wissenschaftliche Forschen selber genährt wird und dieses trägt. Das kann ich hier natürlich nicht durchführen, es war auch nicht mein Thema. Ein Beginn findet sich in einer neueren Arbeit von Paul Lorenzen;[3] das wäre fortzuführen. Ich zeichne hier in ganz groben Strichen wie es gehen könnte:

Vertrauen ist nicht primär eine intellektuelle Haltung, sondern wurzelt im körperlichen Fühlen (in der „Sympathie") und ist in ausgebildeter Form eine feste Offenheit, die auf der Übereinstimmung der Orientierungen mit dem InderWeltSein beruht. Um zu sehen, wie dies Vertrauen im wissenschaftlichen Forschen selbst entsteht, ist nochmals an den oben skizzierten Vorgang der Ausbildung von Orientierungen anzuknüpfen. Für die derzeit dominierende Wissenschaftstheorie sind die erwähnten Kriterien der Vereinheitlichung z.B. Konsistenz, Einfachheit, Fruchtbarkeit usw. Deren Bedeutung läßt sich an Beispielen ganz gut ausweisen. Ebenso läßt sich aber an Beispielen demonstrieren, daß diese Kriterien nicht die letzten Bestimmungsgründe für die Vereinheitlichung sein können.[4] Was kann es sein? Lorenzen meint, es sei die „Transsubjektivität", d.h. der Sachverhalt, daß wir, insofern wir überhaupt argumentieren, unsere Subjektivität abarbeiten. Das geschieht, insofern wir konträre Auffassungen anderer Forscher als Einwände gegen unsere eigene anerkennen und uns darum kümmern, die Einwände auszuräumen. Dieser Zug am Argumentieren verbürgt die tendenzielle Überwindung der Subjektivität der Meinungen bzw. die Ausbildung sachgerechter Orientierungen.

Könnten wir die Wissenschaft in dieser Weise als transsubjektive Orientierungsbildung auffassen und bewußt betreiben, dann könnte das zur Ausbildung eines Vertrauens führen, das nicht so unbewußt und labil ist wie der Fortschrittsglaube; welches aber andererseits auch nicht religiös wäre (nicht im klassischen Sinne, daß dabei auf Gott als auf einen von uns unabhängigen guten Lenker vertraut würde). Es wäre wohl die Vollendung des von den Aufklärern geahnten Selbstvertrauens des Menschen.

ANMERKUNGEN

[1] Vgl. W. Kamlah, *Der Mensch in der Profanität*, Stuttgart 1949.
[2] Vgl. die Arbeiten von J. Mittelstraß über Wissenschaftsgeschichte, z.B. in: ders. *Die Möglichkeit von Wissenschaft*, FfM 1974.
[3] Vgl. P. Lorenzen, „Politische Anthropologie", in: O. Schwemmer (Hrsg.) *Vernunft, Handlung und Erfahrung*, München 1981.
[4] Vgl. die Arbeiten von P. Feyerabend, z.B. in: ders. *Der wissenschaftstheoretische Realismus und die Autorität der Wissenschaften*, Braunschweig 1978.

* * *

PSYCHOANALYSE UND RELIGION

Hans Strotzka
Universität Wien

Nach einer Darstellung der eigenen Entwicklung gegenüber Religion und Psychoanalyse schildere ich meine Praxiserfahrung. Immer wieder, mindestens bei jedem zweiten Patienten, wurde man in der therapeutischen Praxis zwar mit dem Phänomen der ekklesiogenen Neurose (Klaus Thomas), dem Resultat der Diesseits- und Sexualfeindlichkeit der christlichen Kirchen, konfrontiert. (Jedem, der dies für übertrieben hält, sei die Lektüre von Tilman Mosers *Gottesvergiftung* empfohlen.) Es konnte aber nicht verborgen bleiben, daß es bei vielen Menschen durch die Religion zu gelungenen Sublimierungen und erfreulichen Objektkonstanzen kommen kann und daß eine Religion der Liebe unendlich viel Gutes tun kann. Insbesondere sei auch auf die enorme kreative Potenz der Religion hingewiesen, die für den Autor zwischen den Polen Mathias Grünewald und der Kirche von Wotruba in Mauer bei Wien liegt, von der Musik gar nicht zu reden.

In der therapeutischen Praxis hatte sich folgende Praxis eigentlich recht unreflektiert eingespielt:

1) Dort, wo religiöse Phänomene vor allem durch Versündigungsiden und irrationale Strafrituale in der neurotischen Dynamik eine Rolle spielten, wurden sie wie jedes andere „Material" behandelt, d.h. auf ihre Herkunft überprüft, die unbewußten Verflechtungen bearbeitet und im Klima von Widerstand und Übertragung analysiert.

2) Dort, wo eine religiöse Haltung für die Neurose relativ irrelevant erschien, wurde sie nicht mit Gewalt in die psychoanalytische Arbeit einbezogen und sozusagen in einer umgekehrten Fokaltherapie einfach ausgespart.

Gegenüber dieser Technik hatte ich eigentlich immer ein wenig schlechtes Gewissen, bis ich jetzt beim neuerlichen Lesen des Briefwechsels zwischen Oskar Pfister und Freud sehen konnte, daß diese merkwürdigen Freunde dieses Verfahrens als durchaus legitim betrachteten. Zumindest meine ich, das zwischen den Zeilen lesen zu können. Interessanterweise waren bei dieser zweiten Technik nie wesentliche theoretische oder technische Schwierigkeiten aufgetreten. Bei der ersten wurde dem Therapeuten, dessen agnostische Haltung trotz aller Abstinenz natürlich den meisten Patienten bekannt war, oft mit Recht mangelnde theologische Kompetenz vorgeworfen. In dieser Situation hat sich die Zusammenarbeit mit einem der vielen progressiven Theologen ausgezeichnet bewährt, der von seinem Standpunkt die Patienten viel besser entängstigen konnte. Ich habe hier nur gute Erfahrungen gemacht, natürlich ist dabei eine vorherige Information des seelsorgerischen ‚Kotherapeuten' unentbehrlich. Besonders das Skrupelantentum ist die klassische Zielgruppe dieser Kooperation.

Es scheint also eine gewisse Koexistenz zwischen einer sich um Erneuerung bemühenden Kirche und einer Psychoanalyse, die zwar das Konzept der ‚Zukunft einer Illusion' beibehält, aber zu dieser Illusion eine tolerantere Haltung einnimmt, möglich.

Eine sehr interessante Bemerkung Freuds möchte ich wiedergeben — sie findet sich im Brief vom 25. 4. 1928 an Pfister:

> Ich weiß nicht, ob Sie das geheime Band zwischen der ‚Laienanalyse' und der ‚Illusion' erraten haben. In der ersten will ich die Analyse vor den Ärzten, in der anderen vor den Priestern schützen. Ich möchte sie einem Stand übergeben, der noch nicht existiert, einem Stand von weltlichen Seelsorgern, die Ärzte nicht zu sein brauchen und Priester nicht sein dürfen. (S. 136)

Pfister antwortet darauf am 9. 2. 1929:

> Gestatten Sie mir bitte, auf Ihre Bemerkung, daß die von Ihnen gewünschten Analytiker nicht Priester sein dürfen, zurückzukommen!
> Mir scheint, daß die Analyse als solche ein rein ‚weltliches' Geschäft sein muß. Sie ist ihrem Wesen nach rein privat und gibt direkt keine Werte. Ich habe in unzähligen Fällen auch nichts anderes getan, als diese negative Arbeit zu leisten, und nie wurde ein Wort über Religion geredet. Der barmherzige Samariter hielt auch keine Predigt, und es wäre geschmacklos, die geglückte Kur nachträglich durch Glaubensverpflichtungen bezahlen zu lassen. Wie der Protestantismus den Unterschied zwischen Laien und Priestern aufhob, so muß auch die Seelsorge entkirchlicht und säkularisiert werden. Auch der Frömmste muß zugeben, daß der Liebe Gott nicht nur dasjenige entspricht, was ein Weihrauchdüftlein trägt.
> Nun aber scheint es mir, daß nicht nur Kinder, sondern auch Erwachsene sehr oft ein Verlangen nach positiven Lebenswerten geistiger Art in sich tragen, nach Weltanschauung und Ethik, und die Psychoanalyse kann sie wie Hartmann kürzlich so schön ausführte, nicht geben. Viele brauchen schon bei der Erledigung der pathogenen sittlichen Konflikte ethische Überlegungen, die sich nicht einfach auf dem Übertragungswege regulieren wollen. Wenn der Pfarrer nicht analysieren dürfte, so dürfte es doch wohl überhaupt kein Christ, kein religiöser und ethisch tiefgrabender Mensch, und Sie selbst betonen doch, daß die Analyse von der Weltanschauung unabhängig sei. (S. 137)

Erich Fromm, der sich viel mit diesen Fragen befaßt hat, sagt, „daß Gott ein Symbol ist für das Bedürfnis des Menschen, lieben zu können, dürfte leicht zu verstehen sein" (S. 68)

Ebenso einleuchtend: „Der wahre Sündenfall des Menschen ist seine Entfremdung von sich selbst, seine Unterwerfung unter die Macht, seine Wendung gegen sich selbst – auch dann, wenn sie sich in der Verkleidung seiner Gottesverehrung vollzog." (S. 65)

Seine Unterscheidung zwischen autoritärer und humanitärer Religion gibt heuristisch sehr viel her. Fromms Konzeption ist sehr bestechend:

> Freud ist der Auffassung, das Ziel der menschlichen Entwicklung sei die Erreichung folgender Ideale: Erkenntnis (Vernunft, Wahrheit, Logos), Menschenliebe, Verminderung des Leidens, Unabhängigkeit und Verantwortung. Diese Ideale bilden den ethischen Kern aller großen Religionen, auf denen die westliche und die östliche Kultur beruht: der Lehren des Konfuzius und Laotse, Buddhas, der Propheten und Jesu.
> Freud spricht im Namen des ethischen Kerns der Religion und kritisiert ihre theistisch-übernatürlichen Seiten, sofern sie die volle Verwirklichung dieser ethischen Zielsetzungen hindern. Er erklärt die theistisch-übernatürlichen Konzeptionen als Stadien der menschlichen Entwicklung, die einstmals notwendig und förderlich waren, jetzt aber nicht länger nötig und tatsächlich ein Hindernis für weiteres geistig-seelisches Wachstum seien. Darum ist die Behauptung, Freud sei ‚gegen' Religion, irreführend, außer wenn wir scharf auseinanderhalten, *welche* Art Religion oder welche Seiten des Religiösen er kritisiert und für welche er sich einsetzt. (S. 27, 28)

Jung hat die Franklsche Konzeption vorausgenommen: „Die Psychoneurose ist im letzten Verstande ein Leiden der Seele, die ihren Sinn nicht gefunden hat". (S. 134)

Die allzu leichte Eingänglichkeit der Sinnproblematik gestattet es, sich der Bearbeitung von Konflikten in ihren dämonischen Tiefen zu entziehen und billige Oberflächenerfolge zu erzielen, die zwar zugegebenermaßen manchmal sogar dauerhaft sind, aber der Tiefenproblematik nicht gerecht werden.

Von neueren Psychoanalytikern scheint nur Klauber besonders interessant. Glaube könne in psychoanalytischer Terminologie als jene Kraft bezeichnet werden,

> die sichert, daß das Individuum Instinktfrustrationen und Spannungen zwischen Ich und Ichideal etragen kann, ohne die Gefahr einer mörderischen Attacke des Über-Ichs auf das Ich. Anders gesagt, ist es der Glaube in die Unzerstörbarkeit guter internalisierter Objekte. (S. 294)

Während Freud und viele frühe Analytiker sich vorwiegend mit Vaterreligionen befaßten, sehen wir bei Klauber klar die ursprüngliche Mutterreligion: „Religiöser Glaube hat seine Ursprünge in den Phantasien, die sich das Kind schafft um das Vertrauen zu rechtfertigen, daß die Mutter fortsetzen wird, seine Welt zu schützen und zu leiten." (S. 251)

Von theologischer Seite bin ich am meisten beeindruckt von Küng, der den Gottesbegriff in die Nähe von Eriksons Urvertrauen bringt.

Es ist interessant, daß ähnlich wie der Freud-Pfister-Briefwechsel auch zwischen Alfred Adler und einem evangelischen Theologen (Ernst Jahn) eine Diskussion über Religion und Individualpsychologie erschienen ist. Adler nimmt dabei den Standpunkt ein, daß die Gottesidee als Konkretisierung und Interpretation der menschlichen Anerkennung von Größe und Vollkommenheit und als Bindung des Einzelnen wie der Gesamtheit an ein in der Zukunft des Menschen liegendes Ziel verstanden und geschätzt werden kann. Zum Unterschied zum Christentum und bis zu einem gewissen Grad auch zum Freudschen Menschenbild gibt es bei Adler kein in jedem Menschen wirksames böses Prinzip (Erbsünde). Die Frage, wie der Mensch gut oder böse wird, ist ein Grundanliegen der Individualpsychologie.

Der Theologe kritisiert an der Individualpsychologie ihren Intellektualismus, die Auffassung von Neurose als einen Irrtum und das Verharren in der Immanenz, d.h. daß durch vernünftige Erziehung und Heilbehandlung eine gesunde lebensgemäße Haltung erreicht werden kann.

Ich darf nun wieder zum persönlichen Erleben zurückkehren. Etwa Ende der 60er-Jahre war ich persönlich zu folgendem Schluß gekommen: Psychoanalytiker können konservativ und progressiv sein (also herkömmlich rechts oder links), sind aber praktisch immer agnostisch mit einer mehr oder weniger großen Toleranz zu den Religionen. Eine konstruktive Zusammenarbeit ist möglich.

Eine seinerzeitige päpstliche Meinungsäußerung, daß die Ausübung der Psychoanalyse einer Todsünde gleichkomme, wurde von allen belächelt.

Da traf ich (nicht in Österreich) eine Gruppe von Psychoanalytikern, die in der damals gerade akuten Frage des Schwangerschaftsabbruches einen so streng katholischen Standpunkt einnahmen, daß mir schauderte („Das Leben des Kindes habe selbst Vorrang vor dem Leben der Mutter").

Seither weiß ich, daß Aussagen über ‚Psychoanalyse und Religion‘ gar nicht möglich sind, weil unter ‚Religion‘ und ‚Psychoanalyse‘ sich so vielfältige Meinungen und Persönlichkeiten verbergen, daß man bestenfalls für sich selbst und eine kleine Bezugsgruppe etwas aussagen kann.

Mit diesem skeptischen Ergebnis darf ich meine Diskussion zu diesem Thema vorläufig abbrechen.

LITERATUR

Adler A., Ernst Jahn: *Religion und Individualpsychologie*, Frankfurt a. M. 1975.
Freud S., Oskar Pfister: *Briefe 1909 – 1939*, Frankfurt a. M. 1963.
Fromm, E.: *Psychoanalyse und Religion*, Zürich 1966.
Jung, C.G.: *Psychoanalyse und Religion*, Olten 1971.
Klauber, J.: „Notes on the Psychical Roots of Religion, with Particular Reference to the Development of Western Christianity", In: Int.J.Psycho-Anal., 1974, 55, S. 249.
Strotzka, H.: *Fairness, Verantwortung, Fantasie*, Wien Deuticke 1983.

* * *

RESEARCHMANAGEMENT, GESELLSCHAFTLICH-ETHISCHE PROBLEME UND RELIGION

Andries Sarlemijn
Technische Universität, Eindhoven

Traditional religions contained a cosmogony . . . (and) an ethical code . . . Rejecting the biblical ideas about creation led many to question the Christian code of ethics as well . . . We turned science into our God but it still threatens to destroy our cities with fire from heaven if not for our sins then for our stupidity. Nowhere is the action of the science-technology spiral more manifest. (H. B. G. Casimir, *Haphazard Reality: Half a Century of Science*, New York 1983, S. 308f.)

Um was für eine Dummheit handelt es sich hier? Darauf gehe ich in Abschnitt I und II ein. In Abschnitt III wird erörtert, seit wann die Religion im Kontext von Wissenschaft und Technik – wie in diesem Casimir[1]-Zitat – nur noch eine allegorische Bedeutung hat.

I. ‚Researchmanagement' kann verschiedenes bedeuten: 1. eine Klasse von Entscheidungen, 2. die Analyse von Handlungen, über welche entschieden wird, oder 3. die Begründung dieser Entscheidungen. Ob es sich in der 2. Bedeutung um eine Wissenschaft handelt, ist von den Kriterien abhängig, die man dabei verwendet.[2] Fordert man von einer Wissenschaft, daß Gegenstand, Klasse von Problemen und Forschungsmethoden eine Einheit bilden, dann ist Researchmanagement keine Wissenschaft; die Entscheidungen, um deren Begründung es geht, sind sehr verschieden. Dementsprechend gibt es auch verschiedene Arten von mit Researchmanagement zusammenhängenden ethischen Problemen. Für eine nuancierte Analyse ist es erforderlich, daß man ethisch verschiedene Probleme in Schemata einteilt. Einer der Zwecke dieser Schemata ist es, zu verhindern, daß ein Urteil über atomare Rüstung ein Urteil über Kernphysik impliziert. Bei der Annahme dieser Implikation wird übersehen, daß Kernphysik auch bei Isotopentrennung angewandt wird; diese Technologie ist bis jetzt noch für keine Industrie relevant. Zweitens wird übersehen, daß nur ein Teil der errungenen kernphysikalischen Kenntnisse technologisch verwenbar ist. Die genannte Implikation ist also logisch falsch oder beruht auf unvernünftiger Reduktion.

Das Spezifische dieser Reduktion illustrieren die Entwicklungen in den USA. Am 2. 8. 1939 unterschrieb Einstein, dessen Autorität hier Überzeugungskraft hatte, den von Szilard aufgestellten Brief an Präsidenten Roosevelt, so daß dieser die erforderlichen Forschungsgelder zur Verfügung stellte. Die Folge war der Anfang einer Forschung mit unterschiedlichen Ergebnissen: z.B. führte die Beschäftigung mit der Frage, wie kritische Masse zu produzieren sei, sowohl zu technischen als auch zu theoretischen Einsichten.[3] Diese Art von Forschung mit intesiven Wechselwirkungen zwischen Theorie und Technik und mit der Orientierung auf einen wohldefinierten technologischen Zweck (in diesem Falle auf die Möglichkeit einer effektiven Produktion der Atombombe) wird heute im Englischen oft als *target-research* bezeichnet.[4] Auch hier gilt: ethische Urteile über *target-research* implizieren keine derartige Urteile über die Grundlagenforschung. Spricht man sich gegen die 1939 angefangene Forschung aus, dann will man doch damit nicht die davor errungenen kernphysikalischen Einsichten verurteilen, denn die Entdeckung der Röntgenstrahlen (1895), der Becquerel-Strahlen (1896), des Elektrons durch J. J. Thomson (1897), der Quanten-Hypothese Plancks (1900), der berühmten Gleichung der speziellen Relativitätstheorie (1905) usw. gehörten bereits der Geschichte der Kernphysik an. Nicht diese Errungenschaften, sondern zwei besondere Umstände der weltpolitischen Situation haben 1939 zum genannten *target-research* geführt. Für die Beurteilung sind sie wichtig: a) Damals herrschte Krieg, und somit gelten nicht die gleichen ethischen Urteile wie in sonstigen Situationen; sogar viele Vertreter der christlichen Religion halten Töten in solchen Zeiten für erlaubt.[5] b) Zweitens herrschte Angst, und diese beeinträchtigte das vernünftige Entscheidungsvermögen. Deswegen schützt nachweisbare Angst in den Gerichtssälen der meisten Länder vor Strafe. Spätere Entwicklungen überblickend können wir uns fragen, was vernünftiger gewesen wäre, wenn es keinen Krieg und keine Angst gegeben hätte. Hätte man mit *target-research* gewartet, dann wären die Einsichten in bezug auf die Kernfusion mit ihren geringeren radioaktiven Folgen schneller fortgeschritten. Unvernünftig ist somit das übereilte Übergehen auf *target-research* und von diesem auf *development* (Entwicklung der Produktion).[6]

Schematisch sind drei Forschungsebenen zu unterscheiden: a) Auf der Ebene der Grundlagenforschung ist der Wissenschaftler kompetent und kann eine vernünftige Wahl zwischen technologischen Entwicklungen fördern, indem er auf in bezug auf Anwendung miteinander konkurrierende Theorien hinweist.[7] b) Auf der Ebene von *target-research* sind die Möglichkeiten des Wissenschaftlers beschränkter, und er kann sich auf Grund seiner Einsichten nur entscheiden, ob er mitwirkt oder nicht. c) Auf der Ebene der Entwicklung und der Verwendung der Produkte sind die Möglichkeiten des Wissenschaftlers noch weiter eingeengt. Daß *target-research* ein Zwischengebiet bildet, verdeutlicht das Verhalten Szilards. 1939 versucht er erst Juliot Curie und Fermi davon zu überzeugen, daß die möglichen Anwendungen geheim zu halten seien. Einige Monate später überläßt er das Dilemma dem Präsidenten. Sechs Jahre später ist die Produktion im Gange, und man kann über die Produkte verfügen. Mit *strategischen* Argumenten (also nicht mit solchen, die er seiner Kompetenz in seinem Fachgebiet verdankt) protestiert Szilard vergeblich gegen die Verwendung der Bombe.[8]

Die Ergebnisse, die mit der eingeführten Dreiteilung erreicht werden, sind beschränkt. Meistens wird eine nuanziertere Betrachtungsweise erforderlich sein. Diese erreicht man, indem man zwischen klassisch-physikalischer, modern-physikalischer, biologischer und medizinischer Forschung unterscheidet. Auf diese Weise entsteht die Quasi-Matrix von Figur I. Sie ist eine *Quasi*-Matrix, weil die Forschungsebenen und die Fachgebiete zwar zu unterscheiden sind, aber organisatorisch schwierig voneinander losgelöst werden können.[9] Auf den Unterschied zwischen ‚klassisch‘ und ‚modern‘ komme ich später zurück.

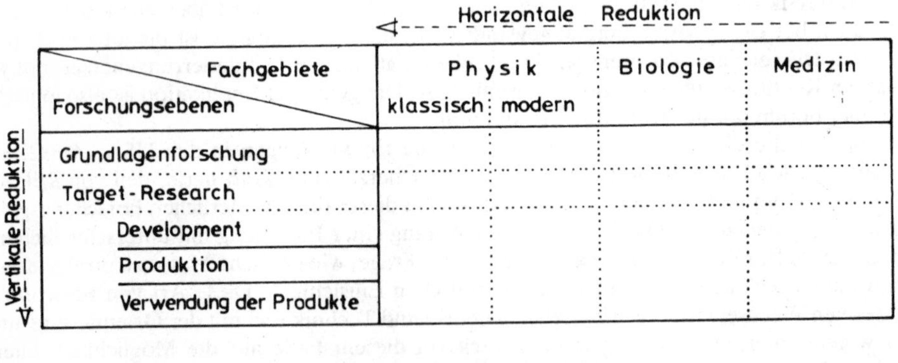

Figur 1: Quasi-Matrix zur Unterscheidung der Forschungsarten

Aus der Widerlegung der vertikalen Reduzierbarkeit folgt: a) Es ist falsch, Grundlagenforschungsergebnisse als Produktivmittel zu betrachten, wie dies in bestimmten philosophischen Kreisen Brauch ist. Erstens sind die Folgen der Anwendung dieser Ergebnisse nicht in dem Maße bekannt und vorstellbar, wie dies bei gewöhnlichen Produktivmitteln der Fall ist. Diese Betrachtungsweise mißachtet zweitens besondere Kompetenzen und ethisch-moralische Werte. b) Das gleiche gilt für den Ausdruck ‚wissenschaftlicher Arbeiten‘, der vortäuscht, daß der Grundlagenforscher Produkte herstellt und wie jeder Arbeiter die Kompetenz, zwischen den in bezug auf die ‚Verwendung‘ konkurrierenden Produkten (Theorien) zu wählen, den ‚Verbrauchern' überläßt.[7] c) Deswegen ist Grundlagenforschungsethik nicht auf gewöhnliche Arbeitsethik reduzierbar. d) Und dies hat wiederum Folgen für den Researchmanager, dessen Mitarbeiter auf Grund ihrer ethischen Einsichten an bestimmten Projekten nicht mitwirken können. Für eine Analyse dieser ethischen Problematik des Managers in bezug auf das Personal sind wiederum Schemata zu entwickeln.[10] Darauf kann ich hier nicht eingehen. Es hat sich gezeigt, daß die Problematik ‚Researchmanagement und Ethik' komplex ist. Deswegen beschränke ich mich auf die Frage, inwiefern die eingeführte Dreiteilung sich mit der Researchmanagement-Praxis vereinbaren läßt.

II. In industriellen Laboratorien setzt Forschung Führung und Planung voraus. Dies wird nicht in Zweifel gezogen. Dennoch gibt es verschiedene Researchmanagement-Modelle; d.h. man ist sich uneinig über die erforderliche Beziehung zwischen Forschung und Anwendung. Für eine globale Einsicht genügt es drei Modelle zu erwähnen. a) Das *ET.-Modell* ist extrem *t*echnokratisch und fordert die Aufhebung der Unterscheidung zwischen Grundlagenforschung und produkt-orientierter Forschung zur Erhöhung der Effizienz.[11] b) Das *GT-Modell* ist *g*emäßigt *t*echnokratisch und läßt eine organisatorische Trennung und methodologische Unterscheidung zu oder fordert sie explizit unter dem Motto „Überlasse die von der Technologie getrennte Grundlagenforschung den Universitäten. Die auf Technologie orientierte Forschung der Industrie verfolgt andere Ziele."[12] c) *Casimirs Spiral-Modell* beruht auf der folgenden Analogie: wie der Löhne-Preis-Kreis durch Produktivitätssteigerung so wird auch die Kreisbewegung zwischen *development* und Produktion durch Grundlagenforschung und *target-research* durchbrochen und in eine Spiralbewegung umgewandelt.[13] Diese Analogie beruht auf zwei Argumenten gegen die ET-Reduktion (Aa und Bb) und auf zwei Argumenten gegen die GT-Trennung (Ba und Bb):

Aa) Die Halbleiterforschung des Philips-Laboratoriums wurde erst durch die Anwendung der Ergebnisse bei der Produktion von Fernsehgeräten kostendeckend, während man zuerst nur an eine Anwendung in der Telephontechnologie gedacht hatte. Nach den Forderungen des ET-Modells müssen die Kosten der Grundlagenforschungsprojekte in den Budgets der Produktionszweige, wo Anwendung erwartet wird, untergebracht werden. Im genannten Fall hätte dies das Ende der Forschung oder der Telephonproduktion bedeutet.[14] Ab) Das ET-Modell beruht auf einer falschen Geschichtsauffassung, nach welcher die für die klassische Periode charakteristische Trennung zwischen Grundlagenforschung und Technik nach dem Vorbild der kernenergetischen und weltraumfahrt-technologischen Projekte aufgehoben werden kann. Erstens wird dabei übersehen, daß solche Projekte die Grundlagenforschung bremsen und daß zweitens diese Projekte die davor errungenen Ergebnisse der Grundlagenforschungsdisziplinen voraussetzen.[15] Diesbezüglich weichen diese Projekte nicht von der elektronischen und elektrotechnischen Technologie ab; diese setzt noch immer die Einsichten von Maxwell, Hertz u.a. voraus, die ohne Orientierung auf eine bestimmte Technik entstanden sind.[16]

Ba) Die GT-Trennung war in der klassischen Technologie durchaus möglich: Galileis Teleskop und Van Leeuwenhoeks Mikroskop wurden ohne theoretische Vorkenntnisse entdeckt, entwickelt und produziert und erst später durch Forschungsergebnisse verfeinert. Die Geschichte des Elektronenmikroskops zeigt jedoch, daß eine solche Unabhängigkeit von der Theorie in der modernen Technologie nicht mehr existiert.[17] Ohne grundlagentheoretische Vorkenntnisse wäre dieses moderne Instrument nicht entdeckt und entwickelt worden. Auch der Transistor wurde durch Zusammenarbeit zwischen Theorie und T*t*echnik entdeckt.[18] Daraus ergibt sich, daß Technologie und Industrie sich in bezug auf die Grundlagenforschung nicht bloß rezeptiv verhalten können. Bb) Das GT-Modell geht an dem Umstand vorbei, daß moderne Grundlagenforschung technologische Kenntnis und Planung voraussetzt. Für die Entdeckung von stets wieder neuen Teilchen in der Hochenergiephysik (50 W-Teilchen und 5 Z-Null-Teilchen) Anfang 1983 reichte die von Glaser 1952 entwickelte Blasenkammermethode schon nicht mehr aus, und es wurde eine elektronische Methode (wobei die Entdeckung der Teilchen dem Computer überlassen wird) erforderlich.[19] Für derartige Entdeckungen benötigt das CERN in Genf Vakuumröhren mit einer Länge von 27 km, die eine Milliarde Schweizer Franken kosten. Dafür, daß diese Anlagen sich für mehrere Arten von ‚Beobachtungen' und ‚Experimenten' eignen, ist Planung unentbehrlich.

Kommen wir jetzt zurück auf die vorher gestellte Frage. Die hier auf Grund von ethischmoralischen Überlegungen geforderte Dreiteilung ist im Casimir-Modell mit den praktischen Aufgaben des Researchmanagements vereinbar (Unterscheidung der Grundlagenforschung von der Technologie, ohne sie von dieser loszulösen); im GT-Modell wird die Absicht der Dreiteilung problematisch (die Trennung bedeutet hier die Möglichkeit, sich vor jeder Verantwortung abzuschirmen), im ET-Modell wird sie unmöglich. Casimirs Argumente sind jedoch auf die Förderung der Technik orientiert: die Entwicklung der Produktion erfordert das Spiral-Modell.[20] Deswegen hält Casimir die Spiralbewegung für einen selbständigen Strudel: die Begründung ist frei von religiösen, ästhetischen und sogar auch von sozialen und politischen Überlegungen.[21] Wie ist diese Situation entstanden?

III. Beschränken wir uns auf die Trennung der Religion von Wissenschaft und Technologie. Das Entstehen der Wissenschaften im antiken Griechenland bedeutet einen Bruch mit vorhergehenden Entwicklungen in Griechenland, Ägypten und Babylonien, wo religiöse, technische, astronomieartige, mathematikartige Einsichten nicht voneinander unterschieden wurden.[22] Bei den Griechen löste sich später die Wahrheitsfindung als Ziel der Wissenschaften von den technischen Absichten. Es entstand auch eine gewisse Spannung zwischen Religion und Wissenschaft; für diese Annahme spricht die Tatsache, daß Plato und Aristoteles des Atheismus beschuldigt worden sind.

Das Mittelalter stellte die Harmonie wieder her. Die Kirche förderte die Kultur, weil die Religion in ihr integriert war, ohne sie zu dominieren. Wissenschaft und Technik wurden in ihrer Entwicklung nicht gebremst. Heute sind sich Wissenschaftssoziologen und -historiker darüber einig, daß im Mittelalter in bezug auf wissenschaftliche Diskussionen und auf technische Entwicklungen große Freiheit von Denken und Handeln herrschte. Die Toleranz verringerte sich später.[23] Ebenfalls sind sie sich darüber einig, daß die christliche Religion die Entstehung der modernen Wissenschaften gefördert hat.[24] Zwar trennen sich die Meinungen bei der Frage, welche religiösen Einsichten den ausschlaggebenden Einfluß ausgeübt haben.[25] Für mein Thema ist diese Frage jedoch unwichtig, weil unterschiedlichste Traditionen (Pythagorismus, Platonismus, Aristotelismus, Atomismus) abwechselnd mit Religion und Wissenschaft verbunden worden sind. Wichtiger ist festzustellen, daß der Bruch sich im 18. Jahrhundert noch nicht vollzogen hatte. Daraus folgt, daß weder die Mathematisierung der Physik, noch deren Orientierung auf die Technik und auch nicht die kopernikanische Wende den Bruch veranlaßt haben. Die Geschichte der Optik zeigt, daß Mathematik, naturwissenschaftliche Theorie, Beobachtung und Analyse der in der Technik produzierten Objekte (Gläser) schon bei den Griechen und auch im Mittelalter miteinander in Zusammenhang gebracht worden sind.[26] Dies gilt auch für die Astronomie: im alten Ägypten und Babylonien wurden mathematikartige Techniken für Voraussagen von z.B. Sonnenfinsternissen verwendet. Dies war auch noch 2000 Jahre später der Fall, als eine heftige Diskussion über das kopernikanische System geführt wurde. Die Heftigkeit war dem Umstand zu verdanken, daß diese Diskussion sich mit der religiösen über die Reformation vermischte.[27] Aber diese Vermischung bremste die Entwicklung nicht ab, sondern förderte sogar die sachliche Entscheidung, denn die religiöse Problematik hatte auch politische Relevanz, und deswegen waren Fürsten und Könige bereit, für das empirische Urteil Forschungsgelder bereitzustellen, was sich in den Biographien über Tycho Brahe und Kepler leicht feststellen läßt.[28] Und obwohl Kepler sich für die Anwendung der Mathematik einsetzte und ein überzeugter Kopernikaner war, befürwortete er nicht die Trennung. In seinen astronomischen Untersuchungen war er bestrebt, eine göttliche Weltharmonie zu entdecken.

Gegenstand der Auseinandersetzungen zwischen den Schülern von Descartes, Leibniz und Newton im 18. Jahrhundert waren nicht die Mathematisierung, nicht die kopernikanische Wende, nicht die Relevanz der Wissenschaft für die Technik, sondern die Frage, inwiefern

Gravitation mit einem Gottesbild in Übereinstimmung zu bringen sei![29] Diese Frage wurde nie gelöst, sondern durch eine Trennung zwischen Glauben und Wissen durch d'Alembert, Lagrange und besonders durch Laplace eliminiert.[30] Historisch wurde die Trennung durch das Aufkommen des Liberalismus und des Positivismus belgleitet. Mehr als ein Jahrhundert später wurde die Trennung von Wittgenstein am deutlichsten formuliert: *in der Sprache der klassischen Physik ist das Mystische unaussprechlich geworden.*[31] Trotz aller Positivismuskritik gilt dies heute in einem stärkeren Maße als damals, denn diese klassische Physik ist inzwischen technische Wissenschaft geworden und ist jetzt weit von weltanschaulichen und naturphilosophischen Fragen entfernt.[32] Die Einheit des Weltbildes (die Einheit zwischen Gravitation, Kernkraft und elektromagnetischer Kraft) steht jetzt in der höheren Energiephysik zur Diskussion; aber das Mystische ist dabei immer noch ‚unaussprechlich‘. Anderseits haben Religion, Ethik, Philosophie der Arbeit und Philosophie der Technik sich von solchen Forschungsgebieten zurückgezogen. Dadurch ist eine Diskrepanz entstanden: Religion, Ethik, Philosophie warnen oft vor der Gefahr der horizontalen Reduktion in der Quasi-Matrix: das Menschliche ist nicht auf das Biologische und dieses nicht auf das Physische zu reduzieren. Wie sich gezeigt hat, ist die vertikale Reduktion eine nicht weniger relevante Problematik. Darüber erfährt man in dieser Literatur jedoch nichts. Vielleicht hat der Mensch geringeren Respekt für seine eigenen Schöpfungen als für die von der Natur gegebene Hierarchie.

ANMERKUNGEN

[1] Als theoretischer Physiker hat Casimir (geb. 1909 in Den Haag) mit Ehrenfest, Bohr und Pauli eng zusammengearbeitet. Seine Beiträge zu den verschiedenen Gebieten der Physik haben inzwischen eine bleibende Bedeutung errungen. Insbesondere gilt dies für seine mathematischen Abhandlungen über die Quantenmechanik. Sie haben veranlaßt, daß nach ihm ein Operator in der Lie-Gruppentheorie benannt worden ist (siehe darüber z.B. H. J. Lipkin, *Anwendung von Lieschen Gruppen in der Physik* (Mannheim 1967)). Als Researchmanager hat Casimir während fast drei Jahrzehnten die Forschung des Philipskonzerns entscheidend beeinflußt. Er war einer der Gründer und der 1. Vorsitzende der EIRMA (European Industrial Research Management Association). Außerdem war Casimir von 1939 bis 1977 Dozent der Universität Leiden und veröffentlichte seit den dreißiger Jahren viele Aufsätze über Wissenschaftsphilosophie und Researchmanagement-Theorie.

[2] Bekanntlich ist man im Englischen mit ‚Science‘ etwas sparsamer als im Deutschen mit ‚Wissenschaft‘. Siehe darüber B. B. G. Casimir, „When does Jam become Marmelade?", in: E. Mendoza (Hrsg.), *A Random Walk in Science* (London–Bristol 1973), S. 1f. Nach Casimir wird die Bedeutung von ‚Science‘ prototypisch (als eine nichtexakte Klasse) und die Bedeutung von ‚Wissenschaft‘ generisch (durch Festlegung des für alle Elemente gemeinsamen Prädikats) bestimmt. In einem demnächst in niederländischer Sprache erscheinenden Aufsatz werde ich auf diesen Unterschied und auf seine Folgen für das Demarkationsproblem eingehen.

[3] Nur ein Teil von dem, was gewöhnlich als ‚Manhattan-Project‘ bezeichnet wird, ist hier gemeint. Der inzwischen popularisierte Term ‚Manhatten-Project‘ steht für alle Forschung (also auch für die, die außerhalb der Universität Manhattan durchgeführt worden ist) und für alle Elemente des Casimir-Spektrums (siehe Anm. 4), insofern sie auf die Produktion der Atombombe orientiert gewesen sind. Für die Geschichte des Projekts siehe M. J. Sherwin, *A World Destroyed: The Atomic Bomb and the Grand Alliance* (New York 1975) und „Niels Bohr and the Atomic Bomb: The Scientific Ideal and International Politics, 1934–1944", in: *History of Twentieth Century Physics* New York–London 1977), S. 352f.; W. de Ruiter (Hrsg.), *Geschiedenis van de kernbewapening; van wetenschappelijk avondtuur tot moreel dilemma* (Eindhoven ²1982). Die Entwicklungen in Deutschland werden von J. Herbig, *Kettenreaktion; das Drama der Atomphysiker* (Darmstadt 1976) analysiert.

[4] Das vollständige Research-Spektrum Casimirs umfaßt: *Fundamental Research* der Universitäten, *fundamental research* der Industrie, *target-research, project-research* (= *advanced devolopment*), *development, factory-engineering, trouble-shooting, application-research.* Im Philipskonzern sind die Aufgaben wie folgt verteilt: „In our organisation each individual division is responsible for its own development, factory engineering and application work, whereas fundamental research, target-research and project-research or advanced development are carried out in our central research laboratory", H. B. G. Casimir, „Science and Industry", in: H. B. G. Casimir und S. Gradstein, *An Antho-*

logy of Philips Research (Eindhoven 1966), S. 75f. Zur Vereinfachung der Problematik introduziere ich im Text nur einen Teil des Casimir-Spektrums (siehe auch Anm. 9). Für eine vm Casimir-Spektrum abweichende Einteilung siehe W. S. Martin, „Research and Development in the 1980's: the need for industry-university cooperation", *Journal of the Society of Research Administrators*, Bd. 11 (1980), Nr. 3, S. 14f. Martin schreibt den zentralen Laboratorien drei Aufgaben zu: *Research, Development*, und *Technical Service*. ‚Technical Service' umschreibt er als „work performed by R&D personnel (usually requested by other areas of a company, such as manufacturing, marketing, or corporate management)". Das Forschungspersonal sieht sich oft gezwungen, bei Aufgaben, für welche es nach der in einem Betrieb akzeptierten Aufgabenverteilung gar nicht verantwortlich ist, auszuhelfen. Außerdem ändern sich manchmal die Arbeitsteilungen und die damit zusammenhängenden Auffassungen über die unterschiedlichen Forschungsebenen. Trotz allen Bemühungen der OECD gibt es immer noch keine einheitliche Taxonomie der Forschungsebenen. Hierdurch ist es schwierig, den ökonomischen Wert der unterschiedlichen Forschungsebeen festzustellen. Siehe auch Anm. 11.

5 Bocheński, J. M., hat − in *Wege zum philosophischen Denken* (Basel−Freiburg−Wien 1959), Kap. VI − überzeugend gezeigt, daß moralische Grundwerte auf einer Evidenz (und nicht auf einer philosophischen Begründung) beruhen.

6 Casimir fordert, daß Grundlagenforschungsergebnisse − wie etwa die des CERN − erst nach einer Periode von 25 Jahren in der Industrie angewendet werden sollten. Siehe H. B. G. Casimir, *De kringloop van natuurkunde en techniek in de 20e eeuw* (Haarlem 1979), S. 26.

7 Herbig (1976), S. 129: „Die Unsicherheit der Regierungen, die neuen Möglichkeiten zu beurteilen, macht sie vom Urteil der Wissenschaftler abhängig". Die Verantwortung des Grundlagenforschers ist deswegen nicht geringzuschätzen.

8 Szilard forderte, daß die Wirkung der neuen Bombe zuerst den Japanern gezeigt werde, damit diese sich − von der Wirkung beeindruckt − ergeben würden. Auf eine ähnliche Weise hat Einstein in den 50er Jahren vergeblich gegen die Produktion der Wasserstoffbombe protestiert. Siehe dazu H. B. G. Casimir, „Physik und Gesellschaft", *Physikalische Blätter*, Bd. 28 (1972), Nr. 11, S. 481f. (insbes. S. 485 und 488).

9 Dies ist auch der Grund, weswegen Casimir seiner Quasi-Taxonomie den Namen ‚Spektrum' gegeben hat (siehe Anm. 3 und 4): „Perhaps the word spectrum is not too badly chosen for there is in reality a continuous transition and just as it is difficult in the solar spectrum to tell whether a certain colour is a bluish green or a greenish blue, one may differ in opinion about whether a certain type is target-research or development, and so on." Casimir (1966), S. 76.

10 Cebik, L. B., „Science, Ethics and Research Administration", *Journal of the Society of Research Administrators*, Bd. 11 (1980), Nr. 3, S. 5f. geht auf diese Problematik ein und unterscheidet in „the range of our ethical involvements" „four levels of activity": (a) the personal dimension, (b) qualitative judgements, (c) conflict settlement, (d) policy formation.

11 In Krisenzeiten gewinnt dieses Modell immer an Popularität. Heute wird seine Popularität von den Ergebnissen der sog. Innovationsforschung gefördert. Diese entstand kurz nach dem 2. Weltkrieg und beschäftigte sich makro-ökonomisch mit Kosten- und Nutzenanalyse von Wissenschaft und Ausbildung. Damals wurden die Kosten für Forschung und Ausbildung in einem Lande mit dem ökonomischen Wachstum verglichen. Die Problematik wurde für spekulativ gehalten und die Schlußfolgerungen fielen für die Wissenschaft immer positiv aus: es würde sich lohnen, in Wissenschaft zu investieren. Inzwischen hat sich das Herangehen bei dieser Forschung geändert: mit komplexeren Methoden wird nach detaillierterer Information gesucht. Und der ökonomische Wert der Grundlagenforschung wird immer niedriger eingeschätzt. So wies das HINDSIGHT-Projekt z.B. nach, daß nur 0,4% der Innovationen einer Rüstungsindustrie der Grundlagenforschung zu verdanken sei. Vor kurzem wies in den Niederlanden eine Gruppe von Forschern nach, daß die Grundlagenforschung auf die Entwicklungen der Matallindustrie überhaupt keinen Einfluß hat (Für eine detaillierte Analyse siehe meine „Toepassing van wetenschap in techniek", in: D. W. Vaags und J. Wemelsfelder (Hrsg.), *Techniek, innovatie en maatschappij* (Utrecht−Antwerpen 1983), S. 98f.). Diese negativen Ergebnisse führen zu der Frage: Könnte der Mangel an Einfluß der Grundlagenforschung auf die Innovationen nicht dem Betriebsmanagement zugeschrieben werden? Mit solchen Fragen beschäftigte sich in den U.S.A. eine Forschungsgruppe unter der Führung von Prof. Ouchi. Sie stellte zuerst die wichtigsten organisationstheoretischen Merkmale japanischer Betriebe fest und untersuchte dann, welche westlichen Betriebe die gleichen Merkmale besitzen. Dann wurde festgestellt, daß diese Betriebe ökonomisch sehr erfolgreich sind. Darauf kam die Gruppe zur Formulierung ihrer Theorie Z, nach welcher jeder Betrieb in 13 bürokratischen Schritten angepaßt werden kann, damit er die gleichen Merkmale besitzt (siehe W. G. Ouchi, Theorie Z (Alphen a/d Rijn 1982)). Die Innovationsforschung stellt also nicht nur die traditionelle positive Bewertung der Grundlagenforschung, sondern auch die Werte der traditionellen Organisationstheorie des Abendlandes zur Diskussion. Casimir protestiert in fast allen Arbeiten, die sich mit diesem Thema beschäftigen, gegen die Ergebnisse der Innovationsforschung; er zeigt, daß die Taxonomie, von der diese Innovationsforschung ausgeht, unhaltbar ist. Insbesondere zeigt er, daß die Trennungen zwischen den unterschiedlichen Forschungsebenen niemals durchzuführen sind.

12 Mit der Idee, nach welcher die Industrie nicht an kritischer Prüfung der Theorien interessiert sei, begründet der Popper-Schüler Hans Albert dieses Modell. Siehe „Aufklärung und Steuerung;

Gesellschaft, Wissenschaft und Politik in der Perspektive des kritischen Rationalismus" und „Wissenschaft, Technologie und Politik – Zur Problematik des Verhältnisses von Erkenntnis und Handeln", in: G. Lührs, T. Sarrazin, F. Spreer und M. Tietzel (Hrsg.), *Kritischer Rationalismus und Sozialdemokratie* (Berlin–Bad Godesberg 1975), S. 103f. und S. 317f. und H. Albert, „Die Möglichkeit der Wissenschaft und das Elend der Prophetie", in: K. Acham (Hrsg.), *Methodologische Probleme der Sozialwissenschaften* (Darmstadt 1979), S. 304f. Insbesondere wäre nach Albert die Industrie nicht daran interessiert, den theoretischen Pluralismus zu fördern und durch ernsthafte Widerlegungsversuche die Erklärungskraft der grundlegenden Theorien zu fördern. Albert setzt dabei voraus, daß der Bereich der Erklärungskraft eine Theorie (der Bereich, der Gegenstand der kritischen Prüfung ist) und der Bereich der Anwendung einer Theorie (in der Industrie) als äquivalente Klassen zu betrachten sind. Diese Voraussetzung könnte vielleicht eine scharfe Trennung zwischen den Aufgaben der Universität und denen der industriellen Forschung begründen. Sie ist jedoch unrealistisch. Mario Bunge („Technology as Applied Science", in: F. Rapp, *Contributions to a Philosophy of Technology* (Dordrecht–Boston 1974), S. 19f., insbes. S. 25 und 27) hat schon auf den Unterschied zwischen „to *test* theories" und „to *use* them" hingewiesen und betont, „that the accuracy requirements in applied science and in practice are far below those prevailing in pure science". H. B. G. Casimir weist darauf hin und zeigt mit vielen Beispielen (1983, Kap. IX), daß die Anfertigungsregeln, die in der auf Anwendung orientierten Forschung gesucht werden, dermaßen konkret sind, daß diese Forschung trotz der weit entwickelten Grundlagenforschung einen ‚alchemistischen' (unwissenschaftlichen) Charakter hat; Grundlagenforschungstheorien begründen nur eine allgemeine Idee und nicht die konkrete Praxis einer Technologie.

13 Siehe Anm. 1.

14 Für noch andere Beispiele siehe Casimir (1966).

15 Daß Krieg und Wirtschaftskrise die Entwicklung (nicht die Anwendung) der Grundlagenforschung bremsen, ist eine von Casimir oft erwähnte begründete These. Siehe Casimir (1983), S. 300f., sein „Physics and Society", in: *Trends in Physics* (Petit-Lancy 1973), S. 125f., „De maatschappij in de maalstroom van de wetenschap", *Wending*, Bd. 25 (1970), S. 23, „Maatschappij, wetenschap en wetenschapsbeleid", *Ingenieursblad*, Bd. 37 (1968), S. 383f., „Industries and Academic Freedom", *Research Policy*, Bd. 1 (1971/72), S. 3f.

16 Siehe Casimir (1970) und (1979) und auch dessen „De natuurkunde ten tijde van Einstein", in: G. Debrock und P. Scheurer (Hrsg.), *Albert Einstein, zijn wereld, zijn wetenschap, zijn denken* (Nijmegen 1982), S. 19f.

17 Der Unterschied zwischen ‚klassisch' und ‚modern' hat nicht nur historische, sondern auch systematische Bedeutung. In einer modern-technologischen Forschung ist das Verhältnis zwischen Wissenschaft und Technik nicht das gleiche wie in einer klassisch-technologischen Forschung. Darauf wird schon in Casimir (1979) hingewiesen. Siehe auch meine *Wetenschap en Techniek* (Eindhoven 1982) und meine *Methodologie van de technische wetenschappen* (Eindhoven 1983a).

18 Siehe C. Wiener, „How the Transistor emerged; a Technical Invention was aimed by Social Inventions, which translated Basic Physics into Practice", *IEEE-Spectrum*, Bd. 10 (1973), S. 24f.

19 Die ionisierten Teilchen fliegen in der Blasenkammer in eine überhitzte Flüssigkeit (z.B. Äther, der bis auf 140° C erhitzt ist), wo sie eine Spur von Glasblasen auslösen; die Blasenspuren können photographisch festgehalten werden. Die hier im Text genannten Teilchen (die ungefähr hundertmal soviel wie ein Wasserstoffatom wiegen) sind erzeugt worden, indem man einen Strahl von Materie mit einem Strahl von Antimaterie zusammentreffen ließ. In der Umgebung des Zusammentreffens sind viele tausend Drähte, die mit einem Rechner verbunden sind, gespannt worden. Entsteht ein Teilchen und fliegt es an den Drähten vorbei, dann erzeugt es einen elektrischen Impuls. Nachher rekonstruiert der Computer die Spuren des Teilchens und das Computerband ersetzt die Photographie der Blasenkammer.

20 Ähnlich reagiert auch H. F. Schopper, Forschungsleiter des CERN-Instituts, auf die Frage nach dem Sinn der CERN-Forschung: „Ich sehe keinen logischen Grund, warum jetzt nicht die Vereinigung der elektro-magnetischen und der schwachen Kraft eines Tages auch zu ganz neuen Anwendungen führen wird"; siehe „Der Traum, Kräfte zur Urkraft zu vereinigen", *Der Spiegel*, Bd. 27 (1983), Nr. 24, S. 184f. Auf die CERN-Forschung geht Casimir in (1979) ausführlich ein.

21 Siehe Casimir (1970).

22 Siehe B. L. van der Waerden, *Ontwakende wetenschap; Egyptische, Babylonische en Griekse wiskunde* (Groningen 1950).

23 Diese Einsicht ist besonders dem Ergebnis von T. S. Kuhns Forschung *The Copernican Revolution* (Cambridge–London 101979) zu verdanken.

24 Siehe W. Büchel, *Gesellschaftliche Bedingungen der Naturwissenschaft* (München 1975), A. C. Crombie, *Von Augustinus bis Galilei, die Emanzipation der Naturwissenschaft* (München 1977), M. Wolff, *Geschichte der Impetustheorie, Untersuchungen zum Ursprung der klassischen Mechanik* (Frankfurt a. M. 1978), B. C. van Houten, „Techniek, wetenschap en samenleving in historisch perspektief", in: Vaags und Wemelsfelder (1983), S. 19f. Weil F. Wagner in *Weg und Abweg der Naturwissenschaft* (München 1970) das Verhältnis zwischen Glauben und Wissen andersartig auffaßt, stimmen auch seine Schlußfolgerungen nicht mit denen der genannten Autoren überein.

25 Büchel (1975), S. 70f. versucht zwischen W. Kern, der die Schöpfung für das am meisten Naturwis-

senschaft fördernde Dogma hält, und A. Kojève, der diese Funktion der Inkarnation zuschreibt, zu vermitteln.

[26] Auf das Verhältnis zwischen Wissenschaft (Optik) und Technik (optischen Instrumenten) bin ich in (1983a) ausführlich eingegangen.

[27] Siehe Kuhn (1979), bes. Kap. IV.

[28] Siehe H. C. Freiesleben, *Kepler als Forscher* (Darmstadt 1970).

[29] Siehe R. Hooykaas, *Geschiedenis der Natuurwetenschappen* (Utrecht 1971), J. Bots, *Tussen Descartes en Newton, geloof en natuurwetenschap in de 18e eeuw in Nederland* (Assen 1972), H. A. M. Snelders, „Das Studium der Physik und Chemie in den Niederlanden im achtzehnten Jahrhundert", *Wissenschaftliche Zeitschrift Martin-Luther-Universität Halle-Wittenberg* (1977), Büchel (1975), M. C. Jacob, *The Newtonians and the Eglish Revolution 1689–1720* (Hessocks 1976).

[30] Das dann entstehende Bild wird von E. J. Dijksterhuis, *Die Mechanisierung des Weltbilds* (Berlin–Göttingen–Heidelberg 1956), S. 548f. wie folgt beschrieben: „Die Mechanisierung des Weltbilds führt mit unwiderstehlicher Konsequenz zur Auffassung Gottes als eines Ingenieurs im Ruhestand, und von da zu seiner völligen Ausschaltung war es nur noch ein kleiner Schritt. Für Naturforscher, die dennoch ihren Glauben behalten wollten, gab es kaum noch eine andere Möglichkeit, als ihn streng von den Naturwissenschaften getrennt zu halten."

[31] TLP 6.522. Oft wird vergessen, daß diese Sätze Wittgensteins sich primär auf die *klassische* Mechanik beziehen (siehe bes. TLP 6.342).

[32] Siehe Casimir (1979) und (1983).

* * *

RELIGION – PHILOSOPHIE – WISSENSCHAFT IM LICHTE DER KRISE DES RATIONALISMUS

Krystyna Górniak-Kocikowska
Uniwersytet im. A. Mickiewicza, Poznań, Polen

Unter „Rationalismus" wird hier eine Haltung verstanden, laut welcher der Mensch imstande sei, die Welt mit seinem *Denkvermögen* zu erklären. Die Gegenposition des Irrationalismus ist die, daß *Gefühl* und *Glaube* die Informationsquellen des Menschen seien.

Um die Welt rationalistisch zu erklären, bedient sich der Mensch sowohl der Vernunft als auch des Verstandes; darum werde ich die Kantsche Differenzierung kaum beachten und bleibe dabei, sowohl die Vernunft als auch den Verstand als *ein* Denkvermögen zu betrachten und beide wiederum dem Gefühl und dem Glauben entgegenzustellen.

Was hier als Krise des Rationalismus verstanden wird, ist die im 19. und 20. Jahrhundert sichtbare Strömung innerhalb der Philosophie, an der rationalistischen Erklärbarkeit der Welt zu zweifeln. Durch eine solche irrationalistische Haltung haben sich die bisherigen Positionen sowohl der Wissenschaft als auch der Religion, sowie die Beziehungen zwischen Religion, Philosophie und Wissenschaft geändert. Meine Frage ist: Kann *die Menschheit* tatsächlich die Welt mittels eines anderen Weges unter Vernachlässigung des Denkens besser erkennen, d.h. der Wahrheit über Welt und Menschen selbst so besser näher kommen?

In der Geschichte der europäischen Kultur spielte der Rationalismus eine wichtige Rolle. Die Aufgabe des rationalen Denkens war die Deutung des Gegebenen mit dem Ziel, ein einheitliches Weltbild zu bauen. Ein solches Weltbild sollte auch als Grundlage menschlichen Handelns dienen. Es zu bauen, war Aufgabe sowohl der Philosophie als auch der Wissenschaft. Auch Religion sollte *die Welt erklären*, und falls dies nicht möglich war, sollte sie wenigstens die *Unerklärbarkeit* der Welt *erklären*. Ist ja auch das religiöse Weltbild von der Art, daß es den Menschen Hinweise für ihre Handlungen liefert. Und gerade die Religion war das Gebiet, auf dem sich zuerst der Kampf des Denkens mit dem Glauben abspielte.

Wenn jemand an etwas (als ein religiös Glaubender) glaubt, ist er davon überzeugt, daß er die *Wahrheit* kennt. Deshalb läßt ein solcher Glaube keine Diskussion zu, denn die Wahrheit braucht nicht diskutiert zu werden. Das, woran man glaubt, läßt sich auch deswegen nicht diskutieren, weil eine Diskussion der Argumente bedarf. „Argumente haben" aber bedeutet *Wissen*. Wenn man aber etwas weiß, braucht man keinen Glauben mehr. Versuche ich aber jemanden von meinem Glauben zu *überzeugen*, muß ich, auch wenn ich ihm diesen Glauben nur umschreiben möchte, den Glauben verbalisieren. Wenn ich ihn überzeugen will – und das *muß* ich wollen, wenn ich tatsächlich *glaube*, sonst geriete ja mein Glaube ins Schwanken – muß ich für diesen meinen Glauben argumentieren können. Aber, wie es schon früher gesagt wurde – *Argumente haben* heißt *wissen*. Wer eine Religion gründet, muß sagen: *Glaubt* mir, denn ich *weiß*. Das war – laut Friedrich Nietzsche – das Verfahren des Paulus. Nietzsche schreibt, daß Paulus der eigentliche Gründer des Christentums war, indem er „das im großen Stile wieder aufgerichtet (hat), was Christus durch sein Leben annuliert hatte".[1] Christus war der Gläubige, Paulus bereits der Wissende. Die Kirche wurde nicht zur Kirche des Christus von Nazareth, sie wurde zur Kirche des Paulus.

Der Weg vom Glauben zur Religion und von dieser wiederum zu einer Kirche, d.h. die *Institutionalisierung* des Glaubens ist ein fortschreitender Prozeß der Rationalisierung dessen. Es ist auch symptomatisch, daß die meisten Reformversuche innerhalb der Kirche mit dem Postulat nach Verinnerlichung und Entrationalisierung der Religion anfingen. Daß diese Versuche aber ziemlich hoffnungslos waren bzw. sind, zeigt die große Zahl der religiösen Sekten, die anfangs immer nach der Innerlichkeit des Glaubens streben, bald aber – jedenfalls der große Teil von ihnen – im Rahmen der organisierten Religion erstarren. Das war auch das Schicksal der ersten großen europäischen Reformkirche. Die bisherigen Erfahrungen scheinen also zu zeigen, daß der Gottesglaube, nur dann *ein Glaube*, und nicht eine Lehre (d.h. ein Wissen) sein kann, wenn er nicht zur Religion wird, d.h. wenn er eine äußerst subjektive, unübermittelbare Erscheinung bleibt.

Mitteilung, Kommunikation bedarf eines Kommunikationsmittels, und das sicherste und auch trotz vieler Mängel eindeutigste Kommunikationsmittel der Menschheit ist seit Jahrtausenden die Sprache. Die Sprache ist wiederum nicht nur aufs engste mit dem sozialen Leben der Menschen verbunden, sie ist genauso eng mit dem Denken verbunden. Die Sprache bezieht sich auf die Welt, aus ihrer Struktur kann aber resultieren, daß das der Sprache eigene Weltbild falsch wird. Im Akte der Kommunikation und durch die ihr verbundenen Handlungen kann das Weltbild korrigiert werden, was wieder eine Korrektur der Sprache selbst zur Folge hat. Es kann natürlich auch das eintreten, worauf Ludwig Wittgenstein hinwies: „Die Sprache verkleidet den Gedanken. Und zwar so, daß man nach der äußeren Form des Kleides nicht auf die Form des bekleideten Gedankens schließen kann" (TLP 4.002) – aber auch hier ist der enge Zusammenhang der Sprache und des Denkens sowie auch ihre soziale Funktion (diesmal eine „negative", tarnende) deutlich zu sehen. Und auch in diesem Fall kann die menschliche Handlung als Prüfstein des Denkens dienen.

Die Erfahrungen, die die Religionen gemacht haben, zwingen sie dazu, sich gegen den Rationalismus als gegen einen Feind des Glaubens zu wehren, obgleich Religion selbst als eine *organisierte, intersubjektive* Form des Glaubens ein Konstrukt der Ratio sein muß.

Die letzten 200 Jahre brachten gewaltige Veränderungen der menschlichen Umwelt mit sich, so daß alle bisherigen Systeme der Welterklärung fraglich wurden. Zugleich wurde die alte Frage nach dem Wesen des Menschen wieder aktuell. Sie muß gestellt und beantwortet werden, denn es ist nicht zu leugnen, daß es *der Mensch* ist, der die Welt so sehr verändert, bis sie ihm selbst als fremd und unerklärbar erscheint. Es entstand eine neue Situation, mit der der Mensch konfrontiert wurde, und zwar als ihr Schöpfer und in gewissem Sinne ihr Opfer zugleich. Der Rationalismus wurde für eine unzureichende Methode erklärt. Mehr noch – man versuchte aus ihm einen Sündenbock zu machen. Die Menschheit war angeblich vom Rationalismus verführt worden, auf rationalen Grundlagen eine Zivilisation zu schaffen, die den Menschen alle Sorgen wegnehmen sollte, was sich aber ins Gegenteil gewandelt hatte. Hat denn die Menschheit vielleicht einen falschen Weg gewählt? Das Problem scheint anderswo zu liegen. Die Frage lautet: War es überhaupt möglich, eine anderen Weg zu gehen? Kann sich die Menschheit beliebig die Welt *wählen*, in der sie existieren sollte, gesetzt den Fall, es gäbe tatsächlich mehrere Welten? Oder wird sie doch durch die Eigenschaften des menschlichen Wesens determiniert? Braucht der Mensch vielleicht ein anderes Vermögen als das seines Gehirnes, um eine andere Welt erkennen oder auch schaffen zu können?

Jene Philosophen, die den Rationalismus in seiner Gestalt aus der Zeit der Aufklärung in Zweifel gezogen haben, suchten also nach neuen Wegen der Philosophie, die sich jetzt dem Menschen zuwandte. Die Ideen der Philosophie wurden auch für die Wissenschaft anregend, in der sich z.B. der Relativitätsgedanke als sehr fruchtbar erwies. Der Mensch als eine „Naturerscheinung" wurde aber auch von der Wissenschaft untersucht, die wiederum der Philosophie wichtige Hinweise und Anregungen lieferte. Es zeigte sich bald, wie unentbehrlich die Wissenschaft für die philosophische Reflexion über das Wesen des Menschen ist. Die Versuche, eine Philosophie „als solche" zu bauen, die frei von den Einflüssen der Wissenschaft wäre, münden im Mystizismus und Spiritualismus, werden also äußerst subjektivistisch, und teilen folglich mit dem religiösen Glauben dessen oben dargestelltes Schicksal.

Das große Problem, mit dem jetzt die Menschheit konfrontiert wird, ist ein neues und kann nicht mit den alten Mitteln gelöst werden. Die Welt, in der wir leben, ist jetzt eine Welt, die von Menschen geschaffen wurde. Aber nicht von *einem* Menschen, sondern von einer Unzahl von Menschen, von der menschlichen Gattung. Die Menschheit war imstande diese Welt zu schaffen, weil sie die Kommunikationsfähigkeit besitzt, und nicht nur in jenem Sinne, in dem

wie Wittgenstein wiederholt betont. Er setzt die Religion der Liebe, also dem am wenigsten von Rationalität gelenkten Bereich, gleich. Für ihn stellt religiöses Handeln eine Basis dar, die nicht mehr weiter hinterfragt werden kann. „Nur beschreiben kann man hier und sagen; so ist das menschliche Leben." (BüF S. 40) Religionsphilosophie wird zu rein deskriptiver Verhaltensforschung, der naturwissenschaftliche Denkstil wäre unsinnig, „da wir ja Naturgeschichte für unsere Zwecke auch erdichten können." (*PU*, S. 368)

In den *Vermischten Bemerkungen* und den *Vorlesungen über den religiösen Glauben* entwikkelt Wittgenstein eine zweite Theorie, die die Religion als ethisches Bezugssystem auffaßt, das Imperative stellt und sie in Bilder kleidet. Nun drängt sich ihm aber folgende Beobachtung auf: „Diese Bilder können nur dienen, zu *beschreiben*, was wir tun wollen, aber nicht dazu, es zu *begründen*." Warum? „Denn um begründen zu können, dazu müßten sie auch weiter stimmen." Diesem Erfordernis entsprechen sie aber nicht, wie er an folgendem Beispiel ausführt: „Ich kann sagen: ‚Danke diesen Bienen für ihren Honig, als wären sie gute Menschen, die ihn für Dich bereitet haben.' Das ist verständlich und beschreibt, wie ich wünsche, Du sollst Dich benehmen. Aber nicht: ‚Dank ihnen, denn sieh' wie gut sie sind!' – denn sie können Dich im nächsten Augenblick stechen." (*VB*, S. 62) Wie kommt es nun, daß Wittgenstein ein solches System von Halbwahrheiten akzeptiert? Kann Wohlwollen ihn offensichtlich Falsches billigen lassen? Nein, denn seiner Meinung nach geht es hier gar nicht um wahr oder falsch. „Es kommt . . . nicht darauf an, ob die Worte wahr oder falsch oder unsinnig sind." (*WWK*, S. 117) Denn auch wenn die Begründungen stimmen würden, so hätte diese Tatsache doch keine Konsequenzen für meinen Entschluß, mich einer religiösen Bewegung anzuschließen, „weil die Unbezweifelbarkeit nicht ausreichen würde, mich mein ganzes Leben ändern zu lassen." (VrGl, S. 92) Religion betrifft das ganze Leben. Ganz andere Grade von Gewißheit erlangen hier Bedeutung: „Nur die Liebe kann die Auferstehung glauben." (*VB*, S. 69) Nicht durch das Angeben von Gründen kann die Religion überzeugen, versucht sie es dennoch, stößt sie ab. „Denn zu jedem Grund, den sie gibt, gibt es einen stichhaltigen Gegengrund." (*VB*, S. 62) Eine Religion, die sich dem szientistischen Druck beugt und ihren Glauben begründen will, ist ein Aberglaube.

Nachdem nun die Religion als Exemtion der Oberhoheit der Wissenschaft entrissen ist, stellt sich die Frage, ob denn diese, das ‚Urteilsspiel', ihren eigenen Idealen der Begründetheit entspricht. Anders formuliert: Findet der Relativismus in Wittgenstein einen Bundesgenossen?

Über Gewißheit behandelt die Begründetheit menschlichen Wissens. Ansatzpunkt von Wittgensteins Überlegungen ist seine Unzufriedenheit mit der *unleugbaren Evidenz* als Rechtfertigung für die Moorschen Sätze: „Ich weiß, daß ich ein Mensch bin.", „Die Erde bestand lange Zeit vor meiner Geburt." Für Wittgenstein ergibt sich die Gewißheit ihrer Wahrheit negativ – nicht durch Evidenz, Falsifikation oder Verifikation – dadurch, daß in unserem Bezugssystem, der Summe all unserer Meinungen, ihnen nichts widerspricht. Wir können uns die durch sie beschriebenen Sachverhalte gar nicht anders vorstellen. „Die Wahrheit gewisser Erfahrungssätze gehört zu unserem Bezugssystem." (*ÜG*, § 83) Dieses System, das Weltbild, nimmt der Mensch durch „Beobachtung und Unterricht" im Laufe der Erziehung auf. „Das Kind lernt, indem es dem Erwachsenen glaubt." (ÜG, § 160) Das Wissen ist seiner Genese nach Glaube. Ein Kind, das von allem Anfang an wissenschaftlich sein wollte, d.h. für jede Behauptung seines Lehrers einen Beweis verlangte, eine Begründung, würde seiner Schulpflicht sehr bald in einer Sonderschule genüge tun müssen. „Der Zweifel kommt *nach* dem Glauben." (*ÜG*, § 160) Das Weltbild gibt nach Wittgenstein den Rahmen ab, innerhalb dessen sich unser Urteilen abspielt: „Es ist der überkommene Hintergrund, auf welchem ich zwischen wahr und falsch unterscheide." (*ÜG*, § 94) „Alles Bekräften und Entkräften einer Annahme geschieht schon innerhalb eines Systems." (*ÜG*, § 105) Insoferne ist alles Wissen relativ zum jeweiligen System. In jedem begründeten Glauben, jedem Wissen, steckt eine bestimmte Portion an unbegründetem Glauben, den ich im Laufe der Erziehung durch die Gemeinschaft erwerbe. „Was ein triftiger Grund für etwas sei, entscheide nicht ich." (*ÜG*, § 271)

Hier hat Th. S. Kuhn angeknüpft. Geht es Wittgenstein um das Urteilsspiel im allgemeinen, so beschränkt sich Kuhn auf ein aktuelles Teilgebiet, das wissenschaftliche Sprachspiel. Es ist ein leichtes, zwischen Kuhns und Wittgensteins Werk einen Isomorphismus festzustellen. Zu jedem kuhnschen Gedanken findet sich ein wittgensteinsches Pendant. Letztlich kommt Kuhn zu dem Ergebnis, daß in der Wissenschaft eine Berufung auf die Wirklichkeit nie voraussetzungsfrei möglich ist. „Meines Erachtens gibt es keine von Theorien unabhängige Möglichkeit, Ausdrücke wie ‚wirklich vorhanden‘ zu rekonstruieren."[1] Bei Wittgenstein lautet das so: „ . . . die Idee von der ‚Übereinstimmung mit der Wirklichkeit‘ hat keine klare Anwendung." (*ÜG*, § 215) Das Kriterium der Berufung auf die Wirklichkeit wird ersetzt durch das feedback der wissenschaftlichen Gemeinschaft. „Es gibt keine höhere Norm als die Billigung durch die jeweilige Gemeinschaft."[2] Wittgenstein drückt das so aus: „Das Wissen gründet sich am Schluß auf der Anerkennung." (*ÜG*, § 378) Der Relativismus beruft sich also nicht zu Unrecht auf Wittgenstein.

Für das jeweilige Weltbild, Bezugssystem ist es nun nicht mehr möglich, weitere Rechtfertigungen zu geben. ‚Richtigkeit‘ ist nicht mehr prädizierbar: „Wenn das Wahre das Begründete ist, dann ist der Grund nicht wahr noch falsch." (*ÜG*, § 205) Auch einer darwinistischen Begründung war Wittgenstein abhold, ohne aber näher darauf einzugehen. „Nein, die Erfahrung ist auch nicht der Grund für unser Urteilsspiel. Und auch nicht sein ausgezeichneter Erfolg." (*ÜG*, § 131) Die Konsequenzen solcher Ansichten für den fortschritts- und wissenschaftsgläubigen Abendländer exemplifiziert Wittgenstein in § 92. G. E. Moore begegnet einem Negerkönig, der in dem Glauben erzogen wurde, mit ihm habe die Welt begonnen, und diskutiert mit ihm. Wittgensteins These ist es nun, daß Moore seine Ansicht über das Alter der Erde nicht als die *richtige* erweisen könnte. Möglich wäre nur eine „Bekehrung besonderer Art: der König würde dazu gebracht, die Welt anders zu betrachten." Wenn sich alles Begründen innerhalb eines Systems abspielt, so kann — treffen zwei Systeme aufeinander — von Begründen keine Rede mehr sein. Dann sind andere Kategorien zuständig, solche die man nur bei der Religion zu finden glaubte. Das Schlußwort von *Über Gewißheit* ebnet alle Differenzen in der Behandlung von Religion und Wissenschaft ein: „Eimal muß man von der Erklärung auf die bloße Beschreibung kommen." (*ÜG*, § 189) Denn nur die Beschreibung, die übersichtliche Darstellung, ermöglicht das Verständnis, nach dem die Philosophie strebt.

Prägnant zusammengefaßt hat Robert Musil das hier skizzierte Anliegen Wittgensteins in folgendem dem Nachlaß entnommenen Zitat: „Die Suche nach der Ursache gehört den Hausgebräuchen an, wo die Verliebtheit der Köchin die Ursache davon ist, daß die Suppe versalzen wurde."

ANMERKUNGEN

[1] Kuhn, S. Th., *Die Struktur wissenschaftlicher Revolutionen* (Frankfurt a. M. ⁵1981), S. 218.
[2] Kuhn (1981), S. 106.

* * *

THE NATURAL ORDER

Adolf Hübner
Kirchberg am Wechsel, Austria

Within us there does exist a *knowing* that nature (being or natural reality) has not come and cannot come to its fundamental sizes (or dimensions) *"by chance"*. Equally we have a knowing that in its roots nature ("the world", being, physical reality) cannot be *chaotic*. We have to acknowledge that an absolute chaos is logically impossible! (We are not allowed to conclude from states of disorder of concrete things to the possibility of an absolute chaos, which would be a state of disorder „without concrete things". All concrete things have, of course, to obey natural regularities and there is no doubt that there do exist natural regularities.)

If, in its very beginning, the world was a *single* thing, a "singularity" (*"the* original black hole"), then we have already a *definite* knowledge of the *logical conditions* of *the world as a single thing.* The world *as* original singularity cannot be only the material ("amorphous stuff") of a future (our) eventful (*ereignishaft*) world in time and space as a variety of many (of course, regularily related) things, but it must necessarily also contain (and be) *the code of a world which it is going to become in the future.*

The world as a single state (the world as the singularity of the world which is now in existence) can, if it follows its "transcendental" *tendency* to develop, become only *a* world in different states. It can, of course, not become world*s*. In other words: one being must remain one being whatever may take place.

Beyond every doubt the following law is valid:

> *One being is exactly one being then, if all its states obey one singular regularity: — one natural order.*

The logical consequences of this law are:

a) The world as we know it, has only one identity. Or: the world is identical with itself.

b) *All states* of a world which has only one single identity are *different* states of that world *within* the everlasting *equality* of *one* natural order.

c) Thus it is logically impossible not to speak of a hierarchical existing order of the world. The connection between more fundamental states of the world and less fundamental states must necessarily have the *logical form*: evolutionary predecessor—evolutionary successor. (Two or more "natural orders" would necessarily contradict each other and thus such a world is logically impossible.)

d) As long as the world is existing as a single state, it can be said that it has not yet *transcended* the threshold to a world "in states". A world, which has become a world as one single state *out of* a world in states by a process of re-volution, *has lost all relations* to a reality outside of itself, because the formerly existing reality in states has been included in toto into it. Since in the same moment, when the world has become a *complete* single state, it has become an *absolute one*, it has (in accordance with the principle of relativity) to start a new evolution "immediately" for *logical* reasons (The principle of relativity is *not* "empirical", it is *logical*. It is a most fundamental error to believe that logics must be "an essence a priori" since it can be *handled* as an essence a priori. On the contrary: reality necessarily must be logical—as far as it obeys rules—and cannot be a—logical. "Earthern heaviness" *does not make logics less logical*. Logic *can* have the property to consume time as essential part of *the* physical reality.)

e) Since the world as a singularity is different from the world in states it necessarily must have a different "archetypical" (original) geometry.

If, what we have said here up to now, is correct, then the world as singularity is the *real code* ("the hardware and software together") of the world in states as we know it, obeying like the latter three forms (aspects) of logic: 1. The *conceptual logic* or the logic of language, which was *transmitted* by nature (being) to us as *its* states—*without* the possibility of "error". The proposition "mankind has developed language" is logically untenable. Rather the proposition "being has developed man and his language" *is correct.* Mankind has acquired language *without any* knowledge of its rules. (See Wittgenstein's Philosophical Investigations.) *To diminish* the natural regularities of language to mere *peculiarities* on the one hand and *to lift* physical regularities up to the *greatness* of "laws of nature" on the other hand is a conceptual *inconsistency* with *severest consequences* with respect to a correct understanding of the world. A *one-to-one-correspondence* between the logical structure of being as a whole and the logical structure of language *is a necessity.* (If it is not a *physical* impossibility to speak of the essences or the logics or orders of a matter—e.g. the matter "being"—then the reason, why this is the case, is: *logical impossibility.* There *are no "other kinds"* of necessities or impossibilities *than* logical ones. We have to lay particular emphasis on the following points:

a) The *minor distinctness* in the recognizability of *committed errors* within conceptual logic *does not* make conceptual logic *"less logical".* Logic is logic and it is *not* something, which could be connected with a "more-or-less-condition". In particular, conceptual logic is *not* inferior to mathematical logic. (The question, whether the conceptual logic or the logic of mathematics has the *higher authority* with respect to a *correct* understanding of *this* world, can be put into a concrete question and *the concrete answer of nature is*: conceptual logic *is superior!* This "new principle of relativity" *underlies* the principle of relativity as it is known to us since Einstein.—The inferiority of mathematical logic in comparison to conceptual logic is dependent on its *"reality-blindness"*: If "g" in the equation $7g \times 7g = 49g^2$ means "gram", then *conceptual* logic tells us that the result is *unrealistic* with respect to the *special case* "world".)

b) Since being (nature, the world) is in a state of *conceptual selfunderstanding*, every conceptually correct proposition *taking fully into consideration the concrete facts of the special case "world"* is undubitably *true.* Thus the logic of language is the *only* and most effective *instrument* in respect to a correct understanding of the world. *Neglecting* this power of the logic of language is the most fundamental *deficiency* in modern science as well as the most fundamental *obstacle* to scientific and "epistemological" progress.

The lack of an education in "conceptually correct thinking" in our present educational system has led mankind into a disastrous, knowledge-inhibiting position.

The paradigm of philosophy is wrong as far as philosophers try to understand the *special* case "world" by a thinking in *generality*—neglecting the very *special* facts of this world. *The paradigm of natural sciences is incomplete* as far as scientists do *not* make use of the power of conceptual thinking. So far (with the exception Einstein) scientists tried to understand the world by using only the logic of mathematics *diminishing* conceptual logic to a "mere absence of contradictions".

2. The world (nature, being) has to follow the rules of mathematical computing. *Nature* as mathematician *cannot* make use of the rules of computing in another way as *we* make use of them. The form of the cooperation of conceptual and mathematical logic which has to be applied in the sciences is: present a concrete conceptual truth of the special case "world" to the logic of mathematical calculating and you will get a result, which necessarily is in correspondence with the physical reality of this world.

For example: Take the concrete conceptual truth that in a world, which has the *property "to be in motion" nothing* can exist in a state of rest (nothing can be static), give this truth the form of an equation by using secure scientific knowledge (phisical *facts*) and you will *not* get a "*new theory*" but the correct picture of physical reality"! (To remove all doubt in our conceptual truth: Can one imagine that a star "is lying about in a corner of the universe"? Can one imagine the existence of a *resting* light-ether if one considers that an ether, because of the existence of conceptual logic, necessarily would be a resting thing, like a star, in a universe which exists by being eventful? Logic can neither know nor allow exceptions! If the world has the *property* to be in motion then "mass" as a resting permanent thing is logically *impossible*. If mass *appears* to be "constant" then the only possibility in accord with the *one and single logic* of the world is, that mass is *produced* at the same speed as it is *transformed* into a state (of energy) which is non-mass (field-energy). This "logical assumption" also fulfills the predecessor-successor-condition, which must be valid "throughout the universe". (Here we have to remind ourselves that quantum-machanics, though in evident accordance with reality *also* leads to the contradiction that the mass of the state 'electron' should not be $9{,}10955 \times 10^{-28}$g but *infinite*.)

If we further consider that the matter "being in states" *starts* out of a being as singularity and, secondly, that we can only talk of the essence of the matter being then we come rather quickly to see that *at the beginning* of a being in states there should stay *an action* (Wirkung) *and nothing else*. Looking back we are able to assert: Because of the one and single identity of the world only *one* elemtary action-quantum could be discovered: for *logical* reason. Since the world is structure and its dynamics and yet must be all the same, the logical structure of the world should equal h^2 (h: Planck's action-quantum). Since a quantum can be permanent only by steady repition, it follows that h^2f^2 must be valid. Since further $E = mc^2$ is a *logical* truth in the same way as h^2f^2 and thus is a correct description of *the* matter being, it must necessarily equal h^2f^2. (There can exist two forms of a correct description of being, but there cannot exist two truth*s*.) $E = mc^2$ is valid for all material states of being and so it must be valid (within the one order of nature) for the elementary state of being "electron", of course. If so, then we get a definite size for f (frequency of h). The time of f then is the time of the most fundamental material event: one time the production and transformation of the elementary mass 1.

The solution of all problems of ontology and of physics *as far as they are logical ones* should, in prinsiple, be given with the equation: $h^2f^2 = m_ec^2$

A critic says: All this seems to me reasonable, but it seems to be too simple and I still doubt the *existence and working* of conceptual logic in being. Our answer is: We doubted it also, since we are weak creatures. Since we are weak but not helpless creatures, we tried to prove the truth of our equation. *Have you*, who possibly may be a gifted physicist, *tried it*?

We tried it and we came tfits a network within which "everything to see together perfectly", but this network is, of course, still very small. You, the reader, who holds these pages in hands, have got from me a short-cut version of a long-way concept, which is written in german language. If you are a physicist, you possibly will be unwilling, and this unwillingness might lead you to a hasty negative judgment of the form: the equation $h^2f^2 = m_ec^2$ is simply false because it leads "to contradictions in dimensions". In this case I will ask for your generosity, to give me and nature a chance to make understandable to you that transformations of dimensions are a logical necessity. (Perhaps it will help you, if you think of the world *as its own code* in form of the original black hole. And, please, don't forget that the logic of *verbal attributes* of numbers necessarily must be another one than that of *numbers*.)

3. The third form of logic with which being has to be in accordance is *the logic of the natural connections between numbers*. We say, the code of the world must be a numerical one and it must be a "united" one. Using the term "united" we want to say that in a code of the world arithmetics and geometry must be one and the same, equally present. Looking into the field of "pure" mathematics we find the equation $e^{2i\pi} = 1$.

This equation has been known since 1748 and was found by Euler. (*e* is the basis of the system of natural logarithms, *i* is $\sqrt{-1}$, $\pi = 3{,}14159\ldots$) Our interpretation of this formula is: "Pointing at its most beloved number, mathematics tells us that the logic of arithmetics and the logic of geometry *are one and the same*." We justify our interpretation in the following way: It seems to us very reasonable, to take into consideration every surprising, unexpected hint which logic is willing to present to us. We further say: Eulers equation shows a *nearly unbelievable* potency of the basis *e* in comparison to the basis 10. If natural logarithms *really* are natural, *then nature should make use of them*. Nature as mathematician very likely is a "natural-logarithmic" mathematician. That this may be the case, is confirmed "somehow" by technical physics: Every vibration of every material in solid state is declining within an *e*-function! We have a conviction, which reads: all mathematicians wherever and whenever they may appear in the cosmos need not necessarily come to the decadic system of numbers but they *necessarily* must come to an *e*-equivalency.

The results of our work show very clearly "that numbers are *not* mere children of human mind, which enable us to describe reality", as Gauß and Dedekind believed, *but that they are part of the abstract aspect of the natural order. The arbitrariness of our measurement-system astonishingly is not able to hinder this kind "of entering the picture" of the natural order.* Looking back from the end of our work, our surprise vanishes and it again turns out that we have a logical necessity in front of us! The *general principle*, which we have discovered *by a conceptual analysis* of nature, is the following:

Nature has to acknowledge any measurement-system not only as A correct one but it has to acknowledge any measurement-system as *THE* correct one!

This wording is the most profound formulation of the *principle of general relativity*. (As we have seen we have made use of the most profound result of the theory of special relativity, E = mc².) The consequences of our principle are the following:

a) Nature as mathematician is *measure-blind*.

b) The utterance of this measurement-blindness is of the kind that the numerals of natural constants do get a general validity, independent of all measurement-units.

c) "Physical size" which we introduce into a correct and consequent description of nature by smaller or larger measurement-units does not take influence on numerals of natural constants (dimensional or not) but influences "*in decadic steps*" only. (The handling of numerals itself is "*reserved*" for nature and its logic.)

d) Because of the general validity of the numerals of universal natural constants, nature is able to tell us, which geometrical element it is willing to take as 1. Nature shows that it is willing to take the circumference of a circle as 1.

e) The key to the code of nature and its carrying basis is *e*.

d) *e* shows us that the *seemingly* arbitrary value $1/hf = \varkappa = 1{,}105174 \times 10^3$ is numerically in correspondence *with its decadic logic*: $\ell n\ 1{,}105174 \times 10^0 = 0{,}1000028$. Here we should see that e^1 shows merely the identy of *e*. Thus $e^{0,\,1}$ is one of the two first decadic steps for *e* to get in touch with the realm of numbers *outside of its identity*. Num $(10 \times \ell n\ 1{,}105174 \times 10^3) = 2{,}7183576 \times 10^{30} \approx e \times 10^{30}$. *This* result means that 10 times ln $\varkappa$ leads to a decadic *self-reproduction of e*. Thus it is shown that $\varkappa$ is also in correspondence with the *numerical logic* of *e* and vice versa.

We may maintain that we have found the *missing link* between the logic of *pure* mathematics and the *physical reality* of our world *by the way of a conceptual analysis*. (Should physicists now feel afflicted or even "offended" by philosophy?)

We conlude by restating: The one and single natural order is resting formally on the one and single logic of *e* and it is resting on the one and single elementary action *h*. Our means of proof is: *pythagorean evidence* (since there is no other).

I believe: God has created man as His (logical) image and He couldn't act otherwise.

* * *

PHILOSOPHICAL IMPLICATIONS OF QUANTUM PHYSICS

Peter E. Hodgson
Corpus Christi College, Oxford

In this paper I want to reflect, as a physicist, on the relation between science and philosophy, and more specifically on the philosophical implications of quantum physics. I am not unaware of the hazards of such an untertaking: it is notorious that scientists are uncertain guides even in their own territory. One can easily find many exemplifications of Einstein's dictum: 'if you want to find out anything from the theoretical physicists about the methods they use, I advise you to stick closely to one principle: don't listen to their words, fix your attention on their deeds.[1]

It is important at the outset to make quite clear what I mean by the philosophical implications of quantum physics. I am not asserting the primacy of physics over philosophy in the sense that somehow, after the physicist has done his work, philosophical conclusions can be distilled from his results. On the contrary, I want to assert the primacy of the philosophical, in the sense that science in general, and physics in particular, is based on certain philosophical tenets about the nature of the material world and man's place within it. Without these tenets science cannot even begin, and indeed the absence of these tenets accounts for the failure of science to develop in all civilisations except our own.[2] Once science is established as a self-sustaining entity the role of these tenets tends to be forgotten, and it is even possible for scientists to give explicit assent to beliefs at variance with those on which science is based.

The thesis I wish to consider is that there is a definite set of tenets about the natural world on which science is based, and that if a scientist consistently holds any contrary tenet then his science will inevitably be impoverished. In this way science serves as a touchstone of philosophical truth: by their fruits you shall know them. It is in this sense that I want to speak of the philosophical implications of quantum physics.

The first of these tenets is that the material entities studied by scientists are real and exist independently of the observer. If this were not so, we would each create our own universe, and there could be no shared knowledge. Furthermore, these entities have an inherent rationality so that they obey laws that can be formulated quantitatively with a validity that extends through space and time. These laws form a coherent whole, so that the entities interact in a consistent way that is to some extent discoverable by the human mind. This order and rationality is not a necessary one, so we have to make observations and experiments to find out what it is.

As science advances, new entities are frequently postulated to account for the results of experiments. Thus we postulate a new particle to account for a track in a cloud chamber that cannot be attributed to any known particle. The accumulation of further evidence and particularly of accurate measurements can eventually lead to the confirmation of the existence of this particle. What started as a hypothesis has become an accepted component of the real world. Many examples of this can be found in the history of elementary particle physics, from electrons and neutrinos to kaons and quarks.[3]

The Copenhagen Interpretation

Around the turn of the century many physicists, particularly on the Continent, were influenced by Mach's sensationalism. Partly as a reaction against the exuberant mechanism of the nineteenth century, and partly because of the economy of thought it undoubtedly brings, they admitted to science only those quantities that are directly apprehended by the senses. Within this perspective, science is reduced to the most convenient and economical arrangement of our sense impressions, and all reference to an underlying reality is excluded. This led Mach to deny the reality of atoms, a denial only shaken when she was shown the scintillations on a zinc sulphide screen due to alpha-particles from a radioactive source. In the following decades, Mach's theory of science was further developed by the well-known Vienna Circle of positivist philosophers of science.

Quantum theory, and later on quantum mechanics, was developed in this philosophical climate, and a comprehensive philosophical interpretation of quantum mechanics was developed in Copenhagen by Neils Bohr, one of the principal architects of the quantum theory of atomic structure. According to this interpretation, physics is essentially concerned with the relations between measurable observables. The values of all observable quantities may be calculated from the wave function of the system, which contains all the information concerning that system. Conjugate variables such as position and momentum cannot therefore have simultaneous sharp values in the classical sense. 'The existence of the quantum of action radically alters the usual distinction between subject and object, the experimental situation being one indivisible whole' (4, p. 75). Quantum mechanics thus demands 'a fundamental renunciation regarding the space-time description' (4, p. 77) which in turn implies 'a radical departure from the causal description of nature.' (4, p. 84).

This interpretation was generally shared and developed further by Heisenberg, particularly in connection with his uncertainty principle.[6] This he interpreted as an unsurmountable barrier between the observer and reality, so that physics had reached the end of the road (4, p. 6). Since it was therefore impossible to reach the ultimate reality, it meant for him that 'objective reality has evaporated' (5, p. 95).

Bohr also accepted quantum mechanics as the end of the road. He did this, in the words of Popper, 'partly in despair: only classical physics was understandable, was a description of reality. Quantum mechanics was not a description of reality. Such a description was impossible to achieve in the atomic region; apparently because no such reality existed: the understandable reality ended where classical physics ended. The nearest to an understanding of atoms was his own principle of complementarity' (4, p. 9).

Einstein's rejection of the Copenhagen interpretation

Initially, Einstein was strongly influenced by Mach, but later on his scientific creativity forced him to repudiate sensationalism and to affirm that 'the belief in an external world independent of the perceiving subject is the basis of all natural science.' (9, p. 60). In his autobiography he remarks 'in my younger years, Mach's epistemological position influenced me very greatly, a position which today appears to me to be essentially untenable' (7, p. 21). Einstein argued that since quantum mechanics does not provide, even in principle, answers to many physically reasonable questions it must be incomplete. It is an essentially statistical theory and gives the average behaviour of a large number or ensemble of systems, but an incomplete account of the behaviour of each individual system. Thus 'essentially nothing has changed since Galileo, or Newton, or Faraday concerning the status or role of the 'observer' or of our 'consciousness' or of our 'information' in physics'. (5, p. 46)

Einstein's repudiation of the Copenhagen interpretation was shared by several other physicists, including Planck, Schrödinger, Von Laue and De Broglie, but the majority of physicists preferred to follow Bohr, and even today his views generally prevail.

Quantum mechanics can be presented as a formal axiomatic theory which specifies how to calculate any experimentally observable quantity. It does however leave unanswered many questions that it is still very natural to ask. The vital point here is whether quantum mechanics is a complete theory, or whether it is a partial or statistical theory. If it is a complete theory, then any questions that it cannot answer must be dismissed as meaningless, and it is a waste of time to try to answer them. If it is not a complete theory, then it is important to see if we can find a way of answering such questions.

This may be illustrated by the phenomenon of radioactive decay. Many nuclei and particles are unstable; after a certain time they decay in a characteristic way. A nucleus may emit an alpha-particle, or a kaon may decay into three pions. There is no known way of predicting the instant of decay of a particular nucleus or particle. We can however establish in each case a half-life, which gives the probability of decay in each instant of time. This half-life can be measured by observing a large number of decays, and in many cases it can be understood in terms of the structure of the nucleus or the theory of elementary particles. The behaviour of a large number of nuclei or particles is thus determined and calculable.

But can any cause be assigned to the instant of decay of a particular nucleus? According to the Copenhagen interpretation of quantum mechanics, all such nuclei at a particular instant are identical, and all possible information that can be obtained from measurements on that nucleus is contained in the wavefunction and this gives only the probability of decay per unit time.

The answer to this question is determined by philosophical and not scientific considerations, although it does inevitably have scientific implications. If we believe that the only admissible statements about the world are those that can be verified by a definite sequence of operations and measurements in the laboratory, then questions about the cause of a particular radioactive decay at a particular instant of time must be dismissed as without meaning. On the other hand, if we believe that the thinking of the scientist should not always be constrained by the theoretical framework existing at the present time, then we will want to persist in asking such questions and in trying to find answers to them.

It is worth remarking at this point that scientists very frequently introduce into their work ideas and concepts that cannot be measured.[8] This has been defended by J. J. Thomson: 'I hold that if the introduction of a quantity promotes clearness of thought, then even if at the moment we have no means of determining it with precision, its introduction is not only legitimate but desirable. The immeasurable of today may be the measurable of tomorrow. It is dangerous to base philosophy on the assumption that what I know not can never be knowledge.' (II, p. 265).

It is indeed evident that there is a considerable jump between the statement 'I do not know of a cause of the decay of this nucleus at this instant of time' and 'there is no cause for this decay.' One can without difficulty postulate a number of possible causes. For example, although all nuclei of a particular type appear to be the same, we know that they are composed of a large number of particles (neutrons and protons) in constant motion, and it is easy to suppose that the motions are different in each individual nucleus, and that the decay occurs when the appropriate configuration is reached. If we knew these motions, and the forces operating in the nucleus, then we could in principle predict the instant of decay. Another possibility is that the decay is triggered by some external influence such as a particle that cannot easily be detected. It will be recalled that Pauli proposed the neutrino to resolve some difficulties with the theory of beta decay, and this particle was not experimentally detected until many years later.

It is not of course maintained that there is much likelihood that such suggestions will in fact prove fruitful. But it can certainly be said that they cannot be excluded and that they allow us to retain our belief in causality and reality besides encouraging further thought and experimentation. The question at issue in the case of the decaying nucleus is whether there is a substratum in terms of which the instant of decay can be related to quantities that are in principle exactly measurable.

Experimentally, this is still an open question, but there has been much discussion of the possibility that the presence of such hidden variables (as they are called) can be excluded on quite general theoretical grounds. As early as 1932 von Neumann [12] devised a proof that no such hidden variables are possible in quantum mechanics. Subsequently however it was realised that his proof is based on unnecessarily restrictive assumptions, and if these are removed the proof no longer holds. There has been extensive discussion of these arguments since then. (10, Ch. 4) It may be doubted whether such general arguments can ever tell us about such a fundamental feature of the world. As John Polkinghorne has recently reminded us, 'if the study of science teaches one anything, it is that it is unwise to try to lay down beforehand by pure thought what will actually prove to be the case. Reality is often so much more subtle than we imagine.' (14, p. 5). Quantum mechanics is certainly not a deterministic theory, but that does not imply that the same is the case for the underlying reality that it partially describes.

The Heisenberg Uncertainty Principle.

Another illustration is provided by Heisenberg's Uncertainty Principle, which is generally understood to say that the product of the uncertainties in the position and the momentum of a particle is always greater than Planck's constant. Similar relations hold for other pairs of variables such as energy and time. The more accurate our measurement of one of these variables, the less accurate the result of our measurement of the other variable. This is sometimes taken to mean that particles do not have definite positions and momenta, and Heisenberg himself said that 'since all experiments are subjected to the laws of quantum mechanics and thereby to the equation $\triangle x \triangle p \geq h$ the invalidity of the law of causality is definitely proved by quantum mechanics.'[15]

If however one goes back to the basic physics one finds rather a different situation. We can for example consider the diffraction of a beam of electrons by a narrow slit, and we then find that the narrower the slit the wider the diffraction pattern, just as the corresponding situation in optics. When they pass through the slit, the directions of motion of the electrons are changed so that they fan out over a certain angular range. If now we consider motion perpendicular to the direction of the beam, then the uncertainty in position is the width of the slit, and the uncertainty in transverse momentum is calculable from the mean angle of deviation. If now we examine these two uncertainties, we do indeed find that they satisfy Heisenberg's Uncertainty Principle.

It is however possible to measure the momentum of each individual electron much more precisely. If we place a particle detector behind the slit we can determine the point of arrival of each electron, and hence we can calculate its transverse momentum with an accuracy much greater than that corresponding to the distribution as a whole. Thus while it remains true that we cannot predict the transverse momentum of the electron after it has passed through the slit, nevertheless subsequent measurements enable it to be determined to an accuracy much greater than that specified by the Uncertainly Principle. (5, p. 54). Thus the physics gives us no grounds for saying that the position and momentum of the particle are unknowable within the limits of the Uncertainty Principle, and still less that it does not have position and momentum. Indeed, it is all perfectly compatible with each electron moving along a definite trajectory determined by forces in the vicinity of the slit that we are as yet unable to calculate or measure.

This example shows very clearly the essentially statistical nature of quantum mechanics. The measurements of the passage through the apparatus of a large number of electrons gives the diffraction pattern; this is a statistical scatter distribution that is calculable by a statistical theory (5. p. 54). A similar situation is found in problems of practical importance, such as the emission of particles from a nuclear reaction. The direction of emission of any individual particle is of no interest; what is important is the probability of emission as a function of angle. This is a statistical quantity, and its measured value is compared with the probability distribution calculated from the theory of the reaction.

Is is also clear that the celebrated wave-particle duality is simply a category confusion. On the one hand we have particles moving along definite trajectories with definite momenta, and on the other we recognise that due to their interactions with the apparatus these trajectories have a certain probability distribution calculable from Schrödinger's equation. The so-called wave nature of these particles is no more an intrinsic property than, for example, actuarial statements are intrinsic properties of a particular individual.

240

A more subtle problem is posed by the two-slit experiment. If the beam of electrons passes through a close pair of narrow slits then an interference pattern is observed on a screen placed behind the slits. (Jönsson, 16) If one of the slits is closed the interference pattern disappears and is replaced by the diffraction pattern corresponding to the single remaining slit. The interference pattern can be calculated quantum-mechanically and so provides us with all the measurable information relating to the behaviour of a large number of particles. There are however other questions that we naturally want to ask, in particular we would like to know which slit a particular electron passed through. We cannot find this out by putting a detector at the slit. (It is frequently stated that this destroys the interference pattern; this may well be so, but in fact the experiment is technically so difficult that it has not yet been done). Since the electron is a particle, it must have passed through one slit or the other, and then why should the interference pattern be affected by whether the other slit is open or closed? There is of course no possibility of the electrons passing through one slit interfering with those passing through the other slit because we can still obtain the interference pattern if the intensity in the beam is so low that the electrons pass through the apparatus one by one.

Stated in this way the problem appears almost insuperable, and indeed to be contrary to the laws of logic. A detailed analysis by Fine [17] led to the conclusion that it is necessary to abandon the distributive law of logic. If this were the case, then it would indeed be an example of a philosophical implication of quantum physics. It was however pointed out by Brody[18] that so drastic a conclusion is not required by the physics. To observe the interference pattern it is necessary for the two slits to be exceedingly close to each other, a point that is not well brought out in the diagrams in many textbooks. It is technically a rather difficult experiment, that was only performed many years after the discussion of the theory had become a familiar feature of expositions of the foundations of quantum mechanics. The separation of the slits must be comparable with the wavelength of the electrons, and then it not difficult to see that the motion of the electron through one slit can be affected by the configuration of the other, thus resolving the paradox. Thus once again we see that a detailed examination of the actual physical situation removes the justification for far-reaching philosophical conclusions that are potentially destructive of knowledge in general.[19] It is only when one adopts at the beginning a particular philosophical view, such as that quantum mechanics is a complete description of what can be known of reality, that one obtains such conclusions.

Indeterminacy and Free Will

The indeterminacy that is frequently associated with the Heisenberg uncertainty relations is sometimes held to provide a loophole for the action of free will. The mind, it is suggested, can operate on matter within the range of uncertainty, and can thus influence events without there being any measurable violation of physical laws. This suggestion is unacceptable even within the framework of the Copenhagen interpretation because if the wavefunction contains all possible information about the system then there is no room for any additional information that may be inserted by a human mind.

It will however be clear from what has been said above that the uncertainties associated with Heisenberg's principle are simply due to our lack of knowledge of the complete state of the system, and do not imply any deviations from strictly determined behaviour. There is thus no reason to suppose that quantum systems provide any more opportunities for the action of free will than do classical systems.

Complementarity

The concept of complementary originates in the Copenhagen belief that it is not possible to measure precisely, or even to speak meaningfully about the values of observables of the same system whose operators do not commute. Thus for example the more accurately we know the position of a particle the less accurately we know the momentum. These are then said to be complementary ways of regarding the same phenomenon; we can use one or the other but not both of them simultaneously.

It will be noticed that even within the Copenhagen interpretation this gives rise difficulties. All we are allowed to mention are the observables, but not whether they each refer to an underlying reality, or whether this is the same reality for both of them. If there is no underlying reality, then only statistical statements are permitted. It was then quite natural that Bohr, Kramers and Slater[21] were willing to envisage that atomic processes are purely statistical, so that the principles of the conservation of energy and momentum are not valid for each individual event, a theory soon shown to be incompatible with the measurements of Bothe and Geiger.[22] This is a telling example of the debilitating effect on physics of the denial of physical reality.

In the hands of Bohr, the notion of complementarity has been widely applied whenever there are two views of a phenomenon that appear to interfere with each other, for example the wave-particle duality, 'the physical and the mental, the animate and the inanimate, the freedom of the will and mechanical necessity, associative thinking and the identity of personality, concepts and their applications, phenomena and the means to observe them, and not least, the celebrated twofold roles of being "both onlookers and actors in the great drama of existence" (Bohr, 23). In these and other roles, complementarity has enjoyed a remarkable career, reconciling irreconcilables in a general atmosphere of confused goodwill.

It will be apparent from what has been said already that complementarity is simply a confusing way of speaking about our lack of knowledge of measurable features of definite entities that have precise values, and that all the subsequent philosophical elaboration is quite spurious.

Bell's Inequality and the Wholeness of Nature

In 1935 Einstein, Podolsky and Rosen[26] proposed an argument showing the incompleteness of quantum mechanics. They considered two systems that are allowed to interact for a certain time interval and then separated. If now a measurement of a particular observable is made on one of the systems, then the value of that observable in the other system is automatically fixed by the conservation laws. Alternatively, we could have made a measurement of another observable, with a similar result. Now these two observables could correspond to non-commuting operators, which according to quantum mechanics cannot have simultaneous sharp values. But the second system has not way of knowing which observable we chose to measure, since by hypothesis the two systems have separated and no longer interact. We thus conclude that quantum mechanics cannot provide a complete description of reality. More precisely, the argument shows that either (1) the quantum mechanical description of reality is incomplete, or (2) two systems that have once interacted cannot thereafter be considered to be separated. Einstein favoured the first alternative, while Bohr in his reply[27] chose the second.

For many years this has remained as a thought experiment, but interest in the argument has recently revived because a way has been found of realising it experimentally. This follows from some work of Bohm[28] who suggested that it be applied to two particles initially bound together in a singlet state of total spin zero. Now separate them so that they fly off in opposite directions. Each particle has spin one half, and in the bound state these spins are antiparallel. Classically, the conservation of spin ensures that when they are separated the spins remain antiparallel; if one has its spin in a certain direction then the other has its spin in the opposite direction, Quantum-mechanically, we can measure the projections of the spins in one particular direction, which may be chosen arbitrarily. If this is done we find that they are equal and opposite, as required by the conservation of angular momentum.

The interesting point arises when we consider the projections of the spins in the two mutually perpendicular directions that are perpendicular to this chosen direction. The corresponding operators S_x, S_y and S_z do not commute, and so according to the Copenhagen interpretation S_x and S_y are essentially undetermined after we have measured S_z. There is thus no correlation between the value of S_x measured on one particle and the same quantity measured on the other particle. And yet we know, again from the conservation of angular momentum, that these two quantities must be equal and opposite for each event. If we interpret the results according to the Copenhagen interpretation we only recover the conservation of angular momentum when we average over a large number of events.

One possible way out of this difficulty is to say that when the measurement is made on one particle a signal is emitted that determines the result of the second measurement so that angular momentum is conserved. This possibility can however be excluded by making the two measurements simultaniously, or at least so close together in time that a signal travelling with the velocity of light from the first measurement would not arrive in time to influence the second. The only way to make intelligible the conservation of angular momentum in each event is to postulate that each particle somehow knows the spin direction of the other, and keeps this information until the instant of measurement. Such information is not contained in the wavefunction, and so we conclude that the quantum mechanical description is incomplete. If we want an easily-visualisable picture of what is happening, we can imagine that when the particles separate they are already spinning in opposite directions along the same axis, and that is why any subsequent measurement shows that this is indeed the case.

This conclusion can only be avoided if we maintain with Bohr that the two particles must continue to be regarded as one single system, even when widely separated, so that the act of measurement on one fixes the direction of both spins, so that angular momentum is conserved. This implies a type of interaction that is called non-local, and has been interpreted as implying a new holistic aspect of reality.[13] It may be remarked that additional difficulties occur if the measurements on the two particles are made a different times. We would have to suppose that somehow the result of the measurement on the second particle is fixed by the result of the first measurement; this is in effect a non-locality in time as well as in space. We could of course say that a signal goes from one measuring apparatus to the other, but then we have the problem of specifying and identifying that signal. In neither case is the explanation a physical one; it is mathematical or hypothetical.[29] There is no way of subjecting them to experimental test, and so there the matter rested. So far this is a hypothetical discussion, since no way of making the required measurements of the different spin projections had been suggested. This was done in 1965 by Bell,[26] who derived certain relations, called the Bell inequalities, between the results of certain measurements on the separated particles. These relations can be compared with experiment and allow additional information to be obtained. The Bell inequalities concern the correlations between the measurements of the spin projections of the particles along the the three independent and mutually perpendicular directions A, B and C. Each such measurement can give the result up $(+)$ or down $(-)$. Let $N(A^+B^+)$ be the probability of finding the first particle in the up state along direction A and the second particle in the up state along direction B and so on. Then for any set of directions A,B,C Bell showed, on the assumption that all hidden variables must be local so that the orientation of the detector used for the first particle does not affect the observation on the second, that

$$N(A^+B^+) \leq N(A^+C^+) + N(B^+C^+)$$

Thus we expect the Bell inequality to hold if the Einstein view is correct, whereas we may expect it to be violated if the Copenhagen interpretation is correct.

Many experiments have been made to test Bell's inequality using photons from atomic transitions and from electron-positron annihilation (the arguments apply also to photons) and from proton-proton scattering (Clauser and Shimony).[31] In nearly every case it has been found that the Bell inequality is violated, thus supporting the Copenhagen interpretation and implying that one or more of the assumptions used to derive the inequality is false. These assumptions have been listed by D'Espagnat[32] as (1) Realism, namely the belief in an objective reality independent of the observer, (2) Induction, the belief that legitimate conclusions can be drawn from consistent observations, and (3) Localitiy, the belief that it is possible to separate two systems so that they can no longer interact with each other. In the context of contemporary physics, this is equivalent to saying that no influence can propagate faster than the speed of light. Since scientists are reluctant to abandon the reality of the world or the validity of their methodological procedures it has been generally concluded that locality must be abandoned.[25]

It is somewhat unsatisfactory that there is no objective way of deciding between these possibilities, and indeed there is yet another possibility that so far has received inadequate attention. It is conceivable that the Bell inequality can be derived from a different set of basic assumptions, and what then would we conclude? There have been many different derivations of the Bell inequality,[33] and one of these, by Peres[34] is of such transparent simplicity that it clarifies the whole problem. Firstly, the proof says nothing about non-locality, and so this is irrelevant to the discussion. Secondly, it brings out the point that is essential for the understanding of the whole problem, namely that the proofs assume that the spin directions can be measured along two different directions for the same particle without the first measurement affecting the second. Now it is a well-known result of quantum mechanics that it is impossible to make a measurement without disturbing the system and hence affecting the result of a subsequent measurement. Since the proof of the Bell inequality assumes that this is not the case, it is not surprising that it is found to be violated. The measurements designed to test the Bell inequality thus show only that quantum mechanics cannot be reduced to local hidden-variable theories if successive measuring processes do not interfere with each other (Brody and De La Pena Auerbach, 35). There is thus no justification for all the wide-ranging philosophical conclusions that have been obtained from the experimental studies of the Bell inequality.

Religious Implications of Quantum Physics

The connection between religion and philosophy is in many respects similar to that between philosophy and science. Science is based on certain philosophical tenets about the material world and man's relation to it. The vitality and fruitfulness of science is a measure of the correctness of these basic beliefs, and of the extent to which they are distorted by contemporary political or other ideological pressures. In a similar way these philosophical tenets form part of a more general world view that may properly be called religious.

This view of the religious basis of the presuppositions of science can be examined in the context of past and present human civilisations (Jaki 36). In only one of these, our own, have all the necessary philosophical beliefs been present, and this makes it possible to understand in some measure the development of science in the seventeenth century. It has been plausibly argued that 'the faith in the possibility of science, generated antecedently to the development of modern scientific theory, is an unconscious derivative from medieval theology' (Whitehead, 37). According to the same writer, 'the greatest contribution of medievalism to the formation of the scientific movement' was 'the inexpugnable belief that every detailed occurrence can be correlated with its antecedents in a perfectly definite manner, exemplifying general principles.'

The main conclusion that I want to draw from this discussion is that quantum physics shares the same essentially realist rational foundations as the rest of science. There is nothing in quantum physics that is contrary to our belief in an objective world existing independently of the observer and behaving in a rational way according to causal laws. The inadequacy of contrary interpretations is shown both by a critical analysis and also by their debilitating effects on research.

Concerning the specific philosophical conclusions that have been drawn from particular areas òf quantum physics, it is well to remember that we are still vary far from understanding the quantum world. There have been already so many twists and turns in the arguments that it seems very unlikely that there are no more surprises in store. Until we greatly improve our understanding it is premature to reach any firm conclusions.

244

Nevertheless, if one were to try to hazard a sketch of the present situation, one might say that quantum mechanics is an outstandingly successful calculational formalism for the quantitative investigation of the atomic and nuclear worlds. It is still incomplete, and there are deeper questions that we cannot yet answer. The belief that quantum mechanics is complete is an error that leads to conceptual confusion and debilitating obscurity, and is at variance with the actual practice of scientific research. The alternative belief, that quantum mechanics relates only to ensembles of systems, is conceptually clear and opens the way to further research. In this area, stochastic electrodynamics already provides an example of a possible line of further advance.[20]

The wider philosophical implications, particularly concerning causality, complementary, free-will and the holistic nature of the universe, that have sometimes been drawn from quantum physics, do not stand up to critical examination. The answers to such problems must be sought elsewhere.

It would indeed be rather strange if such fundamental conclusions could be drawn from one branch of science; if this sort of thing were possible, we might face the problem of reconciling conclusions drawn from different branches of science. If philosophical conclusions are to be drawn from science, they should be drawn from the whole of science, and in particular from an analysis of the methods used to obtain our knowledge of the real world.

ENDNOTES

[1] Einstein, A., "On the Methods of Theoretical Physics", *The Herbert Spencer Lecture* (Oxford 1933).
[2] Jaki, S. L., *The Road of Science and the Ways to God* (Chicago 1978).
[3] Hodgson, P. E., "Existence Criteria in Modern Physics", *Symposium on the Philosophical Aspects of Quantum Theory* (Dubrovnik 1980).
[4] Bohr, Niels, *Atomic Theory and the Description of Nature* (Cambridge 1934).
[5] Popper, Karl R., *Quantum Theory and the Schism in Physics*. Edited by W. W. Bartley III (London 1982).
[6] Heisenberg, W., *Daedalus* 87, 95 (1958).
[7] Einstein, A., *The World as I see it* (New York 1934).
[8] Jaki, S. L., *The Relevance of Physics* (Chicago 1966).
[9] Schlipp, P. A., (Ed.) *Albert Einstein: Philosopher-Scientist* (Cambridge 1970).
[10] Hooker, C. A., Article in *Contemporary Research in the Foundations and Philosophy of Quantum Theory* Ed. C. A. Hooker (Dordrecht 1973).
[11] Rayleigh, Lord, *The Life of Sir J. J. Thomson* (Cambridge 1942).
[12] Neumann, J. von, *Philosophical Foundations of Quantum Mechanics* (1932).
[13] Bohm, David, *Wholeness and the Implicate Order* (London 1980).
[14] Polkinghorne, John, *The Way the World Is* (Triangle 1983).
[15] Heisenberg, W., *Zeitschrift für Physik*, 43, 197 (1927). Translated by S. L. Jaki, in: *Philosophia*, 10–11, 85 (1980–81).
[16] Jönsson, C., (1961), *Zeitschrift für Physik*, 161, 454 (1961).
[17] Arthur Fine, Article, in: *Paradigms and Paradoxes*, Ed. Robert G. Colodny (Pittsburg 1972), p. 3.
[18] Brody, T. A., *The Double Slit Revisited* (Preprint, Mexico).
[19] A further discussion of this point is given by Popper, Ref. 5, p. 59.
[20] Peña, L. de la, *Stochastic Electrodynamics* (Columbia 1982).
[21] Bohr, N., Kramers, H. A., and Slater, J. S., "The Quantum Theory of Radiation", *Phil. Mag.* 47, 785 (1924).
[22] Bothe, W., and Geiger, H., *Zeitschrift für Physik*, 26, 44 (1924)
[23] Bohr, N., *Atomic Physics and Human Knowledge* (New York 1958), p. 81.
[24] Popper, Karl R., *The Logic of Scientific Discovery* (London 1972), p. 248.
[25] D'Espagnat, B., *In Search of Reality* (Springer 1983).
[26] Einstein, A., Podolsky, B., and Rosen, N., "Can Quantum-Mechanical Description of Physical Reality be Considered Complete?" *Physical Review*, 47, 777 (1935).
[27] Bohr, N., "Can Quantum-Mechanical Description of Physical Reality be Considered Complete?" *Physical Review*, 48, 696 (1935).

[28] Bohm, David, *Quantum Mechanics* (1952).

[29] This not by itself a conclusive counter-argument. Classical physicists learned to accept action at a distance for gravitational forces when there was no physical understanding of gravitation. Nowadays a more physical interpretation is preferred in terms of the still hypothetical gravitons. However in the case of the postulated non-local interactions no such physical interpretation has been proposed.

[31] Clauser, J. F., and Shimony, A., *Rep. Prog. Phys.*, 41, 1881 (1978).

[32] D'Espagnat, Bernard, "The Quantum Theory and Reality", *Scientific American*, (November 1979), p. 128. It is notable that beneath the title of D'Espagnat's article there is the sentence 'The doctrine that the world is made up of objects whose existence is independent of human consciousness turns out to be in conflict with quantum mechanics and with facts established by experiment.' This statement goes far beyond the conclusions of D'Espagnat's carefully-worded article. It is presumably intended as a summary of the article and will be taken as such by all its readers, and by the far greater number of people who do not even read the article itself. It thus provides an excellent example of the propagation of a quite unjustified philosophical conclusion, apparently supported by all the prestige and precision of modern science.

[33] These are summarized by T. A. Brody, *Where does the Bell Inequality Lead?* (Preprint, Mexico 1982).

[34] Peres, A., *American Journal of Physics*, 46, 745 (1978).

[35] Brody, T. A., and Auerbach, L. de la Peña, *Il. Nouvo Cimento*, 54B, 455 (1979).

[36] Jaki, S. L., *Science and Creation* (Edinburgh 1974).

[37] Whitehead, A. N., *Science and the Modern World* (Cambridge 1926). In many cases, indeed, the reference to theological considerations was not at all unconscious. See for example E. A. Burtt, *Metaphysical Foundations of Modern Physical Science* (London 1924). See also M. B. Foster, *Mind*, 43, 446 (1934); 44, 439 (1935); 45, 1 (1936).

(The full text of this paper may be obtained from the author).

* * *

RELGIOSITY AND SCIENTISM

Mostafa Faghfoury
University of Ottawa, Canada

The aim of this paper is twofold: first, to show that science and scientific achievements are not *recent* phenomena as some philosophers want us to believe and further, but still on a connected issue, science is not something exclusively Western. Second, science — as a human activity aiming to search for unknowns to the best of our ability — is not in any *radical* way different from other human enquiries. Even though my both aims are directed towards a negative start, as it will become clear I will conclude the paper with a positive remark.

Those who carefully read and follow the history of human civilisation can attest to the excitement that discoveries and achievements have generated. Archimedes, we are told, was taking a simple bath when he discovered the Principle of Floating Objects in Water according to which when a body is partly or completely immersed in a fluid the apparent loss of weight is equal to the weight of the fluid displaced. After such a realization, he ran out of the building naked and started shouting: "I've found it, I've found it." A scientific problem was raised, formulated and finally solved for the time being. Newton's sleeping under an apple tree and Watson's giant ladder are only a few other examples one can cite throughout the history of science as simple instances of opportunities scientists have had to solve some troublesome problems. This may seem an oversimplification of how science and scientists work, but at least, it shows that people who have been interested in finding answers to questions used every possible occasion and worried about them until they found some satisfactory solutions. Scientific search is as much part of a human scientist's life as anything else. The dedicated scientists are not nine-to-five-professionals, rather scientific problems are part of their everyday life. Granted this, science, then, becomes *part* of the real life rather than being opposed to it.

The excitement of settling a problem would then be as important as solving it. There is nothing wrong with a healthy excitement. But what is unfortunate is the *over*excitement of some *philosophers* of science about science. This overexcitement is both damaging to the practise of science and to its reputation.

If we agree that people throughout the history have wondered and questioned issues concerning them. And if we further agree that they have thought and deliberated about them as best as they could, then it would follow that science, as not being anything more than thinking and deliberation, has been always with human race. Therefore, it is not anything recent. Only a glance through the history would further support this conclusion. From ancient Greece to medieval Islam, from India and China to Africa, thinkers from different culture and background have always tried to achieve what is taking place in Western laboratories only in the last three hundred years.

To many non-Westerner's regret science has unjustifiably come to be synonymous with the West. This unhealthy attitude is both discriminating and unproductive. It is discriminating because it only allows what is *ours* and outlaws whatever is *theirs*. And it is unproductive since it denies the possibility of exchange and improvements among people from different perspectives. As a result, what *we* do, as Westerners, would be a search and pursuit of truth, namely science. And what *they* do is non-scientific and in effect superstition. Wittgenstein in criticizing Frazer for a similar attitude toward other cultures writes: "How impossible for him to understand a different way of life from the English one of his time."

Of course, no one can deny what has been achieved scientifically in the last three hundred years with a rapid speed. But what is at issue is that by the beginning of the present century some philosophers in Europe and elsewhere came to the conclusion that science can be THE answer, almost, to *every* possible question. This attitude, what I call scientism, should be distinguished from the practise of science. Positivists, particularly the Vienna Circle Philosophers, went as far as even to show how this can be realized. Popper and the early Wittgenstein, who were not really part of the Movement, the former was not allowed to join and the latter did not want to be associated, drew a sharp line between what is scientific and what is not. This has become the problem of demarcation in the philosophy of science.

Before embarking on the problem of demarcation, let me present my understanding of some general and opposing positions in the philosophy of science. Such a consideration will help us to see how different philosophers deal with the problem.

Popper views science as progressive and as an "unended quest". The way one can account for progression in scientific methodology. The scientific method, according to Popper, consists of the principle of falsification, i.e. theories must be testable through experiments and at the same time may be rejected and replaced by new theories. This process goes on *ad infinitum*. This process is, therefore, open-ended, moves only in one direction—forward—and it produces objective knowledge.

What follows from his position is that science is distinctively different a discipline from any other human activity. If the Popperian picture of science and its method is taken strongly, then it becomes an ideology in the sense Marx used the term. Giving the privileged status to science in expense of other disciplines and using it as a yard-stick for judging the truth of non-scientific claims is what makes science immune from outside criticisms. Rather than being part of human life, science, then, becomes transcendental.

Many philosophers, including Kuhn and Feyerabend, have tried to show that Popper's view of science is neither true nor it should be. Pure objectivity, according to them, is not attainable and claim to it is mythical. They argue that science like any other discipline is influenced by human factors. History, culture, education and the personality of each scientist play a great deal in the formulation of every scientific theory.

Kuhn considers different eras in the history of science. Each era is governed by different "paradigms". What is correct and reasonable in one age may not be said to be mistaken and stupid in another period. Kuhn claims that this is due to, what he calls, incommensurability of paradigms. Even though he talks about different paradigms, but he still worries and accounts for rationality in science.

Feyerabend thinks that in rejecting Popper's views, Kuhn is not *revolutionary* enough and does not really go far. So, he presents a more radical approach than Kuhn's. His position, epistemological anarchism, consists of mainly the following doctrines:

1. Science *is not* a rational enterprise, it does not live up to the philosophical expectations.

2. Science *should not* be rational and rationality is neither a virtue nor beneficial to it.

3. The *status quo* must change, namely the way science is taught and perceived must be replaced with a more honest and open way.

In presenting his views, Feyerabend agrees with Kuhn against Popper that different theories cannot be compared regarding to their empirical contents. He further believes that there is no such a thing as scientific method. He argues that there is no fixed methodology or rules which can claim to explain truth and reason. In short, many have seen his epistemological anarchism as an "everything goes" thesis. It is true that with Feyerabend we have dissolved the distinction between science and pseudo-science, but it seems the price for it is too much. As Popper was not flexible to consider *any other* human search for truth as legitimate, Feyerabend makes an unusual philosophical error of allowing *every* conceivable human enterprise as "scientific". Popper is difficult to be bend, Feyerabend too loose to be hold.

The „*All* or *Nothing* Approach" surfaces once more in the long history of philosophy. There is a very old Persian tale which exhibits this situation very well: there was a child standing on top of a house, his father saw him up there and shouted:

–"Don't come forward, you will fall."

The child *listened* and went back until he fell down from the other side. Popper's picture was wrong because it was too rigid to be true of science, but Feyerabend's picture is so loose, that if it is taken seriously, it will bring life to halt.

The problem of demarcation is not really a problem if we broaden our conception of the human life. The tendency of making an unnecessary distinction between science and non-science may be useful to some philosophers, however it is not helpful if we do want to view and understand humanity in a more than a localized, narrow and also professional way.

The mistake that we have freed ourselves from in the middle-ages from was that the Church and the theologians thought they had a claim over everything and everybody's life. The Church saw itself as a guardian of the people and tried to solve *every* problem in reference to the Bible. If there is anything ideological, in the Marxist sense of the term, about religion, it is exactly on this ground that one aspect of human life cannot, and should not, rule over the rest. The freedom from the religious ideology, *religiosity*, has been for good. However, Feyerabend and Wittgenstein are concerned about the status of science in the post-positivist era. They are worried that we may fall, if we have not already fallen into another similar ideological trap, i.e. *scientism*.

Feyerabend encourages us to "free society from the stangling hold of an ideologically petrified science just as our ancestors freed *us* from the strangle hold of the One True Religion!"[1]

Wittgenstein perhaps was equally afraid of the situation where one authority, religion, could be replaced with another, science, and hence people would lose the chance of thinking on their *own* when he wrote:

> Man has to awaken to wonder — and so perhaps do people. Science is a way of sending him back to sleep again.[2]

I understand both Feyerabend's and Wittgenstein's negative remarks about science are directed towards it as an ideology rather than a discipline. To correct myself, the worries of both philosophers are about, what I have called scientism, rather than against science. The Indian poet, Rabindranath Tagor, has compared science and technology to a tiger. It can be a useful friend to the extent that it can protect you from your enemies, but it has to be constantly watched otherwise it could easily turn its teeth against you.

A Newtonian scholar, R. S. Westfall, recently observed that:

> "Theological depth has become for most scientists irrelevant . . . in the three centuries that have passed since Newton published the *Principia*. Christianity and science have exchanged roles, and natural science today occupies the position in Western civilization that Christianity once held . . . and every other intellectual discipline now measures itself against science . . .[3]

The obsession with division of labor in writings of some philosophers who insist in putting everyone in his/her seat and act as policemen has made us blind to certain undisputed historical facts. We are brain washed to the extend that we believe if someone is a scientist, s/he cannot be a religious person. As if a scientist may not need some spiritual needs, or, alternatively if you like, s/he cannot make a mistake! We often conveniently forget that Descartes was a scientist as well as a believer, The same is the case with Roger Bacon, Newton, Kant, Darwin and Einstein. James C. Maxwell had a firm Christian faith in a creator.

The purpose of this name-dropping should not be missed, i.e. that the above scientists' religious belief in no way worked as a disability in their high achievements. Therefore, history of science itself testifies that the fear of many philosophers nowadays about making a sharp line between science and religion is not a justified one. Both disciplines are parts of human existence in the world and if anything we must have learned by now that neither could be discredited by the other one. Like any other human activity, each has its owns highs and its own downs, each can be good, and can be evil. The aim of maximizing their good and minimizing their evil is what the art of living a social and a political life is all about.

I would like to end this paper, with a conclusion about science, what does it mean to be scientifically human?

It means discovering penicillin, it means making the first phone call, it means walking on the moon, it means putting to use electricity, purifying water, correcting genetic disorders, it means printing Shakespeare's works, it means inventing cars, computers, cameras, stoves . . . it means Noble Prize in physics, it means Albert Schweitzer in Africa, Andrei Sakharov in Russia and it could mean many thousands of other things. But what is more interesting is that it can be any of the following at the same time:

It means building nuclear missiles, aircrafts and submarines ready to go to targets and blow up the world twenty five times over. It means chemical warfare, it means the death of thousands of Japanese in Hiroshima. It means acid rain and many other environmental pollutions. It means Three-Mile-Island. It means Play Boy Magazine. It means Dr. Frankenstein. It means fabrication of data and many thousands of other things.

If we are honest enough and if we accept that there are pros and cons to every human activity and further if we do not want to put a hierarchy either on cultures, people or even disciplines, then the world would be a more pleasant place to live in and we could then take pride in being problem-solvers.

Let me finish on this preaching note.

ENDNOTES

1 Feyerabend, P., *Against Method* (1980), p. 307).
2 Wittgenstein, L., *Culture and Value* (1980), p. 5.
3 Westfall, R. S., "The Career of Isaac Newton", *The American Scholar*, 50 (1981), p. 353.

* * *

LISTE UND INDEX DER VORTRAGENDEN
LIST AND INDEX OF SPEAKERS

251

SCHRIFTENREIHE DER WITTGENSTEIN-GESELLSCHAFT

Herausgegeben von Elisabeth Leinfellner
Rudolf Haller, Adolf Hübner, Werner Leinfellner, Paul Weingartner

 Verlag Hölder-Pichler-Tempsky

A-1096 Wien, Frankgasse 4, Postfach 127, Telefon 0222/43 89 93 △

SCHRIFTENREIHE DER WITTGENSTEIN-GESELLSCHAFT

Herausgegeben von Elisabeth Leinfellner
Rudolf Haller, Adolf Hübner, Werner Leinfellner, Paul Weingartner

---

Band 7

ETHIK – GRUNDLAGEN, PROBLEME UND ANWENDUNGEN

Akten des 5. Internationalen Wittgenstein-Symposiums, Kirchberg am Wechsel, Österreich 1980.

ETHICS – FOUNDATIONS, PROBLEMS, AND APPLICATIONS

Proceedings of the 5th International Wittgenstein-Symposium, Kirchberg am Wechsel, Austria 1980.
Hrsg. Edgar Morscher, Rudolf Stranzinger.
Wien 1981, 525 Seiten, kartoniert. ISBN 3-209-00280-0.

Band 8

SPRACHE UND ONTOLOGIE

Akten des 6. Internationalen Wittgenstein-Symposiums, Kirchberg am Wechsel, Österreich 1981.

LANGUAGE AND ONTOLOGY

Proceedings of the 6th International Wittgenstein-Symposium, Kirchberg am Wechsel, Austria 1981.
Hrsg. Werner Leinfellner, Eric Kraemer, Jeffrey Schank.
Wien 1982, 544 Seiten, kartoniert. ISBN 3-209-00422-6.

Band 9

ERKENNTNIS- UND WISSENSCHAFTSTHEORIE

Akten des 7. Internationalen Wittgenstein-Symposiums, Kirchberg am Wechsel, Österreich 1982.

EPISTEMOLOGY AND PHILOSOPHY OF SCIENCE

Proceedings of the 7th International Wittgenstein-Symposium, Kirchberg am Wechsel, Austria 1982.
Hrsg. Paul Weingartner, Hans Czermak.
Wien 1983, 576 Seiten, kartoniert. ISBN 3-209-00499-4.

NEUERSCHEINUNG 1984:

Band 10/1

ÄSTHETIK

Akten des 8. Internationalen Wittgenstein-Symposiums (Teil 1), Kirchberg/W., Österreich 1983.

AESTHETICS

Proceedings of the 8th International Wittgenstein-Symposium (Part 1), Kirchberg/W., Austria 1983.
Hrsg. Rudolf Haller.
Wien 1984, 262 Seiten, kartoniert. ISBN 3-209-00547-8.

Band 10/2

RELIGIONSPHILOSOPHIE

Akten des 8. Internationalen Wittgenstein-Symposiums (Teil 2), Kirchberg/W., Österreich 1983.

PHILOSOPHY OF RELIGION

Proceedings of the 8th International Wittgenstein-Symposium (Part 2), Kirchberg/W., Austria 1983.
Hrsg. Wolfgang L. Gombocz.
Wien 1984, 252 Seiten, kartoniert. ISBN 3-209-00548-6.

 Verlag Hölder-Pichler-Tempsky

A-1096 Wien, Frankgasse 4, Postfach 127, Telefon 0222/43 89 93 △